EXCELLENCE IN SINGING

multilevel learning and multilevel teaching

VOLUME 5: Managing vocal health

CALDWELL PUBLISHING COMPANY

Pst...Inc. Subsidiary

Redmond, WA

EXCELLENCE IN SINGING

Cover designed by Tom Draper

Interior designed by Robert Caldwell and Tom Draper

Music engraving by Steven Hendrickson

Images and graphics by Robert Caldwell

Also by Pst...Inc.:

Diction for Singers
International Phonetic Alphabet for Singers
Sing! Text and Music for Voice Class
Song: Guide to Style and Literature
Singer's Edition: Guide to Operatic Arias
Guide to Operatic Roles and Arias
Guide to Operatic Duets
Russian Songs and Arias
The Performer Prepares
The Singer's Voice Animation Series

Caldwell Publishing Company
Pst...Inc. Subsidiary
P.O. Box 3231
Redmond, Washington 98073

Library of Congress Catalogue Number: 2001090894

to Katelyn—R.C.

to Ernie—J.W.

TABLE OF CONTENTS

TEACHING AND LEARNING VOCAL HEALTH

The human voice allows us to communicate the intricacies of the human condition—primarily because it has a structure that allows a wide range of variability. It is driven by the human body and its many complex systems—the nervous system, muscular system, skeletal system, circulatory system, and pulmonary system, to name a few. Consequently, a slight change in an emotion, a passing thought, a change in attitude can result in a change in the voice. (See ch. 4, "The body: the vocal instrument," in v. 1.)

Learning to exploit the incredible array of controls for the human voice—the multifaceted functioning of the human body—for artistic satisfaction has been a major focus of *Excellence in Singing*. But just as the voice is sensitive to deliberate changes in the body, it is susceptable to unwanted changes in the body. For instance, the voice will deteriorate when the body has not had enough sleep for one evening.

To reach optimum singing, your student needs a healthy voice. Defining a healthy voice, however, is a challenge. Overall health of the human body affects vocal health, and, as the body ebbs and flows into and out of optimum health, your student's vocal health moves along with it. Her voice can become compromised over a wide range of disorders, from simple swelling to complete paralysis of the vocal folds, from a wide range of causes. (See "Causes of Vocal Health Problems," on page 85).

As her teacher, you normally notice a problem with your student's voice and respond with some form of training. But your student's vocal health may be the cause of her problems, and no amount of training is going to help until she returns to excellent vocal health. In designing the series *Excellence in Singing*, we wanted to help you know how to address issues at this level in particular, which is simple: refer your student to a otolaryngologist.

This should continue to be your basic response to any vocal health problem, but we wanted to give you a picture of what you and your student might be in for if something goes wrong. We wanted to give you an overview, not only to help you know how to respond to your student with a problem such as a hoarse voice, but also to develop a richer sense of how you and your student can take care for her voice when it is healthy—and of the consequences when your student doesn't take care of it or when she suffers another illness in her body that affects her voice.

We also wanted to make sure that the material was relevant to you as a teacher of singing.

This volume was a collaborative effort. From my initial design, scope, and parameters for the book, a team of professionals, led by Christine Sapienza, provided the expert material. This team includes:

Christine Sapienza, Assoc. Professor

Bari Hoffman-Ruddy, Assit. Professor

Judith Wingate, Speech Language Pathologist

Margaret Baroody, Singing Voice Specialist

Jeffery J. Lehman, Otolaryngologist

Savita P. Collins, Otolaryngologist

Jeffrey Fichera, Physician's Assistant

These doctors, surgeons, and therapists routinely work with singers and their vocal health problems. Their clients range from amateurs to celebrated professionals, and they commonly treat a wide range of problems. (See "Vocal health case studies," on page 135.) They perform their work at the Health Center at the University of Florida, which is a major referral center for the entire Southeast and a major center for scientific research. Colleges of medicine, nursing, pharmacy, dentistry, veterinary medicine, and health related professions are all present on the campus. Shands Hospital and Shands Children's Hospital at the University of Florida is a university hospital which offers the entire spectrum of primary, secondary, and tertiary patient care. The otolaryngology service sees 17,000 clinic patients a year and performs 2,400 surgical procedures each year.

Shannon O'Donnell, working as an independent writer, corresponded with Christine Sapienza and myself to produce the first drafts. Then Jocelyn Markey, an editor at Caldwell, worked with me to produce the final version, which was reviewed by the team of health professionals. We followed the same criteria for all writing of *Excellence in Singing*: clear, easy-to-read, and relevant to singers.

Robert Caldwell

THE HEALTHY VOICE

Train your student to care for her vocal health, and she will enjoy many years of healthy singing.

Your student might not be accustomed to caring for her voice. Even when she understands the behaviors that adversely affect the health of her voice, she might not immediately change those behaviors.

In this chapter, we want to give you the tools to impress upon your student how to care for her voice. We discuss concepts, common behaviors, and implications so that you can awaken your student to the idea that her voice is a sensitive musical instrument that needs special care. You can teach her how to maintain good practices that will protect and enhance her voice. And you can teach her to consistently weigh her long-term vocal health against immediate performance demands.

You are your student's partner in managing her vocal health. Part of your role as teacher is to understand the healthy voice and to recognize signs of deterioration, such as hoarseness, throat irritation, breathiness, or any other voice-quality change. (See "Recognizing Vocal Health Problems," on page 42.) Detecting vocal problems early can save time and prevent permanent injury to your student's voice.

As her teacher, you are the first person your student will turn to when she has problems with her voice. If her voice becomes injured or compromised, you will refer her to medical professionals and assist her recovery.

Ultimately, however, your student is responsible for her own vocal health. She must come to know her body and its limits, be aware of her body's changes in different circumstances, be responsible for healthy practices, and seek advice from experts in caring for and maintaining her health.

❋ Remember that your role as teacher is not to diagnose a vocal health problem. Do not try to identify a disease. Your role is simply to refer your student to a medical specialist if necessary and, later, to help in her recovery. (See "Treating Vocal Health Problems," on page 65.)

Health is not a fixed state but a fluid reality that changes with the seasons and events of life. At any moment, your student is moving into or out of some phase of being healthy. How well your student can sing and for how long depends on the quality of care she gives her voice.

To identify the healthy voice, you and your student must understand how the voice works. Without knowing the basic mechanics of the vocal system, you might both have more anxieties and fears about your student's voice. You might even damage her vocal apparatus by straining her voice. (See ch. 4, "The Body: The Vocal Instrument," in v. 1.)

Identifying Vocal Health

Your student sings her best when her sound feels easy to produce: her perceived effort is minimal and her voice quality is superb. She sings her worst when her sound feels hard to produce: her breathing is difficult, her larynx is irritated, or she has some other vocal problem. Her voice might sound raspy, hoarse, or tight. It might vary in performance, and it might be prone to voice breaks and shifts in pitch.

nav to detect

Your first step in assessing your student's vocal health is to identify your student's baseline vocal condition. At the beginning of every lesson, ask your student how she is. Then watch her. Listen to her. Observe whether she is focused or distracted, or holding back to protect something that is beginning to ache. The more ways you can describe your student's voice and vocal habits, the better you will be able to identify changes in your student's vocal health.

When your student is having a vocal problem, you, the teacher, will notice a deviation from her usual performance. You need to find out whether the problem is physical or psychological (for instance, a sore throat or a lack of motivation) and whether it's chronic or acute (for instance, long-term range limitations or a cold). Use the following criteria to help you assess your student's vocal health. (Note that these criteria apply to singers with some training, not to beginners.)

- Energy. A healthy singer is well-rested and attentive. She comes to her work with energy and enthusiasm. Her singing voice keeps its integrity throughout the range. Her speaking voice is supported by a steady column of air and has a consistent range and quality.

- No evidence of misuse. Her voice is not aggravated by tobacco, alcohol, or other misuse. She is not complaining of tight muscles, neck pain, or pain radiating from her laryngeal area to her ear. (See "Causes of Vocal Health Problems," on page 85.)

- Breath. She has efficient, well-coordinated breathing and she exercises good breath control. Her breathing is easy and full. (See the heading "Optimizing the Body To Support Singing," in v. 1, ch. 4, and "What Is the Best Breath for Singing?," in v. 2, ch. 8.)

- Phonation. She speaks and sings with flexible pitches, produces easy changes in tone color, and expresses herself with many tonal inflections. (See the heading "Optimizing Phonation for Singing," in v. 1, ch. 4, and "Focus on Flow Phonation," in v. 2, ch. 9.)

- Resonance. She moves her jaw, mouth, and tongue easily to form vowels and consonants. She can purse and retract her lips. All these maneuvers should be symmetrical and without discomfort or pain. The muscles that control these articulators need to be free of muscle tension, or else her movements will be restricted (See the heading "Optimizing Resonance for Singing," in v. 1, ch. 4, and "Manipulating Resonance and Perceiving the Difference," in v. 2, ch. 10.)

- Supportive body. She stands comfortably, with her posture straight but not rigid. She moves her body fluidly, with her weight evenly distributed. She holds herself easily, using her body to support her breath. (See the heading "Optimizing the Body To Support Singing," in v. 1, ch. 4, and "Calibrating to a State of Readiness to Sing," in v. 2, ch. 7.)

Maintaining Vocal Health

Good vocal care involves a partnership of professionals. In addition to you, this partnership includes medical professionals with specialized knowledge of the body parts that create the voice. Speech pathologists with specializations in voice assessment and voice care might also be included in your circle of support. This team helps your student eliminate bad habits and also identifies good behavioral practices for a healthy voice.

Your student is the most important member of the team, responsible for her health care and good vocal practices. She teaches her body to recognize the sensations of work done correctly. She draws upon that kinesthetic awareness to create a consistent sound. A healthy body will hold these memories and respond well when called upon to perform.

Healthy, balanced living can help your student enjoy practicing and performing throughout her life. Encourage her in good general habits for using her voice, keeping herself hydrated and rested, and staying fit. Along with positive habits that support good vocal health, maintaining good vocal health includes avoiding habits and activities that hinder the body.

We discuss a few key topics that can make a difference in maintaining vocal health. These include:

- Hydration
- Nutrition and Fitness
- Prescription and Over-the-Counter Medicines
- Sleep
- Travel
- Cigarette Smoking
- Substance Abuse

Hydration

Water intake is essential for vocal health. Hydration can reduce vocal effort. If your student is dehydrated, her vocal folds can get stiff, resulting in dryness, hoarseness, and a "forced" quality in the voice. Increasing hydration makes vocal fold movement more fluid and decreases the lung pressure needed to initiate movement of the vocal folds.[1][2]

Voice therapists typically recommend that singers drink approximately six 8-ounce glasses of water a day. A growing body of evidence indicates that drinking more water reduces vocal fold swelling and the size of vocal fold lesions, such as nodules.

The body provides its own basic clue about whether it is sufficiently hydrated. Otolaryngologist Van Lawrence offered the instruction, "Pee pale," meaning that your student's urine should be pale yellow or clear. When her urine is dark yellow, she needs to drink more water.[3]

Your student can also rehydrate her body through the pores of her skin by taking a bath or swimming. Rehydration can take a few days. In a dry climate, she can leave water in the sink or tub to increase the surrounding humidity.

Nutrition and Fitness

Singing is an athletic activity that requires conditioning and good self-care. Because the body is the singer's instrument, a singer must eat nourishing foods, maintain a healthy weight, follow an active fitness program, and rest regularly.

Good nutrition

Your student can help prevent vocal injury and minimize performance-related anxiety through careful dietary practices. Various forms of nutrient deficiency can affect (among other things) disease resistance, nerve function, respiratory strength, and the muscles used for speaking and swallowing.

A good diet provides energy and stamina for singing. The dietary guidelines currently recommended are as follows:

- Eat a variety of foods.
- Balance food with physical activity: maintain and improve weight.
- Choose a diet low in fat and cholesterol.
- Choose a diet with plenty of grain products, vegetables, and fruits.
- Choose a diet moderate in sugars.
- Choose a diet moderate in sodium.
- If you drink alcoholic beverages, do so in moderation.

Fad and alternative diets are available in many different forms, including high-protein, low-fat, low-sugar, vegetarian, and so on. Some diets can result in nutritional deficiencies. Have your student consult with a registered dietitian for information about available food plans.

Maintaining healthy weight

Your student is a vocal athlete and she should maintain a healthy body weight. The stereotype of the obese operatic singer is not a model for good vocal health. A large body does not predict that one will have the large voice needed to fill an opera house. Beyond great singing skills, good muscle tone and overall body conditioning give the singer the ability to produce excellent sounds.

Extra weight can affect your student in many ways:

- It interferes with abdominal breath support for singing.

- It contributes to general fatigue.

- It reduces endurance.

- In extreme cases, it affects resonance by reducing the function of the pharynx. This tissue also plays a role in sleep apnea, which contributes to fatigue and can be quite dangerous. (See "Sleep apnea and snoring," on page 118.)

- It exacerbates reflux. (Weight reduction is often highly recommended in reflux management programs.)

If your student is heavier than twenty percent more than her ideal body weight (according to her doctor's charts), she should consider losing weight. A physician or a registered dietitian is a good partner in developing a careful weight management program. Weight management programs should include training in lifestyle modification with the following goals:

- Gradually increasing the intake of whole grains, fruits, and vegetables

- Knowing what you can eat and how much before your food intake exceeds your energy output

- Gradually working up to at least 30 minutes of enjoyable physical activity each day

Weight loss should occur slowly to minimize any effects on your student's singing voice. Substantial fluctuations in weight can significantly affect your student's voice, although the effects are usually temporary.

Exercise

Singing requires good respiratory support, good cardiovascular health, and adequate respiratory muscle strength. Encourage your student in appropriate exercise to strengthen her body and increase her overall endurance. Emphasize the importance of aerobic exercise to improve cardiovascular health, weight lifting to increase bone strength, and stretching exercises to develop flexibility. Yoga and tai chi can also strengthen your student's body and her spirit.

❊ Refer your student to her physician before she begins a new exercise regimen. Also recommend that she consult a professional trainer to help her design her exercise plan.

To generate the high air pressures and endurance required for singing, the muscles involved in respiration must be strong. By strengthening the muscles of her respiratory system, your student can reduce excessive vocal fold closure, thereby limiting vocal fold irritation. The most efficient way to maximize exhalation pressures *for singing* is to contract the external intercostal muscles to expand the rib cage and contract the abominal muscles to compress the abdominal contents. (See the heading "Optimizing Breathing for Singing," in v. 1, ch. 4.) The second way to develop pressure, which can damage laryngeal tissue, is to increase laryngeal airway resistance by closing the vocal folds for longer periods. Your student should avoid this second option of overcompression, which can contribute to vocal nodules or other vocal fold problems, such as polyps or edema. (For developing strength and flexibility in breathing, see exercises such as "To Pant Like a Dog," "To Use Stop-Plosive Consonants," "To Sip in Air Vigorously," "To Punch with the Arms," on page 60.)

Prescription and Over-the-Counter Medicines

Medicines can have various effects on the singing voice, no matter why they are prescribed. Your student needs to be aware of the side effects of common medicines.

The following medicines have side effects as listed. These medications are the ones most commonly used by singers. For medicines that do not appear in Table 1, have your student consult with a pharmacist or her general practitioner to avoid drug interactions or side effects that could harm her voice.

Table 1: Common Medications and Their Effects on the Voice

Brand Name	Generic Name	Drug Category	Usually Prescribed For	Effect on Voice
Advil	ibuprofen	non steroidal anti-inflammatory	inflammation, including rheumatoid arthritis, menstrual pain, headaches, and other mild to moderate pain	increased possibility of vocal fold hemorrhage
Allegrae	fexofenadine hydrochloride	antihistimine	seasonal allergy symptoms	drying effect, sore throat, hoarseness, laryngitis
Amoxil	amoxicillin	antibiotic	bacterial infection, most commonly of the ear and throat	none on voice or speech

Brand Name	Generic Name	Drug Category	Usually Prescribed For	Effect on Voice
Apro-naproxen	naproxen	non steroidal anti-inflammatory	inflammation, swelling, stiffness, rheumatoid arthritis, bursitis	increased possibility of vocal fold hemorrhage
Aspirin	acetylsalicylic acid	non-narcotic analgesic	fever, aches, pains	vocal fold hemmorrhage or intercordal bleed and stomach ulcer
Astelin		antihistamine	nasal spray prescribed for the relief of hay fever	drowsiness
Ativan	lorazepam	antianxiety	anxiety	slow, slurred speech
Atrovent inhaler	ipratropium bromide	anticholinergic	sneezing, congestion, or postnasal drip	drying or irritating effect, voice change, laryngitis
Augmentin	amoxicillin	antibiotics	various respiratory tract infections, including sinusitis, bronchitis, and pneumonia	none on voice or speech
Azmacort	tiamcinolone diacetate	corticosteroid	maintenance treatment of asthma	complete loss of voice
Benadryl	diphenhydramine hydrochloride	antihistimine	allergy symptoms, including runny nose, sneezing, nasal itching, and stuffiness	swelling of the throat
birth control pills, such as Lo/Ovral	progestin and estrogen	oral contraceptives	birth control, acne. and regulation of monthly menstrual cycles	none on voice or speech
BuSpar	buspirone hydrochloride	non-benzodiazepine antianxiety	generalized anxiety disorder	none on voice or speech

Brand Name	Generic Name	Drug Category	Usually Prescribed For	Effect on Voice
Catapress	clonidine hydrochloride	antihypertensive	high blood pressure	none on voice or speech
Cefzil	cefprozil	antibiotic	bacterial infections of the throat, ear, sinuses, respiratory tract, and skin	none on voice or speech
Claritin, Caratin D 12 and 24 hour	loratidine	antihistimine	seasonal allergic rhinitis	drying or irritating effect, voice change, laryngitis
Coumadin	warfarin	anticoagulant	a blood thinner; used for several types of heart conditions	increased possibility of vocal fold hemorrhage
Daypro	oxaprozin	non steroidal anti-inflammatory	inflammatory conditions such as rheumatoid arthritis	increased possibility of vocal fold hemorrhage
Deltasone	prednisone	corticosteroid	inflammation, severe asthma, and several other diseases and disorders	reduced vocal fold swelling
Dilantin	phenytoin Sodium	anticonvulsant	grand mal seizures and temporal lobe seizures	slurred speech
Elavil	amitriptyline	tricyclic antidepressant	some types of depression	diminished motor coordination
Estraderm patch	estrogen patches	estrogen	symptoms of menopause (osteoporosis)	none on voice or speech
Flonase	fluticasone propionate	corticosteroid	nasal allergies	drying or irritating effect, voice change, cough
Flovent	fluticasone propionate	corticosteroid	rhinitis and asthma	drying or irritating effect, voice change, cough

Brand Name	Generic Name	Drug Category	Usually Prescribed For	Effect on Voice
Fosomax	alendronate sodium	bone growth regulator	insufficient bone density	none on voice or speech
Keflex	cephalexin monohydrate	antibiotic	bacterial infections of the respiratory tract, bones, skin, and reproductive and urinary systems	none on voice or speech
Lasix	furosimide	loop diuretic	pulmonary edema and congestive heart failure	drying or irritating effect, voice change, laryngitis
Levoxyl	levothyroxine sodium	thyroid	diminished or absent thyroid function	none on voice or speech
Lorabid	loracarbef	antibiotic	mild to moderate bacterial infection of the lungs, ears, throat, sinuses, skin, urinary tract, and kidneys	none on voice or speech
Lortrel	amlodipine and benazepril hydrochloride	antihypertensive	high blood pressure	excessive coughing, possibly leading to hoarseness
Medrol	methylprednisolone	glucocorticoid	inflammation such as arthritis, asthma, and laryngeal edema	reduced vocal fold swelling
Norvasc	amlodipine	antihypertensive	high blood pressure, chest pain	none on voice or speech
Premarin	estrogen	estrogen	symptoms of menopause	none on voice or speech
Prilosec	omeprazlone	supress gastric acid secretion	heartburn, gastroesophageal reflux	none on voice or speech

Brand Name	Generic Name	Drug Category	Usually Prescribed For	Effect on Voice
Prinivil	lisinopril	antihypertensive	high blood pressure	excessive coughing
Propulsid	cisapride	gastrointestinal drug	gastroesophageal reflux	none on voice or speech
Provera	medroxyprogesterone	progestational	estrogen replacement	none on voice or speech
Prozac	fluoxetine hydrochloride	antidepressant	depression	drying effect, sore throat, hoarseness, laryngitis
Relafen	nabumatone	nonsteroidal anti-inflammatory	inflammation, swelling, stiffness, and joint pain associated with rheumatoid arthritis and osteoarthritis	increased possibility of vocal fold hemorrhage
Retin A	tretinoin	anti-acne	acne and reduction of fine wrinkles	none on voice or speech
Rhinocort	budesonide	corticosteroid	hay fever and nasal inflammation	complete loss of voice
Robitussin	guaifenesin/PPA	expectorant	congestion and heavy mucus	drowsiness nervousness
Sudafed	pseudoepherdrine hydrochloride	nasal decongestant	nasal, sinus congestion, and allergies	dry mouth drowsiness
Synthroid	levothyroxine	thyroid	hypothyroidism from any of several causes	none on voice or speech
Tylenol	acetaminophen	analgesic	minor pain and fever reduction	highly unlikely but could cause persistent sore throat
Tylenol # 3	acetaminophen/ codeine	analgesic	minor pain and fever reduction	slow, slurred speech

Brand Name	Generic Name	Drug Category	Usually Prescribed For	Effect on Voice
Valium	diazepam	antianxiety	mild to moderate anxiety	slow, uncoordinated speech
Vancenase AQ DS	beclomethasone dipropionate	glucocortoicoid	hay fever and to prevent regrowth of nasal polyps following surgical removal	sore throat, cough
Ventolin or Proventil	albuterol aerosol	direct acting adrenergic agent	asthma	drying effect, hoarseness, soreness
Viagra	sildenafil citrate	erectile dysfunction	male impotence	none on voice or speech
Xanax	aprazolam	antianxiety	anxiety	slurred speech
Zantac	ranitidine	H2 receptor antagonist	gastroesophageal reflux and heartburn	drying effect, sore throat, irritation, laryngitis
Zantac	ranitadine	H2 receptor antagonist	gastroesophageal reflux and heartburn	drying effect, sore throat, irritation, laryngitis
Zithromax	azithromycin	antibiotic	upper respiratory infection, pharyngitis, tonsillitis, and pneumonia	none on voice or speech
Zocor	simvastatin	antihyperlipidemic	high cholesterol	none on voice or speech
Zoloft	sertraline hydrocloride	antidepressant	major depression	drying effect, laryngitis, sore throat, hoarseness
Zyrtec	cetirizine hydrocloride	antihistimine	allergies	drying effect

Singers are prone to fatigue because they juggle busy performance schedules, rigorous rehearsal schedules, and travel. From the very beginning of your teaching-learning relationship, discuss sleeping patterns with your student. Balance her practice schedule with adequate hours of vocal rest.

Consider sleep to be part of your student's overall conditioning. Her voice will be adversely affected by lack of sleep. If your student is chronically sleep-deprived, the quality of her performances will be diminished by the excessive physical and emotional strain. As ENT Robert T. Sataloff states, "General body fatigue is reflected in the voice. Optimal vocal efficiency may not be achieved when a person is tired."[4]

When people are deprived of sleep, they also find that managing their daily routines becomes more tedious, concentrating on immediate tasks becomes difficult, and physical energy seems nonexistent.[5,6]

Sleeping pills

Your student might be more susceptible to sleep problems because of her demands for "time, travel, and the irregular hours of performance."[7] Going to bed late and having to rise early the next morning for rehearsal can lead to inadequate rest. Your student might want to take sleeping pills to facilitate her sleep.

However, sleeping pills are best used with a physician's recommendation. It is too easy to fall into a vicious cycle of taking sedatives to fall asleep and then taking stimulants to manage a performance. If her sleep problems last longer than a few days, refer your student to her primary physician for advice and treatment.

Sleeping schedule

To combat the sometimes irregular schedules of singers, voice therapists recommend that singers follow a consistent sleeping schedule. The following are general guidelines you can give your student for restful sleep:

- Go to bed and wake up at the same time every day.

- Sleep more before heavy voice use.

- Use the bed and bedroom only for sleeping. Do not read, do paperwork, or watch TV in bed.

- Avoid alcohol before bedtime.

- To reduce the potential effects of reflux, don't eat or exercise for two hours before bedtime.

- Before going to bed, relax with a warm bath, reading, or relaxation exercises.

Travel

Travel is a way of life for some singers. It can cause various health issues, including dehydration, jet lag, and fatigue. Although most of the following suggestions focus on air travel, touring by bus or by train also demands attention to nutrition, sleep, and hydration.

Effects of travel

Relative humidity drops in flight, especially on long journeys. The immediate effects of this rapid dehydration are dry skin and dry eyes, and every organ in the body reacts to the lack of moisture by compensating or adjusting its biochemical levels. With significantly less moisture in the air, the vocal folds dry out and get stiff.

Your student might also suffer from the poor air quality in flight. In-flight air contains whatever ozone levels and pollutants exist outside the plane; the body feels them in the form of fatigue or jet lag. In addition, the pressurized air—with its lower level of oxygen—can create light-headedness, difficulty concentrating, shallow breathing, loss of certain intellectual skills, aches in joints, impaired vision, and other maladies.

One of the benefits of traveling in first class is that the air in the front of the plane contains more oxygen than coach.

❋ Because of the low pressure in airplane cabins, your student might need to change the dosages of her medicines. Fo«r example, people with kidney or liver problems might find that their bodies process medicine differently in flight. Have your student consult her doctor or pharmacist for further information.

Combating jet lag and other effects of flying

Give your student the following guidelines to help her prevent dehydration and to ease the effects of jet lag.

- Beverages. Some beverages can result in hoarseness, tongue tension, and limited stamina in higher vocal ranges. Carrot juice increases the oxygen in the bloodstream, and it might help to alleviate the effects of cabin air. But most important, drink *lots* of water to combat the dehydrating effects of air travel. And bring your own bottled water; attendants can run out of water on long flights. After you land, continue to drink large quantities of water.

- Alcohol. Alcohol triples in effect in flight, and it dries out the body's tissues.

- Salt. Avoid salt and beverages such as tomato juice that have a high salt content. Salt increases fluid retention, which bloats the feet and ankles. Also, skip the peanuts and other salty snacks.

- Sodas and seltzers. Avoid carbonated beverages in flight, because they cause bloating. Remember: gas expands at high altitude.

- Tea and coffee. Their diuretic properties increase the effect of dehydration.

- Blood circulation. Stretch, both during and after the flight. In the airport, walk from gate to gate; don't rely on people movers or escalators. While on board the plane, walk the aisles.

- Decongestants. If blocked ears are a problem, take a decongestant half an hour before you land.

- Food. Eat lightly the night before your flight. Also eat lightly during the flight, and choose foods high in carbohydrates, which digest more quickly. If the flight is short, consider not eating at all. And suck on peppermint drops or hard candies during the flight; they smell and taste good, help relax the smooth muscles (including the vocal folds), and help keep other muscles in the throat lubricated.

- Hydration. Rehydrate your body after the flight by drinking extra fluids and by taking a bath or swimming.

- Light. Stay in natural light. The body adapts best to diurnal rhythms if exposed to natural light. However, artificial light can also help, by keeping you alert and combating the daytime slumps resulting from jet lag. Although natural light is better for you, artificial lights can help you keep a regular schedule, which is important for recovering from jet lag.

- Sleep. Go to bed earlier than usual for a few nights before departure. Nap on the plane. After you land, eat dinner early and enjoy a good night's sleep.

Cigarette Smoking

The most immediate hazard of smoking cigarettes is—obviously—the toxicity of the smoke.

In addition, cigarette smoke dries the vocal folds, making them less elastic and less flexible. Smoke irritates the vocal fold mucosa and the linings of the vocal tract and lungs. The vocal tract becomes inflamed, causing the singer to cough and her voice to become hoarse. Excessive coughing causes inflammation, which can lead to infection. Plus, the inhaled tars act on the cardiovascular and nervous systems, hampering breathing.

Nicotine is the addictive substance in cigarettes. Nicotine can also cause cancers in the parts of the body that control the voice. Nicotine intake does not come only from smoking cigarettes. Smoking cigars, chewing tobacco, and taking snuff are other ways to get nicotine into the body. These habits can cause tumors, too.

Aside from the obvious cure—quitting smoking—smokers can help themselves somewhat with proper nutrition, as discussed below.

Infections

Smoking cigarettes affects the lungs and increases the possibility of colds, influenza, acute bronchitis, pneumonia, and chronic lung diseases, such as chronic obstructive pulmonary disease and emphysema. Many of these infections have to be treated with antibiotics and rest. And the antibiotics themselves could have negative side effects on a singer's voice. (xref to medications table)

Cancer

In smokers, the articulators (such as the lips, tongue, palate, and larynx) and lungs are at risk for developing cancer from nicotine. Cancer treatments can include chemotherapy, radiation, or surgery. These solutions permanently affect tissue elasticity in the lungs and the upper airways, leading to changes in voice quality and inefficient breath support.

Kicking the habit

New items on the market provide nicotine to help people avoid the effects of smoke while they quit smoking; these items include nicotine gum, patches, and sprays. Although low-tar, low-nicotine cigarettes may be an attractive alternative for the person who can't stop smoking, there are no safe cigarettes. All cigarettes do damage, and usually the "lighter" the cigarette, the "deeper" your student must inhale to satisfy her craving for nicotine.

To try to ameliorate the effects of smoking, some people simply smoke or inhale less. Smoking less and inhaling less will put your student at a lower risk than someone who is smoking heavily and inhaling hard, but the only way she can avoid the risks is to stop smoking—or not to start. Use your influence as her teacher to help her make the right choices for staying healthy. Refer her to her general practitioner for advice on quitting.

Nutritional help for smokers

No measures can combat the multitude of chemicals that are in cigarette smoke or alleviate irritation from smoking. Some people, however, follow a nutritional approach to try to mitigate the many ill effects of tobacco.

Some people take vitamins; eat a diet low in fats and high in fruits, vegetables, and grains; and drink a lot of water. To neutralize the acid content in the body brought on by cigarettes, some people eat highly alkaline foods; such foods include figs, raisins, carrots, celery, almonds, and lima beans.

Good hydration is recommended to combat the drying effect of cigarette smoke.

Secondary smoke

The damage from secondary smoke carries approximately 40 percent of the effect of actually smoking. Secondary smoke is unfiltered and it contains more tar and nicotine than the primary smoker inhales. Some common symptoms of secondary smoke include exacerbation of allergies, headaches, coughs, and hoarseness.

Sometimes, secondary smoke is unavoidable. Your student might perform at a nightclub filled with smoke. Her friends and associates might be smokers. Although she can't always control those around her, she can limit her exposure somewhat. When she is in smoke-filled places, she can walk out and get fresh air during breaks, avoid standing around and chatting in smoky areas, or use a portable humidifier in a small room. She can also use a humidifier at home before and after the performance. She can ask the management for a quiet and healthy place to rest during breaks. And, as always, she should keep hydrated.

Substance Abuse

Take a firm stand against the abuse of drugs, caffeine, and alcohol. Encourage alternative means for your student to relax and recreate. Reinforce the performance goals she has set, and emphasize those behaviors that lead to success. Refer your student to her general physician or to appropriate drug or alcohol rehabilitation if necessary.

Illegal drugs

Your student should avoid using illegal drugs. Some drugs have a direct effect on the vocal folds; others have an indirect effect on the vocal fold structure. Inhaled drugs such as cocaine and heroin dry out the nasal passages and the vocal tract.

Smoking marijuana can cause the same kinds of breathing problems that plague cigarette smokers, including chronic bronchitis and upper respiratory infections. Lungs weakened by irritation and infection cannot perform at full capacity, leaving the singer without the support she needs for full-voiced singing.

Marijuana also plays a role in developing head and neck cancer along with problems in the immune and reproductive systems. Some of the compounds found in marijuana are of the same types of cancer-causing compounds as in tobacco—sometimes in higher concentrations.

For more information about illegal drugs, your student can log onto the Food and Drug Administration Web site, at http://www.fda.gov, or she can refer to articles and books such as the following:

- *Professional Voice: Science and Art of Clinical Care*[8]
- "Drugs and Vocal Function"[9]
- *The Effects of Drugs on Communication Disorders*[10]

Alcohol

Alcohol acts as a sedative, and it dries out the vocal folds. It also affects motor control, including control of the vocal folds. Drinking alcohol before a performance will affect your student's balance and thought processes, diminishing her ability to perform well. Alcohol use, even in the smallest doses, can decrease awareness, which undermines the vocal discipline and technique that help optimize and protect the voice.[11]

Caffeine

Caffeine may seem harmless, especially in relation to illegal drugs or alcohol use. However, caffeine can become addicting. Caffeine is a stimulant that acts directly on the central nervous system to increase the sharpness of the senses. To try and maintain opening-night excitement for several shows a day, your student might drink coffee, tea, soda, or cocoa; eat chocolate (which contains a chemical similar to caffeine); or take diet pills. Caffeine dries laryngeal tissue, making it stiff and less responsive to the air pressure needed to produce sound. If your student drinks caffeinated beverages, she will have to work harder to produce sound and might injure her vocal folds.

To help your student curb a caffeine habit, have her chart her use of caffeine, and then encourage her to begin to limit its use. When she begins to cut back on her caffeine intake, she may experience headaches, dry mouth, fatigue, and extreme sluggishness. Staying hydrated will help. Tell her to drink a glass of water for every cup of caffeinated product that she consumes.

Using her voice well helps your student maintain vocal health. She should be cautious, however, about *vocal abuse* and *vocal misuse.* Vocal abuse is behavior that results in adverse effects to the vocal-fold structure or function. It is caused by environmental irritants or maladaptive vocal behavior. A change in behavior (such as stopping smoking, avoiding musty places, or giving up a vocally damaging job) can change the effects of vocal abuse. Vocal misuse is the inappropriate manipulation of the pitch, timbre, or dynamic level of the voice. (See "Pitch, Timbre, and Dynamic Levels," in v. 1, ch. 6.)

For either of these problems, recommend extremely limited vocalization or short periods of controlled, soft vocal exercise in the mornings. Give your student short, supervised voice lessons for exercise. Have her sing softly in her normal voice, avoiding extremes of range. Be conscious of her posture and breathing technique. Have her cancel nonessential commitments. And remind her that sleep and good nutrition are also crucial.

After absolute or relative voice rest, have your student return to vocal activities gradually. Athletes return to full performance through exercise conditioning; your student should do likewise.

Vocal fatigue can be a result of vocal abuse or misuse. A singer who uses her voice for prolonged periods or in demanding ways is susceptible to vocal fatigue. Beside singing, your student may need to use her voice to teach or to speak to an audience, which can increase the demands on her voice.

Some symptoms of vocal fatigue include soreness or pain in the throat, hoarseness, and periods of voice loss. When your student vocalizes loudly for extended periods—a common requirement for any singer—her voice wears away and becomes progressively softer or more raspy.[12] Vocal attrition can result in laryngeal tissue pathology, muscle fatigue, and voice disorders secondary to acute or chronic abuse of the vocal mechanism (such as vocal nodules or polyps).

Changing vocalization behaviors and using amplification or self-amplification can mitigate vocal fatigue.

Amplifying the voice

Sometimes your student must overcome the sound of other per-formers or the audience. If, without the proper skills, she contin-ually relies on her own vocal power to overcome other sounds, she will soon tire her voice. Amplifying her voice with a sound system can help preserve the integrity of her voice for a performance and for the length of her career.

Not all singers need to amplify their voices. Some worry that using microphones will make singers rely on the extra help to augment their voices. Consider the following variables when deciding whether to amplify your student's voice: the type of venue, the type of stage, the type of vocal performance, and the size of the audience. A traditional opera performer uses no amplification, yet a pop singer who is singing outside at a music fair needs amplifi-cation.

Clinical experience suggests that many vocal injuries sustained by pop and rock singers may be directly related to an inability to self-monitor their singing voices. A small financial investment in excellent monitor speakers or the new ear monitors could prevent many of these injuries.

In light of these potentially dangerous vocal situations, train your student to sing by feel and not by ear alone. Train her to sing by "muscle memory." Every singer, no matter what her vocal style, should posses a vocal technique that enables her to produce her sound safely, even in the absence of good aural feedback.

Using a good microphone can help your student avoid vocal fatigue and elevate the dynamic level. Several types of microphones are available. The common microphone styles are the lavaliere, collar, head-worn, and boom. These microphones can be found in many stores, from local electronics shops to higher-end stereo shops. According to professors of audiology Carl Crandell, Jim Smaldino, and Carol Flexer, the head-worn microphone offers the most consistent signal.[13] Your student should look for a microphone with a frequency response from approximately 30 Hz to 20 kHz. A quality microphone in this range will maximize and enhance vocal output.

Teach your student how to use a microphone. Singing too closely to a microphone will create sound distortion and alter the sound of her singing voice. Singing too far away will soften the sound of her voice, and she might compensate for the loss of loudness by increasing her vocal fold closure.

Good communication between the sound technician and your student can also help save your student's voice. When a technician works with your student to synchronize the effects of the show, your student can perform without having to strain. A good technician will amplify your student's voice to its maximum quality, and she won't have to drive her voice to fill the room. For example, a sound technician can help a musical theater performer who needs an animated belting quality simply by boosting the amplitude. If a performer does not establish a good relationship with the sound technician, the show could fall flat. (See the exercise, "To Sing an Intense Tone Quality Through the Major Passage," in v. 3, ch. 12.)

Bogart–Bacall syndrome

The *Bogart–Bacall syndrome* is named for the notorious low-pitched voice quality used by actors Humphrey Bogart and Lauren Bacall.[14] It occurs in professional singers, actors, and radio or television personalities who consistently speak at a low pitch. If your student chooses to speak with a low pitch rather than with her natural pitch, she will work harder to produce that voice. Speaking with an unnaturally low voice over time can result in vocal fatigue, laryngeal pathology, and vocal disturbance. (See "**To Locate the Best Speaking Pitch**," in v. 2, ch. 9.)

Excessive vocal use

Singing or talking too much will tire the voice. For instance, those who sing five shows a day, five days a week outdoors can tire their voices and damage their vocal systems. A singer who is abusing her voice in this way might get a sore throat, a pain in her neck area due to muscle contraction and muscle fatigue, and sometimes a pain in her ear.

Every singer has to choose how much to use her voice. People who talk too much can choose to talk less or more quietly. Those who are offered demanding roles, such as two Broadway shows a day for twelve weeks, can either opt out of the role or risk a voice problem.

Excessive loudness

The *acoustic environment* of a performance space can trick your student into singing too loudly and fatiguing her voice. The acoustic environment is the singer's perception of her own voice while she produces it. In a performance space with poor acoustic feedback, your student can easily oversing and strain her voice if she is not amplified by a microphone.

Classical singers are extraordinarily sensitive to the phenomenon of "ring" in their voices. (See the heading "The ring of the voice," in v. 1, ch. 4.) When a classical singer cannot hear or sense this ring, she tends to force the appearance of this quality, usually overdriving the air stream and overcompressing the vocal folds, causing vocal injury. If she gets an immediate sense of the clear presence of her own voice at the onset of tone, such vocal pushing is less likely. She needs to know whether she cannot hear the ring because she is not producing it or because the environment interferes with it.

The size of the performance environment can also be a factor. Many spaces are too large to allow for adequate feedback for the unamplified singer. Working outside at fairs or theme parks, a singer has to project her voice over the surrounding noise. Without walls and ceilings, she cannot hear how her voice really sounds or how loud it is. Healthy and safe vocal practices often suffer.

Voice strain can also happen in other performance environments. Often, vocal performances are held in spaces that were not originally designed for musical performance. Typical examples include high-school gyms, auditoriums, and community gathering rooms in retirement homes. These spaces are frequently designed to absorb noise using ceiling tile and carpeting.

The more noise going on around your student, the louder she will sing. This automatic and irresistible response is called the *Lombard effect*.

Again: always train your student to sing by feel—by "muscle memory"—and not by ear alone.

Self-amplifying the voice

Your student can amplify her voice without electronics by:

- Adjusting her posture and movement

- Increasing her respiratory effort (subglottal pressure)

- Changing her glottal configuration

- Manipulating the characteristics of her vocal tract[15]

When the airflow is shut off faster during voicing, the overall sound pressure level of the voice increases due to an increase in the higher partials. (See "Source-Filter Theory," in v. 1, ch. 6.) The maximum glottal airflow produced during voicing is also important and this is related to the amount of respiratory effort produced. Voice scientists Jan Gauffin and Johan Sundberg found that this value corresponds to the intensity of the pitch of the voice.[16]

Lincoln Center was built to house stage companies but is now the venue for a variety of musical groups, including the New York City Opera Company. Singers must overcome a space not tailored to the needs of singers. Controversy currently exists about the use of sound-enhancing techniques to amplify the voices of the opera performers.

Healthy Practicing and Performing

Every voice has a point beyond which it cannot perform without risking injury, no matter how perfect the singer's technique. Teach this reality to your student, so she will take full responsibility for the health and safety of her instrument. Your up-and-coming singer must learn to maintain the long view when deciding how to use her voice.

Some ways your student can prepare for healthy singing include warming up and cooling down, carefully deciding whether to sing when she is hoarse, and eating a proper meal to enhance her performance.

Warming Up and Cooling Down

Warming up before and cooling down after singing will help protect your student's vocal apparatus from strain or injury. It's a healthy habit for your student to adopt, even before and after light singing.

The purposes of any warm-up period are:

- To adjust the voice from speaking to singing
- To align the body and free the breathing mechanism for singing
- To create physical awareness of the vocal mechanism being used correctly
- To gently stretch and exercise the skeletal muscles used in phonation, as with muscle warm-up before any athletic activity

Just as the voice adjusts during a warm-up from speech to singing, a cool-down returns the voice from the extremes of the singing range to a comfortable speaking range. Cooling down helps return the larynx to more-relaxed functioning.

Some things your student can do to cool down are:

- Soft pitch glides and sighs
- Lowering the voice with nasal quality

- Easy, relaxed voicing (for instance, humming)

- Refocusing to a low-impact voice

- Laryngeal massage

Singing Safely When Hoarse

Your student can sing when she's hoarse, but it is risky for her to do so. The vocal folds are always more vulnerable to serious injury when they are swollen or irritated. A singer must be aware of such risks and must have the technical ability to sing as safely as possible in this situation.

When your student's hoarseness results from an illness or vocal fatigue, it is often difficult to know when she should cancel a lesson, an audition, a rehearsal, or a performance. In the music business, an aspiring singer must often choose between singing a performance or risking losing the job or future jobs.

You must answer two questions to help you decide whether your student should sing while she is hoarse: To what degree does the required singing endanger her voice? Can her voice produce the tonal quality necessary for success in the particular situation? In other words, you must ask yourself whether the ends justify the risks.

Lesson

If your student is hoarse, should she take a singing lesson? Thinking conservatively, consider whether your student should run the risk of injuring her vocal folds when it is not really necessary. In most cases, you can work on other non-vocalizing exercises, such those presented in ch. 1, "Flexibility in teaching and learning," in v. 1, ch. 14, "Teaching and learning the vocal line," in v.

4, ch. 15, "Teaching and learning the score," in v. 4, ch. 16, "Teaching and learning the story," in v. 4, and ch. 17, "Teaching and learning the gestalt," in v. 4.) Otherwise, the lesson is best postponed.

However, there is one justification for your student taking a lesson in this situation: sometime in her singing life, she will have to sing when she is mildly hoarse. You can use this lesson to prepare your student to technically and psychologically handle the situation. Then, when such an occasion arrives, she will be able to sing safely and effectively.

If she can produce an easy voice with no counterproductive compensatory muscle tension (CCMT), and if her voice does not fatigue quickly, then a lesson broken into short segments of singing alternating with rest periods is a reasonable course of action. (See "Clearing Up Counterproductive Compensatory Muscle Tension," on page 43.) If her voice is too fatigued or if further work will only cause injury, however, move on to non-vocalizing work or cancel the lesson.

Knowing how to sing safely under difficult circumstances will give your student greater confidence in her abilities.

Rehearsal

Should your student participate in a rehearsal if she is moderately hoarse? The best answer is, "Only if she can mark safely." *Marking* is the technique of producing a gently sung or inflected spoken voice that is well-supported, is soft in volume, and does not require forceful vocal fold closure or tension.

But, even marking might not make a rehearsal safe for your hoarse student. She might be tempted to mark too loudly for her compromised vocal folds, or the conductor or director might pressure her to mark too loudly. If she has the discipline to resist these pressures, then marking a rehearsal is not dangerous.

Audition

Your hoarse student can audition if she can warm up her voice with relative comfort and no strain and if her voice is a reasonable representation of her talent. The danger in this situation is that, caught up in the excitement of an audition and the emotion of the music, she might abandon safe singing to show what her voice can do. She might end up forcing her singing, which can increase the possibility of injury. Once again, help your student weigh the risks against the possible gain. If she can reschedule the audition, she should do so.

Performance

When your student's voice is hoarse and a performance is not crucial to her career, she should not perform. Help her weigh the benefits of the performance against the risks to her voice.

If she is going to sing, she should vocalize as little as possible in the days preceding and the day of the performance. During the day of the performance, she should warm up gently for brief periods (five to 10 minutes), two to four times. To avoid injury, the singer must focus on technical excellence.

Have her maintain optimum, consistent breath support and a very relaxed throat throughout the performance. She should strictly avoid using her voice during intermission and after performing. Have her follow the performance with a day of vocal rest.

Eating for an Optimal Performance

Certain eating practices can help your student prepare for a healthy performance. A singer needs a reserve of energy for optimum performance, but your student should not have a full stomach before a performance.

Vocal coach Richard Miller suggests a "nourishing, unsalted modest meal several hours before curtain time."[17] Other sources recommend eating a mostly carbohydrate meal at least two and one-half hours before performing. This type of meal will provide energy, is easy to digest, and is a good source for blood glucose concentration.

Counsel your student to avoid fats and protein because they take three to four hours to digest. She should also avoid any foods that are highly seasoned or gas-producing in order to minimize stomach discomfort. Highly spiced foods can directly irritate the mucosa.

In some people, milk, ice cream, and other dairy products have been observed to increase the amount and viscosity of mucosal secretions. With increased or thickened mucus production, your student might clear her throat, lower her pitch, or have noise in her voice because her vocal folds aren't vibrating effectively. (Chocolate might have the same effect.)

She should avoid alcohol because it might cause more symptoms of reflux.

ENDNOTES

1. Katherine Verdolini, Ingo R. Titze, and Ann Fennell, "Dependence of phonatory effort on hydration level," *Journal of Speech and Hearing Research* 37 (1994): 1001–07.

2. Jack Jiang, Jennie Ng, and David Hanson, "The effects of rehydration on phonation in excised canine larynges," *Journal of Voice* 13, no. 1 (1999): 51–59.

3. Von L. Lawrence, "Common medications with laryngeal effects," *Ear, Nose, and Throat Journal* 66, no. 8 (1987): 318–22.

4. Robert T. Sataloff, *Professional Voice: The Science and Art of Clinical Care* (New York: Raven Press, 1991).

5. I. Meney et al., "The effect of one night's sleep deprivation on temperature, mood, and physical performance in subjects with different amounts of habitual physical activity," *Chronobiology International* 15, no. 4 (July 1998): 349–63.

6. T. VanHelder and M. W. Radomski, "Sleep deprivation and the effect on exercise performance," *Sports-Med.* 7, no. 4 (1989): 235–47.

7. Robert T. Sataloff, *Professional Voice,* 334.

8. Robert T. Sataloff, *Professional Voice.*

9. F. Gene Martin, "Drugs and Vocal Function," *Journal of Voice* 2, no. 4 (1988): 338–44.

10. D. Vogel and J. Carter, *The Effects of Drugs on Communication Disorders,* in the *Clinical Competence* series. (New York: Singular Publishing Group, Inc., 1995): 107–35.

11. Robert T. Sataloff, *Professional Voice.*

12. Christine M. Sapienza, Carl Crandell, and Brian Curtis, "Effects of sound-field frequency modulation amplification on reducing teachers' sound pressure level in the classroom," *Journal of Voice* 3 (1999): 375–81.

13. Carl C. Crandell, Joseph J. Smaldino, and Carol Flexer, *Sound-Field Fm Amplification: Theory and Practical Applications* (San Diego: Singular Press, Inc., 1995).

14. James A. Koufman and P. David Blalock, "Vocal Fatigue and Dysphonia in the Professional Voice User: Bogart–Bacall Syndrome," *Laryngoscope* 98 (1988): 493–98.

15. Ron Scherer, "Physiology of phonation. A review of basic mechanics," in *Phonosurgery: Assessment and Surgical Management of Voice Disorders* (New York: Raven Press, 1991): 77–93.

16. Jan Gauffin and Johan Sundberg, "Spectral correlates of glottal voice source waveform characteristics," *Journal of Speech and Hearing Research* 32 (1989): 556–65.

17. Richard Miller, *The Structure of Singing: System and Art in Vocal Technique* (New York: Schirmer Books, 1996).

VOCAL HEALTH PROBLEMS

Singing places physical demands on your student's body, and her body must be healthy in order to respond properly. However, the muscles and tissues your student uses for singing are sensitive to how she uses her voice, the condition of her body, and her environment.

For example, if your student's vocal folds come together too rapidly, rubbing against each other too harshly, or if she sings too long, too loudly, too high, or with too much tension, then her body responds by hurting. The body's responses thus prevent the vocal folds from functioning optimally—or, in extreme cases, from functioning at all.

Your student may develop a vocal problem that is caused by the vocal fold's responses or some pathology in her body—a problem that cannot be corrected with proper technique. With such a vocal health problem, you need to get her to a doctor so he can treat the problem. Your task as a teacher is to notice any change in your student's voice suggestive of a health problem, to refer her to a medical professional if necessary, and to help her with her recovery.

Over time, you will learn to recognize many common vocal health problems. However, no matter how skilled you are, and no matter how many similar problems you may have seen, avoid making a diagnosis. Your contribution to identifying a possible problem is to isolate the "honest" vocal sound from any symptoms of tension and then to determine whether that sound is abnormal.

If your student develops a vocal problem from misusing her voice, you can sometimes help by reminding her about good vocal habits. For instance, you can counsel her not to smoke, to drink enough water, or not to talk too loudly, too long, or too high. But leave anything else to the professional medical community. Your student needs a physician to diagnose any health condition that might be causing her vocal problems.

Recognizing Vocal Health Problems

The first step in helping your student with a vocal health problem is recognizing when a problem is occurring. She may exhibit a number of symptoms—pain, unintended changes in vocal quality, or tension—that could point to the onset of a vocal problem. You and your student can learn to listen for anomalies in her voice, and she can learn to feel sensations in her voice that alert her when something is wrong.

The second step is to isolate the problem from any unnecessary tensions so that you can hear the honest vocal quality. Your student might develop unnecessary tension in her muscles to compensate for a vocal problem, which could mask the true, underlying cause.

Hearing and Feeling When Something Is Wrong

When you hear unintended or uncontrollable tone qualities emerge in your student's voice, you may begin to wonder whether she is developing a vocal health problem. She may sound hoarse, raspy, or breathy. You may hear uncontrolled breaks in or limits to her range—typically, the upper portion. You may hear her voice fail to phonate when she tries to start a tone, or the tones in her middle or upper range may falter.

It is tempting to believe that you will be the very first to detect even a hint of a vocal problem. But your student will often feel symptoms of a vocal problem before it is audible to you. This is *not* an indication that you do not have a good ear or are not a good teacher. You will only fall short in your job if you ignore your student's complaint—particularly if it is a recurring one.

Never ignore a consistent complaint of vocal discomfort from your student. Her complaints might include any of the following:

- Her voice feels "heavy" or "resistant"

- She has lost resonance in part or all of her voice, or her voice has "lost its ring"

- Her voice sputters, clicks, or halts (doesn't phonate) when she tries to start a tone

- Her throat becomes overly tense when she sings above mezzopiano

- She cannot "get her voice forward" (usually related directly to a mechanical inefficiency in her vocal folds)

Even if your student does not complain, if you sense that she is working harder than usual, do not rule out a vocal health problem. And even if your student improves her technique, if her voice begins to sound more "forward" to you and she still complains of feeling the tone "back" in her throat, take note.

Clearing Up Counterproductive Compensatory Muscle Tension

Whenever a singer's vocal folds are even slightly compromised, most singers respond with *counterproductive compensatory muscle tension (CCMT)*, in which she tries to "create" a normal tone by extraneous or excessive muscle contractions. You will only be able to notice an underlying vocal problem after any CCMT is removed.

> ❋ Remember: Any relaxation of vocal tension must always be balanced with active muscle engagement and well-supported airflow. When "trying to get rid of" vocal tension, your student can become so relaxed that her muscle activity and energy decreases too much, and this can adversely affect her vocal quality.

In her struggle to produce a clear voice in spite of a vocal problem, your student can forget or "lose" her point of reference for understanding the sensations involved in free and easy singing. (See the heading "A Baseline State of Relaxation," in v. 2, ch. 7.) You must help her re-establish this kinesthetic awareness, no matter what the resulting vocal quality. Your student must have that baseline point of reference in order to identify the absence of inappropriate muscle tension in singing.

Begin your search for CCMT by carefully checking your student's tongue, jaw and face, neck, larynx and pharynx, diaphragm, intercostal muscles, and back. Look for even the smallest signs of inappropriate muscle tension.

Tension in the tongue

The tongue is a major place for tension to occur. The base or root of the tongue, the mid-portion, the tip, or the entire tongue might be involved. Your student might exhibit common tension responses, including retracting her tongue or squeezing the sides of her tongue. (See the exercises under "The Tongue," in v. 2, ch. 10, including "To Become Aware of the Tongue" and "To Soften the Base of the Tongue.")

To identify these tensions, have your student sing [a] (ah), mezzo-piano, up and down a series of simple scales. Have her start in her lower or middle register and work the entire range of her voice. When sung with truly relaxed muscles, the vowel [a] reveals much about basic vocal fold function, which you hear in the vocal quality.

Observe your student's tongue when she sings [a]. Her tongue should rest undisturbed on the floor of her mouth, with the tip gently touching the back of her lower teeth. As she begins to phonate, the resting position of her tongue should not change; the center of her tongue should not retract or pull down even slightly.

On other vowels, the tip of your student's tongue should not retract away from her lower teeth, nor should there be much (if any) change in the width of her tongue. Her tongue should assume only enough firmness to shape the vowel. Think of your student's tongue as pliable, rubberlike material as opposed to stiff, unyielding concrete.

For many singers, the soft palate's elevation is directly linked to unnecessary tension in the tongue. Often, the back of a singer's tongue presses down while the soft palate lifts. When the singer suddenly releases the tension in the tongue, the soft palate is inclined to drop, resulting in a nasal tone. Your student must learn to allow her soft palate to lift without any accompanying tongue tension.

Tension in the jaw and face

Check for tension in your student's jaw and facial muscles, massaging them in a gentle circular motion while your student sings. The jaw needs to relax to allow the tongue and throat to relax.

("To Become Aware of the Jaw," in v. 2, ch. 10, and "Temporo-mandibular joint dysfunction (TMJ)," on page 111.)

Tension in the neck

Your student may be tense in the area beneath her chin, at the point where the underside of her chin meets her throat. Using a very gentle upward pressure of your fingertips, feel for any hint of downward muscle movement while she sings. (If your student is ticklish, have her place her fingertips on top of yours while you do this.)

Now check the back of her neck while she sings. If it is rigid, softly massage it while your student gently and slowly shakes her head in a small "no" gesture.

Appropriate head and neck alignment are essential to a free, "honest" vocal tone. Inappropriate alignment might indicate the presence of unnecessary tension.

Tension in the larynx and pharynx

It can be difficult to identify exact areas of tension in the larynx. You might be able to hear signs of muscle tension in the larynx when you hear pressed phonation, a tight, strident tone. (See the heading "Focus on Flow Phonation," in v. 2, ch. 9.) If the larynx rises in the throat, it can be a sign of CCMT (although an ascending larynx is acceptable under some conditions and for some styles of singing, such as pop).

It is difficult to quantify muscle tension and constriction in the pharynx, the area above the larynx. However, you can assume that, if a vocal problem does exist, the muscles both inside and outside the larynx and those comprising the walls of the pharynx may be unnecessarily tense. You might be able to help your student relax these muscles with a variety of relaxation techniques. (See the exercises under "Exercises for Releasing Tension," in v. 2, ch. 7, and "To Discover a Low Larynx," "To Relax the Jaw and Tongue," "To Relax the Neck," "To Relax on the Inhalation," and "To Relax the Throat by Suspending the Breath," in v. 2, ch. 9.)

Tension in the diaphragm

Check your student for tension in her upper abdominal musculature, by gently pressing your fingers immediately below her sternum. (Again, if your student is ticklish or if this physical contact makes her tense or uncomfortable, have her place her hands lightly on top of yours while you do this.)

When your student's voice is at rest, this area should be soft and comfortably pliable, not tender to the touch or excessively tense. Even when she is singing, this area should not be "gripped" or stiff.

Tension in the intercostal muscles

Often, the muscles of your student's rib cage become rigidly locked when she tries to produce a "normal" voice with compromised vocal folds. This situation can occur on both inhalation and exhalation.

You can help your student release these muscles by having her gently move her rib cage from side to side.

Tension in the back

You might also find CCMT in the small of your student's back. Have her sit in a chair and collapse over at the waist, hanging toward the floor comfortably with her arms and neck limp. Then have her breathe slowly and quietly into this position. This stretch can help release muscle tension not only in the lower back but also in the shoulders and neck. It can also help release tension in the lower abdominal region, where cumulative tension is often ignored.

Something else you can check for: When your student is standing, be sure that her knees are not locked and that she is not leaning backward. If she locks her knees or leans over, she will create unnecessary tension in her back, legs, and spine.

Referring Your Student to a Doctor

If your student's symptoms seem chronic (having built up over time), or if the problem seems to be long-standing (such as an allergy), then refer her to her primary physician. This is a general practitioner, the doctor who takes care of your student's general health.

If her symptoms seem acute, appearing suddenly, they might be caused by something specific: a strenuous schedule, too much travel, oversinging, or not using her voice correctly. If this is the case, here are some things you can have your student try that might resolve her vocal problem:

- Rest her voice

- Modify her environmental constraints

- Enhance her training methods

- Enhance her vocal hygiene

- Modify her performance program

If her problem is not resolved with these techniques, then your student might need to see an *otolaryngologist*, or an "ear, nose, and throat doctor" (ENT). An ENT is a specialist in problems of the head and neck, along with their related systems. If the ENT is also well-trained to care for singers, your student will be in very good hands.

If the problem seems clearly voice-related and not a general health problem, you can refer her directly to an ENT. However, keep in mind that many health-insurance programs will insist on your student first seeing her primary-care physician for a referral to a specialist.

After the ENT finishes his exam, he might prescribe treatment (see "Treating Vocal Health Problems," on page 65), or he might send your student for further testing to:

- A speech-language pathologist (voice therapist), who special-izes in the voice and the mechanics of making sound

- An allergist, who is trained to identify and treat environmen-tal and seasonal allergies

- A singing-voice specialist, who works specifically with sing-ers, developing exercises so that a singer can sing without injuring her voice

When to Refer

You must decide how long to wait before suggesting a medical evaluation. Your student can harm her vocal apparatus if she waits too long, hoping that the problem will simply go away.

But it's not always necessary to send your student to a doctor. For instance, recovering after an overlong plane trip is usually as simple as getting vocal rest and drinking lots of water.

However, if rest, hydration, or relaxation techniques do not seem to correct even an apparently simple problem (and particularly if the problem continues after several days or weeks), then you should refer your student to an ENT.

✿ Err on the side of caution. Why run the risk of more-serious damage to your student's voice if quick medical intervention could prevent it? The earlier a vocal health problem is detected and treated, the better the long-term outcome.

When in doubt, seek help for your student.

You should refer your student to an otolaryngologist (ENT) immediately if you notice any of the following symptoms:

- Breathing problems
- Significant breaks in the voice without apparent cause
- Deteriorating vocal quality
- Laryngeal pain
- Significant hoarseness that will not resolve

When to wait before referring your student

If you notice a minor problem and if you and your student can wait a little while—for instance, if your student has no upcoming performances—help minimize your student's CCMT, and have her practice relaxed vocal work (brief lessons and short exercises that do not strain the voice) for two to four weeks. During this observation period, have your student sing only for short periods of 15 to 30 minutes, with limited range and volume. If her voice still does not improve, send her to an ENT experienced in voice care.

If your student has a sudden onset of hoarseness or breathiness soon after a damaging activity (such as yelling at a sporting event, oversinging a performance, and so on), and if 24 hours of complete voice rest does not help, then refer your student immediately.

After a particularly demanding rehearsal or performance, your student might experience some vocal fold edema (swelling). This swelling can leave both her singing voice and her speaking voice hoarse. This vocal problem should resolve within 24 hours of relative voice rest (limited voice use). If it takes 48 hours or more to resolve—and especially if this kind of hoarseness is a recurring pattern with your student—then refer her for a medical evaluation.

If your student catches a cold or the flu, and if any hoarseness or loss of vocal range occurs as a result, give her voice seven to 10 days to recover after the other signs of the cold resolve. During this time, have your student practice scales of limited range, loudness, and duration on a daily basis—as long as she experiences no vocal strain or serious fatigue.

If your student experiences one of the preceding vocal problems and she cannot comply with a grace period of gentle voice use (because of performance commitments or because she is simply unwilling), then it is probably best to have the situation medically evaluated.

Whom to Refer To

Before you open the telephone book to look for a doctor and become bewildered by all the many different specialties they practice, start at the very beginning. Ask your student if she has a primary-care physician who oversees her general health care. If she does, refer her to that doctor for an initial evaluation.

After your student's initial examination and some tests, you will begin to hear about medical specialists who are likely to be involved with your student's vocal care. The primary physician might know a good "ear, nose, and throat doctor" (ENT) who is familiar with the particular needs of singers. An ENT is skilled in examining the vocal apparatus.

Your student is likely to be referred to an allergist to see if she has allergies to any particular foods, plants, animals, etc. The allergist may also ask her about her sensitivity to the general environment. Your student will find the allergist helpful in recommending treatment for this common ailment.

Your student may also be sent to a pulmonologist, who will look at how her breathing mechanism is working. If your student's breath is not efficient, she will have treatment and therapy options available to her.

Your student's primary physician begins the referral process. He is the one responsible for her general health care and for referring her to the appropriate specialist(s). His diagnosis and referrals are keys to your student's vocal recovery.

Preparing Your Student for a Medical Examination

In order to diagnose your student's vocal health problem accurately, a medical professional will consider many aspects of your student's overall health during his initial evaluation, including the following:

- Your student's medical history, along with information about her current complaint
- Your student's past and present vocal training
- Positive and/or negative habits that might affect your student's health and singing

You can help prepare your student by encouraging her to keep good medical records and to be honest in her responses.

In addition, take some time to go over the questions that her ENT will be likely to ask.

Your student's doctor her ENT is going to take a medical history, which is a routine part of any comprehensive health examination. If your student has an up-to-date record of her health history, it will save time and eliminate memory gaps.

Remind your student that, although it's called a "history," it includes both past *and present* medical problems, treatments, and symptoms; a background of the student; and a list of any related conditions.

To diagnose a vocal health problem accurately, the more information the physician has about a patient's medical history, the better. If your student will be seeing a physician she hasn't seen in the past, a comprehensive set of notes will be especially helpful. Seemingly unrelated bits of information can often give a skilled professional the right clues for a correct diagnosis.

The following list of topics and questions is not exhaustive, but it will help provide a bank of information for the doctor's use. A specialist will cover more topics and ask more particular questions than a general practitioner will.

- Past surgeries
    - List any surgeries that required intubation
    - List any surgeries on or near the vocal folds
- Past traumas (such as a car accident)
- Are you under a doctor's care for any other medical problems? If so, what are they?

- List your current prescriptions and any over-the-counter medicines you are taking

- Have you been sick recently?

- Did you strain or overuse your voice recently?

- History of speech difficulties / shortness of breath / stridor

  - Describe any previous or present speech difficulties

  - Give a history of difficulty breathing

  - Do you have a history of upper respiratory infection, asthma, or emphysema?

  - Do you have a history of *stridor* (noisy breathing)?

- Emotional status of the patient

  - Are you anxious about anything at this time?

  - What particular stress are you under now?

  ❈ If your student reports or displays any stress or emotional anxiety, pay close attention. Her anxiety may be tied to the fact that performance time or achievement is compromised because of the current vocal disorder. A normal-appearing larynx combined with an underlying psycho-emotional cause can characterize a psychosomatic voice disorder. This is a real phenomenon, and it can be treated effectively when a professional counselor is part of the healing team.

- Allergies (If the history and physical examination suggest an allergy, the allergist will determine the cause using either a skin test or a blood test. But first he will ask some questions.)

  - Have you ever been diagnosed as having an allergy?

- If so, to what and by whom?

- Are there any other family members who suffer from allergies?

- What type of symptoms do you have?

- When and where do these symptoms usually occur and how long do they last?

- Do the symptoms occur daily, weekly, seasonally, or on any other regular basis?

- How do these symptoms affect your singing voice or vocal performance?

- Is your speaking voice affected by your allergies?

- How severe are your symptoms and do the symptoms vary in severity?

- Are you currently taking any medications for your allergies?

- What are the names and dosages of these medications?

- How long have you been taking them?

- Other information

  - What type of work are you doing?

  - What kind of voice do you use during performances?

  - What vocal exercises have you tried to help with the current problem?

  - Physical and perceptual impression of the voice disorder

  - Describe how your voice feels: hoarse, raspy, or breaking apart

  - How long do the sensations last? What brings them on?

Some students will be more articulate than others about how they feel physically. Talk with your student so she can accurately describe her symptoms. The topics and questions listed above are particularly helpful to an ENT or other specialists who deal directly with the voice and who have a common vocabulary to describe how the voice is or is not working.

Help your student to be specific, to go beyond "It hurts." Have her describe to you how it hurts, what other physical sensations she has, and when or where those sensations occur.

Describing Your Student's Vocal Training

Your student's vocal training and previous experience with voice problems will be of special interest to the professionals who examine her. The answers to these questions will reveal how compliant she may be with behavioral therapy and how well she may deal with the stress of an injured voice. The answers will also uncover any patterns that may be damaging her voice without her knowledge.

- Past vocal training
  - Your history of vocal training
  - How long have you been singing?
  - Have there been significant changes in the past few weeks? What are they?
- Current training program
  - Describe your vocal training program
  - How long have you been working with this teacher?
  - What kind of program are you following?

- What kind of singing are you working on?

- What vocal exercises are you doing to help your injured voice?

Describing Your Student's Habits

While a primary physician may cover these topics or ask the following questions, an ENT or a singing-voice specialist certainly will. The effects of abusing the voice during speaking may show up only when your student is singing.

- Describe any abusive voice behaviors at home and/or at work, during singing or speaking activities

- Describe your regular speaking activities at home, at work, and socially

  - Does your job require much speaking?

  - Do you have to yell or raise your voice often to be heard?

  - Have there been incidents of screaming or loud talking recently?

- Describe your sleeping patterns during the last month

- When and where do you usually eat? Do you eat regularly? Describe your diet

- Do you smoke tobacco or anything else?

- Describe your use of alcohol and/or caffeine

- Describe any habitual clearing of the throat or coughing

After the medical history is taken, the physician continues with a physical examination.

The Physical Examination

A primary physician will examine your student and her basic health. An ENT will also use a variety of tests and tools to determine the cause of your student's current vocal problem and to arrive at a diagnosis.

Some tests help the ENT look at the *physical structure* of the vocal folds. Are there visible lesions or malformations? Is infection present? How big are the tonsils?

Other tests help the ENT look at the *function* of the vocal folds. Do the right and left sides of the vocal folds act in symmetry? Are false vocal folds being pressed into service?

The goal of all these tests is to determine what structural or functional changes have occurred in your student's vocal folds. Using a variety of tests and a combination of tools and techniques, the ENT will assess your student's vocal function during singing and speaking tasks.

Visual Examination

There are two primary ways an ENT will look at the vocal folds: either through the mouth or through the nose. The visual exam has been a historic method used by the ENT to determine if the structure is normal or compromised by disease.

Mirror exam

The basic, time-honored test is the *mirror exam.* The ENT places a warmed mirror at the back of your student's mouth, and directs a beam of light toward the back of the mouth. This gives the ENT a top-down view of your student's vocal folds. This test can show whether the structure of the vocal folds is normal.

The ENT uses this test to check for obvious abnormalities and infection. During this exam, your student will be asked to sustain a vowel sound, usually [i] (ee); this will move her epiglottis up and forward so the ENT can see her vocal folds more clearly.

Newer tests have far surpassed the accuracy of the mirror exam, but it remains the first test done because it can reveal obvious problems.

Endoscopic tests

Following the mirror exam, the ENT moves on to *endoscopy*. Endoscopy is a general term; it refers to going inside the body to take an image. Several different kinds of endoscopy are used to examine the vocal folds and their ability to move.

Oral rigid endoscopy. Much like the mirror in the previous exam, the oral endoscope is placed at the back of your student's mouth. A fiber-optic bundle carries light that is directed down onto the larynx. The light is reflected back and the image is projected through a camera to a television monitor. The magnification is on the order of six times better than what is available in the mirror exam, giving the ENT a much better idea of the vocal fold structure. Your student will be asked to sustain the vowel [i] (ee) during this procedure.

Oral cancers, lesions, and polyps are readily visible with this test. It is fairly non-invasive, although some people may experience gagging. A topical anesthetic can desensitize the gag reflex.

Transnasal flexible endoscopy. The ENT uses *transnasal flexible endoscopy* when he needs to see how the vocal folds are functioning. With this test, a flexible endoscope is passed through the singer's nasal cavity. Once again, this test uses light, a camera, and a television monitor to observe the vocal folds. Unlike the previous test, this time your student will be able to use her voice to speak, sing, and whistle.

The ENT may spray your student's nose with a combination decongestant and topical numbing agent. He will then pass the scope beyond the back of her nose in order to see her lower throat and her vocal folds. She should be comfortable during this procedure, and the ENT will be able to see all of the structures with little difficulty. With this test, the ENT will learn more about your student's vocal fold function.

Some risks are associated with this test; nose abrasion and nosebleeds are the most common. Your student may experience discomfort from the tubes passing through her nasal cavity. In very rare cases, a laryngeal spasm may occur, shutting off the airway.

Videostroboscopy. Both of the above tests can be enhanced by an additional test that adds a strobe light. If the vibration of the vocal folds requires assessment, this test can help. *Videostroboscopy*, as it is commonly called, helps determine the movement of the vocal folds. How well do they open and close? Do they open fully and shut tightly? Do the folds move together as a unit? What effect is a lesion having on the vocal folds? If there is a scar on one side and not on the other, how is the movement affected?

This imaging technique allows the ENT to view the movement of the vocal folds in slow motion, making visible what the eye cannot see at regular speed. The ENT looks for the degree and regularity of movement. Compensatory behaviors can also be documented through this technique.

Acoustic Examination

After the videostroboscopic exam, a voice therapist will record your student's voice for an *acoustic analysis*. The voice therapist analyzes what is heard when a disturbance to the vocal fold structure or function exists.

The voice recording serves two purposes: the voice is observed in a relatively natural speaking environment and additional information is gained about the nature of your student's singing problem.

During the acoustic analysis, the voice therapist examines the fundamental frequency characteristics of the acoustic waveform. The acoustic analysis can specify the differences between the speaking voice and the singing voice. Sometimes your student's speech can sound quite normal, but there are breaks in voice production when she attempts to sing. The voice therapist can use this test to find those discrepancies.

Using a head-set microphone connected to a digital audio tape recorder, the voice therapist records your student's speaking voice and her singing voice. From the acoustic samples, the voice therapist can see displays of her vocal pitch, vocal loudness, and timing on a computer. The voice therapist will usually ask your student to perform sustained vowels, counting, glissandos, reading samples, and singing samples for this analysis.

The glissando task is particularly useful, since it provides an index of your student's frequency and amplitude range and her vocal control. When a vocal pathology exists, the vibratory pattern of her vocal folds is typically irregular or aperiodic. Her voice sounds abnormal (hoarse, rough, or breathy) because there is a disturbed acoustic by-product.

The acoustic analysis is an indispensable tool to quantify these perceptual indices.

Aerodynamic Examination

Along with acoustic analysis, *aerodynamic assessment* is a technique a voice therapist uses to test how a vocal disturbance is affecting the vibration of your student's vocal folds. Aerodynamic analysis shows the amounts of airflow and air pressures that are being generated by your student when she is producing sound. Both speaking and singing samples are recorded for this test.

If the vocal folds are not operating optimally, the flow produced at the level of the vocal folds is disturbed. Because the airflow is irregular, the voice sounds abnormal. Your student may generate abnormally high air pressures to help compensate for the inefficient movement of the vocal folds. These compensations may cause even greater problems by setting up a cycle of vocal *hyperfunction*.

Hyperfunction means that your student is working too hard to produce her sound. Increased muscle tension and/or increased respiratory effort are the general clues for hyperfunction. If your student is working too hard to produce her sound, this can result in vocal fatigue or even the development of secondary pathological conditions that coincide with her primary vocal health problem. One common example is the compression of the false vocal folds during voice production. This compression happens as the body attempts to control airflow when the function of the vocal folds is impaired, as in a case of vocal fold nodules or vocal folds weakness.

Pulmonary Examination

Pulmonary function tests are important because they can help determine if your student's voice disturbance stems from a problem with her breathing apparatus. However, a physician will only run these tests if he finds that there may be a problem with the lower or upper airway that could be inhibiting a normal breathing pattern. If the primary physician does not make this referral, the ENT will.

However, you can make a referral for pulmonary function testing if your student complains of breathlessness or if you observe that her breathing is labored. If she describes a feeling of breathing against a resistance or if she feels that she runs out of air after a short period of vocalizing (or maybe even when she walks up a flight of stairs), a pulmonary test may be indicated.

If a pulmonologist gives pulmonary function tests to determine the presence or absence of a disease state, then he needs to complete them during a time when your student is complaining of or reporting symptoms of respiratory distress. A pulmonologist will test the volumetric capacity of your student's lungs, and test the relationship between the amount of airflow and the percentage of lung volumes at which the flow of air is produced.

With such tests, a pulmonologist can rule out pathological pulmonary conditions such as emphysema or asthma that may be contributing to the vocal disturbance. After he runs the tests, he will send a report to the referring doctor, who will then discuss with your student the implications of any condition found.

If your student has a lower airway condition, she may have to change what she sings in performance. She may not be physically capable of performing what she has sung in the past. If she has physical limitations, her original performance goals may be less obtainable.

If this is the case, you can work with her to set reasonable goals so that she does not attempt to perform outside her physiological capabilities. For example, if she has been diagnosed with exercise-induced asthma, she may not be able to sing demanding music while performing active choreography.

If your student has a pulmonary condition, you may need to change the roles you have chosen for her. Consider placing her in roles that do not carry such a demand for physical activity and pulmonary stamina. With your expert guidance, she can become aware of the degree of her functional limitations and, with your caring support, she can become more accepting of these limitations and find creative ways to continue to sing.

Sinus X-ray and CT Scan Examination

The ENT might refer your student for sinus radiography (x-ray) to confirm a diagnosis of sinusitis (she could have a normal x-ray and still have sinusitis). In addition, the ENT might order a CT scan to definitively diagnose a sinus disease.

A diagnosis of acute sinusitis is clinical, based primarily on the history your student provides and the physical findings.

Hearing Examination

A hearing screening test is a standard part of any exam. It is a simple pass/fail test. Your student will be asked for a history of any hearing problems and any results from previous evaluations of her hearing.

This test does not reflect the full status of her hearing acuity, but it does screen for any obvious potential contributors to the vocal disturbance.

The parts of your student's body affected by allergies will be her eyes, nose, throat, chest, and skin. An allergist will probably give her the RAST IgE test; it requires her to give one small blood sample for a chemical analysis. This test is safe, accurate, and relatively painless, and it is widely used to determine specific allergens.

Once a diagnosis has been made, the allergist will suggest a course of treatment that consists of a combination of options, including avoidance, medication, and/or immunotherapy. Immunotherapy involves having regular injections that gradually help your student's body build up a tolerance to an allergen, which minimizes or prevents the symptoms. (See "Allergies," on page 105.)

Treating Vocal Health Problems

A physician skilled in treating vocal health problems uses three main types of therapy: behavioral changes, prescribed medicines, and surgery. He knows that not every treatment is appropriate for every problem.

For a singer who has been traveling extensively, the physician might diagnose severe dehydration, and he might recommend that she increase her fluid intake by drinking lots of water and soaking in the hotel pool (behavioral changes).

If he discovers significant swelling in the singer's vocal folds, he might prescribe certain steroids to reduce the swelling (prescribed medicines).

If the singer has lesions on her vocal folds that do not resolve on their own, he might recommend surgery to remove them.

This section describes the most common ways ENTs put these three treatment therapies into practice.

Behavioral Voice Therapy

Your student's otolaryngologist (ENT) will advocate behavioral voice therapy primarily as a treatment for functional, non-organic voice problems because it is benign.

A licensed speech pathologist (voice therapist) will engage with your student in a behavioral voice treatment program. The voice therapist might recommend various regimens for your student's speaking voice, including concentrating on areas of breathing, working on ease of phonation, working on vocal resonance, building up vocal stamina, focusing on proper technique, and carrying out preventative maintenance (warm-ups and cool-downs). The benefits of good speaking therapies will support singing therapies.

You can help make sure that your student's speech pathologist is well-trained and experienced in the care of the singing voice. Just as there are different types of subspecialties in the area of otolaryngology, there are specialties in the area of speech-language pathology. Your student should work with a therapist who is dedicated to the care of the voice. Make sure she asks the therapist about his or her experience treating the voice and—more specifically—his experience treating singers.

Pharmacological Treatment

Your student's ENT might recommend a pharmacological treatment (the second-most recommended approach), using medicines to alleviate pain and the symptoms of vocal problems.

For instance, the ENT might prescribe corticosteroids, since they can be very useful in the medical management of various vocal problems in singers. Most commonly, they are used to rapidly reduce the inflammatory swelling associated with acute laryngitis. Voice rest with natural resolution is preferred, but steroids can sometimes save the day when an important singing engagement cannot be postponed.

❋ Steroids can give a singer a false sense of well-being, so tell your student not to push her voice too hard. It is important to exercise restraint in these situations, even if the medication seems to have worked vocal magic.

Aside from their short-term use, steroids can also be helpful in the context of a long-term voice therapy regimen. They can shorten the time frame of improvement for certain vocal problems by speeding resolution of some of the more-acute swelling and inflammatory stiffness that can accompany even chronic, well-established pathology.

Systemic steroids are of much greater benefit than inhaled ones. Inhaled steroids can cause voice disturbance in some singers, and more-chronic use can even result in yeast growth on the vocal folds. All systemic steroids also have potential side-effects and must be used judiciously.

An ENT may prescribe other medications when there are medical factors associated with a voice disturbance such as allergies, chronic sinusitis, excess phlegm, coughing, and/or gastroesoph-ageal reflux (acids coming up from her stomach and irritating the back part of her throat and vocal folds). Some of these prescriptions may have side-effects on your student's vocal fold structure and function, such as drying out the vocal folds. If this happens, she may notice decreased flexibility in her voice due to reduced movement in the vocal fold structure.

Whatever the prescription, your student needs to follow the program rigorously. If she does not take her medication as prescribed, or if she stops taking the medication before she is advised to, the therapy may be ineffective. The physician may then decide that pharmacological management is not the best option for her, and the evaluative process will have to start again.

❋ Keep in mind that, if your student does not stick to her behavioral therapy program or her course of pharmacological treatment, then surgery may become her only option—and surgery can be risky.

Surgical Treatment

Your student's ENT will resort to surgery only when other therapies do not or cannot work. Most singers who have undergone vocal fold surgery eventually return to a full schedule of singing. However, whether or not to undergo surgery is a decision that should be made only after all other reasonable, less-risky alternatives have been exhausted.

There are many factors that affect the outcome of surgery, the first being the pre-surgical condition of the vocal folds themselves. For example, the size of a vocal fold mass determines how much tissue disruption must occur during its removal. The more tissue that has to be disturbed—particularly if the mass sits deep in the vocal fold—the more the likelihood of a slower healing process and the increased chance that the vocal fold will be scarred. (Sometimes, scarring has already occurred as a result of the original injury.)

Recovering from surgery

The two most frequently asked questions concerning vocal fold surgery are, "How long will it take my voice to recover after surgery?" and "Will my voice be normal after surgery?"

These are difficult questions to answer, because both the time frame for recovery and the outcome possibilities vary dramatically from patient to patient. In addition, the surgeon's knowledge and experience are important factors in the surgical outcome. Your student needs to choose someone with a good track record in this very specialized field.

However, you and your student must both be aware that, even in the best of surgical hands and with the surgeon doing everything right, a sub-optimum vocal result can occur. For example, some individuals are more predisposed than others to forming scar tissue, and this is not a factor that can be predicted or controlled. Each person has an individualized anatomy that may heal in an unpredictable way. Therefore, the possibility of and timetable for a complete recovery are not that simple to predict.

Your student's pre-surgical vocal technique is a major consideration when estimating healing time and the resumption of a more-normal voice. The better the vocal technique before surgery, the better the chances for a more timely recovery. In the field of sophisticated voice care, it is widely believed that good pre-operative voice therapy and vocal reworking are the best preparation for an optimum vocal recovery. Pre-surgical voice therapy is also an integral part of improving the odds for a good recovery of the singing voice.

In addition, your student's personal attitude during this ordeal should not be underestimated, as it can be a significant factor in the recovery process. The singer who manages to maintain a more-positive outlook during recovery generally seems to reach his or her vocal end result more quickly and with less stress than does the singer who is inherently more negative. The more-positive singer will not necessarily end up with better surgical results, but the vocal journey is often less extended.

The style of music that your student performs may also play a role in determining when she can produce a voice that is viable in a particular performance setting. For instance, an operatic coloratura is expected to produce near perfection of tone in all registers of her voice. Additionally, she must accomplish this without the help of any amplification and with no hints of vocal fatigue. This requires a level of vocal fold functional efficiency that can take longer to achieve post-surgically than the level needed by a blues or a pop singer. For a non-classical singer whose vocal performance success may depend less on tonal perfection in a classical sense and more on a voice that may include uneven or rough qualities and that relies on amplification for projection, the return time to performance can be shorter. This is not an absolute comparison. Again, many other variables enter into the picture and affect the timing.

So far, we've avoided the answer to the question, "How long?" Many singers have already been through a painful and frustrating period of vocal struggle long before surgery occurs. Your student needs to have some sort of time frame in mind when facing recovery, or she may feel that the process is never-ending; however, she is not a failure if her recovery exceeds that time frame.

Be reasonable and conservative. Tell your student that she should not expect to return to fully normal singing for three to nine months after her surgery. Depending on the extent of her surgery, a more-realistic timeline might be nine to eighteen months.

Some singers will sound normal sooner. However, "sounding normal" and returning to performance demands are two different things. Even after they resume a more-normal singing routine, many singers complain of lingering intermittent vocal fatigue. This fatigue should eventually disappear.

If the surgical result is not optimum, then it is likely that the recovery process will be slower. In this instance, it is probably better to mentally prepare your student for a longer recovery time. If improvement occurs faster, so much the better.

Singers are under tremendous pressure to return to singing, auditioning, and performing. Some of this pressure is self-inflicted, and some is a direct result of the realities of the harsh and often unforgiving music business. As her teacher, help your student hold her course toward full recovery, allowing her to do only what is possible without vocal strain or fatigue.

Too many singers make the shortsighted mistake of returning to performance demands before their voices are ready. This can be disastrous. More than one singer has paid a heavy price for this impatience with another vocal fold injury.

Recovery plan after surgery

Remember that there are no one-size-fits-all formulas for designing a vocal recovery plan following vocal fold surgery. You can expect that the vocal fold that was operated upon will have a degree of stiffness and swelling related to the trauma of the surgical intervention. The degree of stiffness and swelling varies among individuals. In some instances, the post-surgical voice will sound distinctly clearer and more efficient than the pre-surgical voice. However, in many cases, the quality of the post-surgical voice will be hoarse with generally decreased volume and resonance.

In the next few paragraphs, we outline a few basic concepts for recovery that you and your student might expect. (See also

"Recovery Exercises," on page 81.) These are not recommendations for your particular student with her particular surgery: you will need to determine those details with your ENT.

Your student's approach to her recovery should be centered upon improving both the stretching and the undulating ability of her vocal folds. This approach must be malleable in order to accommodate the individual healing rate of her vocal folds. Your student should not begin singing again until her physician gives her the go-ahead.

During each post-surgery lesson, you will need to help your student gently explore the boundaries of her voice, always adhering to the adage that "Less is more."

The first lesson can consist of three- to five-minute increments of singing—less if the voice fatigues or strains—and can last as long as 30 minutes. Your student should sing very softly. You can begin on simple three- to five-note scales.

A typical first lesson might consist of two to five minutes of *121* or *12321* gliding, legato scales in the lower and middle range on any comfortable vowel. Your student may require short vocal rest periods even with these limited demands. If her voice permits, add lip and/or tongue trills, again with controlled volume and limited range—whatever her voice will comfortably allow. Very short increments of soft humming on single notes and *121* or *12321* scales can be added if they are not excessively tiring for your student.

Light agility exercises, such as five-note descending scales on consonant-initiated syllables, can also be included in the first three-week period.

✳ Safe recovery demands that you stop a lesson immediately if your student experiences serious vocal fatigue, discomfort, or deterioration of quality.

If your student has had excellent healing of a minimal area of trauma on her vocal folds, she may find that her voice is able to achieve a relatively clear quality and ease of range in the first one or two post-surgery lessons. While this is a very good sign, it is still safest in these exceptional cases to restrict your student's range and volume for the first two to three weeks, to make sure that she does not inadvertently overextend her voice and possibly slow down her total recovery process.

If possible, the ENT should re-examine your student's larynx within two or three weeks after she returns to singing—sooner if her voice seems to deteriorate.

During your student's recovery period, two or three short lessons a week are an excellent way for you to more effectively control her technical progress and to limit any CCMT (counterproductive compensatory muscle tension).

In addition, your student should pursue a daily practice regimen that strictly adheres to the parameters established in each previous lesson with you. Be aware that, no matter how much you warn your student about doing too much too soon, she might nevertheless push her voice past the boundaries you have established in the lesson. When you warn her against this behavior, which can create unnecessary swelling of the vocal folds and delay the recovery process, you might also have her read this book so that she fully understands the kinds of consequences she risks with her vocal health.

In her daily practice, your student should work in limited increments several times a day. She can start with two- to five-minute increments, one to four times a day. In two or three weeks, this can increase to five to 10 minutes, two to four times a day. Eventually, in three to six weeks, she can take on a more challenging routine of 10 to 20 minutes, three to four times a day.

Your student is ready to resume a less-restricted routine when her voice warms up easily; produces an unstrained quality that encompasses more-normal parameters of range, dynamic levels, and agility; and does not tire easily. Keep in mind that the time frames given here are meant only to provide guidelines.

By the third week of post-surgery lessons, simple two-note trills and staccato exercises can be added. If not already incorporated, the third and fourth week can include the use of arpeggios, messa di voce exercises, and scales of greater length, with the option of a sustained upper note at the top of the scale (1234555554321).

Up to this point in the recovery plan, your student produces the only the few vowels that she can sing with the greatest ease and resonance. However, if her voice is continuing to progress at three and four weeks, then it is time to incorporate all of the vowel sounds into your lesson plan.

Although her voice may be improving steadily, some vowels may resonate more clearly and be easier for your student to produce than others. This is a normal occurrence in the healing process. Just as with an uninjured voice, an injured voice can benefit from using the best vowel sound to influence the more difficult vowels.

For instance, if your student's best sound is on an [i] (ee), then, on a single note in the best part of her voice, blend the tone from [i] (ee) to [e] (ay), [a] (ah), [o] (oh), and [u] (oo). This process can enable your student to maintain a better tonal point of reference into more of the vowel spectrum. This exercise concept should be incorporated into all parts of the range. (For a full discussion of singing with favorable vowels, see ch. 12, "Teaching and learning a smooth vocal line," in v. 3.)

Assuming no complications at the level of the vocal folds, extremes of dynamic levels and range can be carefully explored during this initial three- to six-week period.

❀ Remember, the time frames given above are meant only to provide guidelines, from which you can tailor the individual recovery plan of your student. Since different singers heal at different rates, there can be no absolute time frame for the resumption of certain vocal activities.

If and when her vocal folds have recovered enough to sing complete musical pieces, try having your student sing only songs she already knows so that she doesn't have to deal with the stress of learning new material.

When your student can sing with comfort, relative ease, and no fatigue for 10 minutes at a stretch, and when she has access to at least half of her range, then she can begin to learn simple new repertoire. Initially, choose music that does not require extremes of range or volume, particularly with regards to higher notes and louder volume levels.

For some singers, descending passages are easier while, for others, working from the lower range to the upper is less difficult. Start with new music that only demands what your student's voice can comfortably accomplish. As her voice strengthens, and as she gains easier access to greater range with increased flexibility and dynamic contrast, more-demanding repertoire can actually help move your student toward more-normal voice production.

The approach outlined here is an extremely conservative one that some clinicians may deem unnecessarily cautious. If you are inexperienced in working with an injured voice, this more-conservative approach will provide you with a safe structure within which to work. As you continue to work with injured singers and as your experience level broadens in this specialized area, you will feel more confident in your ability to create individualized recovery plans that are both safe and expedient.

Every recovery regimen aims to bring the singer's voice back to its optimum level. This means getting the muscles back to their full elasticity and flexibility, bringing the breath control up to its full capacity, and having the singer produce good, quality sound throughout her whole range.

When surgery fails

Unfortunately, not every vocal fold heals completely after vocal fold surgery. Some singers are left with a vocal fold whose function is permanently compromised.

This does *not* mean that the singer will not be able to sustain a full and productive vocal career. Many singers learn to compensate technically for a vocal deficiency, to the point where the weakness is not identifiable in the finished vocal performance.

It will eventually become apparent if your student is not going to regain a voice that functions normally. If her vocal progress remains at a complete standstill for three to six months and if the ENT feels that her vocal folds have reached their maximum level of recovery, then it is time for your student to consider whether or not she can sustain the demands of a career in light of her vocal health problem.

Common residual vocal deficiencies can include breathiness or lack of resonance, particularly in the middle register. Coloratura sopranos can lose the very top one or two notes in their registers. Instability of tone at register breaks is another common complaint.

For your student to succeed in the face of obstacles such as these, she must keep certain considerations at the front of her mind at all times. Any of these problems can lead to vocal fatigue if your student is employing CCMT in an effort to make her voice feel and sound more "normal."

One thing you must constantly reiterate with your student is the difference between her perceptions of her voice "inside her head" as opposed to the listener's perceptions of the same voice. Your student is exquisitely sensitive to even the slightest change in sensory feedback from her own voice. This makes the permanently compromised singer extremely nervous because of the constant kinesthetic awareness of weakness in her voice. Your student must learn to relax under this pressure and to trust that her voice as perceived by the audience can be a pleasing experience, even if she is not happy with her sensations of singing.

The compromised singer will probably find that she must be even more careful about following the basic rules of good vocal hygiene, since her voice is permanently more vulnerable than a completely healthy voice. She must be more mindful about her voice use on a daily basis. There may be limits to how much her voice can do within a 24-hour period; she needs to learn those limitations and honor them, both in rehearsals and in performances. Even the timing and frequency of her rehearsals may have to be carefully controlled.

For some singers, the performance schedule must be planned in order to allow for needed vocal rest and recovery time. The repertoire must be changed to accommodate the weakness. The keys of certain songs must be adjusted to benefit the overall presentation of the voice.

Obviously, the freedom to adjust and control daily voice use, rehearsal and performance timing, the range, and other vocal demands of repertoire is not easily available to a struggling singer who is fighting her way up the career ladder. This type of control, when available, is usually reserved for the established performer whose reputation and fame allow her to request and often receive special considerations from conductors and management. The up-and-coming singer often has no such clout; therefore, trying to compete with healthy singers who have none of these restrictions to contend with is often a losing battle. This is a disadvantageous position, but it is not impossible to deal with. However, it does require extraordinary discipline, patience, determination, and a large dose of luck.

If you believe that your student's compromised voice can produce a professionally viable performance and that she possesses the personality needed to sustain the effort, then encouraging her to pursue a singing career is a reasonable and responsible decision on your part.

Possible complications from surgery

Any surgery may require intubation, and this can create certain problems with the vocal fold structure or function. Anesthesiologists administer drugs during surgery to reduce the sensory effects on the body; a tube is inserted into the throat to administer the anesthesia. Although this procedure does not appear to have a direct bearing on the vocal folds, the placement of the tube can be traumatic. Cases of arytenoid dislocation can occur when the tube is forced into or not "lined up" with the trachea.

At the very minimum, intubation will always cause some swelling even if it is done perfectly. The singer may complain about a sore throat for two or three days following the surgical procedure.

Although most intubations are done with no complications, possible problems after intubation include vocal fold bowing, vocal fold paralysis, irritation to the posterior vocal fold mucosa, contact ulcers, contact granuloma, arytenoid dislocation, and fixation.

Vocal fold bowing and vocal fold paralysis are usually temporary. The damage tends to be related to peripheral nerve trauma that spontaneously resolves within a six-month to a one-year period. The placement of the tube cuff can compress the peripheral nerve during the surgical procedure, causing nerve damage, but most of the time this is reversible. Behavioral voice therapy is recommended for this condition, since surgical procedures to reposition the paralyzed vocal fold, although often reversible, can still have consequences with regard to voice and airway function. Behavioral voice therapy and vocal exercise can help a singer maximize the speaking voice and reduce the potential of generating compensatory habits because of the paralysis.

A lengthier intubation procedure can irritate the posterior vocal fold mucosa. Patients with some degree of reflux experience greater discomfort than others. Be aware that this condition can often create a vicious post-operative cycle for a singer. The vocal folds require a certain degree of adduction for voicing, and that movement will continue to irritate the area initially injured by the intubation procedure.

A period of vocal rest will help the singer avoid chronic irritation to the mucosal area. Total vocal rest is not prescribed often; this one condition warrants a period of limited vocal use. Since the irritation does not stem from a pattern of vocal abuse, putting a singer on vocal rest will create the opportunity for the irritation to go away. The recurrence should then be minimal.

If the irritation becomes chronic, a contact ulcer or granuloma can develop. If this happens, recommend vocal rest and consult with a physician for some type of pharmacological agent to reduce the inflammation. In a worst-case scenario, granulation tissue will form; more surgery may be required if the granulation tissue becomes too extensive.

In a pre-surgery interview, have your student make the anesthesiologist aware that she is a singer, and have her ask him to use the smallest size intubation tube possible in order to minimize the trauma to her larynx.

Another way to manage the airway without an endotracheal tube is a laryngeal mask airway (LMA). It is not intubation per se, but it is better than mask ventilation. The anesthesiologist places an LMA blindly by simply sliding it along the palate and into the pharynx. As it is inflated, it seals the airway and the patient can be ventilated. A sore throat usually occurs with this procedure as well, but the risk to the larynx is smaller.

However, the best way for your student to minimize damage to her larynx from intubation is for her to communicate with and develop a positive relationship with the anesthesiologist. You and your student need to make sure he knows the risks and the special care needed for singers while performing intubation.

Other than the potential for intubation-related problems after surgery, general anesthesia can cause nausea and vomiting. New medications can reduce, but not eliminate, this risk. The singer might also experience drowsiness for a day or so. Reflux with aspiration is a feared complication, but it is uncommon. With modern monitoring and drugs, a major problem such as stroke, cardiac complications, or death is a remote risk, particularly if the patient is in generally good health.

Part of most treatments for vocal health problems involve recovery exercises, which will involve setting up a restricted regimen of singing. If you understand the nature of a vocal problem and the goal of the recovery exercises, you and your ENT can design a plan tailored for your student and her particular vocal health problem. You are also then in less danger of allowing vocal behavior that might make the vocal problem worse.

During the exercises, you need to keep reminding your student that she is in a rehabilitative process. Help her stay focused on the primary goal of the recovery plan. For example, if the cause of her vocal health problem is a mass on her vocal folds, set as your primary goal the reduction and/or elimination of the vocal fold masses. (See "Organic Disorders," on page 86.)

Some teachers might think there are specific vocal exercises for particular vocal problems and that simply using the right exercise will restore a voice to health. This is not the case. How each exercise is performed, the range of notes sung, the number of repetitions, the length of practice increments, and the dynamic level are essential components in any recovery plan. They may vary dramatically from one person to the next, and from one particular problem to another. (See also "Key Concepts from Exercise Physiology," in v. 3, ch. 13.)

For example, simple hums are gentle exercises that allow your student to concentrate on consistently balancing her breath and her vocal fold resistance. With humming, your student can re-establish the kinesthetic sensations in and around her face, which tends to ease the adductory tension in her vocal folds. However, if she hums with tension in her tongue, jaw, larynx, or pharynx, or if she hums too loudly, she may develop CCMT and hamper her recovery work.

Over time, you will discover that certain exercises work well to overcome a functional weakness or that others will address the CCMT of specific voice problems, but do not think of the exercises as a simple formula. Use the exercises provided in *Excellence in Singing* to help you understand the processes by which certain vocal problems can be eased or brought to full health again.

Following are typical guidelines for recovery exercises. These are not recommendations for your particular student with her particular vocal health problem. You should work out those details with the ENT or voice therapist. (For exceptions, see "Causes of Vocal Health Problems," in v. 5, ch. 22.)

During any period of vocal recovery, your student can benefit from more than one lesson a week. This allows you to continually supervise her voice production. Keep her singing, but in a very careful fashion.

As might be expected, you want to first help your student minimize vocal fold collision impact by reducing CCMT and by singing with careful vocal technique. You should help her reestablish a point of reference for appropriately relaxed vocal production, no matter what the resulting voice quality. (See the heading "A Baseline State of Relaxation," in v. 2, ch. 7.)

The first two weeks

You should have your student sing only breathier exercises with limited duration for at least two weeks. A 30-minute singing lesson with frequent periods of voice rest is a good way to start.

During this recovery effort, she should avoid the extremes of her range, loud dynamic levels, and hard glottal attacks. (See the exercises under "Beginning, Sustaining, and Releasing the Tone," on page 132.) She should also avoid staccato exercises (particularly those that are vowel-initiated). As might be expected, always have her work toward excellent breath support and an absence of tension in her neck, tongue, and throat when she speaks and sings.

You should also have her approach with care any singing exercises that normally help reinforce forward placement (such as humming or singing with [i] or more-closed vowels), so that your student does not try to force the kinesthetic sensations of mask resonance and inadvertently strain her vocal folds.

Light agility exercises and gentle gliding scales are acceptable. Tongue trills and lip trills, for example, are a good way to help maintain breath management, vocal fold stretch, and easy voicing. They can give your student's vocal folds a relatively gentle workout with less impact force. You should, however, be alert to any tongue tension during these trills. (See "Lip trills" in the exercise "To Sustain the Tone," in v. 2, ch. 9, and "To Produce a Tongue Trill," in v. 2, ch. 10. Also see heading "Teaching Agility," in v. 3, ch. 13.)

Between two and four weeks

You can begin to have your student explore her full range over the next two to four weeks—always with the caveat that any strain, any discomfort, or any vocal fatigue means that it's time to stop. (See "The Conditioning Zone," in v. 3, ch. 13.) Encourage your student to practice in no more than five- to 10-minute increments (shorter if her voice shows any difficulty), one to three times a day. Restrict your student's repertoire; utilize simple songs with limited vocal demands.

Even if your student's vocal technique becomes perfect and the reactive area begins healing—if a mass on her vocal folds is the cause of her vocal health problem, though the original mass remains—then her vocal folds can swell from extended or demanding periods of singing, delaying the recovery process, or even creating new vocal health problems. (See "Organic Disorders," on page 86.)

After four to six weeks

After three to six weeks of remedial singing work, the ENT should re-evaluate your student's condition. If there is some improvement in her voice, your student can begin a gradual return to singing. For example, suppose the cause of her vocal health problem is a cyst or polyp. If the reactive area is resolved and the cyst or polyp is resolved (or at least smaller), and if both you and your student are satisfied with her vocal quality, then she can attempt a return to a more-normal singing routine.

If your student is in a situation where she simply cannot stop performing, the prospect for the spontaneous healing of the vocal folds becomes less than ideal. She must eliminate all unnecessary voice use; all unnecessary use of volume and extremes of range must also be eliminated. She should sing with limited warm-up periods. Efficient and reliable breath management becomes essential; your student's breath support must be optimum and never mis-timed, neither delayed nor "locked."

If she is being amplified during her performances, good monitor speakers or ear monitors are critical now. Many vocal fold injuries are likely caused by a singer's inability to hear herself, and much of the vocal over-use and subsequent strain that occurs is a result of this difficulty.

Performers always want to "give their all." Your student must adjust this attitude in light of the need to decrease the risk of straining her vocal folds. Use your best judgment in advising her toward more-careful voice use.

When time is limited, as it so often is for active performers with vocal problems, understand the principles behind what you hope to achieve with an exercise. In that way, if one exercise proves too time-consuming for a student to master, you can create an exercise to accomplish the same results simply by using a different route.

Causes of Vocal Health Problems

An ENT can identify a number of different causes of vocal health problems. With an examination, he can discern whether parts of the vocal apparatus are functioning improperly, if a chronic condition exists that is affecting your student's vocal health, or if a gland is not working the way it should. An ENT can also list illnesses and the results of surgery as possible causes of vocal disturbances.

Following are general causes of vocal health problems. While the list is not exhaustive, it presents a range of causes that will help you understand how dependent singing with excellence depends on a healthy body and why any health issue can cause a vocal health problem.

Functional Disorders

A functional disorder is a problem with the physical function of the vocal folds; the vocal apparatus does not do what it is supposed to do.

For example, if the ENT looks into your student's throat and does not see any lesions or identify any disease process, but the voice is still abnormal, then a functional voice disorder is usually the cause.

An ENT also looks at the parts of the vocal apparatus, searching for the cause of a functional problem. He checks for lesions, polyps, and cysts, as well as tears or hemorrhaging. In addition, he notices the ways in which your student's body has tried to compensate for any pain or pressure that she may be feeling.

Vocal fold swelling. The consequences of congestion and thickened secretions are excessive coughing and throat clearing, which typically result in vocal fold swelling, and possibly even lesions on the vocal fold tissues, which can alter your student's voice quality.

Vocal fold nodules. Nodules are raised bumps on one or both vocal folds. They are often caused by the vocal folds slamming into each other, but they can also develop as a result of gastroesophagal reflux. (See "Digestive system problems," on page 113.) They tend to occur at specific places on the vocal folds.

Behavioral therapy is the first response to vocal fold nodules. As a general rule, increased hydration can immediately help the vocal folds. When the vocal folds lack moisture, they become stiff, and that stiffness may cause more friction as the vocal folds open and close against each other. If your student drinks more water, it may help to relieve some of her primary symptoms.

In addition, a period of modified voice use is a good place to start. (See "Recovery Exercises," on page 81.) However, keep in mind that while a period of total voice rest may improve the symptoms, it will not change the behavior that caused the nodules to form in the first place.

A voice therapist can provide guidance for singing exercises that will do no further damage to the vocal folds. Your student's speaking voice may need to be modified as well, and other behaviors that contributed to the injury should be identified and changed.

You may wonder if surgery should be considered. Any surgical procedure may permanently alter your student's vocal fold structure. While a surgeon always attempts to minimize trauma to the vocal fold edge, there is always the risk of scar tissue or stiffness in the vocal folds after surgery. Surgery should be the last option for treatment. Behavioral changes should be tried first.

Vocal fold cysts or polyps. With vocal fold cysts or polyps, which look like fluid-filled blisters, the symptoms vary widely from singer to singer. Your student might complain of breathiness, particularly in her middle register. She might have trouble with smooth transitions at event areas or when she changes registers. (See the heading "Events and Registers," in v. 3, ch. 11.) She might describe a feeling of instability in any given part of her voice, lose her upper notes, or find it difficult to reach her upper register. *Diplophonia* (two pitches being produced simultaneously) might also occur. Your student's voice might tire after comparatively short periods of singing, with residual hoarseness that could linger for one or two days.

This problem is different from vocal fold nodules, which tend to be related to chronically abusive habits. Quite often, a cyst or polyp will appear on just one vocal fold and will be caused by a one-time traumatic event. Still, your student can try a recovery plan like the one used for nodules in this situation, because the mechanical considerations are similar.

It is common to find a reactive area of swelling—sometimes called "pre-nodular swelling"—on the vocal fold opposite the cyst or polyp. This can be the result of the original mass slamming into the other vocal fold.

The goal is to reduce the size of the cyst or polyp prior to the consideration of surgery. After any prescribed voice rest, your student should resume singing under your guidance. Again, make sure that she uses her voice in a controlled and limited manner.

A true cyst or polyp may spontaneously resolve through a course of rehabilitative voice work alone, but this is unusual. However, more-judicious voice use, tempered with excellent technique, can eliminate the reactive area. It is also possible for the original cyst or polyp to reduce in size when your student improves her voice use.

However, if her vocal folds appear much the same as in the original exam and if her complaints remain the same, then the ENT may suggest vocal fold surgery to remove the mass or masses, or he may recommend another period of vocal recovery work.

Vocal fold hemorrhage. A vocal fold hemorrhage occurs when a blood vessel on the surface of the vocal fold bursts and releases blood into the surrounding area. This is usually caused by a one-time trauma, and it is one of the more serious (although not uncommon) vocal injuries your student can experience.

The immediate course of action is absolute voice rest.

After a prescribed period of total rest, the ENT should re-examine your student's vocal folds. If the ENT feels that enough mucosal wave or undulation has returned to the injured vocal fold for your student to attempt unstrained singing, then she can resume gentle vocalizing. She must *not* return to singing without the ENT's approval.

In many instances, hemorrhages resolve themselves with no permanent damage to the vocal fold. However, permanent scarring of the vocal folds or even a secondary mass can occur because of a hemorrhage, so you and your student must proceed with extreme caution.

Once the ENT gives the go-ahead for your student to begin singing again, her first lesson should last no more than 10 to 15 minutes (less if her voice seems particularly weak), with frequent periods of vocal rest. Practice times should initially be limited to three- to five-minute periods of light singing, one to four times a day.

After a vocal fold hemorrhage occurs, the vocal fold is often stiff, so you need to initiate gentle exercises. Low-volume gliding tones (*121* or *1233321* or other limited excursion patterns) on any vowel that is comfortable for your student can initiate the recovery process. During the first week, limit the lesson(s) to your student's middle range and below.

Your aim is to very slowly and gently re-establish stretch and subsequent undulation to the injured vocal fold by gradually increasing its stretching and vibratory ability. Some clinicians in the field of voice recovery are more comfortable with the initial use of a breathy voice to resolve vocal fold surface injuries. This is a relatively safe concept, assuming that your student does not become *hypo-functional* (too muscularly lax) in her basic technical approach.

When done correctly, forward placement exercises appear to establish a breath-to-vocal-fold connection with accompanying resonance space enhancement of tone that is conducive to efficient, non-traumatic vibration of the vocal folds.

Two weeks of gentle vocal work—avoiding the extremes of register, loudness, and duration—is reasonable. During the second week, you can attempt slight increases in vocal range.

During this process, make absolutely certain that your student sings no note unless she can produce it with complete vocal ease. Try simple, two-note, softly sung trilling exercises in her low to middle range to help her re-establish freer vibratory motion of her vocal folds.

After two weeks, the ENT should re-examine your student's vocal folds. When the ENT decides that relatively normal vocal fold vibration has returned, your student may then begin to explore greater range, volume, and duration.

There is no prescribed time frame for this recovery process. Exercise caution in this dangerous situation. During your lessons, stay alert for any signs that your student is struggling or experiencing vocal fatigue.

Because of the vocal fold's stiffness, your student may lose tonal stability and agility as well as experience problems with tonal focus or resonance. As this stiffness resolves, your student's voice should return to normal. This can take anywhere from 10 days to a number of weeks—and sometimes longer.

Vocal fold tears. A vocal fold tear is just that: a rip in the mucosal covering of the vocal fold. Like a vocal fold hemorrhage, it is a serious (although not uncommon) injury, often related to coughing or other traumatic behaviors of the vocal folds.

A tear in a vocal fold should be treated the same way as a hemorrhage, first with absolute voice rest and then, with the ENT's approval, with a gradual resumption of singing. The guidelines listed above for recovery from a hemorrhage also apply here. Often, the effects of a vocal fold tear will completely resolve more quickly than those of a hemorrhage, but there is no hard and fast rule.

Vocal fold scars. Vocal fold scarring is a dreaded diagnosis. The mucosal layer—the surface covering of the vocal fold—is supposed to move freely in the breeze during phonation. When vocal fold scarring occurs, this tissue adheres to the underlying muscle and no longer floats freely. It occurs when a spot on the vocal folds has been injured too often. (See "The Interaction between the Tissues and the Air," in v. 1, ch. 4.)

Because the scar then becomes a stiff portion of the vocal fold, the resulting vocal quality often includes hoarseness and breathiness, both of which can occur in any part of the voice. Loss of range, both high and low, can also result from this stiffness. Your student might complain about a lack of focus in her voice, as well as feelings of losing breath during singing.

The severity of the effects of vocal fold scarring on the ultimate vocal quality and career potential of your student depends on where the scar is located, how large an area it affects, your student's voice type, and the quality of voice (including range, degree of efficient resonance, and loudness) needed to sing a particular style of music. All of these variables determine whether a vocal fold scar will limit or end a singing career.

This is not a well-studied area; until recently, the medical community could offer little help for the correction of this condition. It is known that the longer a scar has been present, the less likely it is that a singer will be able to improve vocal fold motion through exercises alone. At present, newer surgical techniques, including microsurgery, can help remedied some of the scar tissue stiffness. Each situation should be approached individually, but the sooner you can begin working with the stiff area, the better.

When dealing with a vocal fold scar, both you and your student must take the long view. How long is the long view? It's hard to predict. Within six months, if not sooner, there should be some signs of improvement. But a year or more is not an unreasonable time for rebuilding a voice that has been derailed by vocal fold scarring.

There may come a time, however, when your student may need to consider surgical intervention as an option. This determination is usually made when both the singer and the teacher feel that the vocal progression has stopped and the voice has remained at the same sub-optimum level for three to six months.

During any recovery period from a pathological vocal problem, there will be blocks of time when your student's voice appears to cease progressing. This is a normal part of the process. The vocal system may need time to settle into a new level of accomplishment before it is able to make further strides. However, progress through vocal exercises alone can end, and it is important to be able to recognize when this has occurred.

If you consider that both the stretching and the undulation movement of your student's vocal folds have been compromised by the stiffness of the scarred area, then your job as a teacher is to loosen that stiffness through any reasonable means. A recovery program incorporating a variety of exercises will challenge all aspects of vocal coordination. If your student's vocal folds are very stiff, then her range and resonance possibilities may appear to be quite limited.

Do not be frightened by an initially poor vocal presentation, particularly if it is soon after the scarring has occurred. The vocal folds are capable of extraordinary feats of recovery.

Begin with gentle gliding exercises with whatever vowel provides the easiest and clearest resonance for your student. As you start out, concentrate your efforts on what she can do best. Short scales (*121*, *131*) are a good place to begin. Move from the low to the high range, and do not allow your student to force her voice in even the slightest way.

One to five minutes of these glides will be enough at first. If her voice tires, have her rest for three to five minutes. If her voice subsequently recovers, then you can try lip or tongue trills using the same intervals for similar lengths of time. For some singers, it may be easier to start the lesson with these trills.

In the first few lessons, this may be all that your student's voice is able to accomplish before fatigue sets in, usually in the form of strain or a negative quality change.

Sometimes with a vocal fold scar, the voice quality is so poor that it is tempting to ignore the little bit of CCMT your student may employ when it seems to improve her voice quality. Do *not* allow this CCMT to occur. It is counterproductive to the goal of the recovery process.

Gradually add staccato exercises, preferably using a consonant-initiated syllable such as [bi] (bee) or [ba] (bah). Find a sound combination that is comfortable for your student, and begin with short patterns (*121, 21, 131, 31*, etc.), gradually extending the range as her voice permits.

Throughout this process, there are no specific volume restrictions. The vocal fold's stiffness may dictate that softer volume levels will be easier for your student to produce without strain—at least initially. At some point in the recovery process, include exercises that require increased loudness for brief moments. This can be in the form of a sudden crescendo on a single note, a gradual crescendo to the top of an ascending scale with a decrescendo on the descent, or any other pattern that is manageable for your student. At first, efforts at loudness may tire her voice more quickly than other exercises. If so, save these more-taxing exercises for the end of a lesson.

Sustained humming on single notes or humming on scale patterns, even when done with technical perfection, can be very challenging for the singer who has vocal fold scarring. It may also be quite tiring for her voice. Decide when and whether the price paid for any exercise is worth the assumed benefit. If you try an exercise and find that it is too difficult for your student, come back to it later. Singers will often progress to the point where initially counterproductive exercises become beneficial. Humming can be one of these exercises.

Practice periods should at first be limited to three- to 10-minute periods, one to two times a day for two to four weeks. Your student can gradually increase practice frequency and duration times based on her sense of the ease of response levels in her vocal system. Fatigue and strain are always an indication that it is time to rest the voice.

The effective remediation of any vocal health problem requires that your student apply her discipline to regular practice times that are crafted around careful attention to technical detail. Nowhere is that discipline more important than when she is trying to overcome the effects of vocal fold scarring. This kind of practice is very difficult because the rewards of improved vocal quality can be slow to show up. Your responsibility is to act as the ever-present cheerleader, encouraging your student to work on the process and not to focus on the immediate vocal outcome.

With vocal fold scarring, as with other vocal health problems, working the voice from the top down, beginning in falsetto for males and light head voice for females, then easing into the middle and lower voices, can prove helpful in re-establishing a sense of continuity of vocal tone. This may be easily accomplished on a [u] (oo) vowel, on a descending three- or five-note scale (*321, 54321*). Have your student gently place her hands on both sides of her face near her lips in order to promote greater relaxation. Begin in her middle register, moving the pattern up by half steps. If a starting note is weak but unstrained, do not let this stop your student from attempting the next-higher half step.

Often, the middle voice will prove problematic long after the upper register has begun to resonate with more clarity and ease. For many singers with various types of vocal health problems, the transition from middle voice into an upper register is the most difficult area in which to re-establish a smooth, even voice and it is often the last problem area to resolve itself.

The period for the resumption of repertoire is variable and it depends on your student's level of vocal comfort. The advantage to re-approaching familiar repertoire is that muscle memory associated with a particular piece may re-assert itself and enable your student's voice to produce tonal qualities unavailable on scales or unfamiliar music. When this does occur, it can be a morale booster for the struggling singer.

A different phenomenon happens when certain exercise regimens based on scales become routine and more comfortable, but attempts at repertoire quickly fatigue the voice. In this situation, the time spent singing repertoire must be limited and the repertoire itself should require only what your student's voice can accomplish without strain. The quality of her voice may be sub-optimum, but that is allowable as long as CCMT is absent.

Neurological Disorders

If he believes it is warranted, your student's physician or ENT may also look for problems with the nerves that make the body function. If a singer is diagnosed with a neurological disease, the body's nerves are damaged or disordered and no amount of vocal rest will improve the condition of the vocal folds.

Instead, the doctor will prescribe a regimen of medicine and/or therapy to mitigate the effects of a neurological disease on your student's voice. He will work with your student to find treatment that will help control the symptoms of the disease. He will let her know that some diseases are progressive, gradually weakening the body's ability to function well, and he will give her some guidance in adapting her life to her new circumstances.

This section gives only brief descriptions of certain neurological disorders. Check with your student's primary physician for complete information and prognosis.

Recurrent laryngeal nerve (RLN) **adductor** paralysis

Recurrent laryngeal nerve (RLN) adductor paralysis is a unilateral or bilateral condition, preventing one or both sides of the vocal folds from *closing* because the nerve is damaged.

The symptoms heard in the voice are breathiness and/or hoarseness with possible difficulties in swallowing, depending on the size of the opening between the vocal folds. The paralyzed fold can be positioned close to the midline or far away. The distance away from the midline affects the degree of the vocal or swallowing problems. Depending on the size of the gap, treatment can include surgery to bring the paralyzed vocal fold toward the midline. Recovery prospects are typically excellent.

Recurrent laryngeal nerve (RLN) abductor paralysis

Recurrent laryngeal nerve (RLN) abductor paralysis is another unilateral or bilateral condition: one or both sides of the vocal folds cannot *open* because the nerve is damaged.

Here, the issue is to make sure the airway is open enough for the patient to breathe and swallow. If the airway is not open, surgical treatment is the remedy. A tracheostomy is possible, but unlikely if only one vocal fold is paralyzed. A tracheostomy, which is surgery to place a tube in the throat to create an airway, will probably be performed if both vocal folds are paralyzed and positioned close to midline.

Superior laryngeal nerve (SLN) paralysis

Superior laryngeal nerve (SLN) paralysis is a condition in which the superior laryngeal nerve is injured, either by trauma or because of central or peripheral damage to the nervous system. The superior laryngeal nerve is responsible for giving nerve-to-muscle communication to the cricothyroid, one of the intrinsic muscles within the larynx. (See "The Vocal Folds And the Intrinsic Muscles," in v. 1, ch. 4.) If this nerve is damaged, the singer loses the ability to tense the vocal fold and change its length.

The symptoms can be breathiness and difficulty raising the pitch. Sometimes diplophonia occurs.

A diagnosis of SLN injury should be confirmed with a needle EMG to test whether the muscle is "dead" or "alive." The ENT might suggest reinnervation surgery called "neuromuscular pedicle technique." This technique might mediate the bowing of the fold and lack of glottal closure. The ENT carefully dissects a small mass of muscle from a neighboring muscle and implants it, along with its nerve supply, into the paralyzed muscle.

Behavioral treatments for this problem would be purely compensatory.

Multiple sclerosis

Multiple sclerosis is characterized by lack of coordination, spasticity, and weakness of the muscles. Spasticity and weakness can affect the ability of the vocal folds to adduct efficiently, resulting in an impaired ability to control loudness levels along with a hoarse or breathy vocal quality.

The prognosis for improved vocal quality is poor for individuals with progressive neuromuscular diseases. However, it was recently reported that an individual with multiple sclerosis with a fixed (immobile) vocal fold regained normal laryngeal function for some months following a botulinum toxin injection.[1]

Amyotrophic lateral sclerosis (ALS)

ALS is commonly known as "Lou Gehrig's disease." It is a progressive degenerative disease that attacks nerve cells in the brain and spinal cord, gradually causing them to degenerate. The primary voice symptoms of ALS are hoarseness and breathiness. Speech is also impaired (dysarthria).

The focus of therapy is to employ techniques that compensate for the body's growing weakness. As the voice deteriorates, one option is to use an alternative communication device to augment the voice.

Myasthenia gravis

Myasthenia gravis is a neuromuscular degenerative disease characterized by weakening of striated muscles. This muscle weakness reduces the individual's ability to raise pitch and increase vocal loudness. A decreased ability to maintain the appropriate tension of the vocal folds can result in a hoarse and breathy vocal quality. Little is available for treatment.

Spasmodic dysphonia

The cause of spasmodic dysphonia (SD) is unclear. It is generally agreed upon that it is a central nervous system disorder that causes the vocal folds to either adduct (close) or abduct (open) inappropriately. Adductor spasmodic dysphonia is the most common type, which causes the vocal folds to spasm shut.

The most common characteristic of adductor spasmodic dysphonia is a struggle or strain to talk in association with interruptions in voicing (voice breaks or phonatory breaks). Other associated symptoms might include tremor, hoarseness, and harshness of tone.

Behavioral treatment for SD has traditionally had limited success.

In the 1970s, doctors used surgery to section the recurrent laryngeal nerve—a destructive surgical procedure that worked for some patients. For some patients, the symptoms reappeared as the nerve grafted back together over time.

Botulinum toxin injected into the thyroarytenoid muscle results in the temporary weakness of the muscles, thus relieving the spasmodic condition. Total effects, however, last approximately two to four months. When symptoms reappear, the ENT repeats the injection. This is one of the more current and widely used treatments.

Some techniques that singers found useful in dealing with SD are: talking in a relaxed manner, breath control, maintaining steady subglottal pressure and glottal air flow. Some also found an alteration of pitch and speaking at lower intensities helpful. Many found continued voice modification useful.

After Botox injections, these singers' voice therapy included vocal exercises, relaxation exercises to reduce hypertension in the jaw and the back of the neck, and improved breathing awareness. Voice therapy was an important part of overall therapy, but a singer's satisfaction with the results often depended on the therapist's interaction with her.

Patients with SD have used tranquilizers, especially valium, by prescription. But less than 10 percent reported that tranquilizers resulted in any consistent improvement in their voices. Muscle relaxants, antihistamines, antacids, and antidepressants are other medications prescribed to treat secondary complaints or symptoms.

Illness

Everyone gets sick now and then. The flu makes its rounds, everyone seems to have that hacking cough that lasts for weeks, or maybe it's a bout with the measles. Whatever the case, when illness strikes, your student expects to get better; she expects the illness to go away.

She will survive a bad cold or the flu, even if it lasts for a week. She can stick to bed rest, drink lots of fluids, and perhaps take an over-the-counter medicine to alleviate any pain while the illness runs its course.

Nevertheless, if your student isn't careful, she may discover that even an ordinary episode of the flu can cause damage to her voice. If she doesn't drink enough fluid, she is likely to become dehydrated. At the very least, her vocal apparatus will dry out and be more easily injured.

No matter how common the illness, your student needs to make her vocal health a priority.

Sore throat. A sore throat can have many causes. If her tonsils and adenoids are creating problems, your student may complain of a sore throat or pain when she swallows. When an ENT examines her, he may see enlarged tonsils or smell bad breath (caused by viruses or bacteria that infect the throat or tonsils).

Whatever the cause of a sore throat, keep the water and juice flowing. Drinking water helps to thin the mucus, making it easier to spit out or swallow. Dairy products may make the mucus seem thicker and stickier. If the secretions are unmanageable, your student can ask her doctor for medication to help deal with this problem (on a short-term basis only).

One common misconception is that gargling "washes off" the vocal folds. It doesn't. If any liquid reaches the level of the vocal folds, it will trigger coughing and choking. Liquid (and foods) fall into the esophagus (stomach tube) and should not enter the space between the vocal folds. If this happens, a reflex triggers a cough to clear this area before the material enters the airway.

Gargling does not allow the liquid into the area where the larynx is located; it only washes the back of the throat, approximately where the tonsils are located. It may seem soothing, but it does not have any actual effect on reducing the irritation to the larynx.

One common question is whether to drink hot or cold liquids before singing. As long as your student is well-hydrated, there really isn't a big difference. Hot liquids may help break up secretions or may feel more soothing. The important thing is to keep drinking liquids, regardless of their temperature.

Counsel your student to avoid beverages containing caffeine or those that are high in salt; these tend to dry out the tissues.

Some singers believe that the regular use of cough drops is a remedy for soothing a sore throat. However, there is no real effect of decreasing irritation to the throat through their use. Hard candy or nonmedicated glycerine lozenges will help promote salivary flow, and will help thin secretions and lubricate the vocal folds. Sometimes your student's doctor will prescribe guaifenesin (Humibid, for example) to help thin the mucus, or a cough suppressant such as Tessalon if she is coughing persistently.

Laryngitis. With laryngitis, the mucosal covering of the vocal folds becomes inflamed and swollen. Do not let your student speak or sing during the acute phase of laryngitis because it will increase the risk of a worse vocal fold injury. Absolute voice rest is the safest and most conservative intervention.

"Absolute voice rest" means no coughing, no speaking, no whistling, and no playing of wind instruments (since the vocal folds are still in motion) for at least three days, although your student may need more time to recover. Your student's doctor should not prescribe absolute voice rest for more than 10 days because the muscles may become weak and gets into a habit of disuse or begin to atrophy.

If your student has laryngitis and absolute voice rest is not possible, put your student on limited voice use or relative voice rest. This is a short period with controlled, soft vocal exercise in the mornings. Rest, sleep, and good nutrition are vital during this time.

Give her short, supervised voice lessons for exercise. Have her sing softly in a normal voice, avoiding extremes of range. Be conscious of her posture and her breathing technique. Cancel non-essential singing commitments.

Following the period of absolute or relative voice rest, gradually and carefully approach your student's full return to vocal activities. Athletes return to full performance through exercise conditioning;

a singer should do likewise. A smooth transition to full performance capacity is the goal.

Sinusitis. Sinusitis can adversely affect your student's voice, and it often coincides with a cold. The sinuses are hollow cavities within the skull that are named according to their location. Each sinus cavity (as well as the nasal cavity) is lined with specialized cells; these cells secrete mucus—approximately one to one-and-a-half pints per day.

If the sinuses get blocked with too much mucus, voice quality becomes muffled or "nasal" because mucus accumulates in the sinuses and nasal passages, and the nasal lining, which is part of the vocal tract, becomes swollen. There is impaired clearance in the infected nasal passage. You hear a hyponasal quality—not enough nasal sound quality resonating from the vocal tract. When a sinus infection occurs over a short duration, it is termed "acute sinusitis."

Laypersons have many misconceptions about sinusitis. Often, allergy symptoms are erroneously called a sinus infection. You need to learn how to differentiate between the two.

Your student might begin to notice signs of a common cold, perhaps nasal congestion. This congestion happens because the nasal mucosa swells. The mucosa lines the nose and the sinus cavity. The mucus begins to thicken and the sinus cavities become obstructed. The blockage causes the mucus to become stagnant and bacteria begin to grow. This causes further inflammation and further damage to the cells within the sinus cavity. The thickened mucus causes postnasal drainage and the singer starts to clear her throat often.

Identifying sinusitis early is important in maintaining vocal health. If your student is suffering from acute sinusitis, she will probably complain about nasal congestion, discolored nasal drainage, pain over her cheekbone on one side of her face, toothache, and pressure or pain between or over her eyes. She may also have a headache, and it may be deep-seated with multiple locations. If any of these symptoms are present, refer her to a medical professional for further evaluation.

A common question is, is it OK to sing with a sinus infection? If the drainage is tolerable, encourage your student to sing. The resonance or quality of the tone that you hear may be slightly decreased but, in general, this shouldn't harm your student's vocal folds. Be alert for any sign of vocal deterioration, and have her rest her voice if there is any question.

Tonsil and adenoid infections. Persistent enlargement of the tonsils and/or adenoids can obstruct the airway and cause snoring or sleep apnea. Sleep apnea can also be seen in the absence of tonsil enlargement due to collapse of the airway. Sleep apnea can cause poor sleep quality, daytime fatigue, and—in severe cases—high blood pressure and strain on the heart. (See the heading "Sleep apnea and snoring," on page 118.)

Removal of the tonsils and adenoids can affect your student's upper vocal tract and palatal function. Removal of the tonsils and/or adenoids can also alter her upper vocal tract resonance and change her vocal quality. These changes can be temporary or permanent. Surgery can also cause scarring of the palate, which may change the way the palate moves; this can change the amount of air that escapes from the nose during certain sounds.

While all these changes are possible, many people have their tonsils and/or adenoids removed without noticing any changes to the voice. Select a surgeon carefully, using a voice specialist if possible.

Chronic health conditions

Some health conditions are chronic and your student has already learned to live with them. She may recognize the familiar itchiness of spring allergies, or know immediately what to do when her stomach is upset from too much traveling and too little down time. She knows that chronic conditions don't go away.

She can and does manage these conditions, sometimes with a change in behavior, and sometimes with prescribed and/or over-the-counter medicines. She may be one who lives very well with a chronic health problem that demands a rigorous attention to diet and rest.

However, if your student suddenly develops a brand-new chronic health condition, such as sleep apnea or TMJ, she may be frustrated at the changes in lifestyle that she faces. She may feel limited in her choices or deprived of things she has enjoyed for many years.

Encourage her to look at her health as a whole, doing everything she can to make it easy to sing as she desires. This holistic approach will take the emphasis off the particular condition and put it on the context of living a full and healthy life.

Allergies

An allergy is an overreaction of the immune system to a substance that causes no reaction at all in most people. The term "allergy"—usually used synonymously with the term "hypersensitivity"—refers to an abnormal immune response to an antigen ("allergen").

Symptoms of colds and allergies can look alike. Colds go away after a while; allergies don't, unless the cause of the allergy is removed. Anything that lasts longer than a week is probably caused by allergens.

Allergic rhinitis is a term used to describe a wide variety of allergic symptoms, all involving the nose. Often, associated symptoms are caused by inhaled allergens that affect the eyes, ears, and throat as well.

Types of allergens include plants, flowers, and weeds (wind-borne pollen); animal dander; molds; and dust mites. Allergens typically cause nasal congestion, sneezing, clear drainage, watery itchy eyes, throat clearing, a "scratchy" throat, a sore throat, excessive coughing, pain and pressure in the ears, headache, and/or fatigue.

If your student is allergic to certain environmental irritants, she will have problems, particularly if she is not currently being treated for those allergies.

Two major forms of allergy exist: delayed hypersensitivity and immediate hypersensitivity. Delayed hypersensitivity implies that a longer time is required before symptoms develop. Compared with immediate hypersensitivity, symptoms of delayed hypersensitivity may take hours or days to develop.

When a person is exposed to the same allergen, various chemicals are secreted; these chemicals include histamine. Histamine is largely responsible for the itching, the sneezing, the tearing up, and the runny nose. The nasal congestion caused by allergies may predispose a person to sinusitis.

Even if your student has mild allergy symptoms, she may have subtle vocal complaints—perhaps an occasional voice break, or vocal fatigue from a dry vocal tract. These symptoms are typically seasonal; however, depending on geography and your student's performance travel schedule, these may be year-round issues.

Allergies to dust and mold can be aggravated during rehearsals and performances in concert halls, church choir lofts, and various other types of venues, especially older concert halls. Curtains, backstage trappings, and dressing room facilities are rarely cleaned thoroughly—and when they are cleaned, there can be reactions to the types of cleaning agents used to treat them. Inhaling bleach and other chemical substances can trigger similar effects as stated above.

The simplest and most obvious way to prevent an allergic reaction is to avoid contact with the allergen. However, except in the case of certain foods, animals, and drugs, this method is not very practical. Dust, insects, pollen, and a variety of chemicals will always be present, no matter where your student lives or works.

One of the best remedies for allergy symptoms is the taking of an antihistamine such as Benadryl, Claritin, etc. However, antihistamines can cause excessive drying of the vocal folds; this could be detrimental to your student's vocal health. You and your student need to figure out a balance that will work for her.

Endocrine dysfunction

The voice is sensitive to any type of change in the endocrine system, a collection of glands that secrete hormones directly into the bloodstream, such as the thyroid, pituitary, adrenal, hypothalamus, and pancreas. These problems are generally a result of changes to the fluid content in the laryngeal mucosa. This in turn causes a change in the shape and mass of the vocal folds and alters the voice quality.

Hypothyroidism. Hypothyroidism occurs when the thyroid gland underworks, causing a lower metabolic rate. It can causes hoarseness, vocal fatigue, loss of vocal range, and a globus sensation (the sensation of a lump in the throat).

Cryptorchidism. Cryptorchidism (delay in genitalia/sexual development), along with Klinefelter's syndrome and Frolich's syndrome, all cause a persistent high-pitched voice. These types of disturbances need to be properly evaluated by an endocrinologist. This specialist will evaluate, monitor, and maintain an appropriate hormonal level for your student's body.

Aging. If you have been teaching for a while, you may already know the gifts and talents of a singer who has practiced her craft for years. When she arrives in your studio, you anticipate her pleasure in refining her sills and you hear the freedom in her voice that is unencumbered by worries about her career. You are at ease with her self-discipline, knowing she uses this lesson time to enhance her talent. You may notice a slight breathiness, a phrase sung too quickly, but together you'll concentrate on the problems and resolve them.

Your singer may be getting older, but she is still singing. Her chronological age does not define her as "aging." Your own observations of her will tell you if her voice is beginning to wear the thinness of age.

As you do with all your students, use your skills of observation and trained intuition to identify the student who is beginning to show signs of aging. You'll see some of these signs in your older student, rarely all of them.

As she grows older, her muscles lose their bulk and elasticity. Where she once moved gracefully, she might now hesitate. She may have difficulty sustaining an extended phrase because her respiratory muscles aren't coordinating as well as they once did. She may complain that her hands and feet are cold; her blood flow is slowing down and her extremities are the first to notice the effect. Her muscles can atrophy, particularly if she is not as physically active as before. Her cartilage may turn to bone (ossification); moving her joints can be awkward and painful.

Hormonal changes occur during and after menopause, and you may need to talk with your older female students about these changes.

In addition, you may need to counsel all of your students—both male and female—about the general effects that aging has on the larynx and voice quality.

Some of the more-common characteristics of an aging laryngeal system include a decrease in lung power, atrophy of the laryngeal muscles, stiffening of the laryngeal cartilages, vocal fold thickening, and loss of elastic and collagenous fibers.

The voice changes that occur with aging can also include a decrease of the vocal range, particularly the upper range, a change in vibrato, decreased breath control, vocal fatigue, and poor pitch control.

Even as she ages, you can work with her to keep her voice sounding youthful. When you hear her sing, listen for energy and brightness in her tone. As with any singer, you want to hear good resonance and breath control. Together you can work toward a voice that is agile and capable of extending through its whole range. To this end, concentrate on her vocal folds, stretching them and keeping them flexible, and improving the connection between her breath support and vocal fold vibration.

Instruct her in simple exercises that target specific areas. For example, a glance over the shoulder, held for five to 10 seconds, and then repeated over the other shoulder, can improve the flexibility of her head movement. (See "Releasing Tension," in v. 2, ch. 7 for other examples of helping to keep your student flexible.)

When she does her vocal exercises, concentrate on her vocal flexibility and agility by working on her respiratory system. She should begin with a warm up for 15 to 20 minutes, focusing on her breath support and posture. She can do one to three minute deep abdominal breathing, first with her arms overhead, then stretched out at her sides, and then relaxed by her body. Take breaks to avoid hyperventilation.

Otherwise, you can work with her as you would a younger student. Continue with gliding exercises that reach extremes of her register; have her sing light staccati exercises, as well as those exercises that make her sustain her breath; employ messa di voce exercises; giver her exercises that include difficult patterns of syllable and word combinations, which will also help her improve how she produces both language and voice; use increasingly more rapid scales as you move through the lesson.

You may notice that your student needs more time to breathe, or, on the contrary, she has a hard time slowing down and her breath may be fast and tense. Continue to use exercises that help her to have a regular, sustained breath that can be supported through a musical phrase.

You can recommend your student stay active when she is outside your studio. Encourage her to keep her whole body in mind, knowing that good physical conditioning will always benefit her voice. A good cardiovascular workout will improve her muscle tone and flexibility. Walking, working with light weights, gentle stretching, even swimming, all these will affect her whole body. Remind her to check with her doctor before she starts adding anything new to her program.

You may notice some cognitive changes in your aging student. Take your cues from your student and pace your lesson to accommodate her capabilities. She may not learn new things as quickly as she once did, but don't presume she is failing simply because of her age. Listen, watch, and work with her to keep singing an enjoyable experience.

When she is working on her own, suggest a habit of singing 30 minutes a day, five days a week, with at least 15 minutes devoted to her repertoire. She might enjoy joining a chorus, if she has not been part of one until now. The vocal workout and the social interaction can be beneficial to her. At the same time, she can share the fruit of her long experience to others, and perhaps mentor younger singers who will benefit from her expertise.

Temporomandibular joint dysfunction (TMJ)

Temporomandibular joint pain involves the jaw joints and the muscles that control jaw movement and bite. Specifically, it is pain in the joints between the mandible (the lower jaw) and the skull.

The term "TMJ" refers to a physical disorder or disability that causes pain, spasms, and/or muscle fatigue in and around the jaw joints. The term can also refer to a joint dysfunction, such as the jaw sticking in one position.

TMJ can make it difficult for your student to widen her jaw maximally during certain singing maneuvers; if she cannot "drop her jaw" completely, her sound may end up "trapped inside" her mouth. Singers are not more susceptible to TMJ than other people, but it can definitely affect their performance.

Sometimes, symptoms of TMJ are associated with a motor vehicle accident or some other traumatic event. Ask your student if she has been involved in any such event.

Sometimes, however, the symptoms just appear and are not related to any trauma. TMJ can be caused by poor alignment of the teeth, as well as other disease processes. And there are some things that can make TMJ worse, such as chewing too much gum, nail biting, teeth grinding, or even the way your student holds the telephone between her shoulder and the side of her head.

TMJ is a physical problem that is not caused by stress. However, it can certainly be aggravated by stress and tension.

You may be able to give your student exercises that can loosen and relax her jaw and help her to open her mouth wider, thus "freeing up" her sound. However, if the TMJ is serious, then surgery may be the only answer if your student wishes to continue her singing career.

If you believe that your student has TMJ, refer her to a dentist so that the medical side of her condition can be evaluated and properly treated.

Asthma

Asthma can produce problems in overall health. Specifically, asthma can produce problems with breath support during singing.

Asthma is characterized by lung obstruction because the smooth muscles of the bronchi (the tubes that extend from the trachea into the lungs) are inflamed and excessively contracted. The tubes become very narrow, especially the smallest tubes closest to the alveoli (tiny air sacs).

While difficult to diagnose and define, the working definition of asthma is:

- airway obstruction that is reversible (but not completely so in some)
- airway inflammation
- increased airway responsiveness to a variety of stimuli[2]

During an asthma attack, the patient produces a wheezing sound because high resistance in the affected tubes causes airflow turbulence. The high resistance makes it hard for air to flow, and the patient struggles to breathe. When she tries to force air out faster by contracting her expiratory muscles, the high pressures in the thorax compress the tubes, producing further narrowing. In many instances, air will get trapped in the alveoli because the tubes collapse during the patient's forced attempts to breathe out.

If a singer tries to speak or sing during an asthma attack, she will be limited by the obstructed bronchi reducing the airflow from her lungs. This limits both the intensity and duration of her vocal effort. The overpoweringly distressing feeling of breathlessness that occurs with an asthma attack impairs both speech and singing.

Fortunately, there are good treatments that can stop the inflammation and make the smooth muscles relax, removing the excessive obstruction of the bronchi.

Treatment is any drug that reduces the airway inflammation and relaxes the bronchial smooth muscles. There are a few general classes of drugs: beta agonists, inhaled corticosteroids, theophyllin, ingested steroids (prednisone), and epinephrin are used both as treatments and in emergencies when a person presents with severe bronchoconstriction.

❋   Even when not having an asthma attack, your student may have habits left over from asthma, particularly excessive tension in her neck. You will need to work with her to keep finding the baseline state of relaxation. (See the heading "A Baseline State of Relaxation," in v. 2, ch. 7.)

Digestive system problems

A singer must work to keep her whole body in good condition. Her voice works better when her body is not at war with itself.

Often, something can go wrong with a system that seems to have nothing to do with her voice, at least not directly. Left unattended, her symptoms can lead to the damage of her vocal apparatus. Her digestive system is a common culprit in upsetting the fine balance the body needs to function well.

Gastroesophageal reflux disease (GERD). GERD, more commonly known as *heartburn*, is a serious condition that can hurt or damage your student's voice. GERD occurs when stomach acids flow back up into the esophagus from the stomach, inflaming the esophageal and laryngeal tissues.

The esophagus is the tube that carries foods and liquids into the stomach from the throat. The sphincter located at the upper portion of the esophagus closest to the neck is called the upper esophageal sphincter (UES); the lower esophageal sphincter (LES) is located above the point where the stomach and esophagus meet. After a meal, normally working sphincters should remain closed in order to prevent abnormal movement of stomach acids upward into the throat.

A variation of this condition involves only laryngeal irritation, often with no telltale heartburn, and is referred to as *laryngopharyngeal reflux,* or LPR.

Reflux is common among singers and other professional voice users for many reasons. One reason for the increased risk of *reflux laryngitis,* which is distinct from GERD, is due to the significantly higher abdominal pressure associated with proper breath support. This increase in abdominal pressure places a force against the lower esophageal sphincter (LES), which in turn contributes to the likelihood of reflux.

Some singers are at a higher risk for reflux because of their lifestyles. Often, singers do not eat before they perform, since a full stomach can hinder abdominal support. In addition, most performances are in the evening; therefore, singers often eat large meals late at night before going to bed, after the performance has finished.

The more-common effects GERD can have on the voice are laryngitis and hoarseness. Reflux can also contribute to the development of vocal fold granulomas, Reinke's edema, vocal fold nodules, contact ulcers, and vocal fold carcinoma.

Other signs that GERD may be present include overly prolonged vocal warm-ups, as well as tickling, choking, or pain while your student is singing. Still other symptoms can include dysphagia (swallowing problems) or odynophagia (painful swallowing); globus pharyngeus; chronic throat clearing or coughing; too much mucus in the throat; a sour or bitter taste in the mouth; heartburn; oral symptoms such as tooth enamel decay or gingivitis; a tickle in the throat; and pulmonary symptoms such as chest pain, wheezing, coughing, shortness of breath, or asthma.

If your student has any of these symptoms, refer her to an appropriate specialist for diagnosis and treatment.

A variety of factors might be associated with the onset or continued presence of GERD. Your student's lifestyle, smoking, pregnancy, taking drugs, using hormones, obesity (extra weight places pressures on the upper abdomen), and body position can all increase the risk of GERD. Nicotine and alcoholic beverages relax the sphincters, contributing to reflux. If your student eats certain foods such as chocolate, coffee, or peppermint, these can weaken the sphincters as well as increase acid secretion. A diet high in fatty foods will contribute to reflux because these foods increase the time it takes the stomach to digest.

Treatment for GERD begins with changes in the diet to reduce the foods contributing to the reflux. Counsel your student to avoid fatty foods, spicy foods, chocolate, milk, caffeine, citrus fruits, spearmint, peppermint, alcohol, tobacco, and tomato products, as well as any other foods that increase the severity of her reflux. Decreasing the sizes of her meals and increasing their frequency may alleviate some of the discomfort. In particular, she should avoid eating large meals right before bed; eating or drinking within three hours of bedtime is a very important recommendation for diminishing the effects of GERD.

Your student's physician and/or ENT will also discuss lifestyle changes that will help minimize the effects of GERD. Behavioral changes can include reducing or eliminating smoking and drinking, not lying down or sleeping after meals, and losing weight to decrease pressure on the stomach.

Your student should sleep with her head at an incline of four to six inches to help keep acid from flowing back up her esophagus. Two common methods for elevating the upper body are putting a triangular-shaped wedge under the pillow or raising the entire head of the bed.

Other recommendations may include avoiding tight-fitting clothes and not bending over after eating.

If your student cannot change her diet, or if lifestyle changes are not effective in treating the GERD, then medications can be used to reduce the acidity of her stomach contents.

Surgery is another alternative, but a doctor will only recommend surgery if there is severe damage to the esophagus due to reflux, or if lifelong medications are needed. Before your student ever considers surgery for GERD, make sure that all other treatment measures have been tried.

The most-common surgical procedure to alleviate reflux is called *fundoplication*. This procedure can be done with small incisions in the abdomen. Fundoplication involves sewing a part of the stomach around the esophagus, enhancing the barrier that allows food into or out of the stomach.

By identifying the condition early and by making changes to her eating habits and lifestyle, it should be possible for your student to minimize the effects of reflux. However, with some stomach conditions, surgery may not always be avoidable.

Other gastric problems. Gastric upsets, whether intermittent or chronic, may be troublesome for your student. Since the abdominal musculature is so involved during singing, support for the voice is easily disrupted by gastric problems. Stomach discomfort alone may lead to the use of improper singing techniques, with the possibility of vascular damage to the vocal folds. Constipation may also present problems, particularly for traveling performers.

Constipation. Constipation can be a chronic problem for many singers. An active lifestyle, an active social life, and touring can all lead to irregular meals that are often high in fat and low in carbohydrates. Such dietary habits can lead to decreased intestinal transit times, harder and more formed stools, and constipation. Sensations of bloating, pressure, or cramping can occur.

In general, dietary control with regimented timing of meals, increased carbohydrates (particularly complex carbohydrates), and decreased fats can relieve constipation. Occasionally, utilization of a bulk laxative may be needed. Keep in mind that prolonged use of laxatives, particularly non-bulk ones, should be used with close physician monitoring, because electrolyte and fluid abnormalities typically occur with their prolonged use.

Increased fiber intake is also recommended for relieving constipation. A daily goal for fiber intake is approximately 25 to 30 grams; the average daily diet provides only 12 to 15 grams of fiber. Foods high in fiber include beans, peas, unrefined whole grain, fresh fruit, and raw vegetables.

Eating disorders. *Anorexia nervosa* and *bulimia nervosa* are eating disorders that result in poor nutrition and/or malnutrition. If you notice your student suddenly losing a great deal of weight, you should be concerned. A loss of more than 15 percent of ideal body weight may indicate anorexia. If your student is losing actual muscle mass, she may not be able to support her voice. Plus, dehydration can become a major problem.

Bulimia is characterized by binge eating followed by episodes of vomiting or the use of laxatives. In addition to increasing the potential for reflux laryngeal irritation, bulimia can affect vocal hydration due to the potential for swings in electrolyte concentrations and fluid status. With episodes of repeated vomiting, chronic irritation of the esophagus and larynx results.

Both anorexia and bulimia can lead to dehydration, fatigue, and gastrointestinal problems.

These disorders will be most common in your young female students, but they can occur at any age in either sex. If you believe your student is having any of these problems, refer her to her primary physician or a psychologist.

Sleep apnea and snoring

Sleep apnea happens for two reasons. The first: if the muscles in the throat relax so much that the throat collapses and cuts off the air supply. The second: if the brain doesn't send the right signals to the muscles that control breathing.

Without a regular flow of air, the body rouses itself to near-wake-fulness and the airflow resumes. Someone with sleep apnea doesn't get restful sleep and can be sleepy during the day. In addition, a sudden drop of oxygen in the blood can increase blood pressure.

To diagnose sleep apnea, the doctor will give your student a poly-somnography test, which monitors the heart, lungs, and brain as well as breathing patterns, arm and leg movements, and blood oxygen levels.

Nonsurgical treatment with a continuous positive airway pressure (CPAP) device can be prescribed. This machine delivers air at a pressure somewhat greater than that of the surrounding air, through a mask placed over the nose. The pressure is just enough to keep the upper airway passages open, preventing apnea and snoring.

Be cautious when considering surgery for sleep apnea. Removing part of the soft palate, a procedure known as UPPP (uvulopalato-plasty), affects the working of this articulator. Stiffness of the palate is inevitable, and velopharyngeal closure function can potentially be impaired. Whenever possible, nonsurgical inter-vention should be employed.

Surgery for snoring, although less dramatic in its effect on the palate, also results in stiffening and, in some cases, shortening of the palatal structure. Procedures such as LAUP (laser assisted uvu-lopalatoplasty) and somnoplasty are probably best avoided, unless the negative social ramifications of severe snoring are great enough to justify the risk of intervention.

Other Health Conditions

Your student may face other challenges that affect her voice. She may experience notable side-effects from cancer treatment. She may have some damage to her vocal folds due to anesthesia for a surgery unrelated to her voice. She may be taking a combination of medicines that compromises her vocal health.

No matter what she faces, she will need you to remain alert to the many different influences on her vocal health. She will learn from you the many different ways to identify the factors that can contribute to a decline in vocal health.

Facial cosmetic and reconstructive surgery

Facial cosmetic and reconstructive surgery should have little effect on a singer's voice, except in those cases where the lips are involved, or when a complication such as facial nerve weakness affects these articulators.

Head and neck cancer

Most head and neck cancer is of the type referred to as squamous cell carcinoma. This type of cancer responds well to surgery and radiation therapy, with chemotherapy playing a role only in treatment of very advanced tumors.

Surgery for head and neck cancer has significant and obvious effects on the involved areas of the vocal tract. Early detection of cancer improves the outlook, often making less-invasive, endoscopic approaches to tumor removal possible.

Although usually viewed as less radical and career altering, radiation therapy has a profound impact on the tissues treated. Stiffness, chronic swelling, and dryness due to scarring of salivary glands are all potential long-term effects of radiation therapy, and the negative results for voice quality should be obvious.

Breast cancer and reconstruction

Breast cancer can affect performance ability. Breast cancer treatment may include surgery, radiation therapy, and/or chemotherapy. For breast cancer that is confined to the breast and the regional lymph nodes located under the arm and sternum, and that has not spread through the bloodstream to distant sites such as the bones, the liver, the lungs, or the brain, surgery is the most important of these treatments.

Your female students are far more likely to suffer from breast cancer than any of your male students—although breast cancer does occur in males.

Having breast cancer will affect your student psychologically, but it will also have an effect on the physical aspects of her singing structure.

The surgical removal of breast cancer can affect the breathing mechanism and the muscles involved in respiration. Functional changes to your student's performance can occur depending on the respiratory muscles affected by the surgical procedure. The structural integrity of her inspiratory or expiratory muscles may be limited and cause changes in the mechanisms that drive breathing. On the side not affected by cancer, she might experience hyperfunction in her lung and respiratory muscles. Expect changes in tissue elasticity, creating stiffness in the chest wall. Moving the ribs and abdominal wall is more difficult when the stiffness increases. Generating and controlling volumes of air are harder when these structures move less.

Surgeons use different types of procedures, and your student could experience any one of these procedures if faced with breast cancer. Each affects the respiratory muscles differently.

Lumpectomy. Removal of the lump in the breast and some of the tissue around it. Radiation therapy to the part of the breast that remains usually follows. Sometimes, some of the lymph nodes under the arm are removed.

Partial or segmental mastectomy. Removal of the cancer as well as some of the breast tissue around the tumor and the lining over the chest muscles below the tumor. Usually, some of the lymph nodes under the arm are taken out. In most cases, radiation therapy follows.

Total or simple mastectomy. Removal of the entire breast. Sometimes, lymph nodes under the arm are also taken out.

Modified radical mastectomy. Removal of the breast, some of the lymph nodes under the arm, the lining over the chest muscles, and sometimes part of the chest wall muscles. This is the most common operation for breast cancer.

Radical mastectomy. Removal of the breast, chest muscles, and all of the lymph nodes under the arm. For many years, this was the operation most used, but it is used now only when a tumor has spread to the chest muscles.

Radiation therapy. The use of high-energy x-rays to kill cancer cells and shrink tumors. Radiation may come from a machine outside the body (external radiation therapy) or from putting materials that produce radiation (radioisotopes) through thin plastic tubes into the area where the cancer cells are found (internal radiation therapy).

Chemotherapy. Chemotherapy kills off the white blood cells and makes the patient very tired. It can cause vomiting, which can irritate the esophagus, creating symptoms like GERD. For someone undergoing chemotherapy, the biggest problem is a lack of energy.

Women deal with a variety of conditions simply because they are women. The monthly cycle of hormonal changes, the ability to bear children, and the changes of menopause can all mean significant adaptations to how a woman approaches her lifework.

Your female students will look to you to learn how to anticipate some of these shifts and to give them different ways to achieve their singing goals. They will rely on you to contribute to their continued progress as accomplished singers.

Menstruation

Your student may be unaware of the effects that her menstrual cycle or other hormonal changes can have on her singing voice.

Changes occurred during puberty that affected her overall physical appearance as well as her voice quality. These changes were quite apparent because the effects were significant. As an adult, and as an adult performer, the effects that hormonal changes can have on your student's voice may be less evident.

Hormonal changes can have a negative effect on the singing voice. At the onset of the pre-menstrual cycle, the documented voice changes are a loss of vocal range (especially at the higher end of the register), uncertainty of pitches, reduced vocal power, reduced vocal flexibility, and pitch instability and vocal fatigue. These changes are due to drops in the estrogen levels in the body. This drop typically occurs around the 20th to the 22nd day of the menstrual cycle. As the level of estrogen drops, the tissues of the larynx begin to retain a large amount of water, which in turn causes the vocal folds to swell. Because of this change of mass in the larynx, the vocal folds will not vibrate as well, causing the symptoms.

Your student may also complain of abdominal cramping and excessive bloating during her menstrual cycle. As a result, she may experience less-effective breath support due to the decreased effectiveness of abdominal power. This could, in turn, result in laryngeal tension and squeezing.

Your student may refuse to perform during this time in her cycle, or she may schedule performance dates around it. She must do what she is physically comfortable doing.

Pregnancy

Changes in hormonal levels or body structure and mass during pregnancy have a potential effect on voice quality. Many singers report changes in their voices during pregnancy, some temporary and some permanent; this is "laryngopathia gravidarum."

The vocal changes a woman may experience during pregnancy are similar to those related to menstruation: loss of pitch range, vocal instability, and loss of stamina.

The structure of the abdomen and the strength of abdominal muscle contraction change during pregnancy. Although not discussed widely in the literature, many singers realize the changes to the abdominal support system. Most changes are noticeable during the last trimester and through the delivery process. The effects are abdominal cramping similar to that experienced during the pre-menstrual cycle. Abdominal distension during pregnancy also interferes with abdominal muscle function.

Discourage your pregnant student from singing if the level of her abdominal support is substantially compromised.

Menopause

With older female students, the effects of menopause on vocal quality may become an issue. While there is little research data on this topic, the anecdotal data warrants a discussion.

A typical sign of menopause is the loss of the monthly cycle. However, the termination of the monthly cycle is often a late sign of the menopausal process.

Other common signs and symptoms include insomnia, sleep deprivation, hot flashes, emotional and psychological changes, genital atrophy, laryngeal mucosal changes, osteoporosis, cardiovascular disease, decreased libido, decreased concentration, and other changes.

After menopause, your student can expect changes in her voice. The most common and noticeable hormonal change after menopause is a drop in estrogen levels as well as an increase in circulatory progesterone and androgen. The effects on the voice due to this drop in estrogen levels in menopausal women are similar to the changes occurring during the pre-menstrual phase. Your student may experience a loss of high notes, vocal instability and fatigue, uncertainty of pitch, decreased vocal efficiency, huskiness, reduced vocal power, lower speaking pitch, and reduced vocal flexibility.

There is *no reason* for your menopausal student to abandon her vocal career, to discontinue her voice lessons, or to stop her vocal development.

One option is to refer her to a specialist in hormone replacement therapy (HRT) to explore the possibilities of this kind of treatment.

Help your student build a team of medical professionals (typically endocrinologists) who can facilitate the proper course of treatment and who are sensitive to her professional singing goals. Referrals are important because there are courses of hormonal treatment that may adversely affect the voice. Androgens should not be given to female singers even in small amounts, because they cause irreversible unsteadiness in the voice, rapid changes of timbre, and lowering of the fundamental frequency.

Some of the most serious singers, acutely aware of these hormonal changes and extremely concerned about their careers, will begin to develop baseline estrogen levels in their thirties. This aids in achieving optimal therapeutic estrogen levels during the post-menopausal phase.

If you notice any of the changes mentioned above in your female student, be sure she is not overcompensating to push through voice breaks or pitch fluctuations. These compensations are extremely abusive and can lead to an even more-destructive course.

The Psychological Ramifications of Vocal Health Problems

A vocal health problem is more than just a physical ordeal. You must be ready to help your student handle the psychological impact of not being able to use her voice. She may consider it a mere inconvenience—or it may be a devastating circumstance that takes all of her effort to manage with any measure of confidence and grace.

You are the person your student will look to for information and guidance. Your own experience over years of work will make you familiar with common vocal health problems and their resolutions. If you are aware of the methods of dealing with specific problems, you can draw on the stories of other performers who have wrestled with a weakness that affects both performance and personal identity.

Perhaps your student has been performing, in some fashion, since childhood. She may have rehearsed in the basement or the backyard, performed at school talent shows, and devoted many hours to honing her craft. When asked, she identifies herself first as a singer. For much of her life she has been rewarded, disappointed, and controlled by the pursuit of a singing career.

Was it a good day or a bad day? For your student, she may judge the day on whether or not her voice functioned well and met the demands she placed upon it. Like many others, particularly classical singers, she may have centered her entire identity on being a singer, and singing may be the single most motivating force in her life.

But the human voice is fragile, subject to wear and tear and serious damage. And when a vocal health problem develops, it may threaten the essential sense of your student's very self.

Even before an injury has been confirmed, you'll see some predictable patterns of behavior from your student. Like anyone facing a crisis or chronic illness, your student may exhibit symptoms of denial, extreme fear, guilt, anger, and reluctant acceptance. She may also experience enormous feelings of loss, insecurity, failure, isolation, and stress. These patterns can easily lead to depression, which serves to further complicate and hinder the recovery process.

Part of this reaction comes from a lack of role models. In the past, professional singers did not often make their vocal problems public. More recently, well-known professional singers such as

Julie Andrews, Andy Williams, and Jose Carreras have publicly acknowledged their vocal injuries and have spoken of the choices they have faced for recovery, including surgery. These disclosures, along with a better emphasis on vocal health in college music programs and among singing teachers, have allowed younger singers to become more aware of potential voice problems that may require medical attention.

However, in spite of this information, some singers will avoid contemplating the possible existence of an injury by making excuses about why an unusual disruption of the voice will not resolve. A medical evaluation can ease some of these fears, but your strong example and encouragement will go a long way toward encouraging and supporting your student.

In spite of recent advances, there is still a stigma attached to having a vocal fold injury. Singers continue to resist acceptance of the fact that they are vocal athletes, and they can suffer injuries that are simply the result of the extreme demands placed on an ultimately finite physical system. Instead, the singer (and many of her colleagues) may immediately assume that any vocal injury is the result of poor vocal technique and is therefore her own fault. Then guilt enters the picture.

Some singers do sustain vocal injuries that are the result of a vocal technique that is not adequate to the demands placed on the voice. Injuries can also be the result of vocally abusive habits or poor vocal hygiene.

But even the most technically perfect singer is not entirely safe from a vocal mishap. While excellent technique, combined with a vocally healthy lifestyle and strict adherence to the basic rules of good vocal hygiene, can reduce the chances for a vocal fold injury, no one is completely immune to the possibility.

It isn't hard to understand why your student may not want to accept that the center of her psychological stability is indeed that vulnerable. However, this acceptance can enable your student to take a more-realistic, positive, and ultimately productive route to vocal recovery.

Isolation, Secrecy

Your student may feel utterly alone in this encounter with potential disaster. While the topic of vocal injury and recovery is now more widely discussed in general discourse about singing, individual personal accounts of injury and recovery are rare, particularly in the classical world.

If your student believes that knowledge of her vocal injury will incur negative judgments about her vocal technique, and especially if she faces a potential job loss because of questions about her vocal reliability, she is less likely to share the experience with other singers. Subsequently, the newly diagnosed injured singer is not likely to have anyone to talk to who has gone through the process and who could provide moral support and advice.

The injured singer could very easily adopt a secretive approach to her condition, sharing it only on a "need to know" basis and concocting any number of stories to explain why she is unable to meet certain vocal obligations. This will serve only to isolate the singer, whose personality is often very outgoing and may depend heavily on open social interaction with friends and colleagues.

Do not underestimate the stress, tension, and depression this entire process can cause. Professional psychological counseling can be particularly helpful during this ordeal.

If vocal fold surgery and the subsequent recovery are part of your student's future, it would also be advisable to ask the otolaryngologist (ENT), the singing voice specialist, or the speech language pathologist to recommend a person who has been through a similar event and who would be willing to share his or her insight with the newly injured singer. This personal contact with someone who has been through the experience can be very helpful to your student.

Just make sure that your student talks to at least one person who has had a good outcome! There is nothing wrong with hearing about a poor result from a vocal fold injury and/or surgery; it is important for your student to be fully aware of the seriousness and possibilities of the situation. However, chances are good that the injured singer who receives appropriate medical attention and follows strict recovery guidelines can expect to return to a full singing schedule. She needs as much positive information as possible to make her recovery process less arduous.

Recovery and Despair

The surgical recovery process, particularly for a more-severely injured singer, can seem an endless time of slow, incremental progress interrupted by periods when the voice appears forever stuck at a sub-optimum level. This can be an extremely frustrating situation for your student, and it creates the perfect opportunity for despair to become a constant state of mind.

Again, it is your responsibility as the teacher to establish an atmosphere of realistic positivism. You must encourage your student to take the long view while still giving her permission to express any feelings of fear, loss, anger, and general uncertainty about her future.

However, it is *not* your job to take the place of a trained psychologist or psychiatrist in this process. You are not professionally qualified for this important role, and you can actually hinder your student's recovery with well-meaning but inappropriate psychological advice.

If you think that your student would benefit from counseling, it is your responsibility to inform her of your concern and to encourage her to seek assistance from an appropriate professional in this field.

The Teacher Questions Himself

And what about you? How do you respond to the discovery of a vocal injury or illness in your student?

Like the singer, your first reaction to the suspicion or confirmation of a vocal injury, particularly in a student of long standing, may be one of self-doubt coupled with fear and guilt. You may question your ability as a technical teacher, and you may be afraid of how this information will affect your reputation as a teacher.

Obviously, if you observe in your studio an emerging pattern of singers who cannot seem to avoid vocal injury, then you should carefully re-evaluate your teaching concepts and how they are being implemented by your students.

But, like the injured singer, you must remember that the possibility of vocal injury simply goes along with being a singer. As a teacher, your best defenses against this possibility are the recognition that it exists and the determination to educate your students in every conceivable way so that the chances of an injury are minimized.

Continue to educate yourself on the causes of vocal injury and the many ways to bring your student back to health. The more tools you have at your disposal, the better equipped you will be to deal with any situation.

A vocal fold injury is an extraordinary opportunity for a singer to learn personal skills that can have far-reaching positive effects on the rest of the individual's life. Learning to exercise patience and faith in a process when the outcome is not fully realized is a strength that can benefit the singer as a performer. Realizing that her voice is not indestructible, that she can learn new skills and recovery techniques, that she can develop the patience needed to cope with a long recovery process—all of these can make your student stronger, both professionally and personally.

Another positive result of surviving a vocal fold injury is the insight this gives the individual into going through a disruptive life event. This can be another invaluable lesson—particularly if the singer becomes a teacher.

Following vocal fold surgery, a lingering element of fear may plague your student long after her voice has returned to a full performance schedule. As she begins to resume a more-normal singing schedule, she may be afraid of re-injury. This fear can be fed by very real instabilities in her voice, particularly the sensation of vocal fatigue that some singers experience as part of the normal recovery process. Your student may also experience the fear that her voice will "never really be the same again."

The only sure cures for these fears are time and successful performance experiences.

The first time your student performs after having vocal fold surgery may be a nerve-racking event. Once that first time is complete and she has had some measure of success, the next time should be a little easier. Each following performance will help her learn to trust her voice again, no matter what level it may have reached at that point in time.

After a number of successful performance experiences, your student will really begin to trust her voice and let go of the fear of re-injury and subsequent failure. This process often takes as long as a year, and it is a process that should not be rushed.

Remember that this kind of fear can contribute to muscle tension that may in itself impair vocal quality. Encourage your student to allow herself to be physically and vocally vulnerable during the resumption of singing, so that the very best of her vocal potential can be accessed and realized.

Some singers never regain full use of their voices following a vocal fold injury and/or surgery. Instead, some lack of mechanical efficiency remains, and it always presents a vocal challenge to the singer. The good news is that, in many of these instances, the singer can learn to work around the deficiency, establishing or re-establishing a full singing career in spite of the problem. This takes a particularly realistic, determined, and disciplined mind-set on the part of both the teacher and the singer. Even when any structural weaknesses are such that a singing career can still be created, not every singer has the kind of personality necessary for this special challenge.

There are renowned singers, even in the vocally unforgiving world of opera, who have maintained significant careers in spite of some structural imperfection in their vocal systems. The willpower and determination required by these singers is formidable.

If you believe that your student is technically capable of learning to compensate appropriately for a permanent vocal weakness, then your task is to provide unwavering optimism and patience for as long as your student is willing to attempt this course of action.

Every voice is finite and has a point beyond which it cannot go without the risk of injury, no matter how perfect the vocal technique. The sooner your student accepts this reality, the sooner she will take full responsibility for the health and well-being of her instrument.

You live in a time when advancements in scientific knowledge, technology, and medicine have given singers and voice teachers tremendous insight into the mysterious nature of the voice, along with many new options for dealing with the inevitable injuries that occur in the field.

But for these advancements to affect the world of the voice, you must engage in a lifetime of continuing education and growth. Do not be afraid that all of this new information will negate your previously held technical concepts or make you "too scientific" in your teaching. This information will enhance your abilities as a teacher and will enable you to give your students that more-complete vocal education and understanding that is necessary to excellence in singing.

ENDNOTES

1. Botulinum toxin injection in the treatment of vocal fold paralysis associated with multiple sclerosis: a case report. Journal of Voice, 13, 274-9. Rontal-E; Rontal-M; Wald-J; Rontal-D. (1999).

2. Definition produced by the National Asthma Education Program of the National Heart, Lung and Blood Institute of the National Institutes of Health.

Vocal Health Case Studies

The case studies in this section tell the stories of several singers.

The performers varied in their musical styles and vocal problems. Many of their pathological voice disturbances stemmed from poor vocal behaviors or a lack of awareness of vocal health issues. In some cases, poor vocal health was the result of ambitious scheduling and performances. In all cases, the singers went to an outpatient voice care center in Florida. Some of the singers worked at nearby theme parks, where on-site first-aid station personnel referred them to the voice center. Some were performers whose tours brought them to Florida.

The staff of the voice center is dedicated to treating patients with ear, nose, and throat problems and performing surgery involving the head and neck. Treatments include behavioral changes, prescription medicines, and surgery. Patients are educated in new techniques to care for their voices so that they can continue to perform for many years. Staff members include specialists in a number of fields: otolaryngologists, also known as "ear, nose, and throat doctors" (ENTs); speech language pathologists, with master's degrees or Ph.D.s; physician's assistants (PAs); audiologists; and nurses.

The voice center team interviews and tests patients, recommends behavioral changes and (sometimes) surgery, and prepares plans of recovery. A vocal system evaluation generally includes the following:

- An appraisal of the performance site and demands

- A case history

- Exams such as *endoscopy* (visual examination of the inside of the body using a nasal or an oral scope) and *videostroboscopy* (slow-motion images of the vocal folds, using a scope with a strobe light)

- Acoustic and physiologic recordings and analyses of the voice

During the testing phase, the team uses endoscopy with videostroboscopy to check for the following common vocal fold pathologies:

- Edema (swelling). Generalized fullness of the vocal folds, usually along their entire length

- Laryngitis. Loss of voice

- Nodules/nodular formations. Small, blisterlike lesions

- Polyps. Larger, wide-based, fluid-filled lesions

- Prenodular swelling. Fullness in the anterior portion of the vocal folds

- Rhinitis. Irritation to the nose and drainage from the nasal cavity

- Vascularity. *Vascularity* is prominent blood vessels on the vocal folds. The vocal folds should not be dark red after singing.

- Vocal fold hemorrhage (hematoma). Vascular bleeding with a sac around it, much like a bruise to the vocal folds

The team also tests the singer for deviations from a healthy vocal system, including those listed here.

Healthy vocal folds are pinkish-white with a shiny surface. The folds show no evidence of lesions or visible blood vessels. The edges are smooth. The folds open and close regularly, synchronized with each other. The left and right sides are doing the same thing at the same time, as are the top and bottom. The skin of the vocal folds vibrates loosely and easily relative to the muscle and is pliable.

The voice center team looks for indications of a healthy voice, such as the following. (For more details about characteristics of the healthy vocal system, see "The healthy voice," on page 5.)

- Glottal closure (vocal fold closure). The space between the vocal folds is called the glottis, so when the vocal folds close, the glottis closes. In a healthy vocal system, the glottal closure should be complete.

- Hyperfunction. Under good conditions, the *accessory structures* (false vocal folds, epiglottis) should not assist with voice production. When the parts of the vocal system work too hard, the throat seems to squeeze from back to front and from side to side. False vocal folds tend to move to the middle, and the muscles in the front and back of the throat bulge.

- Maximum phonation time. The *phonation time* for a healthy voice depends on age. Following are some rough estimates of normal phonation times for young adults (ages twenty through twenty-five) and elderly adults (sixty-five and older):

  - Young adult men, approximately 23 to 25 seconds

  - Elderly men, approximately 15 to 20 seconds

- Young adult women, approximately 15 to 25 seconds

- Elderly women, approximately 10 to 15 seconds

- Mucosal wave. The *mucosal wave* is a movement of the skin of the vocal fold moving over the muscle of the vocal fold. If the movement is not fluid, there is stiffness underneath, perhaps from a potential lesion, thickness, or another factor that interferes with normal vibratory amplitude.

- Periodicity. Vocal folds move in phase and are therefore *periodic*. Healthy vocal folds open and close with regular timing and little observable chaos.

- Phase closure. In a healthy vocal system, the right and left vocal folds close simultaneously.

- Phase symmetry. The sides of the vocal folds should move symmetrically as they open and close. The right side's movement should be a mirror image of the left side's movement.

- Phases of vibration. In a healthy voice, more time is spent in the opening phases than in the closing phases of the *phases of vibration*—the four phases of opening and closing the vocal folds (See "Phonation Continuum," in v. 2, ch. 9.)

- Semitone range. The *semitone range* is generally accepted as the best means of comparing pitch ranges. It shows how many half steps of the musical scale separate the top and bottom pitches a singer can comfortably produce. (See "Singing Range," in v. 3, ch. 11.) It is useful to measure at the beginning of a health program and again at the end to measure results. The following are normal ranges of people in the general popultion, not necessarily singers.

- Young adult men, 23 to 47 semitones

- Elderly men, 11 to 35 semitones

- Young adult women, 20 to 40 semitones

- Elderly women, 9 to 41 semitones

- Singing range. The range of half steps that a singer with a healthy voice can produce smoothly. With vocal problems, a singer may have a narrower range. After therapy, she may reestablish her singing range.

- Vertical level of the vocal folds. The *vertical level* and thickness of the upper and lower portions of the vocal folds should be equal in height.

- Vibratory amplitude. In a healthy voice, the vocal folds move easily from midline to their most lateral positions. Neither vocal fold is paralyzed, stiff, or lagging behind the other.

- Vibratory behavior. *Vibratory behavior* relates to how well the tissues vibrate during voicing. Vibratory behavior is normal when all the other items in this list are within normal range. When the vibratory behavior is abnormal, an ENT may see an "hourglass" shape, with an opening at the front and back of the vocal folds and closure in the middle.

- Voice driving pressure (expiratory pressure). Voice driving pressure is the lung pressure necessary to initiate and maintain vocal fold movement. It occurs when the singer exhales.

Because some of the singers in these stories are people you know or have heard of, we have changed their names to protect their privacy. Explanations of the testing and results have been abbreviated or simplified to streamline the stories.

We have chosen case stories from a diverse group of singers—professional, avocational, untrained, trained, adolescent, and vocally-abusive singers—to show the full extent of the body's response to vocal use and abuse. For example, we included an extreme case of a rock singer, whose screaming would obviously create vocal problems. Though most singers reading this book probably wouldn't abuse their voices the way he did, his case illustrates what the body is likely to do under those conditions.

Case One: Outdoor Theater Performer

Janet Casey has spent the past 10 years performing in a major theme park in Central Florida. Her stage is the outdoors, often in 70- to 90-degree heat with high humidity. Working without a microphone, Janet and the rest of the cast present a 30-minute show, as many as nine times a day. At age twenty-six, Janet enjoys the work and its challenges.

When the stage manager noticed that Janet's voice was deteriorating, he referred her to the on-site first-aid station. After an examination, Janet was placed on vocal rest. After a week, her voice loss was still persistent, and Janet was referred to an ENT at the voice center for evaluation.

Evaluation

Janet's voice evaluation included an interview, an assessment of her performance site and its demands, a perceptual assessment of vocal quality, and endoscopy with videostroboscopy.

In the interview, Janet described her musical training to the ENT. She had been formally coached in musical theater, but she was not aware of proper vocalizing and respiratory strategies—skills essential for projecting and maintaining a good voice.

She began a therapy program designed to teach her appropriate ways to generate vocal power. (See "To Develop Singing with

Power," in v. 3, ch. 13.) She also learned to eliminate poor vocal habits that she had acquired over the years. She was motivated to learn new techniques in order to continue her career as a performer in the outdoor theater. The behavioral changes helped eliminate vocal abuse.

All went well until the fall of 1998, when Janet got into a screaming conflict with a family member. At the time, she thought she'd strained her voice. She had some acute voice difficulties but didn't perceive any long-lasting problems.

Then, in the winter of 1999, Janet didn't warm up before a performance. She said she had "no real support" during loud vocalizations and that she had "pushed through her throat" to perform. She felt as though she had "pulled a muscle" in her neck. After completing all nine shows that day, Janet had a vocal breakdown. She had periods of complete voice loss and excessive vocal strain. Janet described this as the time her voice began to deteriorate.

At the same time, Janet was emotionally distressed because she was caring for a critically ill family member. She described extensive crying periods, and she perceived great muscle tension in her throat when she cried. Her stress was further exacerbated by an unusual work schedule: she performed for 10 days without a break.

Perceptual impressions of vocal quality

During her office visit, Janet's speaking voice was moderately breathy and slightly strained, with a low-pitched, gravelly sound throughout a five-word phrase. Some voice breaks were noticed. She frequently "punched" out the sounds (hard glottal attacks) when she started to speak. Her pitch was within normal limits, although her loudness seemed excessive. Her voice occasionally broke during conversation, which probably related to vocal strain.

The doctor palpated her neck muscles and identified tension in her extrinsic laryngeal muscles. Janet reported mild soreness with the palpation of her lower neck.

She could hold a pitch on the vowel [a] (ah) for 12 seconds (maximum phonation time). The highest pitch she could easily sing was E4 (E above middle C) and the lowest was C3 (C below middle C)—an extremely narrow 17-semitone range. Her intonation during this task was fair.

Videostroboscopy results

Janet's videostroboscopy exam showed a wide-based polyp on the left true vocal fold. On the right vocal fold, she had soft, blisterlike swelling with a small nodular formation; this formation seemed to result from irritation from the left vocal fold pathology. (See "Organic Disorders," on page 86.)

The polyp blocked the left vocal fold from closing completely. When Janet vocalized, the ENT saw an hourglass glottal closure, meaning that a gap existed in the forward and back parts of the glottis. Her vocal fold vibratory cycle was predominantly open. Vertical level was equal during her voice production. Her voice driving pressure was moderately decreased.

The mucosal wave was moderately decreased in both her vocal folds, more so on the left. The vibrations of her vocal folds were greatly reduced, also more so on the left. When Janet produced sound, her phase symmetry was characterized as mostly irregular, with one side of her vocal folds closing before the other. Hyperfunction was present as she sang, characterized by squeezing the laryngeal area from front to back and the accessory structures participating to assist with glottal closure.

Treatment for Janet's voice problems involved behavioral changes, voice therapy, and—eventually—surgery. Janet was highly motivated to comply with the recommendations, and she worked hard to change her vocally abusive behaviors.

Behavioral program

Her behavioral program focused initially on modifying the maladaptive behaviors associated with her performance and lifestyle. She began by identifying and eliminating vocal abuse, initiating a modified voice rest program (no more than 10 to 15 minutes of talking per day for one week), stopping her performances, and working in a job that minimized the use of her speaking voice. She did no singing.

Most people must temporarily suspend performing when vocal dysfunction arises. However, complete voice rest was not recommended in this case because of Janet's personality and performance demands. She was likely to take bad habits back to her performance schedule unless she had some new strategies to reduce abusive vocal behaviors.

To help develop a lifestyle more conducive to vocal health, the voice center team provided Janet with information about hydration, nutrition, sleep, and anxiety. Because Janet sang in the heat and humidity, her recovery process required rehydration not only with water but also with an electrolyte replacement drink. (Gatorade® and Pedialyte® are two brands of such a beverage.)

With the speech pathologist, Janet also addressed the sources of stress that were contributing to her voice problems. These included her performance demands, her financial reliance on her job, her difficulty sleeping, and her coping strategies in dealing with her ill family member.

In the first voice therapy session, the concept of the *therapeutic voice* was introduced. The therapeutic voice is soft, relaxed, and breathy. The speech language pathologist taught Janet how to vocalize with an open, relaxed throat, using the breath stream to initiate and carry the tone, using the following instructions:

> Begin by taking in a big breath, then sighing easily, as with relief. Now try that again. This time, as you exhale, add a soft voice during the sigh from a somewhat high pitch. This technique is called "relaxed voicing."

> Repeat the sigh. But this time, as you exhale, count the numbers one through five aloud during exhalation, making each number sound relaxed and breathy.[1] (See the exercise "To Loosen a Tight Onset," in v. 2, ch. 9.)

This exercise helps reduce the collision force during vocal fold closure. The goals are to preserve the normal mechanical properties of the vocal folds, to prevent more damage to the vocal folds, and to restore the vibratory characteristics of the damaged area.

To relax Janet's laryngeal musculature and to reduce laryngeal height and stiffness, the speech language pathologist performed a circumlaryngeal massage. This procedure, similar to massaging other parts of the body, reduces muscle tension and maximizes the movement of the larynx.

Janet was instructed to use an open-mouth posture whenever possible when speaking or singing, in order to lower her larynx.[2] Janet learned to achieve full oral resonance by inhaling deeply and then, while exhaling, dropping her jaw to eliminate tension in her neck, face, and laryngeal region. To help her imagine this position, she was instructed to think of the slack jaw and blank face a child might have when bored or tired.

Janet was trained to use adequate breath before producing any sounds. Concentrating on a large inhalation forced her to breathe to a higher lung volume and helped lower her larynx.[3] This technique is similar to the yawn-sigh exercise. (See the exercise "To Become Aware of the Jaw," in v. 2, ch. 10.)[4]

In addition, part of the retraining was to help her discover the kinesthetic sensations of the tone in and around her face. (See "To Explore Vibrations in And Around the Face," in v. 2, ch. 10.) She helped move the kinesthetic sensations of the tone forward by practicing nasal sounds such as [m], [n], and [ŋ] (ng). Those sensations helped her relax her tongue.

After seven weeks of voice therapy, Janet's vocal folds were reexamined with an oral endoscope and videostroboscopy. (See "Visual Examination," on page 58.) These examinations revealed improvement in the movement of the right vocal fold, increased mucosal wave on the left side, and a decrease in the overall edema and vascularity of both vocal folds. However, the videostroboscopy revealed bilateral polyps, and surgery was recommended.

Surgery, results, and follow-up

Janet was put under general anesthesia. The surgeon found the bilateral vocal fold polyps, worse on the left because Janet's condition had gotten worse before surgery. The surgeon removed both polyps. There were no complications during surgery.

The right vocal fold had generalized and diffuse thickening of the mucous membrane along its entire length, which did not require treatment. The thickened mucous membrane recovered its normal appearance in the weeks after surgery.

After surgery, the speech language pathologist perceived Janet's voice to be without the breathy quality, strain, glottal fry, hard glottal attacks, or voice breaks originally observed. Janet's loudness became adequate.

Janet's maximum phonation time increased from 12 to 23 seconds. Her semitone range expanded from her original 17 to 27.

Videostroboscopy following her surgery showed her vocal fold edge to be smooth and free of laryngeal lesions. There was no edema present. Her glottal closure was complete, phase closure was normal, and vertical level was equal. The vibratory amplitude and mucosal wave were normal, and vibratory behavior was fully present. Phase symmetry was normal, and hyperfunction was not present. Janet was back to normal physical status.

Once Janet's voice began to return to normal, her therapy focused on retraining, strengthening, and balancing the three systems responsible for voice production and quality: breathing, phonation, and resonance. (See "Optimizing the Body for Excellence in Singing," in v. 1, ch. 4.) Janet learned that she could condition the muscles in her respiratory and laryngeal systems.

Just as a runner should not enter a track meet without proper training in endurance, strength, and flexibility, a singer should not return to high-performance work without training her voice. Janet's post-surgery therapy trained her in the proper mechanics of breathing, enabling her to produce her voice in an efficient, low-risk manner.

Return to Performance

Janet returned to work gradually. Although her vocal pathology was eliminated and her vocal function was restored, she needed to build endurance so that she would not harm her vocal system again. Janet worked on familiar music so that she could concentrate on reinforcing good technique without being distracted with learning new material. Vocal warm-ups and cool-downs were mandatory before and after every performance; Janet continued this practice even after she recovered.

Six weeks after her surgery, Janet returned to work on a light schedule. She reported no straining or overcompensating to produce her performance voice, and she felt stronger and more confident. Results of videostroboscopy after the third workweek revealed a good closed phase and intact vibratory function.

Janet had been oversinging in her effort to reach "opening night" intensity for each of the shows she performed every day. The voice center team advised Janet to conserve her energy and find other ways to communicate. By the fourth workweek, she could modify her performance by relying on diction and acting. At her next evaluation, her vocal folds and their functioning were within normal limits. Her vocal fold edges were straight, and the edema was gone. Janet increased her schedule in her fifth workweek.

Throughout her recovery, Janet continued therapy twice a week.

Case Two: Studio, Stage, and Lounge Singer

If you heard Shannon Kinsale's voice, it would sound familiar. She's been in radio and television commercials or on stage in a theatrical production. She has sung successfully without a major vocal injury for 10 years. The thirty-year–old singer and performer now plays a lead role in a popular stage production in a major theme park. She also performs jazz, blues, and soul three nights a week in a lounge setting and she socializes several nights a week in nightclubs.

After the opening night of her stage show, Shannon sang four shows a day. She had voice problems almost from the start. She reported trouble with breath control, she had difficulty hitting high notes, and she couldn't maintain volume without strain. Although she used a microphone most of the time and sang in a comfortable range, she couldn't manage the gospel-style singing without strain.

She went to the theme park's first-aid station and was placed on vocal rest for two weeks. Reevaluation at the first-aid station revealed persistent symptoms of acute laryngitis. The first-aid station sent Shannon to an ENT at the voice center for further evaluation.

Evaluation

Initially, Shannon reported "severe pain in her throat area, loss of voice, and inability to work in her current job." She had excessive neck and jaw tension. She said her speaking voice sounded harsh. Her singing voice tired quickly. As the workweek progressed, the problems increased, and she noticed difficulty in her vocal range. She had no previous history with hoarseness, nasal congestion, increased nasal pressure, or allergy symptoms.

She was unaware of any indigestion or heartburn; however, she did complain of episodes of choking and coughing in the middle of the night. The ENT prescribed Prilosec to reduce stomach acid. Shannon found improvement immediately.

Otherwise, her past medical history was unremarkable. She took Serzone daily for depression. She was on no other medications. She had no known drug allergies. She did not use inhalant drugs, but she smoked cigarettes, drank moderately several nights per week, and drank caffeine often.

The ENT assessed Shannon's vocal quality and performed a laryngeal examination with videostroboscopy.

Perceptual impressions of vocal quality

During conversation, Shannon's voice was moderately breathy with a slightly strained, pressed quality. She spoke with frequent glottal attacks. Her pitch and loudness were adequate. She could sustain the vowel [a] (ah) for 10 seconds. The highest note she could comfortably sing was E4 and the lowest was B2, with an 18-semitone range. When asked to vocalize differently (her first attempts at behavioral change), she vocalized with extreme hyper-function.

Laryngeal exam and videostroboscopy results

The laryngeal examination showed that her vocal folds were mildly swollen but had no distinct nodules or polyps. She was referred for a complete voice evaluation and endoscopy with videostroboscopy.

Videostroboscopy revealed bilateral vocal fold polyps. An hourglass configuration was found in her glottal closure. The open phase predominated and the vertical level was equal. Vibratory amplitude and the mucosal wave were moderately decreased in both vocal folds. Vibratory behavior was partially absent in both vocal folds. Her phase symmetry was regular, and hyperfunction was absent.

Intervention

The initial goal was to eliminate her vocally abusive behaviors through voice therapy administered by a voice therapist. When that did not resolve the problems, Shannon had surgery, followed by another round of behavioral therapy.

Behavioral program

Shannon was directed to eliminate or reduce cigarette smoking and drinking and to follow a prescribed program of vocal hygiene. Shannon had an active social life in which she used her voice detrimentally. She wanted to stay connected with her friends but had to see them someplace other than a nightclub.

She began a modified voice rest program, used a low-impact voice when talking in her optimum speaking range, attempted to eliminate vocal abuse, worked to achieve adequate breath support and control strategies, and focused on relaxing her larynx and refocusing the placement of her voice into the frontal mask.

Her healing process was somewhat slow, but she was determined to avoid surgery and she continued behavioral voice therapy. The ENT prescribed a corticosteroid for a brief time to help reduce the swelling in both vocal folds. However, surgical removal of the pathological condition was deemed necessary.

Surgery, results, and follow-up

Surgeons removed two large polyps, one from each vocal fold. There were no complications during or after the surgery.

After following full then partial voice rest, Shannon's voice no longer sounded strained. She had no hard glottal attacks, and her pitch and loudness were adequate, although she had slight glottal fry (See the heading "Three-Register View of the Voice," in v. 3, ch. 11.) Six weeks after surgery, her voice quality was returning to normal. Her voice was not breathy, and she had no hyperfunction.

Videostroboscopy showed that the vocal fold edge was smooth bilaterally, the glottal closure was complete, and phase closure was normal. The vertical level was equal, and the vibratory amplitude and mucosal wave were only slightly limited in the surgically affected area. Vibratory behavior had slight limitations but was generally increased, phase symmetry was regular, and no hyperfunction was apparent. Physically, Shannon was back to a healthy condition.

Shannon followed a post-surgery behavioral program similar to the one described in Case One. Follow-up treatment centered on continuing to eliminate her vocal abuse and developing coping strategies to help her maintain healthy behaviors.

She complied well with the treatment program, and the voice therapy regimen was successful.

Return to Performance

Her return to work was gradual. Shannon increased her performance schedule gradually until the sixth week, when she returned to her regular schedule. She began working her second job 10 weeks after surgery and reported slight vocal fatigue. Determined to keep this ambitious schedule and maintain good vocal rest, Shannon mostly limited her voice use to those times when she was working. In addition to her two singing jobs, she also completed a series of commercials and voice-overs. She worked these projects successfully without any difficulty with her voice quality.

Eight months later, Shannon had episodes of hoarseness following chronic sinus infections. Antibiotics and vocal rest were prescribed until the symptoms diminished. Voice therapy sessions resumed, with careful monitoring of her speaking and singing voice. Shannon made a full recovery in little more than three weeks and returned to her normal work and social schedule.

Four months after that, she found herself coughing and clearing her throat excessively because of a cold. She could manage a full workday but found her voice to be rigid and extremely fatigued at the end of the day. Her voice quality was moderately breathy, with slightly strained, pressed phonation.(See "Phonation Continuum," in v. 2, ch. 9.)

Endoscopy with videostroboscopy revealed bilateral vocal nodules with generalized edema and an hourglass glottal closure. The phase closure was predominantly open and the vertical level was equal. Vibratory amplitude and the mucosal wave were slightly decreased bilaterally. There was decreased vibratory behavior and irregular phase symmetry but no hyperfunction.

Shannon began a more-rigorous behavioral voice therapy regimen focusing on breath management, relaxed larynx, good vocal focus, modified voice rest, use of a therapeutic voice, and continued counseling on eliminating vocal abuse. She was highly motivated to make these modifications.

Because of her work demands and singing style, Shannon started a voice driving pressure respiratory-strength training program. After completing this program, her pressure-generating capability increased by more than 100 percent. Since then, her voice quality has substantially improved, and she is performing more now than she was before her original vocal disturbance occurred.

Case Three: Musical Theater Performer

Madeleine LaSalle is a musical theater performer working in a major theme park. She toured throughout the United States with a musical theater show, then relocated to her current stage at a park in Florida. There, she began performing the lead in a new stage production.

Her performance site was inadequately amplified during her show. To try to reach her audience, she ended up singing and speaking with a hyperfunctional voice.

The stage manager of the show referred her to the on-site first-aid station because she showed symptoms of laryngitis (dysphonia). Madeleine was placed on vocal rest for one week. The following week, she saw an ENT for evaluation.

Madeleine recalled that her voice had been "normal and serviceable" for her current role for approximately a month, then it became "raspy and deep." She lost her top octave and added some bottom notes. She also had to push to produce any loudness or variability in her voice. As time went on and her performance demand increased, her problems became worse. She began clearing her throat and coughing excessively. Madeleine was a loud and enthusiastic talker, she suffered from poor hydration and nutrition, and she did not get enough sleep.

Evaluation

Madeleine's evaluation included an assessment of vocal quality and endoscopy with videostroboscopy.

Perceptual impressions of vocal quality

Madeleine's voice was moderately to severely hoarse with vocal strain during quiet and loud vocalization, and she had hard glottal attacks. She tended to posture her body in a short phrase as if she were running out of air. Her maximum phonation time for sustaining the vowel [a] (ah) was seven seconds.

Videostroboscopy results

Videostroboscopy revealed moderately rough edges in both vocal folds and generalized edema in the middles of both vocal folds. Madeleine had an hourglass glottal closure and a predominant open phase. The vertical level of approximation was equal, and the amplitude and mucosal wave were moderately decreased in both vocal folds. Vibratory behavior was partially absent in both vocal folds. Phase symmetry and periodicity were irregular. Hyper-function was present.

Intervention

Behavioral and pharmacological treatments were successful, and Madeleine did not need surgery. The voice center team put her on vocal rest for one week. She performed only filing and computer work assigned by the performing company, which involved no vocal demands.

The ENT prescribed an anti-inflammatory medicine for six days to help decrease the swelling in her vocal folds. Madeleine spoke and sang only minimally during this time.

Weekly checkups and treatment sessions included exercises to develop greater stamina, and they helped her continue to eliminate vocal abuse, maintain good vocal hygiene, and develop a more therapeutic speaking voice.

After four weeks of the behavioral and pharmacological treatments, videostroboscopy revealed a slight reduction in the generalized edema. However, Madeleine's vocal fold's vibratory behavior, amplitude, and mucosal wave were still limited. Another four weeks of modified voice rest and vocal rehabilitation were recommended. During those weeks, she continued to reduce her vocal fold swelling through vocal rest, relaxation, and breathing techniques. She was very motivated to follow through so that she could return to work.

Following two more weeks of light duty, her vocal folds were reexamined with endoscopy. There was a significant reduction in vocal fold edema with no observed hyperfunction throughout the examination. Her voice quality was beginning to return to normal, with only a slightly breathy voice and no vocal strain or hard attacks. Surgery was not needed because the voice therapy program was effective.

Return to Performance

After two weeks of a part-time schedule, another videostroboscopy did not reveal any adverse reactions or negative changes in vibratory behavior. Madeleine is currently experiencing good vocal health and performing in her original show, and she has not had another vocal breakdown.

Case Four: Rock Band Singer

Pete Chen had a history of chronic laryngitis and throat pain. He could not perform effectively with his rock band and he needed help.

Pete started having voice problems two to three years before he sought help. He frequently lost his voice, a condition that was occurring more often and for longer periods. In trying to heal himself, he yelled and screamed to "straighten out" his voice problem. After doing so, he naturally felt pain and a stinging sensation in his throat.

He had a history of gastroesophageal reflux disease (GERD) and was taking medication to manage the acid indigestion. He smoked a pack of cigarettes a day.

When he was not performing or rehearsing with his band, he worked as a computer programmer. His work and home life were quiet.

<hr>

Evaluation

During his initial interview at the vocal care center, Pete coughed and cleared his throat excessively. When he spoke, he pushed his voice to overcome the poor vocal quality that he had during singing and speaking. Doctors evaluated Pete's vocal problems through a physical examination, analysis of his vocal quality, and videostroboscopy.

Physical examination

The ENT examined Pete's head and neck. The exam showed a septal deviation to the right and nasal crusting with irritation and nicotine staining. Pete's throat showed signs of prominent redness from nicotine. Through the physical exam and an interview, the ENT found a state of chronic laryngitis, rhinitis, and dysphonia.

Perceptual impressions of vocal quality

Voice therapists found Pete's voice quality moderately breathy with strained voicing, frequent hard glottal attacks, and intermittent glottal fry. His pitch was slightly low, and his voice was too loud, with occasional loss of voice lasting one to two seconds during conversation. His maximum sustained phonation time on the vowel [a] (ah) was, on average, eight seconds.

Videostroboscopy results

Videostroboscopy showed a large mass on the right true vocal fold. Polyps were present in both vocal folds. A glottal gap was present. When the vocal folds closed, the anterior two-thirds of the vocal folds became nonvibratory. Open phase predominated, and the vertical level was equal. The vibratory amplitude was moderately decreased in both vocal folds. The mucosal wave and vibratory behavior were decreased or absent in parts of the vocal folds. Phase symmetry was mostly irregular, and hyperfunction existed.

Intervention

Following the evaluation, Pete started behavioral therapy and pharmacological treatment for two weeks to maximize the benefits of surgery.

Behavioral and pharmacological programs

The doctor put Pete on an antibiotic, a decongestant, and an anti-inflammatory medicine. He told Pete to rinse his nose daily with saline.

He also put Pete on modified voice rest. The voice therapists recommended that he use a low-impact voice, laryngeal massage, better breath support, and vocal hygiene—and that he eliminate vocally abusive behaviors.

Surgery, results, and follow-up

Pete then underwent surgery to remove the polyps on his vocal folds. Pete followed a modified vocal rest program for five weeks, with gradual improvement each week.

Pete wanted a harsh or raspy voice quality for his desired performance effect. The voice center team tried to give him the safest ways to accomplish this goal without a lot of laryngeal tension and strain. Pete used breath management, amplification, softening of the onsets of the voice, and placing the kinesthetic sensations of singing forward in his head instead of backward in his throat. He worked to identify the behaviors that had damaged his voice and then to correct or avoid them. He also learned to identify the boundaries between vocal style and vocal damage.

Return to Performance

Pete's voice quality progressed without excessive laryngeal tension or hard glottal attacks, and he proved capable of monitoring his vocal use to avoid behaviors that were damaging to his voice. However, because of the abusive nature of his vocal style, the voice center team carefully monitored the frequency of his performances and rehearsals.

Pete worked with the team and agreed to peform only his most important gigs, which amounted to one vocal performance every other week, which was workable. The voice center team also taped all of his performances and rehearsals so that he could listen to them later with the therapist. Together, they identified and modified abusive behaviors.

At the end of one-and-a-half months, Pete returned to a regular schedule of one rehearsal and one to two performances per week. He still goes to the ENT office for reevaluations and "tune-up" therapy. He no longer reports vocal breakdowns.

Case Five: Adolescent Singer

Mary Baker is an ambitious fourteen-year–old singer. She has performed with her church choir and school choral group for six years and she is a soloist for her church. She is a competent student, often busy with social and extracurricular school activities. The oldest of four siblings, she is also responsible for babysitting and many family activities. Her school and family environments are noisy places, an important factor in understanding Mary's voice problems.

She reported that her voice was fine until Wednesday or Thursday of each week. Then she would get hoarse and breathy or lose her voice completely. Mary was in good overall health. She was not taking any prescribed medications and had no history of substance abuse. She had a history of chronic sinus infections but no known allergies. She had been involved with a vocal coach from age ten. Her voice was mature for her age.

Evaluation

Mary's primary care physician referred her to an ENT. The ENT initially examined her with endoscopy and then referred her to a team of speech language pathologists for videostroboscopy and vocal function studies.

Perceptual impressions of vocal quality

Upon arrival at the ENT's office, Mary's vocal quality was moderately breathy with frequent voice breaks (approximately two for each five-word phrase) and hard glottal attacks on vowels such as [i] (ee) and back consonants such as [g] and [k].

Laryngeal exam and videostroboscopy results

The laryngeal exam revealed a large polyp on the middle half of the right vocal fold, with possible nodular formation on the opposite vocal fold.

Videostroboscopy revealed an hourglass glottal closure unless she used hyperfunctional compensatory mechanisms. An open phase predominated, and her vertical level was equal. The vibratory amplitude was severely limited in the right true vocal fold and slightly limited in the left. The mucosal wave was severely limited in the right true vocal fold and slightly limited in the left. The vibratory behavior in the right vocal fold was nearly absent, and in the left, it was partially absent. Phase symmetry was always irregular. Hyperfunction was present occasionally.

Intervention

Mary's treatment team recommended an extensive behavioral program coupled with surgery. She participated in voice therapy after surgery.

Behavioral program

The general goals of the behavioral program were:

- To identify and eliminate any forms of vocal abuse
- To initiate a modified voice rest program
- For Mary to use a therapeutic voice, tone focus, breath support, and laryngeal relaxation strategies, as described in Case One

The treatment team started Mary on a behavioral voice therapy program immediately following her examination. Talking with friends in extremely loud environments, between classes and in the lunchroom, strained her voice. The team discussed how to deal with peer pressure and the concept of vocal rest. Mary also learned some strategies to work with her classroom teachers so that she could limit her voice use in class discussions and projects.

The entire family participated in learning good vocal habits. Mary's treatment team found new ways for her to get her family's attention: by using a whistle or clapping her hands. Her younger siblings helped by signaling her when she was talking too loudly or for too long.

Surgery, results, and follow-up

Mary's case required surgery to remove the polyp on her right vocal fold. The surgical procedure was successful, with no interoperative or post-operative reactions.

After four days of complete voice rest followed by three weeks of modified voice rest (no more than 15 minutes of talking per day), relaxed vocalizing, and no vocal abuse, Mary returned for a follow-up examination. Her voice was still slightly breathy from the low-impact voice she had learned to help her heal from the surgery. There was no evidence of hard glottal attacks or vocal strain.

The vocal fold edges were smooth bilaterally and free of laryngeal lesions. The glottal closure was complete, and phase closure was normal. Vertical level, amplitude, and mucosal wave were all normal. Vibratory behavior was fully present, phase symmetry was regular, and there was no hyperfunction.

Mary's voice therapy program after her surgery continued to address the issues of healthy voice use at home, in school, and in social settings and choir singing. Speaking-voice therapy was added because her singing voice was well trained given her age and vocal maturity. Maintaining pitch, loudness, and quality—especially in her speaking voice—were critical skills for her recovery.

Mary also began a vocal endurance and stamina program similar to the program used in Case One: breathing techniques for efficient voice use, vocal rest, and good vocal health practices.

Return to Performance

Mary was able to return to all her daily and extracurricular activities. Her insight into her vocal production and her ability to monitor her voice are now outstanding. She has learned a great deal regarding her vocal health, which will benefit her singing for years to come.

Case Six: Classically Trained Singer

A classically trained singer with a vocal disturbance came to the voice care center, referred by her primary care physician.

Demetria Menotti had sung successfully until 1995, when she had surgery to remove a polyp on her vocal fold. After surgery, she sang successfully for 18 months. Then a new voice problem began, with intermittent periods of a "raspy and breathy voice" with episodes of sudden voice breaks. In the preceding two years, she had had a demanding singing schedule with a great deal of vocal abuse.

When she was not singing, Demetria worked as a court interpreter. The job required excessive talking with loud, authoritative vocal projection. Amplification equipment was not adequate. In addition, she was caring for two small children, so her home was also loud and stressful and Demetria often cried. Her emotional stress contributed to her current condition. When she first went to the clinic, she could not sing or work.

Demetria engaged in classic patterns of vocal abuse: poor hydration because of too much caffeine, too much and too-loud talking, talking over noise, throat clearing, and crying and singing when her voice was already fatigued.

Demetria's evaluation included an assessment of vocal quality and both a laryngeal exam and a videostroboscopic exam.

Perceptual impressions of vocal quality

During her initial interview, Demetria's voice was moderately breathy with vocal strain and pressed phonation. Her pitch was adequate, but her speech was too loud. Her vocal strain was characterized by hard glottal attacks and poor breath support, evidenced by her rapid conversational speech. A maximum sustained phonation time was recorded on the vowel [a] (ah) over three trials, with an average time of 12 seconds.

Laryngeal exam and videostroboscopy results

A laryngeal exam by the ENT revealed a left vocal fold polyplike lesion with generalized edema throughout the vocal folds. A clear view of her larynx was obtained during videostroboscopy, using the oral scope, and it showed bilateral vocal fold nodules. Her glottal closure was hourglass shaped, and her phase closure was predominantly open. Vibratory amplitude and mucosal wave were severely decreased in both vocal folds. Vibratory behavior of the vocal folds was completely absent at times but did return slightly on certain pitches. Hyperfunction was occasionally present.

The voice center team started Demetria on a behavioral approach similar to those in the previous case studies and added pharmacological treatment. She had tremendous success and did not need surgery.

Demetria followed a modified vocal rest program, used a low-impact voice, and received laryngeal massages. She concentrated on developing flexibility in moving the kinesthetic sensations of singing forward in her head and had counseling in vocal hygiene. In addition, she took a prescription corticosteroid for a while to reduce the generalized swelling.

Demetria worked hard at this program in order to avoid additional surgery. She learned to use a wireless personal amplification device, which helped in both therapy and work. Her family and friends supported her vocal rest, helping her to succeed.

In seven-and-a-half weeks, the swelling was reduced and her glottis could close completely. Demetria eliminated vocally abusive behaviors and could identify when she was producing sound safely, without strain or CCMT. Additionally, she was pleased with both her singing and her speaking voices, which she had feared were lost forever. No surgery was required because she was able to reduce her pathological condition through voice therapy.

A spontaneous conversational speaking sample revealed no breathy, hoarse, or harsh vocal characteristics; no hard glottal attacks; and no strained, pressed phonation. Her vocal loudness and pitch were normal. Videostroboscopy showed that her vocal folds looked and performed normally without hyperfunction.

Within three to four weeks, Demetria returned to her regular singing schedule, including freelance work with choirs and singing at local nightclubs.

Demetria returned to court interpreting after eight weeks of the behavioral voice program. She used a wireless amplification unit in the courtroom. In therapy, she focused on slowing down her speaking rate, which gave her better breath control and tone placement. These regimens let her minimize vocal abuse.

At her recheck, she reported no problems with her voice. She sought counseling for the emotional stress and tension at home and reported good results. She also sought training with a vocal coach to improve her singing skills.

Case Seven: Multitalented Professional

Katarina Balthasar has nearly 30 years of professional singing experience. Audiences enjoy her appearances on the Broadway stage, in films, and on television. She has been featured on several recordings and has earned a number of Grammy® nominations as a result. Katarina is known for her jazz and pop-style singing, but she wins her highest accolades for her well-trained coloratura voice.

She arrived in Florida for an engagement suffering from hoarseness, an inconsistent breathy vocal quality, congestion and coughing, and pain and irritation in her throat and neck. She felt she had lost the upper octave of her vocal range, had difficulty with breath control, and couldn't maintain volume without sensing a significant strain. Being aggressively professional in her care of her voice, she had observed a strict regimen of vocal rest and had canceled performances when necessary, but her vocal fatigue had worsened. She referred herself to the voice center.

Evaluation

During her first interview, Katarina described her medical history, which was non-eventful. She had no history of voice problems. She controlled her allergies with medication but took no other prescribed or over-the-counter medicines.

She related her schedule, which included performances in many different cities across North America. She had been on tour for four months, and she had several more weeks to go. A typical day could be packed with meetings with fans, the media, sponsoring executives, and the sound crew.

Perceptual impressions of vocal quality

In her initial interview, Katarina's voice was moderately breathy with very soft volume. She could sustain the vowel [a] (ah) for seven seconds. Her singing evaluation revealed that the highest tone she could sing was B4 and the lowest was B2—a 16-semitone range. She said she felt unstable singing higher pitches.

Laryngeal exam and videostroboscopy results

An ENT did a laryngeal exam, which revealed a mild traumatic vocal pathology consistent with vocal strain and overuse. There were no indications of infection or irritative laryngitis.

Videostroboscopy showed edema on her vocal folds, with prenodular swelling on both folds along the glottal edge. Glottal closure was incomplete and, during louder voicing, showed an hourglass configuration. No hyperfunction was present, but vibratory amplitude was moderately decreased and vibratory behavior was partially absent in both vocal folds.

Intervention

Katarina wanted to maintain her performance schedule. She had a strong loyalty to her audiences and did not want to disappoint them. At the same time, she was determined to actively preserve her voice.

Behavioral and pharmacological programs and results

The physicians recommended oral steroids for six days. Some behavioral strategies were suggested. With her publicist's assistance, Katarina cleared her calendar; all speaking events, and interviews, and cancelled social appointments for the next four days.

Katarina continued her modified voice rest, used a low-impact voice during any vocal production, and eliminated vocal abuse. She worked at managing and controlling her breath and laryngeal relaxation, along with moving the kinesthetic sensations of singing into her frontal mask. This voice therapy was meant to eliminate any poor habits she might have developed from her demanding schedule.

After four days of vocal rest and the steroid treatment, Katarina was re-evaluated with videostroboscopy. Results showed that the vocal fold edema was reduced and she showed better vibratory characteristics. Nevertheless, she still presented mild limitations and reported she felt weak in her vocal abilities.

The team of voice specialists recommended she complete the full course of steroid treatment and take a few more days of vocal rest. At their suggestion, she canceled her opening night performance.

After six days of treatment, on the day of Katarina's first scheduled performance, she was examined again. By now, the vocal fold edge was smooth, with no more evidence of swelling or prenodular formations. The glottis closed completely, with an occasional slight posterior opening on soft voicing. The vibratory amplitude could be fully observed and it appeared normal. The mucosal wave was within normal limits and vibratory behavior was fully present.

Return to Performance

Katarina was examined each day after performing, and she worked to develop her endurance and vocal range. She maintained a modified, easy schedule. Rehearsal time was shorter, approximately 15 minutes—just long enough for the sound technicians to set their levels.

In further conversations, Katarina learned more ways to deal with the demands of her schedule and how to stay healthy. The Florida voice specialists provided a list of referrals for the cities she would be visiting, and they encouraged her to be evaluated regularly and to maintain a limited schedule.

At this date, Katarina reports good vocal health and she continues her successful career. Her commitment to professionalism and vocal care, built over years of hard work and good practice, established the discipline necessary for a good outcome.

Case Eight: Up-and-Coming Operatic Superstar

USA Today identifies Alida Corazon as one of the "singers most likely to be an operatic superstar of the 21st century."

Alida made her debut at the Metropolitan Opera during the 1995/1996 season, and she sings opposite some of the world's most well-known opera stars. Her performance career has taken her to great opera houses and concert halls on every continent, including the Wiener Staatsoper, Royal Opera-Covent Garden, San Francisco Opera, and Opera Nationale de Paris. Her repertoire includes 20 operatic roles, and she regularly performs in concerts and recitals. Offstage, she has recorded many of her classics and has made several television appearances.

After touring both in the United States and Europe, performing on average three times a week, Alida came to Florida for a week of operatic performances. A week before, she had developed symptoms of dysphonia, especially in the upper notes of her range, following an upper respiratory infection. Upon her arrival in Florida, the managers of the Metropolitan Opera Company referred her to the voice center.

Evaluation

Four months before arriving in Florida, Alida developed a right vocal fold hemorrhage (hematoma). An ENT in New York treated her with six days of prednisone and one month of vocal rest. She was treated again with prednisone six weeks later to help ensure an optimal performance for the presidential inauguration. The New York ENT followed her progress with a series of laryngeal examinations. The hematoma appeared to be improving.

During her initial interview in Florida, Alida described a recent history of cluster headaches—headaches with pain similar to a migraine. Headaches such as these can be brought on by stress, overwork, or trauma. She was being treated with Prilosec® for GERD (reflux). She clenched her jaws during sleep and experienced pain near the temporomandibular joint (TMJ) when she chewed. She also related feeling her body swell during a recent airplane flight.

Perceptual impressions of vocal quality

During her initial interview, Alida's conversational voice had a slightly breathy quality with little observable pressing or straining. She had minimal difficulty with loudness or pitch in her speaking voice. Her singing evaluation revealed a loss of the top four or five notes in her upper range.

Videostroboscopy results

The left true vocal fold was slightly swollen. Alida had a hemorrhagic polyp in the right vocal fold. Her glottis closed completely only during lower pitches. As she increased the pitch range, her glottis showed an hourglass configuration.

In general, an open phase predominated. Vibratory amplitude was slightly decreased in the left true vocal fold and slightly to moderately decreased in the right true vocal fold, although the polyp appeared to be very soft. The mucosal wave was slightly decreased in the left true vocal fold and slightly to moderately decreased in the right. Phase symmetry was mostly irregular. No hyperfunction was seen.

Intervention

Alida's program of rehabilitation was comprehensive, treating a number of different symptoms at one time. For this performer, interventions included pharmacological treatment, assistive devices, and behavioral management.

Behavioral and pharmacological programs

Alida was prescribed another steroidal anti-inflammatory medicine for 12 days. Humabid® was prescribed to thin her mucosal drainage.

A dentist examined Alida for TMJ syndrome and teeth grinding (teeth grinding and headaches are typical symptoms of TMJ syndrome). The dentist fitted her with a mouth guard.

Alida was already taking Prilosec® for GERD, so diet modifications were suggested to reduce the causes of reflux. She was also instructed to sleep with her head slightly elevated at night to reduce reflux.

The voice center team recommended that Alida begin strict vocal rest. Because opening night was only three days away, the speech language pathologist supervised her warm-ups to ensure that they were very low impact, were within a reduced vocal range, were not demanding, and did not involve any strain. Alida also went through therapeutic vocal exercises that promoted both respiratory strategies and a forward tone focus to decrease overcompensation in her larynx. Strategies to lower her jaw and relax her tongue were added to her daily routine to prevent any musculoskeletal tension. (See "A Baseline State of Relaxation," in v. 2, ch. 7.)

Alida was counseled on vocal health and hygiene. Emphasis was placed on healthy voice practices during travel. She was taught how to keep hydrated in order to combat swelling and dehydration during airline travel. The voice center team recommended that Alida buy a portable humidifier to wear during long airline trips. She could also use it in her hotel room to keep her body well hydrated. The voice center team reviewed the importance of diet in hydration, especially before a performance and during airline travel. Alida often chose salty snacks such as peanuts, pretzels, and chips—all notorious for disrupting hydration balance; the team recommended alternative snacks.

A portable amplification system was recommended for touring and speaking to large groups. The system's speaker is worn like a small fanny pack and the microphone is worn much like a headband. Alida was able to use this device to talk with groups of people without straining her voice. She even wore the device to dress rehearsals, even though the director had agreed to let her walk through the rehearsals silently. This tool helped reduce the collision force of the vocal folds during vibration, thereby letting her speak without harming her voice.

Finally, general body relaxation techniques were reviewed to help her with the body tension, headaches, and fatigue that were causing her problems.

Laryngeal exam results and follow-up

After opening night, an ENT performed another laryngeal examination. The ENT found the hemorrhagic polyp on Alida's right true vocal fold had dissipated somewhat, and the remainder of the vocal folds and vocal fold function were about the same as in her previous examination. Before leaving Florida, Alida had another laryngeal examination, with similar results. The voice therapists recommended that she continue vocal rest without interruption for a month or two. She canceled a month-long tour because she understood the possible effects of this condition on her career.

Return to Performance

Today, Alida is at home, resting her voice and following a good vocal health and hygiene program. Her local voice care team is following her vocal health, with recommendations from the Florida voice center. She may eventually need surgery, but not until the vocal fold tissues have a chance to resolve any edema and irritation on their own. She will resume her professional touring when her voice problems have been resolved.

ENDNOTES

1. This technique is very similar to the regimen set forth in the "confidential voice" therapy program discussed by Ray Colton and Janina Casper, *Understanding Voice Problems* (San Diego: Singular Press, 1996).

2. Jenny Iwarsson, Monica Thomasson, and Johan Sundberg, "Effects of lung volume on the glottal voice source," *Journal of Voice* 12, no. 4 (1998): 424–33.

3. Ibid.

4. Daniel R. Boone and Steve McFarlane, 5th ed. *The Voice and Voice Therapy* (Englewood Cliffs, N.J.: Prentice–Hall, 1994).

THE METAPHYSICS OF LIBERTY

THEORY AND DECISION LIBRARY

General Editors: W. Leinfellner and G. Eberlein

SERIES A: PHILOSOPHY AND METHODOLOGY OF THE SOCIAL SCIENCES

Editors: W. Leinfellner (Technical University of Vienna)
G. Eberlein (Technical University of Munich)

Scope

This series deals with the foundations, the general methodology and the criteria, goals
and purpose of the social sciences. The emphasis in the new Series A will be on well-
argued, thoroughly analytical rather than advanced mathematical treatments. In this
context, particular attention will be paid to game and decision theory and general
philosophical topics from mathematics, psychology and economics, such as game
theory, voting and welfare theory, with applications to political science, sociology, law
and ethics.

For a list of titles published in this series, see final page.

THE METAPHYSICS
OF LIBERTY

by

FRANK FORMAN

U.S. Department of Education, Washington

KLUWER ACADEMIC PUBLISHERS

DORDRECHT / BOSTON / LONDON

Library of Congress Cataloging in Publication Data

Forman, Frank, 1944-
   The metaphysics of liberty.

   (Theory and decision library. Series A, Philosophy
and methodology of the social sciences)
   Bibliography: p.
   Includes index.
   1. Liberty. 2. Metaphysics. 3. Individualism.
4. Political science. 5. Bunge, Mario Augusto.
I. Title. II. Series.
B824.4.F67 1989   123'.5   88-27342

ISBN 0-7923-0080-7

Published by Kluwer Academic Publishers,
P.O. Box 17, 3300 AA Dordrecht, The Netherlands.

Kluwer Academic Publishers incorporates
the publishing programmes of
D. Reidel, Martinus Nijhoff, Dr W. Junk and MTP Press.

Sold and distributed in the U.S.A. and Canada
by Kluwer Academic Publishers,
101 Philip Drive, Norwell, MA 02061, U.S.A.

In all other countries, sold and distributed
by Kluwer Academic Publishers Group,
P.O. Box 322, 3300 AH Dordrecht, The Netherlands.

Printed in The Netherlands

TABLE OF CONTENTS

PREFACE

Philosophy suffers from an excess of convoluted introspection.
One result is that concepts multiply unchecked. That some events have
observable causes gets reified into a First Cause or, in a more secular
age, to the thesis that every event is fatalistically determined. Another
drawback of convoluted introspection is that tiny but crucial assumptions
slip in, often unawares, with the result that densely argued counter-tomes
are written in reply and no progress is made toward any kind of consensus.
At bottom, subjectivity reigns.

I exaggerate. Toward the other pole of the subjectivity-objectivity
continuum, consensus among scientists is in fact always at a good healthy
distance from compulsive unanimity. New theories replace old, and at any
one time the evidence can usually be interpreted two ways. Indeed, it is
possible to pile epicycle upon epicycle in the Ptolemaic system of the
heavens and approximate the ellipses planets travel in the Copernican
system. What cinched the case for Copernicus was not simplicity—after
all alchemy is simpler than chemisty. Nor was it experiment—there were
no moon shots back then. Rather it was Newton's foundations. He
established a physics for the earth and the heavens alike. Earthly
physics we can verify, and it does not jell with the Ptolemaic system.

Indeed, striving to make subtheories jell with one another is a
major aim of scientific research. Think of relativity and quantum
mechanics in physics, or of micro- and macro-economics. Think also of
why most scientists reject parapsychology as quickly as they do. By the
1890s, the sciences had advanced to the point that the great Charles
Peirce called for a grounding of their underlying assumptions in a
scientific metaphysics.

Some eighty years later, Mario Bunge was the first scientist
to carry out Peirce's program. I shall expound his results in
non-mathematical detail in Chapter 3, but for now only a few remarks.
First, Bunge treats metaphysics as a science and therefore controllable
by the results of other sciences. Bunge's scheme is the _first_ such
carrying out of Peirce's program, not the last. Second, Bunge strives to
keep his metaphysics quite general. For example, his chapter on change
comes before the one on space and time. This way, should relativity
theory get modified, Bunge may not have to revise his concepts and
results on change. He may have to anyhow, which only goes to show that
his whole enterprise is open to revision. Third, science, including

scientific metaphysics, is bound to conflict with naive, however
convoluted intuitions. One resists changing one's intuitions, but this
is what learning is all about.

This book is about liberty, and my basic aim is to set it well
within Bunge's metaphysics. Here are several of his theses I shall be
adopting:

1. Emergentism. The world is layered in systems: physical,
chemical, biological, social, and (parallel with social) human
artifactual. A chemical system is made up of atoms and molecules, but it
has properties, such as a boiling point and availability to participate
in chemical reactions, that are peculiar to it and not to its
constituents. A living organism has properties (metabolism,
reproduction, homeostasis) that cannot be attributed to its constituent
molecules. And a society is more than a heap of people: It has a legal
system and an economic system, things no individual person has. At the
same time, a system is not a holistic entity transcending its parts:
There is no Society apart from its members.

2. Reductionism. While we cannot eviscerate emergent properties by
bulldozing them down to their parts, science strives to explain emergence
by means of lawful interaction among the parts. In other words,
epistemological reductionism, si; ontological reductionism, no.

3. Causality. Each scientific law statement separates the set of
all conceivable things and events into two subsets, the possible and the
impossible. But there is no reason to suppose that the intersection of
the sets of possible things and events corresponding to each law yields a
single, fatalistic outcome. Self-determination and chance, as well as
causes, remain as determiners of events.

4. Free will. Neurologists, unlike mind-body dualists, are busy
studying volition. The answers are not in yet, but given Bunge's views
on causality and self-determination, there is no ontological compulsion
to hold that choice is at best an illusion. A fuller solution to the
problem of free will will make heavy use of the structure of manifold
feedback loops in animal brains and of their consequent extreme
instability as far as action goes. Human brains are even more
cross-wired than those of other animals, and this makes for our apparently

unique ability to be self-conscious, or conscious of our own
consciousness. We can direct our learning, too, and (as Bunge points out)
reason about values as well as evaluate reasons. It is wonderful to know
that the first scientific metaphysics not only allows for the emergent
property called free will but also for its explanation.

5. <u>Values</u>. Animals and only animals evaluate. (Humans can
evaluate values and, to a fair extent, train them, e.g., by taking music
appreciation courses.) It is at best metaphorical and at worst mystical
and holistic to speak of Society valuing. This is not to deny that
individuals can share similar values or that socialization can reduce
conflict. It does imply that social and political institutions must be
systemically rooted in individuals though not ontologically reducible to
them. Champions of "methodological individualism" are never clear
whether they are ontological reductionists who consequently reject
systemic metaphysics. A major purpose of this book is to bring these
issues to the surface.

These, then, are five main theses I have taken over from Mario
Bunge. My aim is to extend the discussion upward to the subject of human
liberty in a way that is consistent with his system. This way, political
philosophy will not have to float above the other areas of philosophy. I
take as my starting point the contractarianism of James M. Buchanan, an
economist and one of the Founding Fathers of the extension of economics to
political behavior that has become known as public choice theory.
Philosophers of the social contract too often <u>tell</u> the alleged
contractors what they have agreed to. An economist far more habitually
reckons in terms of agreement, bargaining, compromise. The economist's
approach is the more metaphysically sound, since only individuals value.
That individuals individually value, that is value differently and hence
need to strike bargains, is an inescapable part of the human condition.
In the course of discussing Buchanan, in Chapter 1, I argue that his
individualism needs to be tempered in order to make a social order
viable, and in Chapter 2, I analyze a broadside attack on the underlying
assumptions of modern individualism by Roberto Mangabeira Unger.
Chapter 3 expounds Bunge's metaphysics, and the last three chapters apply
it. Chapter 4 examines Friedrich Hayek's thesis that social justice is a
mirage and concludes that certain moderate kinds of it need not be
dismissed as resting on bad metaphysics. Chapter 5 examines Ayn Rand on

natural rights and concludes that her arguments, while too weak to compel
wholesale adoption, nevertheless might generally be utilized by social
contractors in their deliberations. Chapter 6 examines what I call the
evolutionary federalism of the social psychologist, Raymond B. Cattell,
and discusses a plurality of social contracts both extending over space
and enduring over generations. Above all, it is up to the contractors
themselves, not to philosophers or economists, to establish their own
political institutions by way of ideally unanimous agreement. (That the
social contract is, of course, a historical fiction, will be discussed
repeatedly.)

To the extent that my general approach and specific arguments
are sound, I shall have laid out a framework for what could, very
dangerously, be called scientific political philosophy. The danger is
that "scientific" much too often connotes socialism, rule by experts, or
just one big scheme for all mankind. This sounds orderly, especially to
those yet to learn that order regularly emerges by processes of
spontaneous self-assembly at all levels of systems, from chemical and
biological on up. (Economics may well be the oldest science of
spontaneous order.) But what looks orderly can mean just being ordered
about. Truly rational planning (meta-planning) should consist of knowing
when not to plan (object-plan), that is, when to call off the bureaucrats.

It's okay to consult experts and even to trust them a little bit.
It's okay, too, to put a little faith in tradition, to wait until a
serious probing of a specific tradition's uses has been undertaken before
throwing it to the winds. Indeed, some people have come to love their
traditions and even want a large hunk of their lives so governed. That's
okay, too, and in a finely enough partitioned federalism, each can seek
out his preferred tradition-experiment balance. It would be most
unscientific to ignore the central fact of both individual and group
differences in this regard, and in all other regards.

It would be no less unscientific to ignore what ever-corrigible
results have come down from the various social sciences, some of which
apply to all men and groups alike. My aim here is not to beat a drum for
any specific economic or social theory or even to claim a single economic
law is true, not even that minimum wage laws cause unemployment or that
rent controls cause housing shortages. I know plenty of people who will
argue both economic laws tirelessly and for free. I could also argue on
either public choice theory or natural rights grounds that education and
money are too important to be left in the hands of the government. And I

could warn against theocracies of all kinds, whether they be any of the
hundreds of possible kinds of egalitarianism or interpretations of the
Bible.

It is altogether too easy to denounce those who disagree with me
as being unscientific. The plain fact is that people vary in their
willingness to get at the truth, and it is they, not I, who will establish
their own polities. I must not get carried away with my own arrogance.
My plea is that others not get carried away with their own <u>metaphysical</u>
arrogance and reify entities like Society and The Good that are detached
from the ontological chain. There are not very many open advocates of
such holism and collectivism anymore, but there are far too many who
assume such things implicitly. It is more muddled than openly bad
metaphysics that is the enemy of liberty.

I hope this book will clear up some of the mud.

****

As it happens, I wrote a short article for <u>Vera Lex</u>, called
"Contracting for Natural Rights," that summarizes many of my ideas beyond
the metaphysical base in Bunge. This article could continue this preface,
but since it can stand alone, I reprint it in an appendix.

CHAPTER 1

JAMES McGILL BUCHANAN AND INDIVIDUALISM

1.1 The Work of Buchanan

"For three millenniums," says H.L. Mencken (1927), philosophers "have
been searching the world and its suburbs for the truth--and they have yet
to agree upon so much as the rules of the search." He adds, "If you want
to find out how a philosopher feels when he is engaged in the practice of
his profession, go to the nearest zoo and watch a chimpanzee at the
wearying and hopeless job of chasing flies. Both suffer damnably and
neither can win." Mencken's diagnosis is that philosophers chase after
The Absolute, which he calls a banshee. He is probably right, since to
validate our understanding, we have to understand how the human brain
evolved. We must therefore independently ground the theory of evolution,
a theory, like all scientific theories, that is constantly changing.
Rather than find The Absolute, we find circularity, but science makes the
circle a virtuous one, one that is ever-expanding. This book will apply
the first system of metaphysics designed to be compatible with modern
science, that developed by Mario Bunge, to the old problem of
individualism and collectivism. But before expounding Bunge's system, let
us examine the works of a specimen individualist and a specimen
collectivist. First, the individualist.
     The writings of James M. Buchanan exhibit a steady evolution from
public finance to public goods to public philosophy and a steady widening
of perspective. His early writings were in the traditional areas of
public finance and dealt with such topics as the incidence of taxation.
His thought progressed from public finance to the public goods so
financed. In 1962 he co-authored with Gordon Tullock The Calculus of
Consent, which went behind the schemes of financing public goods into
alternative constitutions for a government. This book, along with Anthony
Downs, An Economic Theory of Democracy (1957), marked the beginnings of
what is now known as public choice theory, the use of economists' tools to
study nonmarket decision making. A later article by Buchanan, "An
Economist's Approach to 'Scientific Politics'" (1968), contrasted
traditional political science, which is characterized as normative
strictures for "'government for the people,' with the objective approach
of public choice, which endeavors to describe the actual workings of

1

'government <u>by</u> the people.'" It is true that traditional political
scientists would often describe political institutions historically or
comparatively, but always with one eye upon a normative ideal, toward
which it was hoped that history was tending. To the extent that this was
and is the case, political science is not objective and fails to describe
the actual behavior of voters and politicians who in fact have
considerably less than one eye upon an idealized polity.

Governments, the public choice theorists teach, can fail just as
surely as economic markets in private goods, and intelligent choices
should be made between actual market and actual political outcomes instead
of between actual market and idealized political outcomes. It was a great
innovation to say this in 1962; two decades on, it is becoming commonplace
to ask so apparently simple (in retrospect) a question as whether the cure
of government action is worse than the disease. Government failure is
becoming increasingly obvious, and it was the merit of The Calculus of
Consent to treat politicians as just as motivated by their private ends,
in spite of their posturing otherwise, as businessmen. This motivation
had not gone unnoticed before. H.L. Mencken's bitterest book,
Notes on Democracy (1928), was unsparing in its criticism of politicians,
and before him Max Weber (1918) and after him Joseph Schumpeter (1942) had
warned that bureaucrats were on the way to becoming a force unto
themselves. The achievement of The Calculus of Consent consisted in
laying out a theory, parallel to that of economics, describing the outcome
of the process of public choice in taxing and distributing public goods in
a world that does not greatly depend upon huge numbers of persons, either
as voters or politicians, concerned uppermost with the welfare of the
public as a whole.

Buchanan and Tullock's book was very general and discussed the
implications of modifying the constitutional framework within which
collective decisions are made. An increase in the percentage of voters,
or of their representatives in an assembly, required to enact a law
providing for a public good, would decrease the harm done to those
opposing the law, but it would increase the costs of achieving the
required consensus to pass the law. At one extreme, if only one person
were required to pass a law, the amount of legislation would be enormous
(with people constantly repealing each others' legislation?), while the
costs of producing legislation would be trivial. At the other extreme, if
unanimity were required, no one would be harmed by legislation--he need
only veto it--but the costs of reaching unanimous agreement would be

prohibitive. Buchanan and Tullock conceived the idea of minimizing the combined costs of both factors and showed that majority rule (50%) was not at all necessarily the optimum. The optimum becomes a matter for choice at the constitutional stage, and there is no longer anything sacrosanct about majority rule, implicitly when not openly enshrined as it is in traditional political science. Buchanan has often mentioned Knut Wicksell's holding a 5/6 majority to be the optimum; perhaps this is what Buchanan might wish himself, although he makes it clear that fundamentally the decision on constitutional rules is not his alone.

Calculus, while making a fundamental breakthrough into objectivity and a fundamental distinction between alternative constitutions and their operations, left a number of questions (some of which indeed were first raised in the book) unanswered. How might agreement upon a constitution come about in the first place? What about the breakdown of constitutional order? What about government itself violating the constitution? What are the prospects for reform? Buchanan was then led, from public finance to public goods, to public choice, beyond to what might be called public philosophy, to deal with these questions. Deal with them he did in 1975 in The Limits of Liberty: Between Anarchy and Leviathan, a new look at the idea of a social contract, and it is this book, which has easy claims for being his magnum opus, that will form the basic backdrop for this book.

1.2 Buchanan's Individualism

Buchanan announces his individualist perspective on page one of Limits. The first sentence reads, "Those who seek specific descriptions of the 'good society' will not find them here." By this he means that he will seek no ideal truth in politics and that men live together the better to pursue their individual objectives, not to strive toward "some transcendental common bliss." By contrast, a collectivist would either hold some men or groups of men above others or would proclaim the existence of values apart from those held by individuals. Agreements men have with each other, agreements which are necessarily unanimous, not conformity to Buchanan's or anyone else's criteria of the good, are the only means by which good can be judged. Otherwise, when force is used if agreement is not reached, judging action requires some outside standard of comparison of some men against others. Buchanan is emphatically unwilling to invoke such external standards. Later, I shall argue that Buchanan implicitly does and invariably must relax this strict unwillingness

somewhat, but his focusing upon agreements and processes for agreement as opposed to propounding ideal outcomes directs attention to unambiguously desirable reforms and hence toward those that might be more easily implemented. Buchanan does not exactly conceal his opinion that not only he but practically everyone else thinks government has gotten out of control and that while some of us are gainers in some areas almost all of us are losers in the net, when compared to any of a number of reforms. Buchanan nowhere presumes—indeed he denies—that any given constitutional reform need be final; further reforms remain always possible. (LL 39) [1]

If this is the meaning of methodological individualism, it seems unobjectionable, for certainly full agreement is far less problematical than partial agreement, which is not properly agreement at all. Some may cavil that the wishes of some men should never count for more than the wishes of others, but here we are referring to agreement, not to voting shares under an agreement. Buchanan is only contending that the wishes of some do not absolutely dominate those of others. Let the people agree upon whatever social contract they will.

Buchanan also denies the collectivist thesis that there are values apart from (and therefore in conflict with) those held by individuals. It is difficult to imagine what those values could be, however, and to turn up an example of a collectivist who holds to such values and has arguments for them would also be difficult. Perhaps what is meant is the specification of an overriding social objective (such as democracy, equality in one of its many forms, ad majorem dei gloriam, economic growth, or someone's personal list of natural rights), a specification against the wishes of the citizens. Politics involves compromise, to be sure, but compromise applies to the making of laws under a constitution, and not to the making of the constitution itself, which can emerge only by agreement.

Again, Buchanan sees a collectivist as one who judges the constitutions made by others as a presumptuous outsider and not as an insider, not as one of the initial contractors whose consent is needed. Perhaps he means by a collectivist an avowed irrationalist like Hegel. Buchanan is unclear on this point, and necessarily so, for those who might plausibly be placed in the collectivist camp are far from clear about what they do mean. Are they arguing for "some transcendental common bliss," which may turn out to be only a reification of some set of aims individuals might share separately? Are they denying the distinction

between constitution and laws made thereunder, or are they failing to make
the distinction in the first place? If the last, clarification is needed,
for there may be fundamental disagreement. Until clarification is made we
may be sure that each will invent straw men for adversaries.

Buchanan's (methodological) individualism is not reducible to direct
advocacy of individual liberties in the usual sense meant by free-market
economists, whether argued on efficiency or natural rights grounds. (I
shall be examining the case for natural rights in detail in Chapter 5.)
Ordinarily economic liberties are implicitly taken to cover only bilateral
agreements (contracts and exchanges) between two persons, actual persons
or "legal persons" such as corporations. Buchanan explicitly treats
multilateral agreements by all members of society, called social
contracts. While it is automatically understood that a two-person
agreement is necessarily mutual, that is to say unanimous, confusion may
arise if unanimity is not required for multilateral agreement. Buchanan's
treatment recognizes public goods and a constitution specifying the
procedures to supply them from the outset, whereas those who begin with
only individual liberties usually wind up compromising on their principles
on the grounds that protecting of rights and suppling externality-
internalizing public goods necessitate some restrictions on individual
freedom. Theirs is a "natural rights, but..." position, which can be
construed as modestly collectivist. By explicitly allowing omnilateral
(to coin a neologism) contracts, Buchanan is a more thoroughgoing
methodological individualist, in that there is no need to go beyond the
individual's own values to deal with the public goods problem.

The Limits of Liberty applies this basic methodological approach to
the questions of liberty and social contracts by beginning with the most
abstract special case of a two-person, one-good society and becoming
progressively more general. The book discusses the assignment and
enforcement of rights, the limits of collective power, the public goods
aspects of law itself, the capital investment aspects of adherence to
rules, and the question of the control of the government itself. I shall
trace his discussion and try to discern where certain assumptions beyond
strict methodological individualism are implied or warranted.

The second chapter of Limits, "The Bases for Freedom in Society,"
treats the emergence of law out of anarchy. It deals with the most
elementary setting, that of two persons and one good. Before the pair
come to any agreement, each will exert efforts to produce his own
quantities of the single good, efforts to seize the other's output, and

further efforts to prevent such seizure of his own holdings. An
equilibrium will emerge among production, predation, and protection, but
no more needs to be specified about abilities, desires, or selfishness
along these dimensions. It is from this starting point, which Buchanan
aptly terms the "anarchist equilibrium," that the two parties may begin to
negotiate some mutually beneficial pact to reduce their predation and
protection so as better to turn their efforts to production. Among
possible peace pacts, any one might be chosen, if both parties see
themselves as benefiting. The elementary case becomes only slightly more
complicated when more than one good may be produced, for
post-constitutional (post-peace-pact) exchange becomes possible.

An assumption is implicit even in this elementary situation, namely
that making the pact itself is not (or at least is not expected to be) an
empty exercise. It need not be claimed that the signing of the pact is
embellished with sacred rituals, though it may have some kind of
nonrational binding force, but there must be some mutual hope that the
amounts of predation will not continue as before, even if there will be
some cheating. Buchanan is definitely not assuming that anarchists will
become "moral" by the mere act of signing a pact, and he is agnostic on
the question whether human nature is such as to make people want to abide
by their agreements. This has, of course, been argued both ways, but
people can and almost always do set up enforcement mechanisms,
particularly if the population is at all large. As Buchanan notes (LL
188), "The necessity for including enforcement provisions in the initial
agreement distinguishes the social contract from other contracts which are
made within the framework of a legal order."

It is worth stating again that Buchanan says nothing to judge any
particular contract as fair or unfair. Indeed, he briefly mentions the
possibility that one person enslaving another by contract could leave the
latter better off than in an all-out belligerent anarchy. (Whether there
are individuals who would, truly knowingly, sell themselves into slavery
is another matter.) An external observer with pretensions to knowledge of
absolute values may judge the position of the second person here as unfair
both before and after the peace pact, but Buchanan's concern is with the
dynamic processes of mutual improvement, not judgments of any static
present. This may offend our moral sense, at least certain people's moral
senses in certain cases, and Buchanan can be and has been charged with
worshipping the status quo and naively failing to realize that the current
wielders of power are going to get the long end of the stick in any

bargaining over the social contract. Buchanan never quite adequately handles this problem, but it can be mitigated (though not solved in the abstract) with one small, optimistic, but plausible assumption (assuming also that we recognize the problem as real in the first place), namely that unfair advantage dampens over time. We all know the saying, "riches to rags in three generations," and there is suggestive empirical evidence for this in the work of Herbert Simon in "A Model of Business Firm Growth" (1967). He asked the question: How do U.S. firms that have over-average growth rates in one four-year period fare during the next? He expected a certain regression toward the mean, since above average growth can be a matter of chance, but not perfect regression, since it can also be a matter of superior ability. The result of his study was that the ratio of the growth rate of a given firm to that of the average firm in one four-year period would shrink to about its cube root in the next. Thus, a firm with twice the average growth rate in one decade would have 26% over the average the next. (Actually, it was 28%.) This shrinkage should follow a geometric progression, and a firm with an "unfair advantage" whose initial growth rate was double the average initially would hold only a 1.0 percent advantage a century later (1.28 exp $4/100 = 1.010$).

It could be true in other situations, however, that "the rich get richer while the poor get poorer," but it is difficult to figure out how this could come about in a market economy where all exchanges leave contracting parties better off. Political constitutions are the same, except that more than two people are involved, but each remaking of the constitution under the unanimity criterion will also leave everyone better off. (Technically, Buchanan has to exclude eternal and unalterable constitutions from his set of allowable ones. This rules out the use of certain enforcement mechanisms. Also, constitutionally amending the constitution under a less than unanimity rule makes an amendment a law, though one harder to pass than others.) If "unfairness" dampens under bilateral exchanges, it will dampen under multilateral constitutional exchanges also.

The whole issue of fairness is problematic. Those who felt that they got the short end of the stick in the original contract may very well maintain later that their consent was not genuine and attempt to renege on the agreement. Buchanan discusses calculations of prospective revolutionaries plunging society back into anarchy in hopes of securing a new and better contract in Chapter 5 of Limits, "Continuing Contract and the Status Quo." This topic will be discussed further below, and I shall

be examining Hayek on social justice in detail in Chapter 4.

1.3 A First Move away from Strict Methodological Individualism

To this point, the assumptions Buchanan might have made explicit are
not highly controversial. More difficulties arise in "Postconstitutional
Contract: The Theory of Public Goods," which is the third chapter of
Limits. Here we deal with many people and many goods but with an immortal
population, whose membership is fixed in advance. Buchanan concentrates
on the provision of pure public goods and assumes that whatever gains from
trade are to be found among pure private goods have already been realized.
He states that each person has an incentive to consume the public goods
but opt out of cost-sharing arrangements, even if the constitution
specifies unanimity rules to provide public goods. Buchanan is willing to
force recalcitrant members into this social contract if exclusion from
consumption of the public goods is not possible. (As in The Calculus of
Consent, a less-than-unanimity rule to provide public goods might be
agreed upon unanimously.) But what next happens is the beginning of
something very important, a move away from strict individualism by way of
placing restrictions upon the realization of gains (LL 43-44):

> To clarify the analysis, it will be helpful to distinguish two
> institutional structures of departure from a unanimity rule for
> collective action. In the first, collective decisions are made by
> less than full agreement of all members of the community, but these
> rules are externally constrained so as to guarantee outcomes that
> might, conceptually, have been attained under unanimity, without
> bargaining or agreement difficulties. That is to say, outcomes
> generated by collective choices must dominate the prechoice
> positions for all members of the community, evaluated in a utility
> dimension. In this restricted framework, it seems legitimate to
> refer to collective action as indirect contract or exchange. The
> decision rule embodying less than full agreement is necessary to
> avoid the behavioral effects of a unanimity rule, but the intent of
> the substitute rule is to accomplish essentially similar purposes.
> Even if an individual might have chosen differently from that
> outcome which the substitute rule produces, he has made a net
> improvement in his utility through participation in the
> collectivity. As later discussion will suggest, this restricted

departure is not without real-world application.

In the second set of institutions to be examined, collective decision rules are unconstrained, and when unanimity is dropped an individual may find himself actually suffering net utility losses from "participating." That is to say, he may end up at a lower utility level than he might have been able to sustain in the complete absence of collective action....

What happens, even under the first case, is that gains from bargaining over the terms of a multi-person social contract are to be excluded. It sounds wholly reasonable that men should stop their haggling and get on with the serious business of reaching an agreement that will benefit all concerned. Nor is it stretching plausibility to say each man knows when he is bargaining and when he is expressing his true feelings. The problem is whether one man can know whether another man is bargaining. According to the usual dogma about revealed preferences and opportunity costs, strategic behavior cannot be observed. (If we get technical about it, we cannot even observe others making choices, for while we may think we know what the other person's alternatives are, what counts is what he thinks they are, and this, so runs the dogma, we can never know.) Indeed, excluding a person's strategic gains as being somehow illegitimate—which is what it boils down to—is imposing, quite without his consent, an opportunity cost upon him.

This move is a necessary one, however, if the chance of reaching unanimous agreement is not to become practically zero in all but small numbers cases. When we treat Roberto Mangabeira Unger's Knowledge and Politics (1975) in the next chapter, we shall see that the assumption that desires are arbitrarily diverse among persons is a key principle of post-medieval Western thought. What Buchanan has assumed is that we can identify holdouts, although at times quite imperfectly. This assumption strips the analysis of generality, but it does allow us to discuss agreements. Something more is implied however: The assumption suggests that there is a certain core essence of humanity that we have access to, or rather that there is a certain similarity among men. It is not a large step from this to saying that some values are held in common and are, in a sense, objective.

A tyranny could be potentially shoved through this loophole (as some people think the Supreme Court has already managed in the United States). Buchanan proposes a constitution to "The People." They fail to agree.

Buchanan says they would agree if only they would stop haggling. If they
still failed to agree, Buchanan might very well think his constitution had
some objectionable features and propose another one. A different man
might say that the people would agree if only they came to their senses,
which is only subtly different from saying if only they stopped haggling.

   This is not a fatal objection to Buchanan's ideas, however, but it
does embody a warning not to take them to ridiculous extremes. Probably
every social philosophy contains such loopholes. The reason why most
ideas can be carried to ridiculous extremes is that the world is more
complex than our limited vocabularies. Science is the method for
clarifying our concepts as we go along by checking them against reality.
When we speed merrily ahead, piling up deduction upon deduction without
checking against the facts, our ideas will stray away at a geometric rate
from what we are trying to describe.

1.4 New Contractarian Man

   Return to page one of Limits: "My approach is profoundly
individualistic, in an ontological-methodological sense, although
consistent adherence to this norm is almost as difficult as it is
different." Indeed, Buchanan gives only an approximate idea of what
methodological individualism is, and our construal thereof here may be at
variance with Buchanan's, especially when we push the idea out to its
limits. However this may be, Buchanan has frequent resort to the term
"conceptual contract" and the word "quasi-unanimity." Now in all strict
logic, unanimity is either/or: Quasi-unanimity is no unanimity at all,
and a conceptual contract is no contract. I argued earlier that a
contract must not be empty, that each contractor expects the others, more
or less, to abide by its terms. There is, perhaps, something sacred, or
nonrational, about the act of agreeing itself. By a conceptual contract,
Buchanan means a procedure for making collective decisions "so as to
guarantee outcomes that might, conceptually, have been attained under
unanimity, without bargaining or agreement difficulties." (LL 43) What is
crucially important to understand is that Buchanan is not looking for the
social contract and is not attempting by reconstructive reasoning to
figure out what so-called rational men might hypothetically have agreed
to. (In the final chapter, I will argue for a plurality of contracts.)
His contribution to contractarian philosophy is the perspective of the
Public Choice economist that he is, that of thinking about the specifics

of institutional design, such as the constitutional voting rules for
legislators that loom so large in The Calculus of Consent.

Even if we ignore the problems of knowing when these conditions exist
and ignore the problems associated with opportunity costs (both discussed
above), a merely conceptual contract will not have the binding force an
actual one would. It is an imperfect substitute for the real thing.
Ninety-nine times out of one hundred, the charge will be made that
reality, not the theory, is imperfect. It often does seem that utility
theorists berate men for not living up to their axioms of rationality (a
different set of axioms for each theorist), and utopians of all stripes
excuse the failures of their schemes for never having really been tried.
Communism will produce Lenin's New Socialist Man, given enough time. And
so forth.

I shall call Buchanan's conception of a contractor New Contractarian
Man. Indeed, I shall suggest that the broad sweep of human history may be
towards increasingly contractual thinking, and thus Buchanan's
contractarianism may become ever more realistic and less and less wishful.
On the other hand and 71 years on, New Socialist Man seems no closer to
being realized today than in 1917.

Rationalizations become desperate when reality stubbornly refuses to
move into line with the ideal. On the other hand, if reality and ideal
seem not very far apart, and to be moving closer together, then the theory
only fails in the sense that all abstractions must. Buchanan's unanimity
concept could be regarded as either/or, whence in all strict logic it
fails, or it could be taken as an abstraction, whence a 99% unanimity is
very different from a 1% unanimity, which would have been good enough for
Lenin. When the Bolsheviks took over from all the leftist forces
remaining, he explained, "The people wanted the Constituent Assembly
summoned, and we summoned it. But they sensed immediately what this
famous Constituent Assembly really wanted. And now we have carried out
the will of the people, which is All Power to the Soviets." (Shub
1950:152)

Since Buchanan frequently uses the word quasi-unanimity, we shall
consider his ideas as abstractions, as ideals to be approached. The
question is, how close does reality come to the unanimity ideal? Not very
closely at all, if we look to find a historical example of an actual
social contract. Force has been the historical norm, not deliberate
agreement, and this has been the major criticism of contractarian theory
since the day after Hobbes's Leviathan was published in 1651. In Hobbes's

imagined state of nature, so little would be left over for production,
after the energy spent on predation and protection, that individuals would
be better off giving all of their freedoms to Leviathan. Men may not, in
fact, be quite so frightfully warlike, and it would be stretching language
for every dictator who comes along to speak of a "conceptual contract."

The unanimity ideal begins to be approached in the American colonies,
in both senses: Constitutions are in fact drawn up and signed, and an
uncertain but perhaps sizable majority regards the constitution as an
improvement over what went before. The United States Constitution of
1789, however, was not only an illegal seizure of power—the Articles of
Confederation required unanimity among the states for its amendment—but
also there was substantial opposition by Antifederalists, whose writings
were undergoing restudy in the 1980s. On the other hand, the Constitution
of the Confederacy was regarded as building in additional safeguards the
Founding Fathers had neglected. As an improvement, then, perhaps the
Confederate Constitution is as close to the unanimity ideal as has ever
been achieved. [2]

These historical musings, then, have meaning in Buchanan's public
choice version of contractarianism that is lacking in those of earlier
contractarians, for Buchanan is not so much interested in providing a
broad and abstract justification for government per se as in considering
whether the institutional design of specific governments might be
construed to rest upon the unanimous consent of the governed. None have,
in strict historical accuracy, but some have come closer than others. So
while there is a hypothetical element in Buchanan's reasoning (see the
next section) that he is clearly aware of when he uses such terms as
quasi-unanimity and conceptual contract, as a specialist in exchange
(i.e., as an economist) his frame of reference is a specific social
contract that specific social contractors might all agree to.

1.5 The Methodological Meaning of the Unanimity Rule

While Buchanan has not engaged in historical speculation as to which
situations have most closely approximated the unanimity ideal, he might
have said that the historical trend has been towards more popular
government, even if this trend seems to have stopped at majority rule
instead of progressing on towards unanimity. What Buchanan focuses on
instead is the question whether the current situation is one that might
have evolved out of a unanimous social contract. This will necessarily be

a guessing game, but if we ignore this fact and also many other problems,
we have a highly useful perspective with which to judge legislation.
Suppose, to return to the world of The Calculus of Consent, that the
contractors agree on Knut Wicksell's 5/6 majority rule (which Buchanan
mentions in Limits) as the best compromise between too much legislated
imposition of one group's values on the rest and the cost of enacting
laws. Not every proposed law passed will command a 5/6 majority, due to
the formation of logrolling and vote-trading coalitions, and such trading
makes it possible for passionate minorities (actually, passionate
less-than-5/6 majorities) to have their wishes realized.

The voters, all of whom have read Calculus, know all this and opt for
the 5/6 rule rather than a simple majority. We, the omniscient outside
observers, will then judge legislation that could have been passed under
the 5/6 rule as good in a Pareto-efficiency sense and regard laws that
could not have been so passed as coercive. This contract never took place
in our history, but we think or pretend that everyone would have agreed to
the 5/6 rule. It is plain that many laws currently on the books could
never have mustered a 5/6 majority, all the more so since all three
branches of our government have repeatedly exceeded even the powers it
seized in 1789. "The Threat of Leviathan," (Chapter 9 of Limits), then,
is hardly Buchanan's parading his own values; rather it is his considered
judgment of how far government has exceeded any authority it could
possibly have gained under any unanimous social contract whatever. Anyone
who thinks that our government is of optimal size, in any Pareto sense and
not just in his personal opinion, had better be prepared to roll out
powerful arguments in support of his position.

This, then, is the common sense thrust of Buchanan's idea of a
conceptual contract. It is when we get picky about the logic (and
therefore when we lose sight of the common sense thrust) that numerous
nasty problems arise. In the first place, men are, to some extent,
innately disagreeable. In any group of a hundred, the chances are near
100% that at least one person will refuse to sign the contract, and
unanimity minus one is not unanimity. (Adding in minors, the retarded,
the insane, and the just plain ornery makes agreement even less likely.)
Second, as Buchanan himself notes in Chapter 8 of Limits, people are
inclined to regard the social contract itself as a public good and are
therefore disinclined to become informed and make adequate judgments.
Third, Karen Vaughn argues in "Can There Be a Constitutional Political
Economy?" (1983) that not only is very little known about the consequences

of political constitutions, there is nowhere nearly the extensive
self-correcting feedback characteristic of frequent and numerous exchanges
in economic markets. Any convergence to an optimum will be exasperatingly
slow, and equilibrium may never be reached. Buchanan, however, freely
admits that a given constitution need not be Pareto optimal, and so
Vaughn's objection is a matter of degree.

As we have seen, the Confederate Constitution was regarded
(internally) as a major improvement over the illegal U.S. Constitution of
1789. Indeed, were we to renegotiate the Constitution and incorporate
several suggested safeguards discussed in Limits, especially of limiting
the scope of government, the next constitution would be an even greater
improvement. In other words, pace Vaughn, we do learn as we go. Buchanan
might reply that Vaughn's objections are not quite to the point, which is
that (so far at least) no criterion unambiguously superior to the fact of
agreement has been offered. Vaughn's objections would still count, if it
turned out that unanimous agreements were but very slightly better than
useless, so uninformed are the citizens, but the American experience, at
least, belies this. We may not have prevented the coming of Leviathan,
but surely we have retarded it.

A fourth problem with the unanimity ideal is that circumstances
change, as Vaughn says later in her paper. This need not necessarily be a
problem, especially under omniscience and immortality, for the contractors
can theoretically draw up a contract lengthy enough to handle all future
contingencies, or at least do the best job they can. But the best job
might not be a very good one, and in Chapter 5 of Limits, Buchanan
discusses the possibility that changes in technology or other underlying
conditions have changed the perceived anarchist equilibrium out of which
the social contract arose in the first place, meaning that a quite
different contract might be drawn up now. Some will prefer that things
stay put, but they may also fear that changes may be imposed upon the
constitution without their consent and offer some compromises. Perhaps we
are getting sidetracked here, for we are now without the world of
unanimity, but recall that the signing of a contract may have some
nonrational binding force and assume this force decays over time. Then
the problem is a real one, and is usually handled by amendment procedures
requiring less than unanimity but more than that required for the normal
passage of laws. In the United States, the rules of procedure each house
of Congress establishes for itself enjoy a variable degree of respect
intermediate between normal lawmaking and consitutional amendment. These

safeguards are often informal, and public choice theorists could examine whether these informal arrangements might be replaced with more formal ones.

Buchanan does not adduce any historical examples of changing circumstances leading to changes in the (perceived) underlying anarchist equilibrium, and it is not always an easy matter to conceive what they might be. For some, of course, it is very easy indeed, and conservatives and communists join hands in detesting capitalism and its unjustified power. Constitution-making is a serious business--the unanimity requirement will make it one!--and considerable effort will be made to distill the wisdom of the ages into a form of some permanence. Not all of the Founding Fathers foresaw the coming of industrialism, true, but they had reason to hope their attempts to "secure the blessings of liberty to ourselves and our posterity" would suffice, whatever the future might bring.

The future brought an erosion of liberty, even as it brought industrialization, and Buchanan rightly notes that the Fathers concerned themselves with the concentration of power to the neglect of the extent of power. But this shows, it seems, a failure of design. Vaughn thinks changed values are more important, and perhaps she is right. Let us save space by not offering any theoretical or historical arguments for the best candidate yet for an absolute truth, namely that power will accumulate unless fought every inch of the way. Now if values change so that people are less willing to pay the price of liberty, which is eternal vigilance, [3] freedom will decay. This is so regardless of any written constitutional safeguards, as it is a reasonable observation that mere words, while not without their nonrational binding effects, are rarely in themselves so powerful as to override the tendency of power to accumulate.

Vaughn did not suggest how values in America have changed over the past century or so, but it is commonly held that there has been a decline in old fashioned character, a rise in cynicism, a decline in honor, a rise in the willingness of men and groups to use the state for their own ends, a rise in litigiosity, a decline in maturity, and perhaps above all a rise in egalitarianism and the accompanying guilt that reduces the willingness to resist the inroads of the state. These are all value-loaded terms, but they are also descriptive of changes that will erode constitutional safeguards. The perceived moral initiatives have been by those who would enlarge the state, and compromise by compromise the state grows, while

constitutional safeguards are held to be formalities irrelevant to today's
realities.

1.6   Additional Requirements for New Contractarian Man

These objections to the idea of a "conceptual contract"--that it is
wrong to pretend that we could ever get unanimous agreement, that even if
we did it would not correspond to what people really want, and that it
will not last anyhow--are not necessarily fatal, not to the common sense
thrust of the idea. Common sense has it that we do know something about
our fellow men, enough to have some general idea of what would be
acceptable to all men, or at least to all reasonable men. Nor are we
wholly ignorant of how governments operate, thanks in good measure to the
works of Buchanan and other public choice scholars. As to whether a
constitution will be lasting, the price of liberty remains what it has
been, but we can lower the price by installing better safeguards and by
providing for amendments to install further ones as we learn of them.

It may be countered that these claims of so-called common sense are
spurious, that unfreedom is the world and historical norm, that men are
hardly ever so sweetly reasonable. Still, the notion of a conceptual
contract is not without its uses as a litmus test. There remains a major
difference between what ideally reasonable men might conceivably agree
upon and what they never could. Observers will, of course, dispute
specific cases, and part of the dispute will be over what an ideal man
should be taken to be. We must grant him a degree of wisdom and a degree
of thoroughness in his deliberations not much less than that of our
hypothetical outside observer. We grant him maturity not to whine or seek
to undermine a constitutional order that did not meet up to his
expectations. We expect of him a similar patience should his values
change as time passes on. And we expect of him an impartiality or
magnaminity such that he will not exploit the unanimity rule to bargain on
his own behalf.

Of such wise and noble men, then, are Buchanan's conceptual
contractors made up. To these splendid qualities, perhaps two more should
be added. One is that those who are violating the current constitution
with impunity not regard their violations as part of the de facto status
quo and hold out for their "rights" to future predation. Buchanan's
treatment of this problem is ambiguous (LL 96-98), but it is hard to
specify what predation is when it has gone on for so long that it melds

into accepted custom and tradition. Furthermore, while predation or just plain inefficiencies are a net (Paretian) loss, would-be predators compete among themselves to get into privileged positions and eventually drain away all profits to predation. There come to be no winners, only losers (most of us) and those who stay even. Theoretically, there are Pareto optimal ways out, but they can be far from easy to implement. Who is to be compensated? The current rent holders? The ones who invested in but failed to get predatory positions? The rent holders, most of them long since departed, who made a net profit from their rent-seeking? It would seem unfair to take away without compensation a taxi medallion from an owner who paid the market price for one of the 11,772 allowed in New York City. It would also be unfair to tax the citizens the market price and hand it over to the medallion owner, when most taxpayers do not use taxis and it is hard to identify those who do. (In theory, one could set taxi rates between the market and currently regulated prices and pay the difference between the new and market prices to the current medallion owners, but this raises other problems, especially statistical ones.)

To get out of this bind and barring immanent resolution of the problems of economic theory and data collection, we must either presume again that our contractors are impartial or that the reforms will be so broad-based that practically everyone will be better off in the net, that is, after his particular racket is taken away from him. This would be what Buchanan calls a "constitutional revolution," as it is far more encompassing than piecemeal reform. It seems reasonable, however, that Buchanan was momentarily forgetful about just how myopic people are when he wrote "Beyond Pragmatism: Prospects for Constitutional Revolution," the last chapter of The Limits of Liberty, particularly when it comes to their own protected turf. Either that, or they are extemely risk-averse. Not without reason, for reforms have a habit of getting bogged down, and few want only their own privileges taken away.

The other requirement that might be attributed to New Contractarian Man is a lack of petty emotions, such as envy and resentment. These emotions, which can be quite strong, practically characterized democracy for H.L. Mencken (1928 and a sizable fraction of his other works) and brought forth one of Ayn Rand's most splendidly polemical essays, "The Age of Envy" (1971). Buchanan is perhaps equivocal here, for while he evidently does not favor envy, he might be taken as implying that not only might the rich be wise to save their necks by compromising with the howling mob (especially if the perceived underlying anarchist equilibrium

has changed) but possibly there is a certain merit to the mob's
complaints. (LL 80–81, esp.) His argument shifts from the operation to
the violation of the constitutional order and back, sometimes so quickly
that it is difficult to say whether he is speaking ideally or really.

Requiring impartiality of the contractors may lead to a solution to
the question of the legitimacy of pettiness as a factor in constitution
making. Income redistribution, if kept in bounds, is not something that
would have to be excluded here. The reason is that an impartial
contractor would not know for certain that misfortune would not overcome
him; together, the contractors would agree upon some (compromise) scheme
for redistribution or minimum income. There is an argument that, owing to
the declining marginal utility of money, all incomes should be equal.
Such would not be adopted by our wise contractors, for productive
incentives would dwindle. Indeed, the contractors might well put in a
stiff means test to distinguish the unfortunate from the malingerers and,
if they look over many generations, to mandatory birth control at least
for the duration of public payments. (The problem of generations will be
explored in Chapters 4 and 6.) We might, then, expect unanimity here from
impartial contractors, or at least unanimity on some method for
establishing the exact rules and formulae.

Envy and resentment are different and imply an income redistribution
beyond what is rational in terms of the last paragraph. A man quite free
of both envy and resentment now might realize he could become full of them
under changed conditions and not want to arbitrarily block off in advance
their political expression. Officially, economists of the value–free
persuasion would note that the petty emotions are just as real as the more
exalted ones and that they would be imposing their own values to approve
of some and disapprove of others. What value–free economists can make is
a factual claim that contractors who are both wise and impartial would
realize that giving free reign to pettiness would undermine the
constitutional order itself. In the final chapter, I shall discuss the
work of the social psychologist Raymond Cattell and consider how findings
in his field, as well as those from economics, might be utilized by the
contractors.

In all this, we are not asking, we are telling Buchanan what his
contractors must be like and thus moving further away from a
methodological individualism that takes individuals as they actually come
with all their innate quarrelsomeness and other objectionable features.
In some respects we must do this: Men as they in fact are will not come to

unanimous agreement about anything except in very small groups. Some
restrictions on what the contractors must be like must be made; otherwise,
the use of the idea of a conceptual contract to look at legislation has
zero content from the very start. It is vacuous to say that what counts
is the fact of agreement, not the content, if agreements are never
possible. But as soon as restrictions are imposed upon the values and
characteristics of the contractors, possible contents are restricted too
and therefore do begin to matter. The question is how far we may go
adding these restrictions without approaching scholasticism and talmudic
deductivism.

Happily, the question may be regarded as an empirical one, and this
amounts to asking what it takes, for a given population, for a viable
constitutional order to come about, that is, one that will be immune from
violent revolution or the less openly violent but steady usurpation of
power. No constitution can be expected to last forever, but we suspect
that the Founding Fathers, had they had today's hindsight, might have
better prevented the slow usurpation of power. We will get different
answers about what it takes, and the problem is a matter of degree anyhow
(and also a matter of values, since people differ in how sure they want to
be that the constitution will last). Buchanan might find that a rather
minimal set of restrictions on the characteristics of the agreers will
suffice and that our more expanded set demands persons somewhere between
Parson Weems' characterization of George Washington and that given of Mr.
Jefferson each year on Graduation Day at the University of Virginia. One
will simply have to listen to the various arguments and decide what sorts
of rules are needed, at a minimum, for a viable constitutional order.
Then, one may form an opinion as to whether a given law could conceivably
be the product of one or another viable constitutional order.

Again, all this imposing of psychological restrictions upon the
social contractors is moving away from strict methodological
individualism. In fact, Buchanan's own ruling out of strategic bargaining
at the constitutional stage could be read as supposing that social
contractors, rather than somehow pre-agreeing (a social contract to make a
social contract?!) to set them aside, have little propensity to engage in
such bargaining in the first place.

In this connection, it is instructive to note that, whereas Buchanan
devoted only a small space to John Rawls' A Theory of Justice (1971) in
the closing pages of Limits, he was later to write several articles about
Rawls' work. In a recent summing up of his life work, "Better than

Plowing" (1986b), Buchanan remarked that his own constitutionalism (as
opposed to just enacting all laws in one fell swoop) implies an
uncertainty of the future which puts individuals in a state of ignorance
not unlike that under Rawls' veil of ignorance. I will argue in Chapter 4
that this uncertainty is such a broad feature of the human condition as to
be not implausibly called a metaphysical fact.

Let me also note here that Rawls rules out envy from his social
contractors on grounds that those behind the veil will not know how much
of it they will have afterwards, while I am ruling envious persons out of
participating in the social contract in the first place on grounds of an
empirical claim that a contract among the envious will not be viable. I
hasten to admit that I am not offering any body of evidence to back up my
claim, but the reader might consult Helmut Schoeck, Envy (1966).

1.7 Potential Abuses of the Unanimity Criterion

There is something else to consider. Suppose we have pretty much
decided on what is needed for such an order. It might be wise and
impartial men who exclude strategic bargaining and pettiness from their
deliberations, but it need not be exactly this. Still, the preferences of
different groups of such men could vary enormously and the social
contracts that get drawn up would vary only a little less enormously.
Economic theory nowhere teaches how diverse our preferences can get;
rather, and because the theory is designed to be broadly general, it
leaves the impression that they in fact vary widely. This need not be the
case, and the more or less idealized men who are to be the (conceptual)
contractors may share values that are quite close to one another as
compared with non-idealized men as they are in reality. If this is the
case, wise men will come to agree upon more things than actual men. With
lack of pettiness may come certain virtues and preferences for those
virtues. It is an empirical question, of course, and there will be much
disagreement. The point is that as we decide we must place certain
restrictions on the contractors to get a viable constitution, we also cut
down on the range of constitutions they will agree to.

In the limit, these fine, upstanding men will come to agree with--me!
Therefore, any law I don't happen to approve of--I do pretend to be
impartial, however--is necessarily one that could never conceivably have
arisen out of any social contract. This is an easy trap to fall into and
one Buchanan might be said to be not entirely immune from, as it comes out

quite clearly that he holds that the present situation in America could
not have come about by procedures unanimously consented to and therefore
had to have resulted from the usurpation of power. I think I exaggerate
and am being too rough, but it is remarkable that Buchanan holds out
constitutional revolution (that is, unanimously-consented change) as
plausible and not just possible. It is safe to say that he would not so
hold out, had not his learning in economics and public choice theory given
him a good idea in what directions such a constitutional revolution might
go and that they would go somewhere in the direction his learning
suggests. In other words, Buchanan more than hopes that contractors would
not set up a socialist state.

Can Buchanan now stand accused of reversing the very first sentence
on page one of Limits: "Those who seek specific descriptions of the 'good
society' will not find them here"? It is hard to claim that he reverses
himself any more than the inherent difficulties with strict methodological
individualism require. Buchanan's hopes are not germane unless they color
his views of what restrictions will have to be placed on the personalities
of the contractors (such as being agreeable, wise, and impartial) and of
what values are not legitimate (bargaining considerations, perhaps envy).
But place certain restrictions he must, in the only reality we have.
Buchanan's treatment of possible contracts is very broad and there is no
attempt on his part to link any restrictions on the contractors to his
view that constitutional revolution is feasible. It is here, in these
pages, not in The Limits of Liberty, that the need for restrictions is
argued. Perhaps the restrictions we have suggested as necessary in order
to get a workable constitutional order may be acceptable to Buchanan or to
others, and they may entail a sort of contract natural rights holders
and/or certain free-market economists would enjoy. In fact, Buchanan has
been regularly roasted for declining to favor particular schemes (Buchanan
and Samuels 1980), and he is hardly unique in claiming widespread
dissatisfaction with the present mess nor for thinking that there is
something better that virtually everyone should be able to agree upon.
What does set him aside is an awareness that the only reform that could
command nigh universal assent would have to be sweeping and that piecemeal
proposals would surely be resisted by someone, if not a substantial
minority.

What is of more concern here than trying to fix the restrictions on
social contractors and contracts is to consider the implications for
methodological individualism, strictly construed. As said above, it is

difficult to get a fix on just what methodological individualism is. If
it entails that values can be known only in the context of an agreement,
this entails a certain degree of objectivity of values, for (so we have
argued) only a proper subset of all possible agreements can be viable.
This runs head against the doctrine of (absolute) subjectivity of values
that is part and parcel of both methodological individualism and orthodox
economic theory. We also run into the ban against interpersonal
comparisons of utility if we are to exclude pettiness and even strategic
bargaining from having a legitimate place in constitution formation.

1.8 Duties to Obey the Laws?

An additional problem is the temptation disingenuously to imply that
a person has consented to the contract and then hold that he is obliged to
follow its terms. This is quite a bit different from the procedure of
honestly trying to discern whether a law could have been made under a
conceptual contract, even if we try not to stretch said "conceptual"
excessively, for this is our criterion for judging laws. We separate out
the "bad" laws (those that only by an untoward stretch of the imagination
could have arisen under some conceptual contract) from those that are not
"bad." Yet the "non-bad" are not ones that have arisen under an actual
contract, unless there has actually been such a contract, which has
neither been nor is now the case. Under strict individualism, obligation
exists only under real agreements.

It is not clear whether this is a problem for Buchanan, since he
never makes the normative claim that men ought to live up to their
agreements. In fact, he repeatedly deals with the prospect of men
violating their agreements. Yet in Chapter 5 of Limits, he states that if
the government can arbitrarily change rights, "there is no requirement
that its actions be 'honored' with ethical sanctions." (LL 83-84) The
converse statement—that when the government cannot arbitrarily change
rights, its actions ought to be honored—does not strictly follow, but we
do not think Buchanan is making an empty statement, which would be the
case if he never held that ethical sanctions are appropriate, which in
turn would mean that he has no normative judgments at all to offer.

To imply, however, that there are duties of the citizen to the state,
in this world where there are no actual social contracts, is collectivist
at least in some sense, or else the notion involves stretching the idea of
a conceptual contract beyond its methodological value. In the wrong

hands, such duties could be stretched and rationalized to cover
practically any law, and we had better believe that said stretcher is
going to use his veto power under the unanimity rule to block any
constitutional reform that strips him of his "right" to engage in such
justifications of his own power.

Any tool can be misused, however, and effort must go again to find
the common sense of the matter, which is to find some individualist basis
for saying there is an obligation to obey the laws. We cannot do so,
strictly, but just as we have had to modify methodological individualism
in order to come up with a conceptual contract, we might do so also for
obligations to obey the laws enacted thereunder, provided, of course, that
we do not get carried away. When we do get carried away, we arrive at
whole-hog collectivism, or something barely distinguishable from it. One
problem is that there is a range of conceptual contracts and for each
contract various trajectories, each leading to a different set of laws
enacted. There are, then, sets of sets of sets of possible laws under
possible trajectories of possible conceptual contracts. It is a different
thing to assert that an actual given law in question belongs to a set of
sets of sets than to say it was at all likely to have been passed. Laws
against murder? Very likely indeed. Special interest legislation? A
certain amount of it, but wise contractors would try to minimize it.
Prohibition? Hard to say, and remember the issue is not whether that
specific law could ever have gotten unanimous consent but whether it could
have been enacted under a unanimous constitution. The Equal Rights
Amendment? If women belong to the polity, out of which a contract arises,
it is hard to imagine an anarchist equilibrium that could lead to a social
contract that incorporated blatant sexual discrimination. In this
trajectory under the Constitution of 1789, however, the ERA has failed to
go through for fear of judicial activism. And Prohibition might not have
gone through had American history taken a different turn. (Recall that
amendments and ordinary laws both are regarded here as enactments under a
constitution.)

Assume we hold that Prohibition might (but by no means would) have
arisen under at least one conceptual contract. We would then have shown
that it was not a "bad" law, but this is far from saying it is a "good"
law, or one that people are obliged to obey, as unambiguously as one ought
to obey laws forbidding murder. If we actually had a social contract,
Prohibition would be binding. We don't; we live under the illegal
Constitution of 1789, which has been violated repeatedly; and so some sort

of judgment will have to be made whether Prohibition was railroaded
through or whether it had nearly unanimous consent. We maintain the
following principle: Without a social contract, or reasonable facsimile
thereof, in actual operation, a much stiffer test has to be met before one
can speak of a duty to obey a law than would be the case if the law in
question were duly passed in accordance with one. I maintain that
Prohibition, resisted by a huge minority, did not pass the stiffer
test. [4]

   This takes us to the important seventh chapter of Limits, "Law as
Public Capital," and here Buchanan develops an idea which, though this was
not his specific intention, could be used to help settle where to draw the
line between obligations incurred by individuals and duties owed to the
collectivity. We have argued that a limited dose of collectivism will
have to be invoked to get around the problems of extreme methodological
individualism, and so let us consider what Buchanan's idea might suggest.

   In discussing the capital goods aspects of a stock of observed laws,
Buchanan holds that its "benefits are yielded, in enhanced stability of
interpersonal relationships, at an increasing rate over many periods of
time. That is to say, the benefits from law increase in rate as the
investment matures. It is as if, in the numerical example [of the
previous paragraph], investment would yield the full 10 percent return
only if the asset is maintained for, say, ten years, and that this rate
might, say, increase to 20 percent if the asset should be maintained for
twenty years." (LL 125) He adds that it is entirely possible that, once
the public capital embodied in the legal-constitutional structure has been
destroyed, it may be restorable "only over a period that exceeds personal
planning horizons....For all practical purposes, public or social capital
may be permanently lost once it is destroyed. It may be impossible to
secure its replacement at least on the basis of rational decisions made by
individuals." (LL 125-126) If so, "then a recognition of the capital or
investment aspects of the genuine 'public goods' that are being destroyed
makes corrective action much more urgent than any application of a
consumption-goods paradigm might suggest." (LL 126)

   Buchanan, evidently seeing this as a deteriorating era, is looking
more at the erosion of public capital than at its enhancement, but one can
take the opportunity to build upon his distinction between a capital stock
that is characterized by an increasing rate of return over time versus
stocks that are not so characterized, i.e., the ones public goods
theorists usually, if implicitly, talk about. Buchanan seems on the verge

of converting this economic distinction into a moral one, which could
read:

> It is optional whether a society provides for itself ordinary
> public goods, but its members OUGHT to provide for themselves
> public goods whose rates of return increase over time.

I hasten to add that, as there may be several such public goods, the
dividing line will not necessarily be between these and ordinary public
goods but between increasing time-yield public goods and more increasing
ones. It sounds difficult to avoid interpersonal comparisons of utility,
but perhaps the constitution can be drawn up with the more increasing
public goods at a higher level, just as amendments to the constitution
rank higher than ordinary laws. It could be readily argued that freedom
of discussion is very nearly at the highest level, that free speech is a
public good that increases in its return to the capital stock of good
constitutional order as fast or nearly as fast as any other. Besides,
discussion is of the very essence of constitutionalism and cannot be
inhibited if we are to pretend to be having any sort of (continuing)
constitutional order in the first place. If we may speak of a natural
right to participate in the social contract under the unanimity rule, we
may (almost) equally speak of a natural right to free speech. Buchanan
rejects natural rights, apparently, if an extended list is implied
(especially if imposed from the outside), but he should accept at least
two, continuing participation and discussion.

1.9 Contractarianism and Natural Rights

There are, however, advocates of natural rights, and Leland B.
Yeager is among them. In his address, "Contract and Truth Judgment in
Policy Espousal" (1983), Yeager contrasts the broadly conceived
utilitarianism he advocates with Buchanan's contractarianism, giving many
quotations from Buchanan's writings. Yeager notes that Buchanan likens
social contracts to market processes, but truth judgment in politics to
the deliberations of a jury (to find the truth). Yeager quotes Buchanan
as saying, "Once truth is found, there is no moral argument against its
implementation," but that there is no single truth for all mankind.

Yeager has difficulties with the contractarian position. He holds
that while such fictions are useful, one should not become overly

dependent on them. The social contract is such a fiction, as people
rarely deliberate finely on their social arrangements, and, what is more,
pretending that there has been an actual social contract leads to a
glorification of the status quo. Rather, the essence of the state is
compulsion, and any pretending that consent exists when it does not can
only justify such compulsion. Furthermore, it is problematic how an
amoral state of nature can be magically transformed into one of positive
obligations merely by the act of signing a contract, social or otherwise.

Yeager complains that contractarianism is all procedure and no
content: "Rather than suppose that proper procedure exhausts the content
of the good society, it would be more reasonable to emphasize proper
procedure as an important part of that conception." Furthermore
contractarianism is too value-neutral: "The very conception of a liberal
society calls for distinguishing among the particular tastes and values of
individuals, according more to some and less to others, regarding some as
more and others as less worthy of being dignified by basing public policy
on them."

Yeager's own view is that the aim of collective institutions is to
encourage what he so well calls social cooperation, the market being the
premier example of such an institution. He says that his own position is
not so relativistic as Buchanan's, but neither does he wish an
authoritarian regime run by people who think they have all the answers.
Yeager calls his own position "fallibilism" and holds that certain moral
truths may come to be known but that free and open discussion is needed
for their pursuit. Contractarians really wish the same things he does,
but his own position is free of their drawbacks.

I have voiced several of Yeager's objections earlier, and my
resolution of the dilemmas has been to construe contractarianism as an
ideal to be approached and also as a tool to be used in judging
legislation. It does not seem that Yeager would prohibit any law that
genuinely had completely universal approval, even if he thought the
citizens would come to grief. This situation is, of course, hypothetical,
but we have construed Buchanan's notion of a conceptual contract as a
basis for judging that a given law might have been made under a
constitution established by somewhat idealized men. Laws against murder
are very different from the whims of a dictator or even special interest
legislation, the merits of which are at best ambiguous. Some such
legislation is inevitable, but it can be kept to tolerable levels. We
have justified Buchanan's use of the word conceptual so that the set of

good laws (in the sense that the machinery for their establishment is
approved) is not the empty set. Certainly the word can be so distorted as
to rationalize everything, but so can every other word.

The charge that Buchanan's contractarianism glorifies the status quo
involves a more subtle difficulty. It is one thing to contemplate
idealized contractors in a state of nature cogitating upon a social order;
it is something quite else to think about getting unanimous agreement to
reform the present mess, especially as those on the take are far from
idealistic and can be expected to block reform.   It would seem that we
are stuck with the present, unless we are willing to coerce some groups
for the benefit of others. This need not be the case if the reforms are
broad (Buchanan's "constitutional revolution"), however, as it can be
argued that few if any are really ahead in the net with gains from a few
privileges outweighing many losses elsewhere. (Getting people to realize
this is another matter, but one of the jobs of <u>Professor</u> Buchanan is to
educate!) Another way out is to hold that certain values are not to be
included as appropriate for public policy, which is exactly what Yeager
advocates. As already seen, Buchanan does seem willing to make strategic
bargaining illegitimate, and other factors (e.g., envy) may well have to
be excluded, on <u>this</u> Earth, to allow either a viable constitutional order
or viable constitutional reform or revolution.

Buchanan seeks a high degree of generality and thus a correspondingly
relatively relativist position on specific values. Yeager thinks moral
truths, while not given to us by revelation, can be learned approximately
and better and better as time goes on, much as scientific knowledge is
gained in the non-moral realm. (Chapter 6 will discuss knowledge in
social psychology, Chapter 5 the possibility of knowledge of natural
rights.) Buchanan may think my own speculations about which social
contracts will not work are premature, and more so Yeager's. At the same
time, Buchanan would seem to be more enthusiastic than Yeager about
different peoples experimenting with different social arrangements. A
nation made up of those who are rugged individualists by temperament may
very well be so jealous of their individual liberties as drastically to
chain the constitution to disallow not only those public goods provided
under another nation's constitution, but also those which, on their own
preferences, they should appear to want. On the other hand, Yeager might
protest a nation setting up a state that is "too large." (Federalism will
be discussed in Chapter 6. I am not implying, incidentally, that either
Buchanan or Yeager advocates forced imposition of his own conclusions upon

other peoples. The question of when one nation might liberate the
oppressed peoples living under a far-from-unanimous dictatorial regime is
a separate, and difficult, problem. I have no hints to offer here, and
neither do Buchanan or Yeager.)

The difference between Buchanan and Yeager is not that one is all
procedure, the other all content, but that each has a difference of
emphasis, there being a greater agnosticism and recognition of differing
regards for individual liberties over different nations on Buchanan's
part. Both, it is fair to say, see free and open discussion as near
essential to a free political order, and certainly neither is happy about
the present. (Who is?) And both are quite aware of the compulsory nature
of all past and existing states.

1.10 Conclusion

I have attempted to elucidate Buchanan's contractarianism as a
methodological principle to distinguish laws that might have been passed
under a social contract drawn up by somewhat or even highly idealized men
from those that never could. This requires a certain historical judgment,
but it is a useful guideline. I have called such an ideal New
Contractarian Man and have considered what characteristics he must and
might have. I have further distinguished between a law that might have
been enacted under some constitution and one that appears to one's best
judgment likely to have been enacted under most if not all constitutions.
In the latter case, it may be held that there is a moral duty to obey laws
of this sort, even if there has been no actual formal social contract,
which of course there never has been. It is also true that some laws,
especially in their fine details, will be arbitrary but necessary and that
there is a (weaker) duty to obey them also. Furthermore, the entire body
of law has certain "holistic" properties (after discussing Bunge, we will
be able to replace the mystical notion of holism with an ontologically
meaningful one of emergent properties of a system) obliging the citizens
to some extent, perhaps small, to be law-abiding generally. Finally,
those laws and public goods whose rates of return to enhanced stability of
interpersonal relationships (another "holistic" property) increase over
time are much more important than ordinary goods, so important that we
might even say the constitution ought to be constructed in such a way as
to facilitate their provision.

At each point in the discussion, we have noted inadequacies of strict

methodological individualism. Buchanan himself modifies his individualism by ruling out strategic bargaining at the constitutional level. Even in making this slight modification, he could be taken as making interpersonal comparisons of utility, since bargaining opportunities that are foregone are, strictly speaking, subjective opporunity costs. But I have gone further and claimed that in order to get any contract at all, a fictional New Contractarian Man has to be invoked and, it seems in places, endowed with virtues so splendid that few actually possess them. This could be a weakness as great as that of Lenin's New Socialist Man, and it remains to be explored whether there has been an evolution toward New Contractarian Man in actual human history. One also has to ask whether contractarianism is mandated by, or at least is tolerably consistent with, human nature. Both involve difficult questions.

A grave defect of this discussion of Buchanan's methodological individualism is that the concept is not clear. My arguments that methodological individualism needs to be modified may or may not apply to the precise claims and statements made in The Limits of Liberty, to Buchanan's own conception, or to the (varying) conceptions held by others. To quote Limits, page one again: "My approach is profoundly individualistic, in an ontological-methodological sense, although consistent adherence to this norm is almost as difficult as it is different." Buchanan is here contrasting his approach to the normative one that infuses political science, where an author tells (and not infrequently attempts to intimidate) the reader about what the political order should be like. Such arrogance Buchanan will not abide; for him it is up to the people themselves to come to their own agreements on what the political order should be. Perhaps Buchanan is too reticent when he says, again on page one of Limits: "I claim no rights to impose [my] preferences on others, even within the limits of persuasion," but the contrast he makes with the way political scientists usually operate is emphatic.

What is not so clear is whether those who parade their values openly reject methodological individualism, partially or totally, and in what respects. Buchanan is indeed different in the degree to which he strives to be objective, but perhaps many of his underlying premises are not so greatly at odds with those of conventional political scientists as they may appear. A man's biases are not impossible to fathom, though this has not been an easy nor an unquestionably successful task with respect to Limits, and men from the same culture, at odds with each other as they

often are, may share more in common than they disagree over. From a
larger perspective, "there ain't a dime's worth of difference between
'em."

Let us, then, look for a larger perspective. We modern Westerners
may all be methodological individualists, contractarians,
constitutionalists, upholders of reason and science, to varying degrees
and even (perhaps especially even) when in ostensible revolt. Searching
for a larger perspective, I shall examine a book by a member of the
Harvard Law School faculty, Roberto Mangabeira Unger, Knowledge and
Politics, which was published in 1975, the same year as The Limits of
Liberty. We might imagine we would want a book totally at odds with
Limits, but that would be Zen Buddhist puzzles, shrieking, or silence (all
about the same thing). Rather, Unger's book dissects the paradoxes of
post-medieval thinking in the West, but the probably inevitable result is
that his ultimate conclusions, after much fanfare and promise to go beyond
modern thought, lie very safely within it. No matter, for one should
learn what one can from books, and it is to Knowledge and Politics that we
next turn.

CHAPTER 2

ROBERTO MANGABEIRA UNGER AND COLLECTIVISM

2.1 Unger's Characterization of Individualism

Knowledge and Politics, by Roberto Mangabeira Unger, came out in the
same year, 1975, as The Limits of Liberty by James M. Buchanan. While
Buchanan attempts to ground our understanding of liberty and the role of
government upon methodological individualism, Unger attacks the whole
individualist body of thought that has grown up in the modern West from
Thomas Hobbes in the seventeenth century onward. Unger elucidates this
tradition of thought and, in drawing out its background assumptions more
thoroughly than was done in the last chapter, argues that individualism is
in a state of crisis, similar to the one in ancient and medieval thought
which led to individualism in the first place. Unger argues that
individualism, taken as a whole, fails both to be internally consistent
and to correspond with life as it is in fact lived. He offers an
alternative to both ancient and medieval thought and modern individualism
which may be regarded as collectivist, and thus a suitable adversary to
Buchanan's individualism, but which is, as we shall argue, more muddled
than collectivist. In the next chapter, we shall expound the ontology of
Mario Bunge and later apply his systemic world view to discuss social
justice, natural rights and federalism, taking the best features from
atomistic individualism and holistic collectivism, the better to have a
common framework to discuss all viewpoints.

   Unger argues that post-medieval individualism [5] came about in the
seventeenth century as a reaction against the world view of the ancients
and medievals. This earlier view saw human nature as timeless and unitary
and furthermore subscribed to the existence of what Unger calls
"intelligible essences," a term he defines twice: "Something has an
intelligible essence if it has a feature, capable of being apprehended, by
virtue of which it belongs to one category of things rather than another,"
(KP 39) and "The theory of intelligible essences states there are a
limited number of classes of things in the world, that each thing has
characteristics that determine the class to which it belongs, and that
these characteristics can be known directly by the mind." (KP 79) Under
this doctrine, a thing can be distinguished from its essence, that is,
from what it should be. Hence, there is room for objective values.

Essentialism is also compatible with the organization of society around fixed estates, the idea that a man is born into a fixed place in society.

Under individualism, Unger argues, the notion of intelligible essences is wholly rejected and replaced with the notion that the whole is nothing but the sum of its parts. The particular is no longer seen as a (flawed) instance of the universal; rather, universals are arbitrary groupings of particulars. Individuals are concretely real and radically different from universals, which are mental constructs with nothing necessary or essential about them and hence just names. Although Unger traces individualism back to the seventeenth century, some of its roots go back to the great William of Ockham and his nominalism (Latin, "name"). Ockham criticized only part of the older view, and it remained for Hobbes to criticize the remaining aspects of the doctrine of intelligible essences. (KP 5)

The rejection of intelligible essences has implications for the psychology of the individual person. The individual is no longer seen as a particular representative of an essentialist human nature; rather, he is seen as a bundle of desires. If there were rhyme or reason to these desires being what they are, then reason could dictate which desires a person ought to have. But then we are back in the normative world of intelligible essences, with its judgmental comparisons of the actual with the essential. Desires, if we follow this line of reasoning, are purely arbitrary and should some men share similar desires, it is purely by coincidence. Reason, says the essentialist, can lead a man to his true desires; to the nominalist (or individualist in the sense used here), the role of reason is the purely instrumental or practical one of showing what it takes to satisfy these desires. But the laws of nature are the same for everyone, and so there is only one reason. Hence reason and desire are separate, just as separate as universal and particular. Men are individuals, with nothing else in common except an ability to reason about the means to ends and never about the ends themselves.

The line of reasoning in the above paragraph is somewhat specious, and it smacks more than a little of medieval scholasticism, as arguments using more than a few abstract nouns are prone to. Nor is this a good empirical argument based on the facts; in fact, men share far more values than random chance alone would imply. We primates share a number of biological and sociobiological needs, and most of us are conformists.

Unger draws a second analogy, that between the split of reason from desire in individualist psychology and a split between rules and values in

individualist politics. Recall page one of The Limits of Liberty: "We
live together because social organization provides the efficient means of
achieving our individual objectives and not because society offers us a
means of arriving at some transcendental common bliss." In other words,
our individual objectives (particular values) can be anything at all, but
we use rules, universally applied to all, to provide the minimally
required social order for each to pursue his own objectives. Rules vs.
values is the political counterpart of the metaphysical separation of
universal and particular.

2.2 Buchanan's Implicit Agreement with Unger

The Limits of Liberty argues strongly that only agreement is needed
for a social contract, not any general uniformity or non-discrimination of
the operation of the government under the constitution. Indeed, the "leap
from Hobbesian anarchy" (LL 28) can result in a very lopsided constitution
(and possibly even slavery (LL 59-60)), with one party getting for himself
most of the gains from trade enabled by the social contract. For
Buchanan, there is officially only one requirement of "uniformity," that
of all-or-nothing agreement by each person to the contract. Yet he
remarks on "the basic principle of collective political order, that of
equal treatment..." (LL 39) and that "the law or rule must be generally
applied to all citizens." (LL 112)

Buchanan thus assumes unawares, and in spite of the thrust of his
other arguments, the radical separation of universal rules and particular
values and thus agrees with Unger's characteristization of individualism.
(He also assumes that nations are territorial, and of course the entire
book is atheistic.) It is hardly surprising that Buchanan should make
generalizations from his own culture, and if it were pointed out that
transcendental beings play a central role in Mohammedan law (Coulson 1968)
or that that law covers only those who submit (which is what "Islam" means
in English) and not those who dwell on a specific piece of real estate,
Buchanan would not be moved to rewrite his book and at best would add a
footnote. However, when he speaks of the necessity that laws be uniform,
he is showing that he is an individualist in Unger's sense as well as one
of the methodological variety. The three radical separations of
individualism given by Unger (theory vs. fact, reason vs. desire, rules
vs. values) do indeed hang together in some kind of analogizing reasoning,
and we produce James M. Buchanan as Exhibit A in evidence. If these

separations hang together for a careful thinker, trying hard to make
distinctions, they must be tightly fused in the rest of us.

It is this hanging together that Unger calls the unity of
individualist thought. In the last chapter we examined Buchanan's
methodological individualism from its own standpoint and concluded that it
was more applicable in a world inhabited by New Contractarian Man than in
the world of today, but nevertheless the notion of a conceptual contract
is highly useful--though also subject to abuse--in distinguishing a law
that might have been passed under a constitution agreed upon by somewhat
but not ridiculously exemplary men from a law that could only have been
imposed coercively. We also argued that these exemplary contractors would
most likely wind up discovering that a large measure of individualism in
the natural rights sense was desirable, that it happens that men will best
pursue their ends in a society where men are largely individually free.
Here we tackle the problem of individualism as a world view in Unger's
sense. (Note that a world view is held together neither by strict logic
nor by empirical laws--Unger's order of ideas and order of events--but by
analogous reasoning.) Buchanan is most clearly an individualist in the
methodological sense, a good measure of an individualist in the sense of
personal liberties, and also a post-medieval individualist in Unger's
sense. I hoped I vindicated whatever personal libertarian sentiments
Buchanan may have, though both I and Buchanan refrain from nailing down
what the optimal amount of individual freedom is.

2.3 Unger's Criticisms of the Individualist World View

Unger argues that, since individualism as a world view forms a unity,
efforts must be made to grasp it entire and not to single out a particular
aspect of it for criticism, leaving the others untouched. Nor can
individualism's "true nature be understood, and its secret empire
overthrown" (KP 8) merely by standing each of its doctrines on its head,
for the same reason, we add, that anti-clericals in Roman Catholic
countries are just as caught up in Christianity as the Pope. Unger's
achievement is to grasp this unity of individualist principles, and push
them to absurdity. From page 8:

> There is no one thinker who accepts [individualist] theory, in
> the form in which I present it, as a whole, or whose doctrines are
> completely defined by its tenets. If one looks at the writings of

the philosophers most closely identified with the beliefs I examine,
one finds a family of ideas rather than a unified system. There
appears to be analogy instead of sameness. Hence, it might be
objected that the view I discuss is a view nobody has ever held.

   Practically any doctrine can be pushed to absurdity, and the reason
is that the human brain is not very big. Our concepts never quite
dovetail with reality and as we pile up deduction upon deduction, no
matter how exact our arguments, we get carried away from reality at a
geometric rate. Men are far better than other animals at making concepts,
but they are also far more able to reify. The uniqueness of the West
consists of a willingness by many, and an insistence by some, to put the
deductions to the test and go back and refine the concepts. No other
society, save the Classical, came even close, although today the rest of
the world is rapidly imitating what has proven manifestly successful. The
world might have droned on until the Sun died, with man being only a
populous primate that managed to make a desert out of a huge part of the
Earth's land surface.
   It is meet to push the individualist world view to absurdity, for
doing so brings to light mistaken directions which we willy-nilly follow.
Unger entitled his book Knowledge and Politics to emphasize that theory
and practice go hand in hand as part of a world view held together by
analogies and that neither theory nor practice can be changed alone. Let
us follow Unger along his path, ask ourselves which of his conundrums we
really want to get out of, crying out from time to time that no one ever
meant for individualism to be taken that seriously (i.e., that absurdly),
and learning what we can. Later, I shall present and criticize Unger's
own proposed resolution of the paradoxes of individualism and his plan for
the future. By way of anticipation, Unger does not revive intelligible
essences, at least directly, and sees human nature as evolving and
emerging over time. (As we shall see in Chapter 5, Ayn Rand subscribes to
an essentialism, of an epistemological sort.) This hardly conforms to the
desire to define things exactly, but in a world of change this is not
always possible. Alfred Marshall had a different idea of what economics
was about than did Adam Smith, and Marshall's work itself changed the
definition. On today's understanding, economics is decidedly less a moral
enterprise than it was to either Marshall or Smith, but the economic
approach has been extended to cover parts of politics and even
sociobiology.

Unger also holds that the domination of some men over others inhibits the full expression of human nature. Buchanan, as we have seen, is professedly agnostic about human nature (LL 63) and its evolution, but we have argued that Buchanan implicitly holds a contractarian ideal and something of a hope that man is evolving toward it. Buchanan's value-free stance does not enable him directly to decry domination, which for him would be non-unanimous putative "contracts," but it is safe to say that he regards the coming together of men to make an agreement as something more than a theoretical tool of analysis. Men express their potential more fully when they act agreeably than when they resort to force.

Unger criticizes individualist doctrine on grounds of the untenability of the radical separations of universal and particular made in each of its three aspects: theory vs. fact, reason vs. desire, and rules vs. values. With respect to the first, if things lack intelligible essences, our words are at bottom names of arbitrary groupings of things. Our theories stand upon these arbitrary groupings and are therefore arbitrary themselves. If we take arbitrary not to mean provisional but randomly chaotic, then theory is completely separate from fact. This is in plain opposition to our merry optimism that science is progressive. In practice, we sneak intelligible essences in by the back door, and "it is not surprising, then, that language should become an obsession of the [individualist] thinker, for he worships it as the demiurge of the world." (KP 80) Moreover, he who has the power of making definitions has real power indeed (as Hobbes noted in <u>Leviathan</u>), as was also (we add) noted in a certain book that has had an appeal across a far wider spectrum of readers than Hobbes: [6]

"And only <u>one</u> for birthday presents, you know. There's glory for you!"

"I don't know what you mean by 'glory,'" Alice said.

Humpty Dumpty smiled contemptuously. "Of course you don't--till I tell you. I meant 'there's a nice knock-down argument for you!'"

"But 'glory' doesn't mean 'a nice knock-down argument,'" Alice objected.

"When <u>I</u> use a word," Humpty Dumpty said, in a rather scornful tone, "it means just what I choose it to mean--neither more nor less."

"The question is," said Alice, "whether you <u>can</u> make words mean

so many different things."

    "The question is," said Humpty Dumpty, "which is to be the
master--that's all."

    The rejoinder to Unger's criticisms is that no one, or at least
certainly no one today, espouses such an extreme nominalism. (But recall
Unger's own strategy of pushing individualist ideas out to absurdity
(KP 8)). In the realm of set theory we may speak of arbitrary sets with
complete generality, [7] but when we deal with the factual sciences our
concepts are partly if not largely controlled by the fact that they should
be useful. Our theories in general, and their concepts in particular, are
provisional and revisable, and both do get revised, in ever closer
approximation to the facts. (The doctrine that concepts are true to the
extent that they are useful as parts of true theories is the pragmatism
of the great Charles Peirce.) [8] Thus, universal and particular are
intertwined. Nevertheless, they are separate in accordance with
pre-Peirce individualist doctrine and remain partly separate still, since
one hopes it is the theories that get adjusted to the facts and not vice
versa. (However, facts do not stand completely by themselves and are in
fact interpreted and understood in the light of some theory or other.
This intertwines theory and fact all the more. Examples come readily to
mind: Interpretation of tracks in Wilson cloud chambers uses a great deal
of physical theory, as the empirical investigation of the effects of
minimum wage laws uses economic and statistical theory.)

2.4   The Factual Basis for the Separation of Theory and Fact

    The question remains: What is the world out there like, with respect
to universal and particular, or theory and fact? Our sciences seem to
describe the world well with a handful of very general concepts, such as
charge, spin, mass, length, etc., in physics, and the stuff out there is
made up of combinations of elementary things, in a bewildering variety of
mixtures. Scientists might as well assume "that there are a limited
number of classes of things, that each thing has characteristics that
determine the class to which it belongs, and that these characteristics
can be known directly by the mind," (KP 79) disputing only the word
directly. As we shall see, Mario Bunge advocates something similar,
which he calls "natural kinds," in The Furniture of the World (1977).

    Now, it could be argued that the number of general concepts needed
to describe the world is infinite, but it is hard to see what sort of

evidence (very indirect, as Bunge said to me in a letter) could support
this view, and, infinite or not, science does succeed in reducing all the
possible things to more manageable combinations of things. That the
things of the world are clustered and not chaotic does not seem to be just
an artifact of the human brain, though its limited size will mean a
failure to make all the distinctions and refinements necessary, which fact
we are reminded of every time science advances. Our brains, it might also
be claimed, have a bureaucrat's preference for ordering reality into a
hierarchy: In cosmology, it is planets, solar systems, galaxies, clusters
of galaxies, and so forth. But: There are arguments as to whether there
are superclusters of clusters of galaxies (pretty much accepted) and
super-duperclusters of superclusters (hotly debated). What is of extreme
importance here is that such arguments today do not proceed by a priori
reasoning but rather upon modern probability theory coupled with elaborate
catalogs of observed galaxies. (The Greeks knew of a galaxias kyklos,
"circle of milk," as early as the sixth century, B.C., but that this was a
galaxy of stars, our Milky Way, was not established until Sir William
Herschel mapped it with a telescope in 1785). [9]

Whatever reality is like, the individualism Unger describes asserts
that theory and fact are entirely separate. Those living in individualist
society make such a separation, Unger claims, because philosophy and life
are intertwined. If our psychology and politics accord with individualist
premises (i.e., reason and desire are separated as are rules and values),
our views of theory and fact will also come to share this same radical
separation. Unger may well be correct here, though we think the
correlation is not 100%, but what is missing is a good, solid materialist
explanation. (My reasons for adopting Bunge's materialist metaphysics,
i.e., its compatibility with science, will be discussed in the next
chapter.) It is not enough just to analogize one mode of separation with
another.

Let us hazard an explanation in the way the brain is divided, being
mindful that such an explanation is almost certainly only partly true but
nevertheless illustrates that human behavior need not be mysterious. We
begin by borrowing from Stuart J. Dimond's 1979 anthology chapter,
"Symmetry and Asymmetry in the Vertebrate Brain." Dimond observes that
animals tend to be symmetric along one of the two axes perpendicular to
their line of motion. This is true also of the brain, but there are
certain asymmetries, such as the heart being on one side, as well. In
vertebrates with two eyes, the brain integrates the information from both

eyes to form a three-dimensional picture. Dimond also argues that such
animals' brain halves duplicate functions to a large extent and he
observes that this excess capacity can be useful in case of accident.
What he does not show is that this excess capacity is worth its cost in
calories. In any case, there is a certain division of labor as well as
duplication. Among other things, the integration of information from the
eyes takes place on one side of the brain and not the other.

When we come to humans, we know from the work of Julian Jaynes (1976)
and others that the left hemisphere of the cortex (in right-handed
persons) is more concerned with fact and the right with patterns or
theories. According to Jaynes, modern schizophrenics and
pre-self-conscious men before the Greeks heard voices from the right side,
which were often felt to be messages from the gods. With the coming of
consciousness, men heard these voices less, but with a nostalgia remaining
for the good old days when men did not have to think. Thought requires
effort (free will!) to stimulate the feedback between the fact and theory
sides.

On this view, the bifurcation of the cerebral cortex is (perhaps) the
material basis for the bifurcation of our thoughts into theory and fact
and, correspondingly, the splits between reason and desire and rules and
values. Once one bifurcation gets going, so do the others, though we
hardly understand the details. Why did these splits really get
going--nay, get exaggerated--only after the Middle Ages? On the contrary,
if Jaynes is correct that consciousness means the integration of the
hemispheres, then these artificial (brain-artifactual) distinctions should
be eroding.

In fact, the bifurcations made in the post-medieval West are less
rigid than those made by earlier men with less integrated hemispheres. In
the Middle Ages, the overwhelming bifurcation was between God and man.
God was wholly transcendent, except for Jesus, and this was an important
exception. In "heretical" Christianity, that is, the losing side (losing
because it was too radically separatist for the emerging Western
mentality), Jesus was wholly God and nowhere material (Jesus only
pretended to suffer on the cross). Some of these Levantine throwbacks
went so far as to claim Jehovah was but the demiurge, or sub-god, who
created the foul material things of the Earth, while the true god sent his
son to redeem the chosen of mankind to participate in the wholly separate
realm of the spirit. (Pagels 1979)

Individualism represents a big step forward, a secularization of

transcendence in Unger's term (KP 161), though with lingering, even large, bifurcations still present. The Darwinian revolution, which is at bottom materialist and should do in the mind-body distinction, is still running its course. Even in our enlightened age we still have an America that is at least 80% Christian and more than enough spiritualists as well as mystics and irrationalists, even among physicists.

What is remarkable--and deserves careful neurological study, much of which will have to be speculative--is that Indo-European religions have always tended to be trinitarian rather than dualistic. (Dumézil 1959 and Littleton 1973) Furthermore, it is in the modern West that fiction (the novel) was added to truth and lies, the stranger to friend and enemy (Cuddihy 1976), not guilty to innocent and guilty (Scottish law), nonrational to rational and irrational (Pareto). As we shall see, Unger proposes his own thirds in between the bifurcations he discusses. Let us remark now that there is a basis in reality for some of the many bifurcations men have invented down through the ages. Some will collapse into unities (e.g., spiritual into material, mind into body, i.e., brain), and others will split into trinities and (more rarely) foursomes. So far, formal logic is two-valued, true vs. false.

2.5 Unger on the Separation of Reason and Desire in Individualism

Having covered Unger's first bifurcation, theory vs. fact, let us discuss the second. As we have seen, under individualist doctrine, the individual person is not seen as a (flawed) representative of an essentialist mankind but rather as a bundle of arbitrary desires. Reason, which is unitary for all men, stands utterly apart from these desires and is solely an instrument for their satisfaction. Thus Thomas Hobbes (1651): "The Thoughts, are to the Desires, as Scouts and Spies, to range abroad, and find the way to the things Desired," and David Hume (1739): "Reason is, and ought only to be the slave of the passions." Reason cannot tell a man what his desires ought to be. Man, says Unger, is an incurably moral animal, and individualist man will try to ground morals either upon the principle of desire or the principle of reason. According to the principle of desire, good is the satisfaction of wants. But the paradox is that, since desires are arbitrary, a morality based thereupon is blind and cannot choose among competing desires. Any such morality would collapse into subjective choices. A morality faithful to reason, on the other hand, appears more promising, for reason can determine the

necessary rules that enable men to live together in society. The problem
is that, as the commands and prohibitions of reason are made more
concrete, here too, judgments will have to be made among conflicting
goals; but this, says the doctrine of the subjectivity of values, reason
is powerless to do. A morality of reason is inert, while a morality of
desire is blind.

The upshot is that, too often, reason is confined to public life,
desire to private life. The bifurcation of reason and desire destroys a
unified self and shared commitment to universal ends that gives moral
significance to community life. "Schizophrenia brings to light the hidden
moral truth of the moral condition [individualist] psychology
describes." (KP 58) Cognitive incoherence, personal distrust, social
competitiveness, and natural disharmony all follow from this separation of
reason and desire.

Economists will see themselves here, for it is true that economic
theory is designed to be so general that wants could be completely
arbitrary. And we also see in the economist's use of Pareto optimality an
unwillingness to compare one man's utility with another's. It is further
true that reason is regarded by economists as purely instrumental, that
rational action is geared to the satisfaction of (arbitrarily) given ends.
But the economist also has his morality of reason, the non-coercion
principles of the market, which can be conditioned by public goods
arguments, but still within the bounds of Paretian criteria. Buchanan
does not advocate non-coercion in bilateral economic exchanges
(laissez-faire) but he does keep the non-coercion criterion in his
unanimity principle for a multilateral social contract.

2.6 Response to Unger

How apt are Unger's criticisms of individualist psychology and the
corresponding moralities of desire and reason? Strictly speaking, it can
be held that if one man wants to rob another, a morality of desire cannot
gainsay his wish. This does not carry the usually intended connotation,
however, which is that a man may satisfy his desires if he harms no one
else. This is not quite right either, for a businessman outcompeting
another is doing him harm, but this is regarded as permissible, part of
the rules of a fair game. Attempts may be made to restrict other
externalities, such as noise (often by redefining property rights), and
still others will be permitted, such as the right to publish ideas that go

against conventional dogma and upset the dogmatists, and perhaps also
nudity. (The issue of public nudity will have to be decided as long as
there is a government that occupies space large enough to fit in a human
being, and naked people can often be seen outside their own property.
Question: Could militant Puritans and militant nudists ever work out a
social contract?)

This only implies that lines of permitted and prohibited will
have to be drawn somewhat arbitrarily, and from some perspectives, very
arbitrarily. The use of a morality of reason, such as Kant's maxim of
universality, or the familiar dictum, "your freedom ends where my nose
begins," suffers from the problem that those "long chains of deductive
reasoning" Alfred Marshall grew to detest are not sufficient when it comes
to giving exact specifics. The best we can hope for is to learn from
experience what kinds of social arrangements help keep the social order
viable and progressive. It would be nice if there could be universal
agreement about the lessons of history, but, as I have argued, such
unanimity is only something to be approximated.

Concerning Unger's charge that individualism leads the individual to
an atomistic life, the terms are loaded. One could draw the choices the
other way: proud and sovereign independence vs. cowering and coerced
conformity. Let it simply be noted that a free society does not prohibit
cooperation, only the spurious cooperation that is not for mutual benefit.
It would not be fair, however, to set up Unger as an example of someone
who favors conformity for its own sake; rather he sees the doctrine of
individualism as leading to too much competition and too little
cooperation, certainly from his own standpoint and possibly from that of
the people concerned, if they could see themselves truly. Perhaps the
hypothetical wise and impartial contractors in the remote and future world
of New Contractarian Man could arrange a political constitution so that
the predicted outcome is an optimal blend of competition and cooperation,
but who is this Roberto Mangabeira Unger to have a ready-made answer in
the present? I maintain that it is presumptuous to tell apparently happy
people that they are miserable and would place the burden of proof
squarely upon such claimants. Nevertheless, there are plenty of people
who claim that they themselves are alienated (as well as claiming
alienation for others but rarely on any other basis than loose
observation). Buchanan himself sees the taxpayers as feeling remote from
a monstrous and bureaucratic government. (LL 91-92) This has come about,
Buchanan says, precisely because the government has usurped power.

Unger's charge can be phrased empirically, using Buchanan's contractarianism as a controlling ideal: Will cooperation, provided under a constitution, induce further efforts to increase it when new laws are contemplated or the constitution itself renegotiated? Contrariwise, will people living under a regime of rugged individualism be inclined to extend individualism further? Or will a balance be struck, a convergence to an equilibrium? And how far will this balance vary with time and peoples? Unfortunately, both Unger and Buchanan make only occasional noises about a federal structure of governments and societies, a topic which will absorb us in Chapter 6. Any optimum would be such a structure, one which, however, could not and should not be planned from the ground up, but one whose evolution could be (weakly) directed.

Freedom comes at a price, for some a very heavy price, since men living in a free society cannot easily get away with blaming their failures on others. Resentment just does not wash. On the other hand, one man or group's resentment is another's legitimate grievance. The grievers will claim the rules of the game, i.e., the social contract they did not sign, are stacked against them. Such claims, of course, can be hypocritical posturing and often call for redistribution of wealth and income instead of modification of the rules of the game. (LL 81) This is the usual procedure of egalitarians. On the other hand, libertarians and near libertarians will note the great amount of protectionist legislation, but will not try to get their group protected, instead urging deprotection of the protected, which will amount to calling for Buchanan's constitutional revolution. [10] Egalitarians want to increase radically the role of the state, and some go so far as wanting to abolish the family and even, if they only could, nonrandom mating in the population. It can be safely said that the chance of such drastic reforms achieving anything like unanimous consent is microscopic. Again, Unger may think he has found the truth, but his job remains to persuade the rest of us.

2.7 Unger on the Separation of Public Rules and Private Values

As we have seen, Unger draws a third application of the individualist split between universal and particular, finding one between public rules and private values in an individualist political order. Just as men are seen to be but the sum of their desires, societies are seen as but the sum of individuals and their peculiar values. Page one of The Limits of Liberty again: "We live together because social organization provides the

efficient means of advancing our individual objectives and not because
society offers us a means of arriving at some transcendental common
bliss." Precisely, and for this reason objective public rules are drawn
up so that men may live together. Unger: Individualism "defines order and
freedom as the master problem of politics." (KP 63) Oddly, Buchanan the
economist is greatly concerned with this problem too, odd for one of the
economist's great jobs is to show how individual freedom promotes a
spontaneous order and is therefore not in conflict with it. But Buchanan,
when he speaks of order and freedom, is referring to the "freedom" to rob
as well as the freedom to trade and make contracts, while many regard the
freedom to rob as a spurious one and not at all in keeping with
enlightened self-interest. This leads to the problem of defining the
location of the nose in "your freedom ends where my nose begins." We have
argued that probably every society will have laws against murder, and it
is not stretching plausibility to include robbery.

It might also be held that every society will pass laws against
exploitation. This is problematic: First, very few societies have
anything like a social contract, whose main job is to limit the greatest
exploiter of all, government, and no society has been very successful here
for any sustained period. Second, the definition of non-coercive
exploitation is either so broad that it includes almost every intelligent
use of opportunity or so personal that no consensus on its meaning can be
achieved. Third, we have an intuitive idea of exploitation as occurring
even under voluntary agreement for mutual benefit when one party almost
always gets the long end of the stick or rather most of the total gains
from trade. Such cases are very hard to prove and may very well result
from existing regulation or other rigidities rather than from a deficit of
government involvement in the economy. Fourth, if prices are free to
fluctuate, most of the effects of biases in the laws will be counteracted,
though deadweight welfare losses may remain.

Nevertheless, most (if not all) industrial nations have laws against
"exploitation," such as anti-monopoly, labor union, and workingman's
compensation laws. How far the exploited benefit from these laws in the
net (i.e., after prices and wages have adjusted) is a moot point, and
their prevalence is worth pondering. No state is wholly legitimate, there
being no actual unanimous social contract anywhere, but no state that lets
its members leave is wholly illegitimate either. It is therefore
problematic whether Buchanan's "conceptual contract" should be extended to
include such anti-exploitation laws. If the conceptual contractors all

had to be as steeped in the public choice literature of the past two decades as Buchanan himself, such legislation might very well not have been permitted under the constitution. This is asking entirely too much of the conceptual contractors--who knows how poor today's cutting edge in economic understanding will look several decades down the road!--and such things as exploitation are often far more subjective than objective anyhow. (In the final chapter, we shall examine the work of Raymond Cattell and consider how much knowledge of his field of social psychology our contractors might utilize.)

Under strict methodological individualism, all values are subjective, and Buchanan wishes his treatment of constitutionalism to be so broad and general as to allow for any possible social contract, so long as it be agreed upon unanimously. As we have seen, however, Buchanan himself winds up placing restrictions on full generality, and we have added others, which in our judgment are necessary if the constitutional order is to be viable. Here is the dilemma: If we can judge that certain anti-exploitation laws have passed the Buchanan litmus test (i.e., could have been passed under some conceptual contract), what is to prevent the state from invoking anti-exploitation each step along the path of the politics of resentment to Leviathan? On the other hand, could the state come to be viewed as a tool of the exploiters and thus illegitimate if it failed to pass anti-exploitation laws demanded by the voters, illiterate in economics though they be? The constitutional order may not be viable then, either. The spread of economic literacy will help resolve the dilemma, and our hidden assumption is that New Contractarian Man is versed in this discipline. Until this golden age arrives, the already existing understanding of the role of flexible prices in greatly nullifying exploitation can be used as a debating tactic to shift the burden of proof onto those who claim (non-government) exploitation is important.

For Buchanan, one of the great merits of individualism is precisely that of its generality, though we have argued that this generality must be tempered in the interest of a viable social contract. On the other hand, Unger sees this generality as implying that individualist politics is contentless, that no conclusions can be drawn from it about what the laws ought to be. As we have seen, Unger holds that, just as under individual- ist psychology a man is the sum of his particular desires (with reason being instrumental to the achievement of these desires and also as being universal over all men), under individualist politics, society is the sum of individual men (with universal rules being instrumental to the

achievement of particular values of individual men). Individualism thus
posits an extreme dichotomy between general public rules and particular
private desires. The political order, then, must be made up of rules that
are neutral with respect to individuals. Unger's claim is that this is
not possible, that laws will unavoidably benefit "the purposes of some
individuals more than those of their fellows." (KP 66-67) More generally,
not even just enforcement of the laws is possible, for once a judge goes
beyond the strict letter of the law to its purpose, as he surely on
occasion will, he becomes capricious or else starts imposing his own view
of the good society in his decisions, and this means that he ceases to be
neutral about the merits of particular men's values. The ultimate upshot
of individualist politics is that we nevertheless pretend to an
unbreachable split between public and private and this destroys a feeling
of unity in the individual.

2.8 Response to Unger

To respond to Unger's criticisms, let us begin with the last and
state that it is an awfully good thing that public and private are
separate. The alternatives are that everything be private or that
everything be public. An entirely private society would consist of not
more than one person making choices. If two or more did, disagreements
would arise and be up for adjudication. If judgments were always rendered
in one person's favor, we would be back in a world of only one person
exercising choices. Therefore the judge must be, to some extent, neutral
or what might as well be called a public figure. The other alternative,
that everything be public, is hardly a way to chain Leviathan, a problem
Unger rarely worries about. It may very well be true that the law cannot
be absolutely impartial, but Unger offers only leftist sentimentality in
evidence that modern individualism makes too much of a fetish of the
separation of public and private. If anything, and given the nearly
absolute truth that power tends to accumulate, the tendency that any
blurring of public and private will be exploited is ever present.
     More to the point as telling against Unger's criticisms of
individualism generally is his own admission: "There is no one thinker who
accepts the [individualist] theory, in the form in which I present it, as
a whole, or whose doctrines are completely defined by its tenets." (KP 8)
In other words, reality puts a brake upon an ever present tendency to
reify, more so in the scientific age (so we have argued) than in the past.

Moreover, Unger's three divisions of universal and particular (theory and
fact, reason and desire, rules and values) have a great measure of truth
in reality. Furthermore, as evolution proceeds, the harmony between
reality and our world views grows, although there have been awakenings of
interest in the "Wisdom of the East," apparently more than once a
generation since at least the Age of Discovery began in 1492. The
neurological explanation is simple: Thinking takes work! There has been
a spate of books in the last decade declaring that subatomic particle
physicists have just been rediscovering what the East knew a long time
ago, to wit, reality is an ineffably, interconnected One, conveniently
forgetting that Newton's law of gravitation had things connected up over
three centuries ago, and, as Lawrence R. Brown states in The Might of the
West (1963), only Westerners conceived that the same laws could apply to
terrestrial and celestial things alike.

Unger would be quite correct to say that our (roughly) quart-sized
brains do not describe reality very well, individualism being just the
latest example. One wonders about Australopithecines' pint-sized
ideologies, but even Buchanan's three-pint contractarianism has problems
if carried out literally. Such criticisms are often far from useless,
but the critic is at his most useful best when he hints at things to
come. Unger does so, and let us examine his suggestions.

2.9 Unger's Evolutionism

"Man cannot yet be fully known, because, in a sense, he does not yet
fully exist," says Unger. (KP 234) Ordinarily, we get a more or less
firm handle on what we are trying to describe, because the thing we are
describing obligingly stays put. Our concepts evolve because we and our
theories evolve, not the things out there. When we come to defining
human nature, however, both we, the theoreticians, and we, the objects of
our theories, change, and it is no easy matter to say which "we" changes
the faster. Lenin's New Socialist Man did not arrive on schedule, and
Brennan and Buchanan, in "Is Public Choice Immoral?" (1982), expressed a
real fear that the sportsman cum cynic of The Calculus of Consent might
arrive well before New Contractarian Man, who would bring about the
necessary constitutional reforms to chain down this amoral cynic.

If man cannot be fully known, we will have to define human nature as
something evolving, which Unger does. He then proceeds to define the good
as that which hurries this evolution on. This definition is dangerously

circular, for how can one recognize whether change is actually evolution
unless one has an idea of the good to check the change against in the
first place? If one does not fall into this trap, there is another: We
conclude, rightly or wrongly, that human evolution, as represented by man
at his best (a third trap), is headed in a specific direction. The trap
is arbitrarily to approve of this direction or to equate the good with the
inevitable (if one sees these changes as inevitable, which Unger, by the
way, does not).

I may have fallen into this trap myself, when speaking of the
evolution toward New Contractarian Man. Recall that majoritarian
democracy was once (and by many still is) regarded as the ideal of
responsive government; what we got was rampant pressure groupism, a
decidedly negative sum game with mostly losers and precious few (net)
winners. A similar impasse may be reached with New Contractarian Man, and
it is just as lame to blame the failings of contractarianism on the
populace as it is to blame the failures of communism on the failures of
empirical man to become New Socialist Man. There is a point to both
excuses, but not a very large one. One should never become so enamored of
one's pet theory as to push it out of harm's way into the zone of the
non-falsifiable.

Unger has an idea, rather vague, of what the future of human
evolution will bring, and he couches it in terms of a harmonization,
though not a full resolution, of the radical splits of universal and
particular he sees in the individualist world view. Under individualism,
"Man stands before nature and society as the grand manipulator." (KP 153)
Unger would replace this separation with an ideal of a natural harmony
between the two and sees such a harmony already existing in love, art,
religion, and work, with the last being (ideally) a harmonious blending of
a self and the things found in nature rather than a mere domination over
them. Second, rather than individual ends being arbitrarily diverse,
Unger envisions an ideal of sympathy and a sharing of ends, or individuals
complementing rather than competing with each other. (See the section of
Chapter 6, "The Self of Self-Interest.") His third ideal, that of
concrete universality, will be approached when people see themselves as
specific instances of human nature and as helping that nature evolve (just
as each paper in Public Choice helps direct what the discipline of public
choice is and is becoming).

These ideals of harmony seem hardly objectionable when the alternative
is extreme belligerency. In fact, we are partly along this road, even

under the rule of individualism. We do, partly, live in harmony with
nature ("Nature to be commanded must be obeyed"), and, learning some of
the laws of nature and society, we are backing off from the extreme
enthusiasm for social planning that was embraced before it got put into
practice. (But some will never learn.) We do share some ends, else civil
society would nowhere exist, not even one ruled by Hobbes's omnipotent
sovereign. And most of us, whether Christians or Darwinians, see
ourselves as part of an ongoing process.

The question is, when does this evolution stop? Unger himself says
these ideas are never to be fully realized in history. If so, what is the
optimum, and is it not close to what would come about under individualism,
under "the Enlightenment dream of free relations among free men," (LL,
closing page) or under Buchanan's contractarian ideal? Unger is richly
unclear here but he obviously thinks there is much room for improvement,
as he holds that human nature will not become fully expressed so long as
some men dominate others. So what is domination? Unger is not at all
helpful when he says, "Domination is defined simply as unjustified power"
(KP 167), but he gives a hint when he derides "domination" resulting from
genetic advantage: "The lucky ones can then cash in on the favors of
nature like prostitutes whose price depends on whether they are fat or
thin." (KP 173) [11]

Unger gives another hint of what the elimination of domination might
be (KP 183):

> One can imagine a condition under which the distribution of
> power within the bureaucracy would not involve personal dependence
> and domination. It might be called the condition of democracy. The
> exercise of power based on merit must be subordinated to the
> democratically established common purposes of those working in the
> institution. For this subordination to be effective, a number of
> requirements have to be satisfied. The chief of these is the
> availability of an independent mechanism through which all members
> of the institution participate equally in the formulation of common
> ends [other than profitability, one presumes!]. An ever broader
> scope is given to these common ends in determining the aims and the
> internal structure of the institution. For the purposes of
> participation, the distribution of talents is disregarded.

This fits in with Unger's ideals of sympathy. But: Unger professes

not to wipe out individuality altogether; indeed, individuality is all the
more brought out when individuals complement each other rather than
coexist in a state of mutual antagonism barely contained by the police.

The question now boils down to which ends people will come to share,
presuming Unger wishes this sharing to be genuine and not forced.
Buchanan, the orthodox economist, may not have an answer here, for
economists have blown up the word taste, a common word in their lexicon
which no longer refers to idyosyncratic expressions of individuality, into
an all-purpose term for preference, including a "taste" for committing
murder and mayhem. But Buchanan, the constitutionalist, does have an
answer: The shared ends are whatever are agreed upon in the signing of
the social contract.

Unger can reply, of course, that the social contract is a fiction,
but so are Unger's own ideals. To be fair, we must either push them both
out to their limits or hold both to the realm of common sense. If the
ends to be shared are not to be forced, we are squarely in Buchanan's
world of unanimity. Unger speaks darkly of "the implacable stratagems by
which one mind becomes the master of another," and warns that "the
classical arguments in favor of slavery show that even the harshest forms
of oppression may appear justified." (KP 244) Buchanan would not entirely
reject this argument, for he deals with the question of people treating
the social contract itself as a public good and therefore making
insufficient investigation before submitting to its terms. (LL 145) We
may feign, if we wish, that this will not be a problem for New
Contractarian Man or that, if it is, any initial unfairness will have
largely been eroded within a few generations, but we could also feign
something similar as we approach Unger's ideal world.

Unger approacheth Buchanan, in so far as both see human nature
evolving, but is the converse true? Buchanan is emphatically not an
egalitarian in the usual sense of being willing to impose an external
norm. A social contract may look quite lopsided to someone outside, but
for Buchanan the fact of agreement alone is what counts. But in another
sense, Buchanan is just as much an egalitarian as Unger is, i.e.,
perfectly. Unger, from the third paragraph above: "For the purposes of
participation, the distribution of talents is disregarded." Now Buchanan
on page two [12] of The Limits of Liberty: "Each man counts for one, and
that is that."

Thus Buchanan approacheth Unger with respect to the fundamental
equality of men (even if not exactly in the same senses), if only Buchanan

could be sure Unger would adopt the placing of ends to be shared in and
only in the social contract itself. But there is another sense in which
Buchanan approaches Unger's egalitarianism: the historical. Now, <u>Limits</u>
is not very obviously a historical book. There are fleeting references to
history, but Buchanan's treatment is mostly abstract. It can be
considered downright provincial, concentrating not merely on modern
Westerners but quietly assuming that most people are sharp enough to get
tenure in a university economics department. (Unger's men are near
geniuses, too. It is a common presumption.) Unger's treatment, while
also very abstract, is more oriented to history: He speaks of the idea of
intelligible essences held by ancient and medieval philosophers, the
individualism held in the modern age, and the philosophy to come in the
next age. Nevertheless, the two authors may be joined, for one of the
broad changes in history (of man at his best!) is that of increasing
participation in the affairs of government. Majority rule may not be
unanimity, but neither is it monarchy or aristocracy, and Buchanan is no
more a champion of the latter two than Unger. As unanimity has been
approached historically, the progressively less powerful have come into
the polity and have made it more egalitarian, in the sense of more
universal: "Each man counts for one, and that is that" used to be <u>some</u>
men count as one. Indeed, one kind of domination or power, the only kind
for Buchanan, is that of operating the political machinery without the
consent of the less powerful. But if the formerly powerless (i.e., the
excluded) can then run the political machinery so as to take power from
the incumbents, then the incumbents are the dominated. Unger may try to
play Robin Hood but not when pretending to reduce domination at the same
time.

 Through this thicket of tortured reasoning, then, do Buchanan and
Unger approach each other, in the sense that both want participation by
all. To the extent either has come to his abstract theories as a way of
grounding previously held values, and to the extent either finds our
reasoning dubious, he will not see any such convergence. But perhaps the
road to convergence is rendered a bit more easy, considering that both
Buchanan and Unger have remarkably little to say when it comes down to
specifics. For Buchanan, this silence is wholly deliberate, and it is the
present writer who has had to make recommendation <u>for</u> Buchanan, with the
aim of achieving some minimal level of viability in the social contract.
Unger's approach is very much different. He does reject the ancient and
medieval notion of objective values, but his depiction of the good as

reducing domination, and thus letting human nature express itself more
fully, has an insistence about it not entirely unlike the insistence made
by those who think they have truly found objective values. Unger
describes the method for muddling through as "practical reason," and he
confesses: "I have no worked-out account of [practical reason] to offer,
not because I believe such an account impossible or unimportant, but
simply because I have not found one." (KP 258) This is hardly a statement
Buchanan would make.

We have added content to Buchanan, to ensure that we will in fact get
out of anarchy in the first place. We now need to add content to Unger,
for the opposite reason of chaining Leviathan. This is a problem Unger
(and, as we shall see in the final chapter, Cattell) scarcely recognizes,
though Leviathan is on the march almost everywhere. How can Unger see to
it that the government is restricted to do just what he wants it to do?
In our country what began as efforts to redistribute income from the rich
to the poor (or from the productive to the unproductive) has ended up
today with very little of this kind of redistributive activity taking
place, in comparison with redistribution to members of organized pressure
groups whose sole merit consists in being organized. (Tullock 1983)
Moreover, what net redistribution by income class does take place is
managed with incredible waste. And whatever unjust power was held in the
bad old days of monarchy and aristocracy has been replaced with the far
larger power of Leviathan. Lastly, if Unger had his way, envy would
become the master principle of politics, despite any wishes on his part to
have only the grievances he himself thinks are legitimate given a voice in
politics.

2.10 Conclusion

Is Unger a collectivist? The hope was to pit a collectivist against
Buchanan the individualist. This would have helped us understand both
better. Now Buchanan is an individualist very strongly, but is he not a
little bit of a collectivist, too? The first page of The Limits of
Liberty denies the existence of a "transcendental common bliss," but the
last page invokes "the Enlightenment dream of free relations among free
men." But we are out of luck if we hoped to find in Unger a collectivist
anywhere so pure as Buchanan is an individualist. The reason is that,
ever since The Wealth of Nations was published in 1776, explanations as to
how order emerges upward from the interactions of individuals have had a

place in our thinking and no longer do individuals dwell in an inferior, mundane realm of sub-reality, above which hovers the true reality of collective Platonic essences. This was a mystical notion all along, but when economics became a science, or at least began to become one, mysticism lost out in the competition to explain things. It is no doubt true that the first observers of the operations of exchange markets regarded them as a mystery. Now we understand how markets work, though not as well as we would like. And what we do not understand we give a name, transforming ignorance into mystery and paying our respects towards it. The newly named mystery is as often as not something collective, and the market itself was once turned into a mystery for the present writer when he was urged to overcome certain doubts by "putting faith in the market"!

The great danger to liberty is not from collectivists (who are hard to find) but from muddled metaphysics. It takes clear thinking as well as eternal vigilance to keep Leviathan at bay. Unger's unclear vision of the future will be no more successful at maintaining liberty than the great Canute was at stopping the tide. Extreme individualism, as I have argued, is not the answer, and it is useless to answer leftists' insistence on objective values (to which they alone possess the key) by denying them entirely. I shall argue, when discussing Hayek in Chapter 4, that the notion of social justice, which some consider to be entirely objective, should be reconstrued so that the only just societies are those with the (ideally unanimous) consent of the governed. And in the final chapter, I shall argue that certain values and/or laws take on the character of objectivity to the extent that they turn out, in fact, to be required for the maintenance of the social, what Cattell calls maintenance values as opposed to experimental values. The test, however, should remain agreement, with what are persuasive arguments and not just authority.

Collectivists, then, are not so much those who hold to a Platonic metaphysics about Society, but rather those whose policies would lead to Leviathan. The best way to put them on the run is to demand empirical evidence and clarification of their background assumptions, not to try to make them vanish by an a priori ruling out of court of the issue of objectivity altogether or by some sort of semantic trickery. The point is to root everyone's values out, no matter their persuasion, question the bases for the values (which so often are just personal whims), and try to see which are true (or true for some men at some time). But we need a language to discuss these issues and hence first a long discussion of the ontology of Mario Bunge.

CHAPTER 3

MARIO AUGUSTO BUNGE AND SCIENTIFIC METAPHYSICS

3.1 The Aim of Bunge's Philosophy

Metaphysics became an exact science in 1977, the year of publication
of Mario Bunge's The Furniture of the World. Bunge, of German descent and
born in Argentina in 1919, began his career as a physicist. He brought
with him to philosophy the perspective of a practicing scientist (much as
Buchanan came into political philosophy as an economist), and his chief
goal is to develop a philosophy that is compatible both with the current
body of science and with the ways scientists go about their work. While
philosophers continue to debate the existence of external reality and the
possibility of human knowledge, scientists proceed to learn about that
reality.

The honors for the idea of developing a philosophy consistent with
science go to the great Charles Peirce and his program for a "scientific
metaphysics" (the title of the sixth volume of his posthumously collected
works), but the sciences were nowhere as advanced then as they are today.
Even more decisively, the language of mathematics, set theory, and
symbolic logic did not yet allow for the kind of precision needed to do
the task. Bunge's work represents the first carrying out of Peirce's
vision, and this first effort should never be construed as claiming to be
the last effort or the final word on any of its subjects.

Mario Bunge's magnum opus is his Treatise on Basic Philosophy,
published by D. Reidel in Dordrecht, Holland. Seven of its eight volumes
had appeared by 1988. To place the ontology volumes, which are the ones
most important to the present discussion, in the context of his work, as
well as to beat a drum for them by way of advertisement, the volumes run
as follows:

Volumes 1 and 2
(Semantics I and II)

Sense and Reference (1974, 180 pp.)
Interpretation and Truth (1974, 210 pp.)

Volumes 3 and 4

(Ontology I and II)

The Furniture of the World (1977, 352 pp.)

A World of Systems (1979, 314 pp.)

Volumes 5, 6, and 7

(Epistemology and Methodology I, II, and III)

Exploring the World (1983, 404 pp.)

Understanding the World (1983, 296 pp.)

Philosophy of Science and Technology (1985)

       Part 1: Formal and Physical Science, 263 pp.

       Part 2: Life Science, Social Science and Technology, 341 pp.

Volume 8

(Ethics)

The Good and the Right (too long in forthcoming!)

    Bunge conceives of ontology (or metaphysics) as the most general of
the sciences and of particular sciences as special ontologies. While
Peirce coined the term "scientific metaphysics," Bunge was the first to
build a system describing the way reality is structured in a manner fully
informed by contemporary science. Doing so will bring philosophy up to
date with the separate sciences and put the latter on firmer foundations.
As such, the general science of ontology is no more completed and
infallible than any of the particular sciences: "It is hoped that this
system will not be ridiculously at variance with reason and experience."
(FW xiii)

    Bunge's system is exact in the sense that much of it is expressed in
the symbols and terminology of modern logic and mathematics. While none
of his proofs of theorems are particularly difficult in themselves, his
Treatise will be inaccessible to those without the mathematical
prerequisites. Plato's Academy allegedly bore a sign over the entrance
forbidding those ignorant of geometry to enter; Bunge's academy would
replace geometry with topology. Bunge's works have a rigor and exactness
that engender an aesthetic pleasure and a sense of rightness that is
paralleled in the great masterpieces of classical music. His works are
free of (substantial) mathematical errors that bulk irksomely in the

writings of other philosophers, who belong to what C.P. Snow called the
First (i.e., "humanistic") Culture. It is hard however, to convey the
pleasure of reading Bunge, much as no book devoted to Beethoven's string
quartets could substitute for hearing them. Instead, I shall sneak past
the sign about topology and try to sketch his central arguments in
nontechnical language and offer justifications for them.

Bunge argues that all thinkers with any pretense to being scientific
and exact have at least an implicit metaphysics or a broad background view
of the objects of their study. His purpose is to bring out these implicit
views, clarify them, and try to improve them. It is certainly the case in
economics that the background assumptions are hidden, for economists
rarely define, for example, what choice is or argue against determinism.
From one of Buchanan's essays (1969b): "In a wholly determinist universe,
choice is purely illusory, as is discussion about choice. I do not treat
this age-old issue, and I prefer to think that the subject discussed as
well as the discussion itself is not illusory." As we shall see, Bunge
will define and defend the reality of choice and free will, resolving it
to the satisfaction of economists perhaps, though not necessarily of
all philosophers.

In The Limits of Liberty, it seems that Buchanan holds the view that
society is the sum of its individuals, but he does not treat the matter at
length. That he is not altogether satisfied with extreme methodological
individualism is clear enough, but his fear seems to be for the opposite
of extreme collectivism. Those he calls positivists, who equate values
with whatever the powers that be propound these values to be (LL 51), are
bad enough, let alone outright collectivist mystics like Hegel, whom
Buchanan does not even bother to dismiss. As we shall see, Bunge's notion
of a system, and in particular of a social system, is a way out of extreme
individualism that does not embrace collectivism.

Regarding the scientific status of his own system, Bunge states that
"there will never be any metaphysical laboratories" and that "metaphysics .
can be checked solely by its coherence with science." (FW 15-16) So while
his metaphysics is not directly an experimental science, it is designed to
be compatible with all the ones that are experimental. It is this
feature, plus its revisability, that qualifies (so far only Bunge's)
ontology as a science. Though economics is not as full-fledged a science
as physics, Buchanan also argued that compatibility with other branches of
science is a virtue in one of his most inspired and inspiring essays,
"Economics and its Scientific Neighbors" (1966). I shall adopt Bunge's

metaphysics, then, but as always with all sciences, until further notice.
My aim here is not nearly so much to defend Bunge against all comers as to
exploit Bunge's <u>results</u> for the purpose of developing a metaphysics of
liberty and discussing its implications for the problems of social
justice, natural rights, and federalism (Chapters 4-6).

3.2 Bunge's Furniture

<u>The Furniture of the World</u>, the first of Bunge's two volumes on
ontology, reads like a mathematical theory of the building blocks of the
universe, complete with definitions, postulates, theorems, proofs, all
intermixed with remarks about what is going on, traps to be avoided, hints
to help one understand, and discussions of the virtues and drawbacks of
earlier philosophers along the way. Much of this first volume will not be
of direct concern to the issue of liberty, and mostly I shall sketch the
development of his ideas in summary form.

Chapter 1 of <u>Furniture</u>, "Substance," lays down in precise language
the notion of bare existents (also called substantial individuals), as yet
to be decked out with any attributes. Bunge elucidates how one object is
part of another, how two things may be placed side to side, and how they
might be mixed. He also discusses how an object may be (conceptually)
decomposed to certain levels: a social system to people, at the living
level, and to all the atoms of the people at the atomic level. This
concept of level will come into play throughout, but the first chapter is
mainly of technical and aesthetic value (substantially so) rather than of
value for the prime concerns here.

"Form" is the title of Chapter 2 and fleshes out bare existents with
properties. Here Bunge takes pains to distinguish the properties of
substantial individuals, composite or not, taken singly or multiply, from
our statements about them. Properties are always properties of something:
"There is no substantial property apart from entities, let alone prior to
them and dwelling in a separate Realm of Forms." (FW 64) We can make
negative statements <u>about</u> properties, but the properties themselves are
always positive. Thus, the statement that neutrons are electrically
charged happens to be false, but this does not mean that neutrons have the
property of not-being-charged, let alone of being anti-charged. Some
properties are frame-dependent (as in relativity theory), and some are
even observer-dependent, but only in psychology and definitely not in the
most general science, ontology. "A scientific metaphysics must be just as

objectivisitic as science itself, i.e. thoroughly." (FW 67)

Bunge postulates the existence of only a finite number of very general properties (like mass and charge) but an (uncountably) infinite number of particular properties of special cases (e.g., properties of a specific atom at a specific time, there being a continuum of instants of time). This is a critical assumption, and here is his justification (FW 72-73):

> It seems reasonable (and comforting) to assume that the set of substantial properties in general, though extremely numerous, is finite. Thus one thinks of an animal as having different weights, metabolic rates, and ages at different times; yet all these are just different values of only three general properties--weight, metabolic rate, and age at different times and relative to different frames. In any case we stick out our necks and assume:

> Postulate 2.3 The set of general substantial properties is finite, and that of substantial [particular] properties...is non-denumerable.

There are certainly more than three ways to characterize an animal, and Bunge is postulating that the number of ways is limited, although perhaps in the billions. The number could be infinite, though it is hard to conceive how, except mathematically, for it would be impossible to classify things in a finite amount of time. We do so classify, and the hope is that we do not always leave important characteristics out.

Compare now Unger's second statement of the doctrine of intelligible essences: "The theory of intelligible essences states there are a limited number of classes of things in the world, that each thing has characteristics that determine the class to which it belongs, and that these characteristics can be known directly by the mind." (KP 79) In Bunge's view, much of our knowledge is indirect, mediated by scientific theories, rather than being directly perceptible, and so his notion is not quite the same as that held by ancient and medieval philosophers. Bunge's definition of a natural kind, to be discussed shortly, is also connected to the idea that there are only a finite number of general properties. Bunge defines the scope of a property as the set of individuals for which the property holds and postulates a principle of lawfulness, which states that the scope of any property either contains or is contained in the

scope of some other property. In other words, there are no stray
properties unrelated to everything else in the universe.

Bunge then gives the important definition of an emergent property as
one that is true of the whole but of none of its parts. Equilibrium is an
excellent example of an emergent property economists are familiar with.
Bunge postulates that all composite things have some emergent properties
but that these properties are epistemologically analyzable with reference
to the parts. This latter contradicts holism and its discussion of wholes
apart from their parts. Bunge allows for the explanation of ontological
novelty and warns that "a mountain is not explained away when explained as
composed of atoms." (FW 98)

In other words, epistemological reductionism, si; ontological
reductionism, no. It is the lawfulness of the world, of things being and
becoming and of processes, that makes epistemological reduction possible,
at least in many cases. (Bunge does not claim that we will someday
understand everything.) Later Bunge will view the world as made up of
layers--physical, chemical, biological, and social--and protest the
"ontological bulldozing of reality" to a single level.

Stated in such a summary fashion as we have done, it may seem that
Bunge's development of his system is arbitrary, full of unnecessary
technicalities, and bound to do nothing but add to the bulk of pointless
argumentation that is philosophy. Philosophy hitherto has never been
conclusive, as the quote from Mencken at the beginning made clear, but
Bunge's program is to make philosophy consistent with science, and this is
perhaps the only way any consensus can be reached. Consensus may never
become unanimous, however: "We cannot prove the existence of concrete
things any more than we can prove the existence of deities or of
disembodied minds. What can be proved is that, unless there were things,
other items--such as acting on them and investigating them--would be
impossible." (FW 112) Bunge frequently intersplices the formal
mathematical exposition of his system with discussions of previously
advanced solutions, what is objectionable (in part) about them, and how
they might be modified so as better to conform with science and the way
scientists operate. He is uniquely qualified for this task, for he was a
practicing scientist (physics), and his Foundations of Physics (1967b) is
still the only book to lay down the implicit background assumptions of
physicists in an exact way. Bunge has also written extensively on the
philosophy of science, and his Treatise might be viewed as an extension of
Foundations of Physics.

Chapter 3 of The Furniture of the World is entitled "Thing," which is defined as an individual (simple or composite) together with all its properties, known or unknown. Bunge distinguishes real things from our concepts and ideas of them: "The failure to distinguish the thing represented from its model is not just a form of mental derangement: it is also at the root of black magic and subjectivism." (FW 121) Part of modeling something is to characterize the states it can be in from one of many alternative viewpoints. Scientific laws restrict the possible states a thing can be in.

Several definitions: A class of things is not an arbitrary set of things but a set that is the scope of some property. (Recall that the number of properties is finite.) Several properties taken conjointly (e.g., human = rational and animal) determine a kind, and a set of properties, each of which is also a law, determines a natural kind. All of this, however, is just a framework: "We shall not list the kinds of constituents of the world but shall leave that task to the special sciences. For no sooner does the metaphysician pronounce the world to be 'made of' such and such kinds, than the scientist discovers that some of the alleged species are empty or that others are missing from the metaphysician's list." (FW 153)

"Possibility" is the title of Chapter 4 of Furniture. Bunge conceives of reality as the union of the actual with the really possible. A conceptual possibility could be any characterization (what Bunge calls a state function) of some thing, but real possibility must also conform with scientific laws. What actually happens depends on possibility and also upon circumstances. Laws plus circumstances may force a unique fact or they may not. Bunge's world is not a rigidly deterministic one and he allows for chance propensities. Looking at it mathematically, each law divides all conceptual possibilities into two subsets: the possible and the impossible. All the laws (known and unknown) taken conjointly reduce the domain of the possible to the intersection of a number of subsets. Rigid determinism would assert that this intersection has one and only one member: that there is but a unique outcome. However, there is no a priori reason to suppose this in advance, and so Bunge leaves open real possibility. The ideas in this chapter will become useful when discussing choice and free will later.

Chapter 5 is called "Change," and it is a thing of beauty to behold the way Bunge can define change without introducing time. This chapter paves the way for the final one of The Furniture of the World,

"Spacetime," and he is able to conceive of time with sufficient
abstraction as to be compatible with relativity theory. These last two
chapters are bound to be controversial among both philosophers and
physicists--or if we agree with him, he sets things right at last. Of
interest here is Bunge's simple and elegant definition of causality: One
event in a given thing causes a (later) event in some other thing if the
difference the first thing has on the (otherwise free) trajectory of the
second thing includes the later event. But there is no necessity in
postulating that every event has a prior cause, as this would arbitrarily
rule out spontaneity or self-causation, and thus free will.

3.3 Bunge's Systemism

    The second of Bunge's two ontology volumes, A World of Systems
(1979), is of more immediate concern here. While Furniture gives the
basic structure, vocabulary, and postulates, the companion volume applies
the basic notions to the actual world, albeit in a very general fashion.
Bunge begins with a description of systems in general, treats chemistry,
life, mind (brain), and society in specific, and wraps up the book with a
discussion of the systemic world view. Much of the book is not relevant
here, even while it does present nice resumes of several scientific
disciplines and supplies clarifications and exactifications of their basic
concepts.
    Chapter 1 of A World of Systems is called "System" and begins with
noting that all the sciences study systems of one sort or another. There
is even a field called "general systems theory," which purports to study
features in common to all systems, the principle of least effort being a
good and familiar example. Systems theory and ontology have a great deal
in common, both being very general disciplines, but the two differ in that
ontologists do not take for granted such notions as possibility, change,
and time, which systems theorists do. The latter tend to focus on
input-output models that are largely at the mercy of their environment
while ontologists can also study free systems. And ontologists study
stochastic systems as well.
    Bunge distinguishes conceptual (e.g., mathematical) systems from
concrete (material) systems and further distinguishes an aggregate (or
random heap) from a system (SW 4):

        Because the components of an aggregate do not interact--or

do not interact appreciably--the behavior of each is independent of
the behavior of the others. Consequently the history of the
aggregate is the union of the histories of its members. On the
other hand the components of a concrete system are linked, whence
the history of the whole differs from the union of the histories of
its parts. We shall take the last to be an accurate version of the
fuzzy slogan of holistic metaphysics, namely The whole is greater
than the sum of its parts. But we shall go far beyond this
characterization of wholeness or systemicity.

Concrete systems are made up of at least two different connected
things and are described by a triple consisting of the system's
composition (the list of its parts), its environment (the list of all
other things that act upon or are acted upon by the parts of the given
system), and its structure (the set of relations among the system's parts
and among them and the things in the environment). Bunge postulates that
all systems (not just living ones) are subjected to selection by the
environment. Systems can be made up of subsystems, but the more stable
the subsystems, the less stable the system itself.

The general discussion of systems is wrapped up with a discussion of
how the author differs from holists, at one end, and from the atomists, at
the other, while recognizing the partial merits of both. Holism is overly
vague when not downright mystical. Bunge characterizes some of the
doctrines of the holists, one of which follows (WS 40):

Wholes emerge under the action of agents that transcend
both the actions among the components and the environmental
influences. For example, morphogenesis is guided by an entelechy,
or elan vital, or morphogenetic field external to its components.
In sum, the formation of totalities transcends their components and
is traceable to inscrutable entities. Thus far the holistic
account of the formation of wholes. Needless to say, science has
no use for such secret hence incontrollable principles of
organization. Instead, science acts on a principle of immanence,
not transcendence, namely this: Only the components, the way they
come together, and the environment determine what kind of thing a
totality shall be. (Hence our representing a system by the ordered
triple: composition-environment-structure.)

Atomism, by contrast, ignores wholes altogether, or rather engages in ontological reductionism, which is the doing away with emergent properties. Our job is to explain, as best we can, these emergent properties, not to explain them away. Bunge is a moderate epistemological reductionist: Some such explanations are forthcoming, but not necessarily guaranteed. Bunge's position in a nutshell: "The world is material but not just a lump of physical entities: it is composed of systems of a number of qualitatively different kinds." (WS 44)

"Chemism," the title of the second chapter, is the first of four to deal with the special sciences going up the levels of reality. Not many things here concern us, but it is worth noting that a body of water has properties (such as a boiling point) that individual H_2O molecules do not have and that a water molecule is a system, differing from one oxygen and two hydrogen atoms separately. It may be interesting to know that we can now predict the boiling points of (bodies of) small chemical compounds on the basis of the physical structures of the atoms making them up, not very accurately yet, but within a factor of two or so, measured in absolute degrees Kelvin. So far, there is no deep theory to base the predictions on, just a growing body of experiments and measurements. Science often begins with some odd data (and how odd it is that hydrogen and oxygen are both gases with very low boiling points, while water boils at 373° K.) that eventually fall into some sort of pattern. Theories may eventually be advanced to explain the patterns and then be tested on new compounds. Depending on how successful the theories are, epistemological reductionism will have been achieved, but not ontological. [13]

Bunge gives us a warning (WS 48):

In ontology we take such [chemical] bonds for granted and let chemists inquire into their nature. (Remember the fate of Hegel's alleged refutation of Berzelius' brilliant hypothesis that chemical bonds are electrical.) The metaphysician accepts gratefully what the chemist is willing to teach him about the spontaneous formation (self-assembly) of molecules out of atoms, or of other molecules, as well as about the breakdown or dissociation of such systems as a result of their interaction with the environment (in particular thermal motion). The philosopher's task is not to compete with the chemist but to try and discover the structure and peculiarities of chemical properties of chemical processes vis a vis other kinds of

process. If in the course of his work he comes up with results
helping to clarify the foundations of chemistry, so much the
better.

One more point of considerable interest is a simple remark: "But of
course not all conceivable [chemical] compounds are really possible, i.e.
lawful." (WS 49) Bunge limits the diversity of things (recall Unger's
intelligible essences) in two ways, by admitting of only finitely many
general properties and by distinguishing conceivable from lawful things.
He notes that "there are about 4 million known species of chemicals" (WS
48), a huge number, to be sure, but still finite if not manageable.
Presumably, even the ones chemists do not know about would still be finite
in number: Well before a molecule got to be as big as the Sun, it would
collapse.

Chapter 3 of A World of Systems, "Life," gets us closer to our
concerns with economics and the foundation of a state that provides
collective economic goods. Bunge states his approach well toward the end
of the chapter: "Biosystemism recognizes the bios as an emergent level
rooted to the chemical one." (WS 119) He details the origins of life,
built up subsystem by subsystem, and remarks (WS 77):

> Nowadays we know that chemical and biochemical systems cannot
> help but self-assemble under the actions of bonds of various kinds.
> Moreover we know that such self-assembly processes are more likely
> to occur in stages than at one stroke. In particular, the formation
> of primitive proteins may have proceeded in two stages: amino acid
> synthesis followed by polymerization. Therefore the first
> biochemical systems, and even the first organisms, may have formed
> on our planet and elsewhere as soon as the requisite conditions were
> met. This explains the short time span between the origin of rocks
> and the appearance of the first bacteria and blue-green algae.

Bunge goes on to draw some careful definitions and make numerous
distinctions (WS 83):

> Definition 3.4 A system is
>> (i) a biopopulation iff it is composed of individuals of
>>   the same biological species;
>> (ii) a community or ecosystem iff it is composed of

several interacting populations of organisms
belonging to different biospecies;
(iii) a <u>biosphere</u> iff it is the largest system in which a
given biosystem participates.

It is also important not to rush in and attribute higher level
properties, such as goal directed behavior, to all life forms: "There is
no evidence of goal directed behavior except for certain features of the
behavior of animals equipped with an advanced brain." (WS 92)

3.4 <u>Bunge on Mind</u>

There is much more of general interest in the chapter on life, but as
it is not of immediate concern, we pass to the fourth chapter, "Mind."
Once again Bunge presents a careful development of his emergentist
materialism of mind out of (some) living things: "This kind of
materialism is monistic with respect to substance and pluralistic with
respect to properties." (WS 126) This chapter was expanded into a whole
book, <u>The Mind-Body Problem: A Psychological Approach</u> (1980), which
supplies a superb resume of neurology and the brain; here the treatment is
more sketchy. Bunge discusses neurons, neuron assemblies, and nervous
systems and divides neural systems into two kinds, those that are
<u>committed</u> (or wired-in, prewired, or preprogrammed), i.e., that are
"constant from birth or from a certain stage in the development of the
animal," and those that are <u>plastic</u> (or uncommitted, modifiable, or
self-organizable), whose "connectivity is variable throughout the animal's
life." His postulate: "All animals with a nervous system have neuronal
systems that are committed, and some animals also have neuronal systems
that are plastic." In the first group belong "apparently worms, insects,
and other lowly animals." He further postulates (not without substantial
supporting evidence, but only to enable him to get on with his axiomatic
treatment) that "every animal endowed with psychons (plastic neuronal
systems) is capable of acquiring new biofunctions in the course of its
life." (WS 132-133)

Learning consists of "the formation of new neural systems, i.e. in
establishing permanent connections among neurons or facilitating ephemeral
(but repeatable) neuron interconnections." (WS 132) Bunge defines <u>mental
activity</u> as brain activity of plastic neural systems and distinguishes
this from the activities of pre-wired systems. "Every fact experienced

introspectively as mental is identical with some brain activity; this, in
a nutshell, is the neurobiological or materialist hypothesis of the
mind." (WS 138) He later notes: "Mind and brain are not identical: there
is no more brain-mind identity than there is lung-respiration identity,"
(WS 141) though, of course, he will equate the two as a manner of speech.

Bunge has a witty discussion of various dualist objections to
materialism, two of which are worth mentioning here. One is that pain is
indeed perceived in a limb that has been amputated (phantom limb), but
only in adults who from childhood have formed a comparatively unalterable
map of the body. Dualists cannot explain both this and the lack of
experiencing phantom limb in young children. The other is best given by a
quotation (WS 148):

> Another, related objection to the identity thesis,
> and one commended as definitive by Popper (Popper and Eccles,
> 1977 [The Self and its Brain]), is as follows (Kripke, 1971
> ["Identity and Necessity," in Milton K. Munitz, ed., Identity and
> Individuation]). If the identity is to be taken just as seriously
> as "Heat is the motion of molecules", then it must be a necessary
> identity, in the sense that it must hold in all possible worlds--
> whatever these may be. However, this cannot be, because "it seems
> clearly possible" (to Kripke) that M (e.g. pain) could exist
> without the corresponding brain state N, or that the latter could
> exist without being felt as pain--whence the identity is contingent
> and therefore flimsy. Rejoinder: (a) scientists and science-
> oriented philosophers do not waste their time speculating about
> (logically) possible worlds: they want to explore the real world
> (Bunge, 1977a [Furniture]); (b) the difference between necessary
> (or strict) identity and contingent identity does not occur in
> ordinary logic or in science. In sum, the sophistic objection to
> materialism holds no water.

More pertinent than either of these objections to dualism is the
general position that scientific models of reality ought to be capable of
explaining things. The chief difficulty with a separate realm for the
mind, to say nothing of Popper's "World 3" of the disembodied "products"
of human thought and artistic endeavors, is that there is no theory about
these separate realms and hardly any hope for discovering any scientific
laws about either their own operations or the interactions between these

realms and the material world. It is not wholly unreasonable that men
would have conceived of a separate realm for the "mind," and it is often
convenient even today to feign such a realm: Ideas remain brain
processes, but when we are considering these ideas largely if not wholly
apart from who thought them up (i.e., when we are not resorting to
ad hominem or its more sophisticated variety disguised as the "sociology
of knowledge"), we abstract and pretend that the ideas are "ideas in
themselves."

A Carbon Chauvinist Pig (my term for someone who generalizes from
life on Earth to all possible life in the universe) could argue that
certain concepts, such as numbers, have universal validity (i.e., for the
entire universe) and hence are independent of any particular kind of mind.
This is just supposition, thought not bad supposition, but another problem
is that in the past century or so, several definitions of numbers have
been proposed and it is by no means certain that the set theoretician's
definition of, say, 3, as "the set consisting of the empty set, the set
consisting of the empty set, and the set consisting of the empty set and
the set consisting of the empty set," [14, for this book's only equation!]
will be the standard one in the future. Besides, there are many different
rival logics and set theories, when it comes to the more technical axioms,
with no particular version winning anything like a consensus. None of
these foundational disputes has much bearing on the way scientists operate
(yet), and it is not clear what it would take to make us adopt a different
logic, whether different beings could or would use different ones, or
whether we (i.e., men) have to assume some particular background logic
before investigating the world. In any case, not even logic provides a
clear-cut case for brain-mind dualism. If it did, the problem of making
any lawful statements about the mind would remain. (Bunge 1981: Ch. 8,
"Popper's Unworldly World 3")

Bunge goes on, in his chapter on mind, to build up concepts from
perception to the self. His treatment is, like all of science,
preliminary and revisable, and we detail his definitions for the purpose
of showing how at least the outlines of a materialist and emergentist
conception of mind are possible. Economists might feel uncomfortable with
many of his distinctions, such as between value, choice, and decision. If
so, here is hoping that Bunge's efforts will stimulate improvements.

Bunge begins with the old problem of sensation and perception and
gives some definitions. "A system detects things or events of a certain
kind (or is a detector of them) if and only if it reacts to them only."

"A detector is a neurosensor (or neuroreceptor) iff it is a neural system
or is directly coupled to a neural system." "A sensory system of an
animal is a subsystem of the nervous system of it, composed of
neurosensors and of neural systems coupled to these." "A sensation (or
sensory process, or feeling) is a specific state of activity (or function
or process) of a sensory system." (WS 150-51)

The brain processes this incoming data through these sensory systems
in a chain. In the primary stage not much processing takes place, and
the processor tends to become rigid as the animal grows older. Not so
with later stages called perception. These perceptual sensory systems
remain plastic, combine with one another (e.g., sight and sound), and can
intersect both with the body's motor units and with ideational units. The
integration of what becomes a whole system of maps of the external world
requires both physical development and learning.

Behavior is defined: "The set of motor outputs of an animal, whether
global as in locomotion or partial as in grasping or grinning, moving the
eyeballs or excreting, is called its behavior." (WS 156) This behavioral
repertoire is made up of inherited and learned components. A drive
consists of the detection of an imbalance, and Bunge postulates that for
each drive, there is a corresponding type of behavior that reduces such
drive. Such behavior need not be explained by resort to teleology,
however, nor is it necessarily the case that the behavior resulting from
an evaluation coming from a drive is the right one to further the life of
an organism. Much less is it the case "that all animals are conscious of
such evaluations and can make value judgments. Only a few higher mammals
can form value judgments: in all others, and even in man most of the
time, valuations are automatic. What distinguishes man from the other
animals, with regard to evaluation, is that he can reason about values
as well as evaluate reasons." (WS 159, my emphases)

Bunge next defines an animal as having a value system over a set of
items provided the animal can detect and distinguish among the items and,
of any pair of items, prefers one to the other, or values them equally.
Postulate: "All animals are equipped with a value system, and those
capable of learning can modify their value systems." (WS 160) An animal
chooses an option out of a set of alternatives provided that it is
possible (recalling that in Bunge's ontology real possibilities exist) to
select any alternatives in the set, that it prefers the given options to
any of the others in the set, and that it actually picks that option.
Then follows (WS 161):

Note the difference between preference and choice: the former underlies and motivates the latter. Choice is valuation in action, or overt valuation--hence an indicator of valuation not a definition of the latter. And note also that not every choice implements a decision. Decisions are deliberate or reasoned (if not always rational), and reasoning is the privilege of only a few animal species. Most choices, even in daily human life, are not preceded by any decision-making process.

It is clear that Bunge's concepts are not those of the revealed preference school in orthodox economics. But, then, the orthodox position is more a series of slogans than a worked out metaphysical position. Hence Bunge's ideas, which are informed by a study of the neurobiology of animal brains, do not necessarily clash irreconcilably with the orthodoxy either. Once more, let us hope that work in the sciences and metaphysics (the most general science) will help clarify the foundations of economics.

We must proceed further before we get to man, the ostensible subject of our inquiries. Bunge distinguishes memory, which magnets can have, from learning, which as we have seen involves the modification of a plastic neural system in an animal. If an animal can learn, and all vertebrates seem to be able to, it can develop expectations about the future. Such animals are "said to behave in a goal seeking or purposive way." (WS 164) His definition and comments (WS 164, my emphasis):

An action X of an animal b has the purpose or goal Y iff
(i) b may choose not to do X;
(ii) b has learned that doing X brings about, or increases the chances of attaining, Y;
(iii) b expects the possible occurrence of Y upon doing X;
(iv) b values Y.

Notice the conditions for purposiveness: freedom, learning, expectation, and valuation....The claim that purposes defy scientific explanation and call for the hypothesis of an immaterial mind was downed by cyberneticians, who suggested a precise general mechanism of purposive action, namely the negative feedback loop.

Bunge next turns to thinking and deals with two basic types of "thought processes, namely concept attainment and proposition formation.

We shall conceive of the former as the process of forming kinds, such as the class of cats or that of triangles. And we shall conjecture that forming a concept of the 'concrete' kind--i.e. a class of real things or events--consists in responding uniformly to any and only members of the given class." (WS 165) He postulates that there are animals equipped with plastic neural systems (psychons) to do just this job of recognition. Recalling that Bunge uses the word class in a specialized way--a class is not a random collection of things, but one that can be characterized by obeying one or more scientific laws--Bunge's statement here is more or less equivalent to saying that Unger's intelligible essences are intelligible (i.e., knowable by the human mind). Bunge's formulation is not quite equivalent to Unger's, for ancient and medieval philosophers, especially the Christian ones, thought there were a great many essences besides those corresponding to material things!

The operation involved in forming propositions is that of psychon pairing, and Bunge postulates that "thinking up a proposition is (identical with) the sequential activation of the psychons whose activities are the concepts occurring in the proposition in the given order." (WS 165) (This postulate is not as much a summation of the present state of neurology as are his other postulates, for Bunge notes that how propositions are formed is far from understood. Nevertheless, we will maintain that this postulate is good enough for the purpose of illustrating generally a materialist conception of mind.)

A decision to choose is different from just choosing, as discussed above, in that in deciding the animal has knowledge or cognition of the alternatives as well as merely being presented with them. Some more comments from Bunge (WS 167):

> The ability to make decisions is restricted to animals capable of knowing. But not all knowledge is of the same grade, nor all valuations correct. When they are, they constitute the basis of rational decision:

> Definition 4.39 A decision made by an animal is rational iff it is preceded by
>   (i) adequate knowledge and correct evaluations, and
>   (ii) foresight of the possible outcomes of the corresponding action.

(Economists, especially, will object that adequacy comes in degrees and at a price. But we should be concerned more with the concepts that Bunge is offering here than with adjusting them. Ditto for the word compulsion two paragraphs below.)

Bunge distinguishes awareness, consciousness, and self-consciousness. An animal is <u>aware</u> of a stimulus (internal or external) if it feels or perceives it. <u>Consciousness</u> is awareness specifically of a brain process (by another part of the brain), and not all animals are capable of it. Another postulate, or rather finding of animal psychologists, is widely known: "In the course of the life of an animal capable of learning, learned behavior, if initially conscious, becomes gradually unconscious." (WS 172) And we know the (alleged!) story of the centipede, attributed to one Mrs. Craster, who died in 1874: [15]

> The Centipede was happy quite,
> Until the Toad in fun
> Said "Pray which leg goes after which?"
> And worked her mind to such a pitch,
> She lay distracted in the ditch
> Considering how to run.

Two more definitions from Bunge: "An animal act is <u>voluntary</u> (or <u>intentional</u>) iff it is a conscious purposeful" act and "An animal acts of its own <u>free will</u> iff (i) its action is voluntary and (ii) it has free choice of its goal(s)--i.e. is under no programmed or external compulsion to attain the chosen goal." (WS 172-73) For Bunge, "all animals capable of being in conscious states are able to perform free voluntary acts. If consciousness is not exclusively human, neither is free will. And both are subjects of scientific research." (WS 173) And a last definition (WS 175):

An animal
   (i) has (or is in a state of) <u>self-awareness</u> iff it is aware
      of itself (i.e. of events occurring in itself) as
      different from all other entities;
  (ii) has (or is in a state of) <u>self-consciousness</u> iff it is
      conscious of some of its own past conscious states;
 (iii) has a <u>self</u> at a given time iff it is self-aware or
      self-conscious at that time.

He adds: "Possibly animals other than humans have self-awareness but, so far as we know, only humans have self-consciousness, at least when normal and past their infancy." (WS 175)

I have dwelt on Bunge's chapter on mind at length because the philosophical issues are important and hope to have shown that Buchanan's worries that choice and free will might be illusory may now at last be dropped. To repeat myself, and Bunge's many remarks to this effect, his treatment of general ontology in his furniture book and applied ontology (systems) in the companion volume are sketches and not pretentions to being the final answer. I have also dwelt on the subject of mind at length in order to exhibit the evidence that a materialist philosophy is not "ridiculously at variance with reason and experience." (FW xiii)

3.5 Bunge's Systemic Conception of Society

The fifth and penultimate chapter of A World of Systems is entitled "Society" and deals actually with human societies. "We shall argue that every human society, no matter how primitive or evolved, is composed of four main subsystems: kinship, economy, culture, and polity. We submit that all four are already found in nuce in some prehuman societies." (WS 182) What is unique about man is not so much a bigger head, per se, but the (emergent) properties of his cultures. Bunge best speaks for himself (WS 186-187):

> Whereas to biologism human society is just one more animal society, according to spiritualism it is nothing of the sort because it is guided by ideas and values. We take the alternative view that human society is an animal society with many and remarkable novel properties, only a few of which it shares with animal protoeconomies, protocultures, and protopolities. We assume that man is neither an animal at the mercy of its genetic makeup and its environment, nor a free spiritual being akin to divinity: man is, instead, the primate that works and strives to know, that builds, maintains, and transforms social organizations far beyond the call of the gene or the environment, and that creates artistic, technological, and intellectual cultures, and also plays. Man is faber and sapiens, oeconomicus and politicus, artifex and ludens....

        We should distinguish three modes of evolution:
"blind", animal, and social. "Blind" evolution is evolution by
mutation, recombination, and natural selection; it is the way
molecules and plants evolve. Animal evolution combines genetic
change with behavior: the environment selects not only phenotypes
but also behavior patterns, and animals adapt not only phylogenet-
ically but also ontogenetically by learning adaptive behavior.
Finally social evolution proceeds not only by genetic change and
behavioral change, but also by social creation and selection.

        In all three cases the individual proposes and the
environment decides--metaphorically speaking. But in the cases of
animal and social evolution the individual learns and the
environment, rather than being given to it, is partly chosen and
partly even remade by it. And in the case of social evolution there
are not only biological and psychological factors but also economic,
cultural, and political ones. Moreover, thanks to language and
social life, some of the learned skills and some of the products of
human activity are transmitted to the new generations: here we can
speak of the (social) inheritance of acquired characters. But even
this inheritance is plastic, for we are free either to disregard or
to enrich our heritage.

    An interesting anthology chapter by David O. Oakley, "Cerebral
Cortex and Adaptive Behaviour" (1979), discusses the apparent excess of
intelligence in primates, in defiance of the usually conservative
processes of evolution, and explains it as due to the rather greater
demands imposed by social interaction as opposed to the physical
environment. "The computing capacity required to handle social
interactions with even a limited number of self-regulating individuals of
the same species is likely on a number of grounds to be greater than that
needed for interaction with the physical environment." Carleton S. Coon,
in The Origin of Races (1962), held that this process of "evolution by
social adaptation" as opposed to "evolution by environmental adaptation"
(the terms he uses) has gone particularly far in man, whose brain consumes
one-eighth of the body's calories but represents only two percent of its
mass. The brain is a very expensive organ, and it is the job of
evolutionists to figure out how the benefits equal the costs. Too bad the
brain rots and we can't find out from fossils the details of its

structure, especially with regard to free-will feedback loops.

Bunge's chapter on society is chock full of the symbols of set
theory, and the purpose of all this symbolism is to show that society,
too, can be conceived as a system in the sense he has defined it. He
divides the active population into primary laborers (who transform the
environment), secondary cultural workers (whose work "is an activity
capable of evoking feelings or thoughts, or supplying ideas intervening
in the primary production" (WS 200)) of the social system, and tertiary
managers (whose work "is an activity contributing to controlling some
primary or secondary work"). (WS 201) These three groups do not
constitute subsystems in themselves; rather, each provides inputs to the
economic, cultural, and political output systems.

Any such scheme of dividing up society into such a criss-crossing
network is, of course, fraught with difficulties--Bunge lumps financing
in with primary production, which may make him a closet Misesian--but few
economists tackle such problems as the differences among primary and
secondary production, holding such terms to be meaningless.

Better typologies of social systems will have to come along, and
perhaps there are certain stochastic regularities in the way activities
are organized that could be used to suggest that some typologies are
better than others. Bunge's economy, culture, and polity are all
represented by academic disciplines, but there is nothing corresponding
to sociology. Nevertheless, one may often resort to sociological
explanations of, say, economic problems (e.g., alienation is more
responsible for the decline in economic growth rates in the United States
than government regulation). Sociology has great pretensions to being
the discipline that can subsume all the others, but economists--who study
choice--have made similar noises.

Bunge's typology is probably just as good as any, but going through
it in detail would be not nearly so useful as showing that an emergentist
view of society is possible, as he showed regarding an emergentist view
of mind. What is of greater concern for us are several philosophical
remarks he makes along the way, five of which we shall proceed to relate:
[16]

(1) Every society has emergent properties. We hasten to
note, though, that 'emergent' does not mean "unexplainable" or
"unpredictable". Firstly, because "emergence" is an ontological not
an epistemological category. Secondly because it is the business of

science not only to acknowledge emergence but also to incorporate it into theories and thus to render it understandable and sometimes also predictable.

   (2) Social philosophers are divided over the nature of institutions, hence over the proper way of studying them. The two classical doctrines in this field are holism and [atomistic] individualism. The holist regards an institution such as the Law as a disembodied corpus of rules or laws that individuals enforce, obey, or violate. According to this view the institution hovers above the persons and moreover is superior to or more valuable than them. No wonder holism, in some form or other, is inherent in totalitarian ideologies. The individualist rejects such an abstraction and regards the Law as the set of judges, lawyers and policemen—with total neglect of the subjects of the Law, namely the common citizens. When confronted with a sentence such as 'The Law compelled X to do Y', the individualist translates it into 'Judge (or policeman) U forced X to do Y'. But of course this is a poor substitute for the original sentence, as the person U in charge of enforcing the law behaves as he does because of what he is, namely a member of a certain legal system with a code of legal procedure. Different individuals might have behaved in roughly the same way. On the other hand the same individuals, in a different legal system, might behave differently. In conclusion, the legal system in question is neither the set including the individuals U and X nor a set of supraindividual rules. Hence although both holism and individualism have their points, neither is competent to account for the behavior of the individual in society. Holism fails because it postulates totalities transcending the components, and individualism fails because it ignores totalities. [17, my emphases]

   (3) Of all the aspects of the economic system, those of greatest philosophical interest are perhaps technology and the artifacts it produces and employs. Both raise numerous philosophical problems of all kinds, hardly investigated. Let us say a word or two about artifacts, i.e. things fashioned by rational beings with the help of some technique, whether primitive or advanced. An artifact is not just one more thing but a thing belonging to a kind that did not exist before the emergence of man

or some other rational being. Artifacts may be regarded as
constituting a whole new level of reality, namely the
artiphysis....Far from being contemptible entities whereof a
philosopher does not deign to speak, artifacts are at the heart of
human society and have properties absent from natural things.

(4) The matter of personal freedom constitutes the center of
ideological debate in our time, yet it cannot be argued with profit
on the ideological plane. On the other hand the systemic view of
the political system can shed some light on that debate, namely as
follows. A normal person is a component of some society or other.
To survive, he or she must keep some measure of individuality or
autonomy as well as engage in some synergic (harmonious)
interactions with other components of the system, for otherwise the
latter would break down. Indeed, exaggerating the autonomy of the
individual would lead either to his or her breaking away from the
system, or to subjecting the latter to the tyrannical control of the
individual at the expense of the freedom of the other components.
And overstressing the synergy of the whole may lead to depriving
their components of creativity and thus to impoverishing society.
So, if we care for both the system (not necessarily the
"establishment") and the individual, we had better devise a
political regime combining the good points of individualism with
those of collectivism. But the matter of political regimes will
have to be deferred to Vol. 7 [now Vol. 8] of this Treatise.

(5) We have introduced a method for both describing the
structure of a society and keeping track of its multifarious
changes, namely the social structure approach. The [atomistic]
individualist is bound to dislike it because it achieves what he
holds to be impossible, namely describing the state, and the changes
of state, of a society as a whole. But he cannot in good faith
dismiss it as being "merely a holistic confusion", for it is based
on a conception of society which, being systemic, is neither holist
nor individualist. Besides, the method is mathematically
transparent, so it cannot be branded as confused--in particular
because it does not involve the individualist confusion of a
sociosystem with its composition.

The sixth and final chapter of <u>A World of Systems</u> is the only one of either ontology volume with more than one word in its title. "A Systemic World View" provides a summary of both ontology volumes, offers some broad speculative generalizations characterizing the systemic make up of the universe we live in, and wraps up the book with a showing of where his own philosophy stands with respect to others.

First, the speculative generalizations: (1) Every concrete thing is either a system or a component of one. (2) These systems come in Chinese boxes or nested layers, and the universe is itself such a system, namely the system such that every other thing is a component of it. (3) At the present state of evolution of the universe, there are five system genera: physical, chemical, biological, social, and technical (artiphysis). (4) The more complex a system, the more numerous the stages in the process of assembly and its possible breakdown modes. (5) Physical things take part (either as components or as agents) in the assembly of chemical things take part in the assembly of biological things take part in the assembly of both social and technical things (man—made artifacts).

For a recapitulation of this chapter, we can do no better than quote the final section entire (WS 251–52):

6.6 SYNOPSIS

It is closing time. We close by characterizing the ontology presented in this volume and its companion, <u>The Furniture of the World</u>, in terms of a few traditional <u>isms</u>. (A single <u>ism</u> is bad because it is one sided and rigid. Many—sidedness and flexibility can be achieved only by a system of matching <u>isms</u>.)

Our ontology endorses

(i) <u>naturalism</u> or <u>materialism</u>, for it countenances only material existents and discounts autonomous ideas, ghosts, and the like; but <u>not physicalism</u> (or <u>mechanism</u>), as this denies that all things are physical entities;

(ii) <u>systemism</u>, for it holds that every thing is either a system or a component of one; but <u>not holism</u>, as it rejects the myths that the whole is incomprehensible, prior to its components, and superior to them;

(iii) pluralism as regards the variety of things and processes, hence the plurality of kinds of things and laws; and also monism as regards the substance that possesses properties and undergoes change (namely matter) as well as the number of worlds (just one);

(iv) emergentism with regard to novelty, for it holds that, while some bulk properties of systems are resultant, others are emergent; but not irrationalism with regard to the possibility of explaining and predicting emergence;

(v) dynamicism, for it assumes that every thing is in flux in some respect or other; but not dialectics, for it rejects the tenets that every thing is a unity of opposites, and that every change consists in or is caused by some strife or ontic contradiction;

(vi) evolutionism with regard to the formation of systems of new kinds, for it maintains that new systems pop up all the time and are selected by their environment; but neither gradualism nor saltationism, for it recognizes both smooth changes and leaps;

(vii) determinism with regard to events and processes, by holding all of them to be lawful and none of them to come out of the blue or disappear without leaving traces; but not causalism, for it recognizes randomness and goal striving as types of processes alongside causal ones;

(viii) biosystemism with regard to life, for it regards organisms as material systems that, though composed of chemosystems, have properties not found on other levels; but neither vitalism nor machinism nor mechanism;

(ix) psychosystemism with regard to mind, for it holds that mental functions are emergent activities (processes) of complex neural systems; but neither eliminative nor reductive materialism, for it affirms that the mental, though explainable with the help of physical, chemical, biological, and social premises, is emergent;

(x) sociosystemism with regard to society, for it claims that
society is a system composed of subsystems (economy, culture,
polity, etc.), and possessing properties (such as stratification and
political stability) that no individual has; hence neither
individualism nor collectivism, neither idealism nor vulgar
materialism.

The reader accustomed to dwell in a single ism or in none is
likely to throw up his hands in despair at the multiplicity of isms
embraced by our ontology. Let this be said in defense of such
multiplicity. First, it is possible to synthesize a variety of
philosophical isms provided they are not mutually inconsistent--
i.e., provided the result is a coherent conceptual system rather
than an eclectic bag. (We tried to secure consistency by adopting
the axiomatic format.) Second, it is necessary to adopt (and
elaborate) a number of philosophical isms to account for the variety
and multiplicity of reality--provided the various theses harmonize
with science. Third, tradition can be avoided only at the risk of
unfairness and ignorance: rather than dismiss our philosophical
legacy altogether, we should try and enrich it.

3.6 Conclusion

I have taken the reader through Bunge's ontology volumes for a
variety of reasons, the chief one being to exhibit the carrying out of
what Charles Peirce called "Scientific Metaphysics," a systematic
description of how reality is made up that is both internally consistent
and in accord with modern science. Peirce lacked the tools to do the job
himself, and Bunge has now made the first systematic attempt. Later
hands, with access to better tools and future findings of science, will
improve upon his work, but Bunge has put the sciences on firmer ground
than before.
This is particularly true of the social sciences. A good many, but
by no means all, social scientists and social philosophers have presumed
that human action, choice, and free will are real and have proceeded
accordingly. Yet they have been uneasy in so presuming, even as they
attack the views of those who are not convinced that choice is real as
"scientism," "positivism," and "aping the physical sciences." It is

Bunge's position that positivism is inappropriate even to physics and that, at bottom, scientific understanding is much the same in the physical, chemical, biological, and social sciences. It is his notions of emergent properties and ontological layers that make this general view possible, and it is of the utmost significance that Bunge's ontology affirms the existence of free will without invoking god or a separate realm for mind. Social scientists may now accordingly proceed with good conscience--as always, until further notice.

Bunge is at best on his home ground, physics, and some of his definitions and concepts in psychology and the social sciences may seem deficient. But even his physics is fallible. Furthermore, his characterizations of individualism and collectivism may sound absurd, but they are only caricatures of seldom articulated positions. Caricature is often the first step to goading those so portrayed to clarify their positions. In the next two chapters I will employ Bunge's ideas and terminology to Buchanan's contractarianism and examine the issues of social justice and natural rights. Unger will reappear in the last chapter, when I shall argue for a plurality of social contracts.

CHAPTER 4

FRIEDRICH AUGUST VON HAYEK AND THE MIRAGE OF SOCIAL JUSTICE

4.1 Hayek's Own Argument Against Social Justice

This chapter will apply Mario Bunge's systemism to the notion of
social justice. The key idea argued here is that, while society is a
system, whose composition consists of individuals who have and pursue
values, to claim "society" itself has values is to endorse a holistic
metaphysics. Social justice is an emergent property of a social system
and not a property of individuals living outside of society; it will be
an ontologically viable concept only if it can be shown to arise from
individual values and not float independently above them.

Both justice and freedom are emergent properties of the structure of
a social system. Freedom--the set of one's choices for action which
others may not interfere with--is empty in the case of the lone
individual living outside of society. Now which freedoms to protect, and
how far to protect them, is up to the social contractors, as discussed in
Chapter 1. The same is true of justice, both the older notion of the
impartial administration of impartial laws and the new one called
"social" justice, which may involve redistribution of income, wealth, and
opportunities.

The metaphysical issue here is how far social justice can be rooted
in an agreement among men to empower a government to further this kind of
justice. Anyone can form his own private notion of what social justice
is and can attach a value, even a supreme value, to it. But if he manages
to get the government to carry out his personal ideal alone, we have a
dictatorship, not a social contract. (As with the production of public
goods by the productive state, and we may wish to regard social justice as
a kind of public good, what is to be agreed upon is a constitution, with
full awareness that not every law passed by the legislature will itself
pass the unanimity test.) Friedrich Hayek, in The Mirage of Social
Justice (1976), has delivered a strong attack on the whole notion of
social justice. I shall summarize his argument, connect it with the
unanimity requirement, and assess its metaphysical implications.

Hayek argues that men developed their moral intuitions when they
lived in small groups. In these pre-capitalist societies, the chain of
cause and effect of human actions was limited. Who kills what animal can

83

be easily determined and the effect of making better flints fairly well
understood, even if the capital value of such technological innovations
was grossly underestimated. (After all, there were no markets that
established interest rates!). But despite this error about capitalization,
which he does not deal with, Hayek holds that Dawn Man had a tolerably
reliable sense of desert based upon immediate consequences of human
action.

Modern society is organized very differently. Human actions,
especially in the production and exchange process, have secondary and
tertiary consequences that are far removed from easily graspable primary
consequences and indeed overwhelm them. Rewards for productive efforts
are not determined by men sitting around a campfire but by profit and loss
in the marketplace. Profits consist of revenues from a wide variety of
sources minus expenditures on a wide variety of inputs. Prices for goods
sold and inputs purchased depend on the goings on elsewhere in the economy
and these goings on depend on remoter ones still, almost ad infinitum.

What profits are actually earned, then, bear only a remote
relationship to any Dawn Man feelings of desert that pertain to the
immediate consequences of action. In modern societies, who gets what is
determined by men sitting at a distance, in accordance with abstract rules
governing property. The Dawn Man's sense of justice is replaced by an
abstract justice of impartial administration of impartial rules.
Nevertheless, Hayek goes on, the earlier sense of justice lingers on.
(How far this is due to innate factors talked about by sociobiologists or
to our continuing experience with small groups, especially the family,
Hayek does not say.) And there is an ever-present tendency to personify
the network of abstract laws as "society" and demand that rewards be
re-tied to immediately graspable desert.

This re-tying is what Hayek calls "social justice." It is a mirage
precisely because, in advanced societies, immediate consequences are very
minor and no one could conceivably analyze all the remote effects, add
them all up, and come up with true deserts. Hayek's fundamental point is
that suppressing these Dawn Man intuitions is the price that has to be
paid if an advanced society is to operate. Otherwise, there will be
continuous interference in the profits dished out in the market at
virtually every turn. To give an example (my own), it seems clear to many
people that many rock "musicians" receive outrageously high salaries, even
if all the rock fans voluntarily paid to hear them. (To invoke this fact
of voluntariness is indeed to consider one's willingness to abide by

abstract rules.) It also may seem that nurses and secretaries are
underpaid, even if (abstract-society-oriented) economists can find no
market failures: it is the market itself that gave out rewards that are
counter-intuitive.

Hayek sees no stopping point to Dawn Man demands for case-by-case
rectification. So not only is social justice impossible to determine, but
trying to achieve it could undermine almost every exchange in the market.
This is gloomy enough, but Hayek could have added the Public Choice
question of who would make the decisions for case-by-case redistribution
of rewards by the market. Since the chains of consequences of human
actions are too complex to be gone through, in practice anyone can advance
whatever claim he feels like; and no doubt there are plenty of moon-eyed
teenagers who wish their favorite rock stars were billionaires rather than
merely hecto-millionaires. In practice, allowing for endless
rectification in the name of social justice would mean a field day for the
power hungry and the upshot of all this activity would be redistribution
by pressure group, or what Ayn Rand called "the Aristocracy of Pull." But
then, Hayek wrote The Mirage of Social Justice (1976) before Gordon
Tullock wrote Economics of Income Redistribution (1983). I remark here
only that America has stopped short on the Road to Serfdom.

4.2 The Metaphysical Issues in Hayek's Argument

But what is the metaphysical problem in all of this? It is true
enough that men in abstract societies still often think as if they lived
in primitive times. It is also true, as Hayek warns, that this
inappropriate thinking can be dangerous, in that personifying this larger
society and demanding social justice from it is to ask the
epistemologically impossible or at least computationally impossible. But
metaphysically the problem seems to be one of degree: social justice in a
small society also involves a pretense that men can calculate deserts. It
is Hayek's implicit assumption that this can be done. But how? The
answer must be that the rules and procedures men in small groups use to
arrive at the distribution of rewards are based on some sort of consensus.
Men sitting around a campfire no doubt argue, but we may suppose that they
also agree to present their cases to the leader of the band and accept his
decisions. (Or perhaps the band may vote.) And it is quite possible that
the man who developed a better flint would refuse to accept the leader's
decision if he were a budding capitalist who appreciated the long-term

impact of his innovation and wanted to be excused from having to take part
in hunts in the future. So even in primitive societies, unanimous consent
is an ideal. But let us suppose that there is an unanimous contract
nevertheless.

Hayek's claim that social justice is a mirage in large abstract
societies, then, reduces to the factual issue of whether there can be a
unanimous social contract allowing for a leader or a legislature to
administer the specific kind of social justice Hayek has in mind, namely
case-by-case rectification of rewards in large societies as well as in
small ones. This factual issue becomes a metaphysical one, if we remember
Bunge's dictum that metaphysics is the most general science. We are
dealing very generally with the nature of man, the nature of human action,
the nature of agreements, the issue of the possibility of agreements. Now
dissenters even in small societies will have their own conception of how
rewards should be distributed, case-by-case. They will disagree over
matters of fact about who bagged which animal, and whether a large capture
was due to luck or skill. They will disagree subjectively over how far
both luck and skill are to be redistributed to the unlucky and the
unskillful.

Now in small groups today, agreement will often emerge from a mutual
recognition of the price of continued disagreement. We are not inclined
to really believe that juries, judges, and legislators arrive at final
truths. On the other hand, Dawn Man was more inclined to worship his
rulers and manufacture gods, who deserved thanks for correcting his errors
about justice and desert, either now or in the life hereafter. The
ontological existence of gods goes against all that can now be established
by scientific metaphysics, [18] and trust in the leader of even a small
group to find some higher Truth in matters of justice is more than
tenuous, a perennial theme in Buchanan's writings (e.g., Limits, p. 1).
But what there can be is a consensus to abide by the decisions of a
leader, who may or may not be hallucinating or pretending to. It is the
fact of acceptance of authority that counts, not whether the authority
figure or those who accept him is a bad metaphysician. Buchanan does not
think politicians arrive at the Truth, but he never says that citizens
must not. [19] Whether bad metaphysicians can be said to consent to a
social contract, or whether people have been bamboozled through false
consciousness into accepting the welfare state—-Unger is plainly behind
the times if he thinks that business advertising has anything like the
force of the Human Betterment Industry, and public education in

particular, in shaping false consciousness--is deeply problematic and, like most things, a matter of degree. [20]

Thus the metaphysical question of social justice is whether there can be a social contract to administer it. A key fact about men (as opposed to creatures in other galaxies whose machinery for concept formation and all the other paraphernalia for determining how the world works may be quite a bit different from ours, and about which we must largely speculate, all the more so since we know so little about ourselves) is that our brains are sharply limited, especially when it comes to knowing second-order and remoter effects of our actions. Beyond a very small society, and I might as well advance a figure of population of one or two hundred, there simply can be no consensus on how to redistribute rewards on a case-by-case basis. This kind of social justice, then, is a metaphysical mirage. [21] All that need be assumed is that there are enough men who would resist the nightmare state that would ensue to block unanimity (or quasi-unanimity, ignoring here the lone hermit). These men need only have a fraction of the insights and virtues I attributed to a hypothetical New Contractarian Man in Chapter 1.

It could be argued that men are indeed as frightfully warlike as Hobbes imagined and that they would surrender all their liberties to a Hobbist sovereign, even in the case of a large population. The sovereign could, if he chose, redistribute rewards and such redistribution could be called by definition social justice. I am not qualified to engage in a scholarly exegesis of Leviathan, but a common reading is that the job of the sovereign is largely if not entirely to keep peace. If he deems redistribution that appears to be social justice is necessary to keep the peace, then he will impose it. On the other hand, his redistribution may be regarded as an efficient way of bribing troublemakers, as opposed to fining or imprisoning them. But to say that justice is whatever the sovereign decrees is just as problematic as to claim, in Christian theology, that good is what God wills as opposed to claiming that God wills a good that is independent of Him. In any case, the men in Hobbes's fearsome state of nature are contracting for peace, not for case-by-case redistributive social justice.

4.3 Progressive Taxes Not Necessarily a Mirage

I have been deliberately adding "case-by-case redistributive" to "social justice" to make it clear that this is the kind of social justice

Hayek says is a mirage in any advanced society. And I have argued that
this kind of social justice is a metaphysical mirage, in that there would
never be any method for bringing it about in a manner arising from
individual values, that is to say, in a social contract. The reason is
Hayek's: The computations are too difficult for men in a society where
remote consequences of human actions loom large. But what about a simple
scheme like a graduated income tax? The tax laws are indeed complicated,
but at least not so hopelessly so as to render a social contract
impossible. Moreover, all countries that have income taxes have
progressive ones, so one should pause before dogmatically claiming such
progression absolutely cannot rest upon a constitution that has the
consent of the governed. This is not to claim that such taxes were passed
by legislators under unanimously-approved constitutions, but does call for
pause before rejecting social justice by way of progressive taxation as a
mirage.

We should now make just this pause. The case for progressive
taxation is indeed quite obscure, for as Tullock (1983) points out, rarely
is what constitutes a "just" concentration of income ever articulated.
Tullock cites Lester Thurow, who "feels that the highest income an
American should receive is no more than five times as much as that of the
lowest income American" (p. 195). But Thurow advances no reason for the
factor of five, nor what and why the factor might be in other times and
places. Now the actual statistical distribution of income depends on many
factors, among them: 1) the institutional laws governing property rights,
2) the structure of initial endowments, 3) inheritance laws and taxes, 4)
the entire social situation beyond politics, especially how the culture
inspires (though far from determines) efforts to produce income, 5) the
statistical distribution of said inspiration, and 6) the actual efforts
individuals put forth.

This is a positive formula, a matter of the facts, hard though they
may be to unearth. [22] But behind the factual account of income
generation, there lies a normative formula that will state what amount of
effort it is reasonable, all things considered, to expect various
individuals to put forth. One may not, for example, think it reasonable
to expect children on welfare to behave like rugged individualists, if one
believes the incentives built into government programs run heavily the
other way. This can and does lead to demands for reforming the welfare
system rather than to redistribute money to the victims of that system.
Such reformers can and do argue that to engage in redistribution would be

to entrench disincentives all the more thoroughly.

This leads into a deep paradox that will be dealt with later, namely the problem of generations. The reformers do sense a societal injustice, namely that welfare children, who did not consent to being born, are unfairly disadvantaged in that they were not only not properly brought up to hold the capitalist virtues but also that the state itself put positive roadblocks in the way. In later life, they may very well put forth all the effort that may humanly be expected of them to better their condition, even though such efforts will be less than those of other young adults. Social justice, then, might be taken to mean that income be redistributed to bridge that gap between reward for effort in fact put forth and reward for effort that would have been put forth had the roadblocks to the development of a normal personality not been artificially put in the way.

But there are (at least) two arguments against this rectifying redistribution. The first is that redistribution to these victims will perpetuate the cycle of poverty. A trade-off must be made between justice to specific victims in the present and breaking up the perpetuation of welfare culture, which would reduce injustice in the future. (I assume very few would opt for a third alternative, for the government to take welfare children away from their parents.) The other argument against rectifying redistribution is Hayek's: It may very well be that welfare programs reduce effort put forth, but the connection between effort and reward is necessarily and substantially reduced in any advanced market economy. Furthermore, administrators are fundamentally incapable of gathering the knowledge necessary to make all the case-by-case corrections of reward to desert.

However, no such wholesale case-by-case redistribution is being proposed. Rather, there is a feeling that a certain class of persons, namely those brought up in the welfare culture, have been damaged unfairly by it. [23] While knowledge of injustice to any one particular individual is at best knowable only within extremely broad limits, the overall statistically average impact could be known within narrower limits. How much to redistribute to these victims involves normative considerations as well, especially that of how much effort is reasonable to expect those victimized by welfare to make. And how far rectification should be allowed to run into conflict with other goals and values is also a personal matter. I am not sure how a social contract would be reached among those with diverse subjective trade-offs, but then the literature is silent on how the amount of production of one public good would be decided

upon, as opposed to the voting rules in <u>The Calculus of Consent</u> for the production of many public goods. Very possibly, the median voter rule would be the only one the voters could reach an agreement upon. [24]

Hayek's argument can still come back to haunt us: There can be an endless procession of other groups with claims, many of them dubious but hard to refute, to being victims of injustice. And there is still the problem of <u>who</u> is going to pay for the rectification. Given the fantastic opportunities for hypocrisy and rent-seeking on the part of power brokers and guilt mongers, one could argue that a social contract empowering a state to even begin doing these things would never be signed unanimously. But this is a prudential objection--and hence an argument to build in severe constitutional safeguards--more than a metaphysical one.

Still, a case can be made for a very general progressive income tax, as opposed to a particular scheme of rectification aimed at a specific group. First, people might come to a factual conclusion that there is a broad correlation between enculturation into the capitalist virtues and income that is significantly greater than zero. (One argument is that capitalism perpetuates a permanent underclass.) Second, undeserved luck is also positively correlated with income. Third, people want a certain amount of insurance against unexpectedly low incomes, as witnessed by the (actually fairly modest) markets for disability insurance. Now normative as well as factual judgments are involved here, and there are moral hazards as well as trade-offs involved also, which may well lead to <u>regressive</u> income taxes. [25] Whatever the upshot, social justice is something that emerges from a social contract and does not reside on an ontological plane hovering above individuals and their values. Social justice is inherently limited by the social contract and is not something to be used as moral blackmail.

I find no basis in Bunge's emergentist metaphysics for Rawls' allegedly contractarian claim that justice, however defined, is the first order of business of any society. Rather, justice is <u>a</u> value, one kind of public good, to be pursued jointly among many others. The rights to be protected by the protective state are also species of public goods, and if people want to <u>create</u> a right unknown to other societies, such as the right to privacy, they may do so. Furthermore, it is up to them how strongly to enforce this right, at the expense of other rights and at the expense of other goals, such as economic growth. Similarly, it is the social contractors who are the ones to <u>define</u> justice. They may read inconclusive arguments of social philosophers, from Hobbes and Locke to

Rawls, and adopt wholly or partly their arguments. (I shall examine
natural rights arguments in the next chapter.) But it is fundamentally
the social contractors who are to decide, not outside critics.

4.4 Multi-Generational Social Contracts

A major problem for social philosophers comes in small packages
weighing some eight pounds on the average and measuring some twenty inches
long. These packages have blue eyes at first and come into the world
kicking and screaming, even though their life support systems will last
another ten minutes. Over three and a half million times a year in the
U.S. alone, every ethical system ever advanced is refuted. Not only is
one ethical system urged upon all mankind, with major variations rarely
considered, but everyone in it is presumed to be over 18 and of sound
mind. The Limits of Liberty has a fleeting reference to the descendants
of the founding fathers losing respect for the earlier social contract,
and Knowledge and Politics has not even this much. In neither book are
there any children! The philosopher's world, unlike the real world, is
peopled with immortals. Buchanan is careful to assume as much openly at
the beginning of Chapter 5 of Limits, but he does not dwell upon the
implications of relaxing this assumption. [26]

In later papers, Buchanan (1984 and 1985) does take future
generations into account, although as far as one can tell new members of
society spring into the world full blown. Employing the distinction
between subjective costs at the time a choice is made (opportunity costs)
and objective choice-influenced costs afterwards (an obligation to make
payments) expounded upon in his Cost and Choice (1969a), he argues that
there is a trade-off between present consumption and investment in capital
stock bringing future returns that applies to individuals and collective
bodies alike. The papers mainly treat deficit financing of government,
but in fact many government policies, as well as private choices, affect
consumption versus investment. Much of the papers is given to arguing
that accounting practices, to say nothing of politicians' rhetoric,
disguise this distinction between consumption and capital investment.
What is important here is the idea of taking the future into account, not
the specifics of the two papers.

In a society of immortals, there is no conflict between generations.
It is difficult to gather all the living together to agree upon a social
contract; to gather all generations can only be done conceptually. I

propose doing so by extending Rawls' "veil of ignorance" approach. Most
of the discussion Rawls' book has generated is over the thickness of his
veil! Buchanan and Faith (1980), for example, treat an imagined situation
where a person does not know who he will be after the social contract is
signed but is nevertheless a concrete person beforehand, with his own
ideas about how various alternative contracts will work out. Being
ignorant about who but opinionated about how, he will opt for the
constitution that provides, in his opinion, the highest average payoff. A
person differently opinionated about the how may choose a different
constitution.

In a world of generations of men, the veil can be extended to include
the when dimension. In each generation, the people then alive will wish
that past generations had invested more and consumed less. At the same
time, each generation would rather consume now than make investments whose
payoffs come in the distant future. Under a when veil of ignorance, [27]
a balance can be struck. As with public debt and capital investment, so
with eugenics and genetic engineering (DeNicola 1976 and Fletcher 1974).
In the euthenics case (i.e., improvements in the structure of the social
system as opposed to its composition), there will be disputes as to where
to invest (education vs. scientific research vs. reforestation, etc.) and
imperfect knowledge about the effects of such investments. So also with
eugenics. In both cases, a unanimous social contract--between
generations--is called for, and in both cases more perfect knowledge will
produce better decisions. A healthy but not morbid regard for the worst
unseen consequences is called for, which is why diversity in both
euthenic (non-human animal and plant) and eugenic (human) gene pools is
desirable, but not pan-mixia. Numerous agriculturalists have warned
against too narrow a diversity of crops, and a much smaller number of
biologists (e.g., the discussion in Ortner 1983) has warned against the
destruction of varieties in humans through the more and more random
intermixing of populations that has been accelerating since 1492.
Whatever the methodological use of Rawls' veil of ignorance, it should not
extend to willful and wanton disregard of consequences.

Babies clutter the tidiness of a world of supposedly fixed
composition. In addition to rates of growth of various things, their
existence has consequences for justice. These involuntary immigrants were
not asked whether they wanted to be born, nor what particular society to
be born into. The society can ask them to undergo rites of passage in the
form of agreeing to the social contract and kick them out if they refuse.

(That a social contract need not encompass all mankind will be dealt with
in the final chapter.) But this is not obviously fair, for emigration is
not free. (It would seem even less fair to demand that an emigrant repay
those who had invested in his upbringing, though many countries have
emigration taxes, some of them effectively infinite.) In addition, it is
not obviously fair that some babies come into the world with more initial
endowments than others. The inheritance may be of genes, property,
business connections, parental provisions, or just an environment
conducive to success. But on the other hand, neither is it obvious that
"social justice" demands their rectification, especially totally at the
expense of everything else, and in particular through interference with
the right of those who have earned wealth to pass it on as they choose.
It is even less clear why the government should tax people not responsible
for bringing disadvantaged babies into the world to pay for the
rectification. Philosophers debate these matters incessantly, and the
publication of A Theory of Justice has only stimulated the debate.
Indeed, certain free-market advocates, e.g., Ayn Rand (1973a), have
denounced Rawls in no uncertain terms.

Once again, Bunge's metaphysics demands that justice, although an
emergent property of a social system, be rooted in individual values.
Rawls' veil of ignorance construction, while exceedingly useful, can be
abused if it is made so thick that individuals are virtually stripped of
having values or else made so ignorant about their particular values that
their individuality is suppressed. By contrast, the contractarian
approach of an economist (Buchanan) will keep exchange and therefore
individuality and individual differences uppermost in mind. However,
Buchanan's constitutionalism, as opposed to his contractarianism
generally, does effect something of a veil of ignorance, inasmuch as the
workings of the legislature, and the gains and losses therefrom, are less
predictable than if the constitutional stage were bypassed and specific
provisions of every public good decided upon once and for all. As people
and situations change unpredictably over longer and longer periods of
time, later and later pieces of legislation will look more and more random
from the standpoint of individuals at the moment of agreeing to the
constitution. To this extent, the social contractors will want to design
a constitution that will be expected to pay off impartially.

In Chapter 1, I quoted Herbert Simon's finding that the growth
of business firms regressed toward the mean (geometric as the cube root
every four years), thus swiftly dampening any initial advantage a firm

might have. Incomes of persons, and of generations of persons, do not regress to the mean at anything like this rate. For social contractors of life spans near three score and ten, the veil of ignorance will not be thick enough to guarantee impartiality regards children, grandchildren, and great-grandchildren, none of whom consented to be born. It is in order not to impose a social contract upon them that I invoked a when veil of ignorance above. A person under the when veil would trade off his right to pass on his advantages to his heirs and assigns against the value he would place upon having initial advantages distributed more equitably. He would also consider the effect upon incentives, and hence upon economic growth, that such redistribution would entail and, in addition, the value he might place on living in a more equally-advantaged society. (We need not assume independence of utility functions when a person evaluates some measure of an emergent property of an economic system.)

Matters are otherwise, if it turns out that advantages accumulate over time rather than dissipate. The social contractors may wish to simply set up a progressive tax, but they might well undertake a searching examination of how the particular institutions of property rights generate this accumulation and consider modifications. Some modifications may slow down economic growth, but so does progressive taxation. In addition, in case there is no progressive accumulation in the same hands, but still a tendency for concentration to grow over time, with the wealthy (and wealthy families) rotating, some may want taxes to become more progressive over time, or a procedure for doing so to be somehow established at the constitutional level.

On the other hand, if concentration decreases over time, the contractors may wish progression to lighten, though this is rarely advocated. It is the downward redistributors who generally have the moral initiative, regardless of what the concentration is at the moment, regardless of how much economic mobility there is, how much opportunity, or how initial advantages are distributed, and regardless of any costs to liberty and prosperity. Such is the moral power of egalitarianism. This power, I submit, rests upon bad metaphysics: an unexamined claim that there exists a thing called social justice on an ontological plane transcending individuals, and not rooted in individual values, to be decided upon by the contractors themselves. The cost of this bad metaphysics is not so much the net amount of downward redistribution that constitutes (according to Tullock (1983)) only a small percent of taxes, and perhaps not even the cloud of guilt of never doing enough that hangs

over us all, but rather the unleashing of the transfer state. Transfers
constitute the overwhelming bulk of the activities of governments in
"advanced" democracies today, and the costs besides the transfers
themselves are those of rent-seeking activity and the inefficiencies
generated by protectionism and other disguises of transfers.

Many observers are wondering, along with Tullock, whether the poor
would be better off if the government did no transferring, as compared
with the present situation, that the wants of the poor would be better met
directly through private charity, and if not, then through greater
economic growth. Observers are also wondering whether the support for
downward redistributive programs rests in no little part on the interests
of those who are paid to administer them and who in consequence
manufacture and propagate what amount to ontologically spurious
conceptions of social justice. In any case, the social contractors may
not accept, say, Rawls' thesis on the centrality of what he calls "the
least advantaged," perhaps as a result of reading Nozick 1974. Rather,
if Bunge's metaphysics is adopted, the contractors would see that
justice--and just as important, how much is going to be spent on
it--emerges out of their contract. The existence of generations makes it
impossible to gather together all those who are to be part of the society.
Consequently, I invoked a fictional when veil of ignorance. Of course
perfect unanimity, even among immortals, is a fiction. Therefore when
invoking a contract as justification for conformity to law, one must be
honest with oneself and not try to pass off an arrangement that
lop-sidedly benefits oneself as having been agreed to. The same is true
of social justice: One must pay as much attention to the future as one
wishes that the past had paid to the present. But not a whole lot more.

4.5 Elitism

Conceptual confusion and bad metaphysics make it easier for
rent-seekers to justify transfer programs in the name of social justice.
Confusion is also psychologically useful to those whose ideological bias
is toward expanding the state: Clarity would result in cognitive
dissonance and would require a wrenching reexamination of their premises.
It is just as well for them that education, largely a state activity, is a
superb example of a government failure that does a poor job generally and
in teaching scientific metaphysics in particular. It may be too much to
expect Mario Bunge's The Furniture of the World to have filtered down

fully since 1977, especially since the present essay is the first attempt
to present it in a non-mathematical fashion. Nevertheless, powerful
interests (whether rightly understood or not) are served by keeping the
populace perpetually uneasy as to whether social justice is a bottomless
pit, in which the notion of choices and trade-offs is somehow inapplicable
to issues of social justice or of any kind of justice.

As a result, spokesmen for social justice become an elite who have
the moral initiative to direct the activities of society and yet are
relatively immune from criticism. Now a contractarian agreement to have
an elite is not logically impossible: People do in fact turn to and even
pay all manner of experts to give advice, and this advice very often goes
beyond just laying out the likelihoods of various consequences of choices.
People regularly pay lawyers and physicians to _tell_ them what is in their
legal and medical interests, and there is nothing stopping them from
turning to pastors and philosophers for allegedly expert moral advice.
The field of medical ethics is growing, and it is just possible that
someone, somewhere read an editorial in The New York Times to be
persuaded as opposed to finding out what the Times' latest line was.

It is also logically possible that people would sign a social
contract to empower a state to engage in wholesale case-by-case
redistributive social justice. I argued, however, that limitations on
knowledge of remote consequences of human action constitute what could be
plausibly called an ontological barrier to carrying out this sort of
social justice. This grandiose conception of social justice is a
metaphysical mirage since social contractors would not empower a
government to attempt the ontologically impossible, logically possible
though it may be. (People regularly ask the impossible from government!
What I am claiming is that there are enough New Contractarian Men who
won't to block a unanimous social contract.) On the other hand, a social
contract allowing for progressive inheritance and income taxes is not to
be blocked on metaphysical grounds. It is up to the contractors, not to
outside observers, to decide how much progressivity there is to be and
indeed whether the net result might be regressive, all things considered,
including economic growth.

The question is whether people might hand decisions on the extent of
progressivity over to experts. Now economists might well be consulted on
the trade-offs between progressivity of income taxes and economic growth,
and sociologists on inheritance taxes and intergenerational social
mobility. But this is asking experts to supply the facts, not to make

the actual choices, which rest with the people themselves. Under constitutional government, however, the people do not have to unanimously approve every piece of legislation, and ordinarily the constitution will specify procedures for representation. [28]

Now representatives do indeed represent their constituents' interests, and hence they act like Downs-model politicians. But the goodness of fit is never perfect, because of a two-way limitations of knowledge problem: The representatives know only imperfectly the desires of their constituents, and the constituents know what they want and what their representatives are doing about it also only imperfectly. This gap can be grounds for distrust, but it can also be grounds for trust: Voters can hope that their representatives will act like statesmen and do what is right and, moreover, decide what is right, inasmuch as voters (like everyone else) do not have perfect knowledge of the right. Inasmuch as one's vote has a negligible chance of overturning an election, what Hartmut Kliemt (1986) has called the "veil of insignificance" is operative. This means that it is practically costless to vote for what one thinks is right rather than for what is actually in one's self-interest. In practice, people vote for a combination of both.

So there is plenty of room for an elite of moral experts. This elite will not, in general, coincide with the set of representatives, since they also have problems of moral knowledge, but can also consist of the intellectuals to whom the politicians, and the voters, listen. However, motives to be moral are not usually overwhelming, and this opens up room for another batch of experts, those who claim to know what the "true" interests of various individuals and groups and humanity as a whole are, as opposed to their expressed and revealed preferences.

Elites in this country, at least, emerge spontaneously more than come about by planning or imposition. There are elements of conscious intent, where like-minded people try to help each others' objectives and careers along, and hence there is an element of conspiracy (whose Latin root means "breathe together") though it is mostly decentralized.

From a contractarian standpoint, the issue is not so much whether people want to delegate moral issues to an elite, but rather how to keep the elite in check. A large part, indeed, of The Limits of Liberty is given over to the problem of keeping the state in check, but it is worth asking whether the author of Limits is so extreme in his desire for small government that he might as safely be ignored when denying any claim that near-unanimity exists about the size of government (plus or minus ten

percent) in this country as one would dismiss an occasional hermit. Gargantuan government is here to stay, in other words, because that is what the people want.

The way out is simply to insist that gargantuan government is not what the people want. This can be done by asserting that wants have been perverted: People have become addicted to big government, public education has instilled false values, and people have been intimidated into silence, fail to appreciate the price the state exacts, are too unimaginative to conceptualize alternatives, and are hopelessly out-organized by myriad special interests. All of these charges have been made repeatedly, and Buchanan has let some of these sentiments slip into the pages of Limits, and arguably he is not entirely free from pretensions to be an expert himself, not so much on morals, but on what people "really" want. It is very hard to fight experts without thinking oneself to be a better expert.

Buchanan's method is not to make any of these claims; rather it is to search out a basis for what he calls a constitutional revolution. This means to begin at the present and obtain ideally unanimous agreement on a wholesale package of reforms. In perhaps most cases, individuals are so harmed by all the other laws, institutions, rigidities, and inefficient transfers that they lose in the net, whence no compensation will be needed. In other cases, one-time side-payments will be necessary. But reforms will have to be wholesale, as they have a habit of getting bogged down and few want to go first.

Robert Whitaker (1976) argued that the cycling of elites has happened twice in American history and that a third cycling is now underway. The Virginia planter aristocracy was once in the vanguard of helping the country expand westward, but it degenerated into a slaveocracy and resisted further expansion, since new states were more likely to vote against slavery, the drier soil in the west being unsuitable for cotton. They were replaced with another expansionist power, industrialism, which degenerated into high tariff protectionism, which was replaced by the Human Betterment Industry, now degenerated into what public choice scholars call the transfer state, which is slowly on its way out, to be replaced by something we cannot yet envision. [29]

From the standpoint of a political (as opposed to a social) contract, the Human Betterment Industry is far more powerful than Big Business, which merely got protectionist legislation. Aristocracies of old, however, were the government. It is hard to conceive, however, of

what a social contract would look like that would speed up the cycling of moral elites, including those based upon religion. Certainly, there are those who are impatient at the slowness at which the transfer state is being reduced--it is still actually expanding, though its intellectual basis has been undermined--but from a larger perspective perhaps the cycling is proceeding apace. In any case, it would probably take a super-elite to control the cycling of ordinary elites.

Elites, then, come into being by offering something (it is probably safe to say citizens do want at least some state-provided welfare benefits and progression of taxes to continue, even if they come to agree that much of the transfer state should be reduced), by promulgating a moral theory, and by convincing people of where their "true" interests lie. Challenges to ruling Establishments are made by contradicting these claims on all three levels and getting rival claims accepted. Thus Big Business was attacked for failing to provide effectively for welfare needs, for failure to provide for social justice, and for manipulating consumer wants (Marx's false consciousness). It is very interesting that the current human betterment elite is still justifying its expansion by attacking the business elite of the 1920s! Today, the tables are being turned around: It is the Human Betterment Industry, especially public education, that is promoting false consciousness. The transfer state is being attacked for being ineffective and wasteful. But so far, it is more that the reigning morality of (unlimited) social justice is being undermined than that a new one, or a revival and improvement of an old one, is ready to be implemented. I have no single morality to offer the world; indeed, I will argue for a plurality of social contracts in the last chapter. The next chapter will consider the revival of natural rights.

CHAPTER 5

AYN RAND AND NATURAL RIGHTS

5.1 Similarities and Differences with Contractarianism

In the language of set theory, contractarianism and natural rights
theories have a very large intersection but neither is a proper subset of
the other. It might seem that the unanimity requirement of Buchanan's
contractarianism, the one being examined here, incorporates natural
rights. After all, it is unanimity that distinguishes the social
contract: no one is forced into it, and it is precisely the ban on
initiating coercion that characterizes or is a principal conclusion of
natural rights theories, and in particular that of Ayn Rand. The
difference is chiefly one of emphasis: natural rights theory emphasizes
bilateral exchange in the economy, while contractarianism emphasizes
omnilateral exchange in the polity. At first blush, the two theories,
except for emphasis, are identical.

On the other hand, what rights are to be protected by the protective
state is one of the things social contractors decide upon. They may write
into their constitution rights like those of paid vacations (United
Nations Universal Declaration of Rights), or they may fail to include
rights that natural rights theorists insist ought to be protected, such as
freedom of religion. Natural rights, then, exist whether any group of
contractors recognizes them or not.

Yet the social contract is a fiction: neither Buchanan nor anyone
else is busy collecting signatures! Rather, and as I argued in Chapter 1
in the section on the methodological meaning of the unanimity rule, a
given piece of legislation can be judged, not as having been approved by
everybody, but as having been duly enacted under a constitution that in
the ideal might have been agreed to by everyone. I added to the fiction
of a historical strict unanimity assumptions about the hypothetical
contractors, whom I called New Contractarian Men. These men were to
refrain from strategic bargaining at the constitutional stage, lest the
contract never be made, and perhaps also had to be willing to set envy and
other corrosive emotions aside. They were also presumed to be
knowledgeable about the economic point of view and of the necessity of
building in constitutional sageguards to keep Leviathan at bay.

I can't get absolutely precise about just what New Contractarian Man

will be like, for otherwise I could be charged--quite correctly--with
supposing that every New Contractarian Man subscribes to Frank Forman's
world view (whatever that is) lock, stock, and barrel, if not to his
specific utility function as well. It does no good at all for me to <u>tell</u>
social contractors what constitution they have agreed to! Some
restrictions, like those on strategic bargaining, seem essential for the
contract to be viable, and others like the ban on envy are arguably
plausible, given what we know about human nature. Requiring a knowledge
of economics is asking a lot, but one need only assume either that
those contractors who do not have this knowledge are reasonable enough to
pay heed to arguments coming from those who do or else that the economists
among the New Contractarian Men are numerous enough to form a veto
coalition that will render (quasi-) unanimity impossible. In any event,
which subset of all conceivable social contracts will be viable is an
empirical question, and I hope it is plausible to maintain that a social
order based on bad economics would either have to be imposed by force, as
the Bolshevik takeover was, or would disintegrate, as utopian communities
have.

In the last chapter, I took science at the most general level of
ontology and argued that a contract aimed at wholesale case-by-case
redistribution was a <u>metaphysical</u> impossibility, since it would place
demands upon not-so-large-brained humans that are impossible to be met.
There should remain a fairly wide zone of possible social contracts, and
the question for the present chapter is how closely one might expect to a
social contract to adhere to natural rights.

If New Contractarian Man can be hoped to listen to economists, he
might also listen to natural rights theoreticians, as both speak in a
broad and abstract way about human nature. There are many theorists of
natural rights, and I single out Ayn Rand's philosophy of Objectivism for
discussion, like I singled out Buchanan as an individualist and Unger as a
collectivist. I do so even though her thought is largely outside
mainstrean philosophy for several reasons. Like Bunge, she is a system
builder rather than an analyst or a worker on the superstructure. Bunge's
great project is to bring philosophy in line with contemporary science.
This entails sweeping under the rug many old philosophical issues, like
the existence of an external world (FW 112), but it also means that
philosophy can come up with <u>results</u> of the sort science comes up with, in
his case results of the very general science he takes ontology to be. Ayn
Rand's method is different: to keep going back to basic definitions

and rebuilding from the ground up.

Another reason for discussing her, as opposed to another natural
rights theorist like Nozick, is that she is far from being a perfect
specimen of a modern individualist as described by Unger. As we shall
see, she reaches back to Unger's intelligible essences of the ancient
philosophers, though not in exactly the same way the ancients used the
concept. Finally, her largely deductivist approach about the nature of
man and his rights—she does not use "natural rights," but "man's rights"
or just plain "rights"—may be compared to the empirical scientific
approach of Raymond Cattell, whose efforts at deriving ethics from social
psychology will be discussed in the final chapter. I have chosen her,
then, as with all my authors, for comparison and contrast with one
another.

5.2 The Arguments for Natural Rights

Values, we will recall from the discussion of Bunge's A World of
Systems in Chapter 3, are emergent properties of certain animals. That
an animal has a value system over a set of items means that it can detect
and distinguish among the items and, for each pair, prefers one to the
other or is indifferent. Bunge further argues that animals capable of
learning can modify their value systems. The supreme end for which these
values serve is the homeostatic one of maintaining life (cf. Rand
1961:17), a systemic or emergent property of the organism. Values exist
in this homeostatic context and are not absolute in themselves.

Ayn Rand proceeds from this notion of the end of sustaining the life
of a person, and her notion of rights is based upon very fundamental
considerations of just what a man is. Men need food, clothing, shelter,
but more basically men must exercise their reasoning powers to obtain
them. Men's brains are not hard-wired together, and each must learn [30]
for himself what he needs to do to further his own life. She also holds
that the exercise of reason is a voluntary act, and that this too is a
part of essential human nature (Rand 1961:19). Natural rights doctrines,
then, stress that a man ought to be free to follow the dictates of his own
reason as long as he respects the equal rights of others (Rand 1961:22).
This definition is not circular, she argues, for it is the use of
coercion, and only this use, that can block a man's exercise of reason.

Now, according to Unger, modern individualism entirely rejects the

notion of intelligible essences and therefore any notion of essential
human nature that informs natural rights doctrines. This denial of
essences leads to a radical separation of reason and desire, as discussed
in Chapter 2, and renders any sort of morally derivable basis for a social
order impossible. Unger claims that any set of general public rules will
unavoidably benefit "the purposes of some individuals more than those of
their fellows" (KP 66-67). If we should choose to evaluate some kinds of
behavior over others, we are willy-nilly heading toward conceiving the
essence of goodness.

I shall be arguing later that the case for essences can be made in a
provisional way, at least. Regards Unger's claims of a bias in any set
of rules, this may simply be unavoidable in our imperfect world, and he
never states how big a molehill is involved. Fairness could instead be
regarded as an ideal, much as Buchanan's unanimity criterion is an ideal.
The impossibility of perfection does not entail giving up. [31] The
argument for natural rights--zones of action with which it is wrong for
anyone to coercively interfere--begins with the value of human life and
happiness and proceeds to derive these rights from the essential nature of
man. In a nutshell: 1) essences are real; 2) the essence of man consists
in his being a rational being; 3) rights exist since there are no long-run
conflicts of interests among men.

This last step is necessary, for value is related contextually to the
homeostatic end of a system maintaining itself. Two or more men are so
many separate homeostatic systems, and it must be argued that, rightly
understood, the maintenance of these systems does not conflict. There are
four ways out of this dilemma. The first is to argue the case directly,
which Ayn Rand (1962:50-56, emphases added) does:

> To claim that a man's interests are sacrificed whenever a desire of
> his is frustrated--is to hold a subjectivist view of man's values and
> interests....In choosing his goals (the specific values he seeks to
> gain and/or to keep), a rational man is guided by his thinking (by a
> process of reason)--not by his feelings or desires. He does not
> regard desires as irreducible primaries, as the given, which he is
> destined irresistibly to pursue....The mere fact that two men desire
> the same job does not constitute proof that either of them is
> entitled to it or deserves it, and that his interests are damaged if
> he does not obtain it....Both men should know that...their
> competition for the job is to their interest, even though one of

them will lose in the <u>particular</u> encounter....All of the above
discussion applies only to the relationships among <u>rational</u> men and
only to a <u>free</u> society....In a <u>nonfree</u> society, <u>no</u> pursuit of any
interests is possible to anyone; nothing is possible but gradual and
general destruction.

These are mighty claims. What is going on is deductive argumentation
proceeding from a concept of the essence of man as being contained in his
rationality. Yet men as they actually come, all mortal and many far from
being wholly rational, do stand to gain from coercive rent-seeking.
Rational Man is every bit as much an idealization as New Contractarian
Man, if not more so.

Something else is added, a second way out of the dilemma of potential
conflict of interest: The quotation states that competition, or rather a
free society, is in the long-range interests of everyone. This claim is
not so mighty, and it has been put forward in milder versions by
economists ever since Adam Smith, if not before. Men are no longer so
drastically idealized, although sometimes the long run will come sometime
between when the Sun dies and Hell freezes over. But now the claim is
empirical, not a priori deductivist from the essence of man. As it
happens, proponents of laissez-faire among economists tend to take a
highly deductivist approach in their writings (Mises 1949 and Rothbard
1962), whence the venerable issues of monopoly, intellectual property
rights, and public goods are swept under the rug.

A third way of dissolving potential conflicts of interest is to
invoke a psychology of Rational Man such that his well-being depends upon
his commitment to reason and his respect for reason in others and their
rights. According to this idea--here I follow Ayn Rand and Nathaniel
Branden (the author of several articles in Rand 1964c)--one must earn
one's self-esteem by using reason to be productive. Getting something by
stealing or cheating is taking a short cut that undermines self-esteem.
This means that, contrary to Unger, means and ends are not separate, that
the choice of means matters to well-being. This accords with Bunge's idea
that animals capable of learning can modify their value structures and
that men can "reason about values as well as evaluate reasons" (WS 159).
Or as Buchanan (1978) has put it, "Man wants freedom to become the man he
wants to become." What this means is that reason programs the emotions.
Magda B. Arnold gives the neurological evidence in her <u>Emotion</u>
<u>and Personality</u> (1960).

Unfortunately, while reason and desire are not as separate as Unger claims modern individualism holds them to be, no very specific values, such as which career to pursue, can be deduced from the essential rationality of man alone. Much more needs to be known generally about man the rational animal, in Aristotle's famous formulation, as opposed to man the rational being, in Ayn Rand's fomulation. It is an empirical question how far the pursuit of rationality, shaped by our evolutionary past, eliminates potential conflicts among men and thus makes the case for natural rights.

A fourth way of dissolving potential conflicts is to brush them aside by proclaiming that morality has to do with fairness and that moral rules must apply equally to one and all. The problem is, of course, circularity and, further, that certain kinds of seemingly general rules, such as "Subsidize all economists whose first and last names correspond to unmarried presidents of constitutional republics," should be eliminated. Time was when defining the exact location of the nose in "Your freedom ends where my nose begins" did not seem too problematic; but when United Nations documents speak of the right to a paid vacation, clarification is in order.

A further defense of natural rights, running like a thread through all the others, is that men must act on moral principles. Now in set theory, shoes and ships and sealing wax and cabbages and kings can be gathered together into a set. In Bunge's ontology, on the other hand, there are collections which are not arbitrary but rather are natural kinds arising from the systematic lawfulness of the world (FW 143). The concept of a moral principle could be parallel here and would entail that not every arbitrarily dictated norm of behavior is a principle. Friedrich Hayek's The Road to Serfdom (1944) essentially advocated this and claims that a mixed economy is inherently unstable, or that, in present-day jargon, no (rather inefficient) equilibrium among competitive rent-seekers is possible. It can also be claimed that a moderately dishonest man must either completely reform or go downhill to ruin. This is to claim that, as science is a well-ordered body of lawful principles and not just a catalog description of events, morality is also based upon principles and is more than pragmatism in the negative sense of short-run expediency.

To return to the arguments for natural rights, the second step, that the essence of man consists in his rationality, also raises problems. That men need to exercise their reason is true enough, as it is true that human babies come very underdeveloped and with few wired-in programs to

help them survive. But men are not blank computers--tabula rasa is how
John Locke put it--and many of our drives and values are shaped, though
far from totally determined, by our animal, vertebrate, mammalian, and
primate heritage. Charles Lumsden and E.O. Wilson (1981) use mathematical
arguments based upon evolutionary genetics to argue that tabula rasa is
not efficient and give estimates of the (short) time it would take before
a mixture of wired-in and open programs would come to the fore. [32]

   With the issue of essences, the first step in the argument for
natural rights, I have no fundamental quarrel, even though most thinkers
today reject essences and subscribe to some form of William of Occam's
nominalism, wherein concepts and ideas are just arbitrary names we assign
by convention. (Similarly, economists conceive of values as subjective
and arbitrary.) Charles Peirce, the inventor of pragmatism, hinted at a
way out. [33] I expand upon his hints and hold that, yes, our concepts
are somewhat arbitrary and do have a random component. They become
pragmatic or useful as they fit into scientific theories. Science, or the
study of reality generally, shapes and controls our ideas and definitions.
The deeper and truer the science, the more a preliminary working
definition gets at essential characteristics of things. The idea that
carbon is element number six may not be the last word, but it is far from
an arbitrary change from the old idea of something hard, black, and
lightweight and therefore not a diamond.

   If we view essences not as something eternal but rather as an
ingredient in a helpful definition of a concept, then the case for liberty
as stemming from man's nature as a creature with a reasoning faculty is
not preposterous. What is preposterous, or rather presumptuous, is to
press an idea into service too far, and this is what natural rights
advocates do, especially when they rely upon arguments that are full of
holes; there are disputes even in mathematical logic. This is a fact of
life, but we should be suspicious of those "long chains of deductive
reasoning" that the great Alfred Marshall grew to detest. Such deductions
get carried away from reality at a geometric rate as one proceeds from
link to link in the deductive chain.

5.3 The Advantages of Contractarianism over Natural Rights

   A process approach is deeper than a static one, and this is the
principle advantage of contractarianism over natural rights. A social
contract is an agreement, and an agreement connotes the meeting of the

minds of those who do not share identical views and values. Even if there
is some objective truth about how a society ought to be ordered, men will
come to grasp this truth at different rates. Meanwhile, something
provisional will have to be adopted as long as some social contract is
perceived by all as being superior to the anarchist equilibrium.

Buchanan generally assumes that the rights to be protected by the
protective state are all exactly defined and that their enforcement could
be turned over to an outside agency, but in practice the contractors will
have to strike a balance between rigidity and so great a flexibility that
Leviathan could sneak up unawares by degrees. Natural rights advocates,
by contrast, rarely consider the procedures for refining and redefining
rights as men come to a better understanding of some objective truth about
natural rights. When natural rights advocates discuss a social contract,
they do not consider it as a bargained compromise among diverse interests
but rather as all men coming to the same truth in accordance with right
reason about the essential nature of man. [34]

A second advantage of contractarianism is that it explicitly handles
public goods. Natural rights advocates officially cannot gainsay a
unanimous and uncoerced multi-person agreement to constitute state
machinery to provide public goods, but, unlike Buchanan, they do not dwell
upon the issue. Similarly, they avoid the problem of externalities or
else brush it aside with an a priori conviction that somehow property
rights could be redefined to handle the problem. Even granted that this
be the case, they do not describe the machinery to redefine property nor
argue that redefinition will not be coercive. Legislators and jurists can
undertake the necessary sort of cost-benefit analysis (which is foreign to
deductivist natural rights theories stemming from the essence of man),
even though the problem of keeping these same legislators and jurists
under control remains. Natural rights advocates, when confronted with
particularly severe paradoxes in their beliefs, are prone to retreat to a
"natural rights, but..." position, while contractarians handle these
problems square on.

A third advantage of the contractarian approach is that it pays
attention to institutional design. While natural rights authorities clash
over whether, say, intellectual property (patents, copyrights, trademarks,
and trade secrets) is a genuine natural right (compare Rand 1964b with
Rothbard 1962), social contractors can simply (!) weigh costs and benefits
of establishing rights in intellectual property. Moreover, they can
empower a legislature to set the duration of patents, something that

natural rights theories are utterly incapable of doing. Social
contractors can also set up machinery to make trade-offs between the
costly accumulation of evidence in criminal cases and the probability of
wrongful conviction. Economists habitually, even compulsively, reckon
with trade-offs, a perspective generally absent among philosophers.

A fourth advantage is shown by the first study of Nietzsche in
English (and quite possibly still the best), that of H.L. Mencken (1908):
"With the clash of authority came the end of authority." He was speaking
of Nietzsche's early rejection of religion on the grounds that there could
not be more than one absolute Truth, but the statement may apply to
natural rights doctrines as well. There are just too many philosophers,
from Hobbes and Locke to Rand and Rothbard, laying down diverse
pronouncements, each of them final, about which of the various natural
rights are the true ones. Might it not be better for the people
themselves to make up their own minds about which rights to protect,
whether they call them natural or not? After all and unless we adopt a
holistic metaphysics alien to Bunge's and believe society is some god or
some transcendental object and rights only a manifestation of its glory,
then rights ought to benefit people. And who is in a better position to
know which rights are beneficial than the people themselves?

Yet "authorities" known as philosophers take over and tell the people
which rights they have agreed to. Thomas Hobbes, for example, tells them
that they are so frightfully warlike that the only right they have kept is
to remove a sovereign who fails to keep the peace. (Hobbes is not usually
classified as an advocate of natural rights. But the one right, that
of revolution, is of the highest importance.) John Locke, who holds a
less fearsome view of human nature, lets them keep a good deal more. John
Rawls, as East Coast liberals read him, says the people have agreed to
East Coast liberalism, though my own reading of A Theory of Justice (1971)
makes me think he moved in a libertarian direction during the twenty years
he spent writing it. (I got this impression by reading it cover to cover
in a week, or about 1/1040 the time he spent writing it.)

Objectivists also invoke contractarian arguments. Thus Peter
Schwartz (1986): "Obviously, in a system based on objective procedures
for uncovering the truth, some defendents will ultimately be acquitted.
But even they, if they keep the full context in mind, will understand that
such a system serves their true interests and protects their freedom, even
though it can at times apprehend the wrong man."

This all would seem to mean the end of authority, too, but the

merit of <u>Limits</u> is that it moves away from authority in the direction of
realism, a fifth advantage that sees the social contract as economists see
contracts: as agreement, exchange, bargain, compromise. Compromises can
be made, and we don't have to wait for everyone to agree with every jot
and tittle that John Rawls, or John Locke, or Thomas Hobbes wrote. Maybe
even this distinguished trio could come to some sort of agreement, if only
to stop fighting one day a week and hold a pow-wow on the ideal social
contract. Buchanan, it will be recalled, very definitely recognizes that
a social contract need not at all be the best one possible.

5.4 Value and Fact Again

In practice, the sort of political order set up by social contractors
in anything approaching unanimity may differ only very slightly from a
natural rights order. Natural rights arguments from the <u>nature</u> of man as
a rational being have a plausibility about them that social contractors
might well come to follow closely. Any society based upon natural rights
will, in practice, have to keep redefining rights (sometimes coercively),
and some sort of consensus regarding the legitimate authority of the
redefiners will emerge, lest anarchy and blood feuds come to prevail.
Regards the productive state, given the unanimity requirement, it is
likely that someone will use his veto power to assure that the rules of
procedure for providing public goods will not depart too drastically from
unanimity. So could someone favoring big government, but the costs of
remaining in anarchy should result in his not holding out for very long.
Big governments, so natural rights advocates seem to assert from first
principles, are not stable. Buchanan might sadly retort that an
inefficient equilibrium--in the sense that unanimous and wholesale
revision of the constitution is possible--might be long lasting anyhow and
that corrupt communism in the Soviet Union might drone on for a very long
time without a relapse into the terrors of Stalinism. (That this has
actually happened is described in Simis 1982.) The Soviet government is
the result of a social contract only under Lenin's stretched conception of
one. Perhaps the only viable polities that will remain constitutional are
those whose protective states approximate the night watchman state and
whose productive states are very small. <u>If so</u>, then describing the subset
of viable constitutional orders in fundamental (essential) terms could be
similar to the task of defining natural rights. And <u>if so</u>, the difference
would then be more metaphysical, regards the kind of thing rights are,

than practical.

Ayn Rand has argued that active [35] rationality is the major, if not the only, means to serve the good and that the values men pursue, when rightly understood, do not conflict. I have argued that these arguments are full of holes, but my purpose here is not to engage in the easy task of nit-picking but rather to show that the case for natural rights needs to be supplemented with assumptions—by no means ridiculous ones—to complete the case. Natural rights theory postulates an abstract Rational Man that is a considerable idealization of the actual animal that evolved into homo sapiens. The jump in the argument is that actual man <u>should</u> behave like ideal man. Who would have qualms about such noble aspirations? <u>Still, the jump is made</u>, and while any natural rights derived from the essence of man should consider his essential animality as well as his essential rationality, the animality too often gets dropped.

Natural rights advocates run into difficulties, even if men strive toward enlightened rationality. Reasonable men will still have disputes; the concepts of rights and property will change; the public goods problem remains. Contractarians try to handle these problems, but they encounter difficulties when they assert that rights are wholly arbitrary and have existence only as the people unanimously agree to them, which unanimity will almost never happen anyhow. Even Buchanan temporizes when he excludes strategic bargaining—how much bargaining he will allow is moot—as a legitimate factor in pronouncing a social contract to be unanimous. We may also have to rule out social contracts that will not last, such as perhaps those that legitimate envy. In short, we have to demand that actual man behave like the New Contractarian Man of Chapter 1, a creature not very different from Rational Man. So, even in contractarianism, a jump must be made from theory to practicality.

Buchanan, our specimen of a contractarian, similarly tends to conceive of man as a rational <u>being</u>, as he explicitly states in <u>Limits</u> that he is being agnostic about human nature. He does not rule out that human nature may be any of a variety of things, unlike Ayn Rand, who positively asserts the <u>tabula rasa</u> doctrine, and this agnosticism serves the purpose of keeping his discussion general and of avoiding strife over the nature of human nature. But by saying nothing, Buchanan could be taken as agreeing with his fellow economists that fact and value are wholly separate.

Unger apparently does not realize it, but the acceptance of the radical separations he speaks of has passed a peak. Karl Marx, although

he ballooned a partial truth out to fatalistic proportions, popularized the notion that a man's station in life influences his political ideology. But far more scientifically, studies of neurology and evolutionary psychology have again mingled fact and value, although at times, seemingly, to replace Marx's environmental fatalism with genetic fatalism. It is the merit of Raymond Cattell, whose work will be discussed in the last chapter, to break free of these two prisons and to hold that heredity, environment, and choice are all mutually interacting determinants of individual and group behavior. Economists study choice, to be sure, but the objects of these choices are usually confined to marginal adjustments, and even there choices are seen as determined passively by "given" utility curves.

Some libertarians tend to exaggerate the importance of free will to the point where a person can choose to be anything he wishes. Objectivists, however, posit a less pliable human nature and stress the importance of the pursuit of integrated, rational knowledge in giving the individual a sense of efficacy and self-esteem. On this view, emotions function as a warning signal that something is amiss with the cognitive structure, by which the emotional network is programmed. Economists would instantly quarrel with this conception, not only because they have adopted the split between reason and value in its possibly naivest form, but also because their studies are geared to the fine details of marginal adjustment. It is hard to see what applicability this broad conception of the link between cognition and emotion has to do with choosing among brands of cereal. From a fine perspective, values do indeed seem wholly idiosyncratic, but, if values were wholly objective, there would be no room for exchange, the bread and butter of the economist's work, nor for the multilateral exchange of the social contract.

CHAPTER 6

RAYMOND BERNARD CATTELL AND EVOLUTIONARY FEDERALISM

6.1 The Self of Self-Interest

The self of rational self-interest, like every other concept, gets
fuzzy and elusive when examined up close. The reason is that making and
refining concepts is a part of science, a part every bit as important as
theory building with these concepts and testing out such theories. It is
an ongoing activity and takes hard work. Mario Bunge devoted a large
hunk of his Scientific Research (1967a) to the matter of definition and
James Buchanan wrote a whole book, Cost and Choice (1969a), which he
regards as his most important contribution to economic theory, to
elucidate just one idea. Concept formation is no more to be completed
than is any other scientific activity. As an economist would put it,
concepts get refined until the marginal costs of further refinement start
exceeding the marginal benefits. What saves this statement from being a
pure tautology is the fact that foundational crises periodically take over
and once again it becomes profitable to push for new ideas and further
refinement.

There is a veritable industry attacking atomistic individualism
these days. I examined Roberto Mangabeira Unger's Knowledge and Politics
in Chapter 2. Mention should also be made of Alasdair MacIntyre,
After Virtue (1981), and Robert Bellah, et al., Habits of the Heart
(1985). All of these books pound away at what is now a commonplace thesis
in sociology, that of John Donne's Devotions, "No man is an Island, entire
of itself," oft repeated since Donne's death in 1631.

Yet none of these recent books offers much in the way of a solution
to the paradox of how people might organize their government when said
government will change said people. Thus, it can be charged that having
the government protect "capitalist acts among consenting adults" (Nozick
1974) will result in the Consumer Society and turn people, who naturally
yearn for cooperative community, into dog-eat-dog competitors (Kohn 1986)
and/or self-satisfied pigs who denude Nature's Gifts. Thus, it can be
contrarily charged that the Welfare State breeds dog-eat-dog rent-seekers
and, through public education, dupes people into acquiescing in
ever-larger government bureaucracies. (My case for the latter,
"Egalitarianism as a Morality Racket," an address to the Southern

Economic Association, is reprinted in the Appendix.)

These books, as well as a flurry of other recent writings, invoke
(often explicitly) the Greek ideal of the good life and argue that man is
fulfilled only when he actively participates in the polis. According to
Aristotle, man is by nature a political animal. Such is his natural end,
toward which, moreover, he ought to strive. Ayn Rand also invokes
teleology when she distinguishes keeping the heart pumping from "man's
survival qua man" (1961:24) and argues for the three cardinal values of
reason, purpose, and self-esteem and the three corresponding virtues of
rationality, productiveness, and pride (1961:25). She builds her theory
of rights upon the claim that the virtue of productiveness is undermined
when a person takes a short cut of obtaining something by force or fraud.
It is this grounding of politics and natural rights in ethics that makes
her philosophy an important attempt at system-building.

But while Ayn Rand regards government as absolutely necessary to
protect rights, and has devoted some space to the challenges of
developing good government and laws (e.g., 1963 and 1964a), and while
talent of high order will no doubt be necessary to hammer out the
details, the overwhelming mood of her writing is that the productive and
virtuous life is not to be found in politics, at least not for very long.
Basically, she wants to be rid of politics, as indeed do most writers of
the Public Choice school. This again is the overwhelming mood of these
writers, who implicitly look upon rent-seeking as the bad life, harmful to
the psychological well-being of people so engaged. It is difficult to
document this mood, at least in scholarly writings, and when Dwight Lee
(1987) tries to correct the impression of Public Choice scholars as being
entirely negative toward government, he does not provide documentation
either.

Officially, claims Lee, Public Choice scholars are upbeat when it
comes to government. This is true of Buchanan's contractarianism,
especially regards the productive state in its provision of public goods,
but also regards the protection of rights by the protective state. True
enough, the illegal Constitution of 1789 plus all the usurpation of power
since has turned our government into something richly deserving of
criticism, but still, engaging in politics could be an important component
of the good life were there a good (unanimously approved of) government in
place. And I daresay that had Ayn Rand thought about it, and even while
she holds there to be knowable principles concerning what in truth
government should be doing (which is quite distinct from Buchanan's notion

of government as omnilateral <u>exchange</u> not at all aimed at some truth),
challenging opportunities to both get closer to the truth and carry out
the details of its implementation would always remain, just as creative
opportunities to better production in the economy always remain.

Unger, MacIntyre, and Bellah are not, then, so completely wrong about
the polis playing an important role in the ideal of the good life. They
may be naive optimists, they may be too little concerned about chaining
Leviathan, they may even have few objections to the transfer state except
that it doesn't transfer enough. They may, in short, be grievously
underexposed to the public choice literature (or even the daily
newspapers!) about how far politics has degenerated into <u>bellum omnium in</u>
<u>omnes</u>; still, they do not have to embrace a woolly collectivism to hope
for the day when politics can help transform the self into a better self.
The optimism of these authors is, shall we say, premature and, in the case
of case-by-case redistributive social justice, asking for the impossible,
even for the metaphysically impossible, as I argued in Chapter 4, based
upon the sharp finitude of the human brain in grasping remote consequences
of human action. I do not want to exalt our present difficulties with
keeping budgets and deficits under control to the level of ontological
gloomism, at least not yet.

At this point I must repeat the lesson of Bunge's scientific
metaphysics: <u>No values outside of individuals</u>. This rules out any
conception of the good that does not redound to the benefit of, ideally,
each and every one of the individuals who form, in Bunge's term, the
composition of the social system. This does not rule out politics making
political animals better animals, but it is just and only the animals
themselves that are to benefit. Now there is truth in the statement that
not everyone always knows what is good for himself--the limitations of our
brains guarantee as much--but there is an ever-present temptation for
those removed from any given individual (namely others) to claim to know
what is in the given individual's best interests. I direct the reader
back to the section on elitism in Chapter 4 and insist that anyone who is
so keen upon politics making better men that he has a specific and
detailed constitution for forcefully implementing his hopes be prepared to
argue his case, not on the basis of hope and/or so-called good intentions,
but on the basis of actual understanding of how human psychology and
public choice interact. This is asking a good deal, but subjecting the
unwilling to risk yet another failed utopia is asking much more. Strict
contractarianism--notarized signatures of every last person--can stand a

certain amount of compromise, but the sheer scope and quantity of
government failure in the twentieth century suggest that compromises be
made reluctantly.

6.2 Teleology

Teleology is dubious business. Some want to strip even man of this
holdover anthropomorphism. Biologists look upon evolution as short-run
opportunistic rather than goal-directed. This means that, while wings
have an obvious function and survival value for birds now, each stage in
their development had to have had additional survival value for the bird
at the time. (The problem of wings is unsolved, at least using the
unanimity criterion, and conferences are held to discuss it.)

Functional explanations in the social sciences are similarly found
suspect, especially by Jon Elster, in favor of microfoundational
explanations as to how individual goal-seeking leads spontaneously to
overall regularities (often unwanted or even diswanted) that, to be sure,
can look as if they were consciously planned. Elster may be going too
far, since individuals can and do aim at collective results, such as a
target rate of economic growth. Also, our readiness to attribute
unconscious or concealed motives to people need not be entirely amiss just
because as yet we have no really good theory of human hypocrisy. After
all, public choice scholars and Marxists alike routinely unearth
self-interest explanations for behavior, oftentimes much too quickly.

The reason why the free-rider problem is so often solved beyond any
sufficient explanation from self-interest (think about just how often it
is!) is because men are language- and symbol-using animals. We
conceptualize some group to which we belong as having interests. We then
identify our self, or part of it, with the group in a way economists would
call an interdependence of utility functions. Call this a corruption of
the true, primordial Ur-self, whose drives are somehow "given" (Unger's
arbitrary desires, again), if you wish, but it is just as probable that
language co-evolved with our emotions and drives. If so, the mere
cognitive act of identifying oneself with a group brings with it a desire
to further the interests of the group as such, thereby changing one's self
and one's self-interests in the process. This is plainly not supposed to
happen, and economists will look very hard for explanations other than one
so patently irrational as this one. But why not? Why not become an
enthusiastic joiner and forego free-riding in the full awareness that

joining will both alter one's desires and satisfy them too? Nothing wrong
with this at all, except that Unger's description of individualism fits
economists to a T: Reason and desire are supposed to be utterly separate,
with desires arbitrarily gushing out of the limbic system and/or reptilian
brain (terms, by the way, Unger never uses. He actually wrote a whole
book on emotions, Passions (1984), fully one hundred twenty-five long
years after The Origin of Species, without any discussion of biology!)

      I am not sure how it could be tested, but it could well be that words
and symbolic constructs do not just sit on the top layer of the brain but
go all the way down. See Yeo 1979 for evidence generally that the
evolution of vertebrate brains involved changing the older parts of the
brain as well as tacking a penthouse on top. Individualism, in other
words, got its neurology wrong. Some separation, no doubt a very great
deal, remains between reason and desire (similar to the specialization of
the hemispheres of the cortex for theory and fact I discussed in Chapter
2), and so there is likewise no automatic justification for the other
extreme of a collectivism that proclaims we'll all be happy if only we
love one another. In other words, joiners and free-riders will always be
with us.

      Now, to wend our way back out of these digressions: Man is a
symbol-using animal, and this confounds reason and desire. (Other animals
use symbols, too, and I'm not at all clear how men differ.) This has
potentially powerful implications for the design of institutions,
especially as far as the propensity to identify one's self and one's
self-interest with one's group goes. Social contractors who understand
this may well want institutions that nudge them into being joiners. On
the other hand, Robert Nisbet has argued in many books, beginning with The
Quest for Community (1953), that we join readily enough as it is and that
the real problem is that both radical individualists and totalitarians
alike despise associations (Edmund Burke's little platoons) between the
individual and the state, individualists because they despise associations
of all kinds and just barely tolerate the state as a protector of
atomistic individuals' rights, and totalitarians because guilds, churches,
clubs, and the like get in the road of the state's total power. Nisbet
doubts that isolated individuals can be much of a bulwark against
Leviathan on the march. Clearly there are problems of constitutional
design (checks and balances) here.

      The role of symbols, besides changing utility functions, also allows
interests to be pursued, and teleological ends to be promoted, without

full conscious intent. Thus, the systematic downplaying of the role of religion in American history textbooks used in public schools need not be the result of a conscious conspiracy of Secular Humanists (implausible, given the tiny circulation of their publications). More likely is that "religion" is a trigger-word, a symbolic construct that sets off a negative reaction in those who, if they reasoned the matter through the way Nisbet does, would see in religion an intermediate body between the individual and the state that blocks their aggrandizement of power.

I am not postulating a sort of unconscious Public Choice homunculus (whose knowledge is two hundred years ahead of the authors of the journal Public Choice) inside every brain, in a manner parallel to Freud's superhuman id. Going along with the findings of modern sociobiologists and ancient Greeks that men are incurably moral, most of us (as with public school history teachers above) would be appalled at the very idea that we are power hungry. The homunculus must work by stealth and therefore not very efficiently. Besides, it seems unlikely on evolutionary grounds that the homunculus would be a better reasoner than the conscious brain. On the contrary, the homunculus is a very sentimental creature, one that spews out bad vibrations whenever the word religion pops up, inappropriately or not.

I am sure the metaphors and speculations I have been making recklessly will correspond with neurological reality at best tolerably, but my point is metaphysical: Contrary to Elster, we can speak of teleology in the context of group action. The microfoundations Elster seeks are to be found in the way the brain uses words, making use of hypocrisy and self-delusion when overcoming the free-rider problem. These explanations should not be overdone, but neither should appeals to self-interest by public choice scholars and Marxists agreeing with Unger's depiction of individualists, appeals that too often stop at the first explanation that comes to mind. As in so many other cases, a judicious assessment, never easy to confirm, of the strengths of various forces impinging on the human personality (raw self-interest, moral scruples, a propensity to identify with the group) must be made.

Teleological, or functional, explanations of group behavior, then, are not entirely out of place. But what about what Unger calls "intelligible essences" and the idea that there can be a gap between what a thing is and what it ought to be? Ayn Rand distinguishes man from "man qua man" and uses this distinction to derive natural rights. Alasdair MacIntyre unearths the Aristotelian doctrine of man the political animal

and sees his fulfillment in the polis. I detailed objections to Ayn
Rand's arguments in Chapter 4 and could do much the same with MacIntyre's.
But social contractors are free to implement either or a mixture of both
without waiting around indefinitely for philosophers to plug the
arguments' holes. Moreover, they are free to ignore the teleology and ask
why a man should strive toward his natural end just because it is his
natural end. Instead, the contractors might learn about psychology,
neurology, and evolutionary history and build their social contract upon
this knowledge. In Chapter 4, I argued that the theory of psychology
behind Ayn Rand's Objectivism contains the claim that there are no
long-run conflicts of interests among rational men. This claim, I argued,
has been far from completely established. Yet to the extent social
contractors come to think it is true, to that extent will they enshrine
Ayn Rand's natural rights in their contract.

I propose next to rope a sixth thinker into the discussion, the
social psychologist Raymond B. Cattell, who is best known for his theories
of human personality and as a pioneer in factor analysis, a statistical
method for letting the data emerge with the dimensions or axes of
personality rather than say what the major groupings are in advance.

6.3 Cattell's Morality from Science

Let us recall Bunge: "What distinguishes man from the other animals,
with regard to evaluation, is that he can reason about values as well as
evaluate reasons." (WS 159, my emphasis) Buchanan 1978 says it
differently: "Man wants liberty to become the man he wants to become."
Buchanan does not mean that men can sprout wings. In Bunge's terms, the
laws of systems, individual human and also social, allow only certain
becomings (lawful changes of state) out of all conceivable and wishful
ones. These limitations are by no means as well understood as they might
be, and it is the business of psychologists and sociologists, as well as
economists, to try to find them out. In particular, it is the job of the
social psychologist to study the possible (i.e., scientifically lawful)
interactions between the individual and society. One of the best known
social psychologists is Raymond B. Cattell. He has written a book
combining his insights into social psychology with an ethical view, A New
Morality from Science: Beyondism (1972). This book is hardly informed by
the general view of economists that desires are arbitrary, and in fact
Cattell seems regularly to underestimate the random component of human

wants. But with this caveat, his insights into the lawful formations, or becomings, of desires are worth investigating, and we now turn to his book and its potential usefulness to the present discussion.

Cattell argues that a morality from science is at last becoming possible. Previous efforts foundered on excessive deduction, with too little feedback from empirical reality. Religion and art have made claims to understand life, but at best they have discovered only emotional "truths," with some value in providing for emotional integration with life. Religious values are not to be discarded lightly, for some have stood the test of time. Cattell's views here are similar to Hayek's. Both decry the undermining of values and a sense of social obligation in the wake of Reason. Being sentimental about religion, however, is not very helpful, for one still needs to choose which religious values to retain. Anti-rationality is not one of them!

Cattell is an explicit evolutionist and holds that evolution is the overriding theme of the universe. This may not be so, but we need to evolve further to find out. Cattell gives an argument similar to Pascal's wager that little will be lost by trying evolutionary experimentation, while much stands to be gained. While Unger, in his discussion of evolving human nature, fails to mention biological evolution, Cattell places biological on equal footing with cultural evolution. He urges the deliberate formation of new racial and cultural units, their isolation, and their eventual careful cross-fertilization.

Cattell sees evolution primarily as competition between groups. His book appeared before the term sociobiology gained currency, and much controversy over the reality of group selection in animals has raged since in efforts to reconcile what appears to be altruism on behalf of the group with the necessary diminution in genes fostering altruism left behind as altruists sacrifice themselves, and thus their numbers of offspring, for the group. [36] When it comes to humans, however, institutions and ideas can be passed along outside of biological reproduction, [37] thus allowing for group selection.

For Cattell, the final arbiter of a moral system is its survival. Knowledge of the social sciences, especially of social psychology, can be utilized to help foster the survival of each group and also to ensure a variety of man-made moralities in different groups so that evolutionarily diverse directions can be pursued, evaluated, and learned from. Cattell, himself a pioneer in factor analysis, proposes using this technique to find the factors that influence such dimensions as affluence, morale,

social pressures upon individuals to make cultural advances, solidarity, order, and so forth. It may happen, for instance, that a high divorce rate has side effects on morale but that deaths from alcoholism have greater side effects (138). There will be costs and benefits of altering these causes, and what actions to recommend will depend upon the total situation of each particular society. In general, there will be maintenance values all societies share but plenty of room for values to experiment with in each society as it pursues its own evolutionary destiny.

Cattell claims that his morality differs from previous ones in that it is to be grounded on science rather than revelation or abstract reason, which more often than not assumes Christian values by default. (He views modern Humanism as taking tolerance to the extreme.) But more important, Cattell's morality is not universalist: "It is an easy intellectual and emotional mistake to suppose that what is super-personal, transcending the individual, ought to be universal." [38]

Cattell sees the selective effects of war as far too haphazard and random in character to serve as an evolutionary test of a society's moral value, and consequently he would have a world government. Beyond keeping the peace, the world government would also serve as a data collection and evaluation agency for each country's bio-social experiment. Just when Cattell would have the world government intervene in the internal affairs of a country is unclear, though he discusses the possibility of intervention in case of unambiguous racio-cultural disaster. [39]

The central aim of a world government is to foster <u>cooperative competition</u> among countries and the production of variation and natural selection. He would have countries much smaller than at present, and so would Buchanan and Unger. [40] Cattell would at times reduce cultural borrowing and immigration, both of which cloud the effects of selection, but would allow for a certain hybridization, carefully watched, to alternate with these periods of isolation. He would restrict international aid to alleviate poverty when such aid would have the perverse effect of perpetuating it.

Such is the basic outline of Beyondism in the abstract. Cattell has opinions aplenty about what maintenance values will be necessary for any society. He would have the government divided into a branch of experts, to decide means, and another branch, in which "every individual counts equally," [41] to decide ends. It is unclear how free a hand the second branch would have, for he also states that "toleration of differences over <u>ends</u> should have a limit." (450) In case there is too much disagreement

over ends, Cattell sees a solution in migration or the formation of
splinter groups. (450-1) He sees a basis for such legislative separation
in the brain, where wants come from autonomic systems and means from the
central nervous system. (345) Nevertheless, desire must be tempered and
channeled by reason, for any emotion can err, since our past genetic
endowment is inadequate to our modern needs. (329)

Of specific emotions, Cattell sees as particularly dysfunctional
in the modern age envy (156,301,331,360,442,454), sexuality, [42] and
pugnacity. [43] But more generally, he comes across as a stern moralist,
who regards altruism as a necessity. [44] He comes down against senseless
luxuries [45] and even just wasting time and against hedonism generally.
[46] He stresses the importance of character education (371) and claims
that the modern view that what is degenerate or in bad taste is just a
matter of opinion is valid only when it comes to values derived from
intuitive religions as opposed to empirical science. (394)

This stern and moralistic life has its payoffs, however, and Cattell
waxes enthusiastic about the excitement to be found in communities of
astronauts, scientists, and artists (430) and holds that the emotional and
aesthetic quality of science is fully equal to that of the arts. (209) In
general, Cattell says "feeling must adjust to reality," (441) and "the
Beyondist says, 'This is the nature of the universe and my position in
it. If my feelings do not fit this, it is because my emotional structure
has not yet evolved harmoniously with my capacity to understand.
Therefore I need to evolve and learn emotionally.'" (427) He also states
as a fact that "evolution toward greater cognitive understanding is also
evolution toward richer emotional life." (105)

Cattell's intertwining of reason and desire and his opinions about
what the Greeks called the good life (which implies the existence of
rational ends) go strongly against the radical separation of reason and
desire Unger described as characteristic of the individualist world view.
More problematic still is Cattell's belief in authority for morals,
(421-2) with an implied trust in experts. (424) He states: "The greater
fraction of the possible diseases of authority is eliminated when
authority itself is built for constant research and movement" (425) and
also, "If morality becomes a branch of science it has the authority of
truth." (440)

Such statements will hardly sit well with a contractarian like
Buchanan! However, there is no automatic reason why agreement could not
be achieved on some, maybe much of what Cattell has to say, particularly

if the adoption of his values becomes generally recognized as necessary for a progressive society. Cattell fully appreciates the underdevelopment of the social sciences and it may turn out that some of the values he treasures are optional or even counterproductive, either in every society's common maintenance values or in the context of the experimental values particular societies may wish to adopt provisionally. In either case, it is not necessary to push any specific value to the extreme. Each society will make its own decisions, subject only to limitations on such matters as waging war.

Cattell, like Unger and unlike Buchanan, does not develop his ideas within an explicitly contractarian framework, and his views on contractarianism are bound to be somewhat unclear and inconsistent. Yet he does espouse contractarianism explicitly in places: "Now the position of evolutionary morality is that definable rights can be set up by a contract between the individual and his government; but there are absolutely no such things as 'man's rights' in the abstract." (266) He later says, "The control of a society regarding those to be born into it is at present so weak that no responsible party representing society could enter a contract. Certainly, society cannot be said to have chosen with whom it will enter a contract." (286) Cattell embraces a contract theory beyond that of most contemporary contractarians when he states that Beyondism "asks the state to recognize the rights of the unborn and extends morality to genetics." (270) More problematic, but still possible, would be the adoption of his position that inherited wealth "should be phased out at the same rate as that with which genetic eminence disappears in families, which is fairly fast." (152; see also 322). Also problematic in today's welfare state environment is his multi-generational contractarian perspective that enables him to say that "any realistic ethical system must regard a man who begets eight children on public welfare as someone as socially dangerous as any criminal." (355) [47] Cattell's morality explicitly goes to the composition of a social system, in Bunge's sense, as well as to its structure. On the other hand, support of free speech, fair play, mutual respect even in sharp disagreement, and the Golden Rule are much less problematic.

Many of the values Cattell sees as desirable within nations carry over to relations between nations, and he urges that no single nation have a monopoly of power or culture. Cattell even goes beyond the generations of humans and of new human races when he speaks of new species beyond man and invokes a "transcendental conscience which is the individual

conception of purpose as it exists outside any human group." (439)

6.4 Criticism of Cattell

    Such, then, is an outline of Cattell's "new morality from science,"
Beyondism. It has contractarian elements in common with Buchanan, an idea
of diverse moralities in a federated structure, the concept of which lies
implicit in Bunge, and the notions of an evolving human nature and of a
remixing of reason and desire found in Unger. Cattell goes beyond Unger
and Buchanan in applying results from social psychology to arrive at
specifics, and he emphasizes the genetic half of genes and environment
which Unger totally ignores. And his metaphysics, while never explicit,
need not clash with Bunge's, although a familiarity with the latter's
writings could well have obviated certain statements that smack of holism.
    All of this means that Cattell's efforts are pioneering, but how
valid is his achievement? From a contractarian, the question to ask is,
How likely are Cattell's proposals to be adopted unanimously? The answer
is, of course, not very likely and surely not immediately. But neither is
the whole world going to adopt Buchanan's unanimity rule and stop imposing
values on others. Nor will Christians adopt Bunge's metaphysics or
right-wingers Unger's radical egalitarian vision. A conceptual agreement
would be possible for Cattell's vision only if the contractors are placed
behind a veil of ignorance of suitable thickness: If a man, say, did not
know whether he was going to be a hedonist, he might well take the risk of
having to live in a society, such as the one Cattell advocates, that
clamps down on hedonism, assuming that he accepts Cattell's findings in
social psychology.
    A much more pointed question can be asked: Is Cattell behind a
veil of ignorance? Probably everyone imposes his own personality on the
utopia--in Cattell's case, utopias--he constructs. When Cattell states
that "all progress, as far as we can control it, should be at a maximum
pace" (277, my emphasis), he is exposing his own values, and not even his
own, if he has any use for simple loafing and enjoyment of life. Cattell
himself may not waste much time, [48] but a multi-generational social
contract will compromise between the desire to loaf and each generation's
wish that past generations had wasted less time. The fear that Beyondism
will degenerate into a regime imposing harsh and arbitrary Puritanical
values on an unwilling citizenry is a real one.
    But Cattell's calling for a maximum rather than an optimum rate of

progress may be more a lapse in reasoning than an imposition of his own values. More telling are his strictures against sexuality, which he scolds for much more than merely taking up time. He offers some evidence for this (396-7), but it strikes me at least as rather weak. Here he pitches the optimum amount of Puritanism too high, compared to what might be reasonably expected under a multi-generational social contract. If it is simply economic growth that is the multi-generational issue, any good free-marketeer could quickly reply that too much sex could be efficiently counteracted by changing the tax laws, not by regulating sex. Furthermore, coitus can be one of life's finest rewards and stimuli for some, though ruinous for others. Yet Cattell shows no recognition of this variability. It is not clear, however, whether Cattell is advocating government intervention in this area.

In general, Cattell has too much naive faith in experts, whether to legislate in the area of government having to do with implementing means, to speak about rational ends, or even to evaluate bio-social experiments, without grossly abusing their powers. Experts disagree among themselves, and the studies he refers to are often based upon small-numbers psychological experiments, which, although usefully indicative, are far from conclusive about peoples or countries as a whole. Cattell is also far too optimistic about controlling the experts, a problem he only vaguely alludes to. Unger is also optimistic, and both could do well to absorb Buchanan's Limits.

A more general problem is that, for all his talk about different countries having different values, but a few maintenance values in common, Cattell gives no real flavor of these differences. It seems that each value he does invoke is universal both in its validity and in its extent. If there is any point to having many countries, it is that their affairs be run differently, as best suits the social contractors in them.

To see how this might turn out, let us take a leaf from a constitutionalist of a wholly different sort than Buchanan. He is William H. Sheldon, best known for his classification of human physiques into strengths along the three dimensions of endomorphy, mesomorphy, and ectomorphy. The extremes of human constitution or body types are represented by the fat man, the strong man, and the thin man, respectively, but every person is a mixture of all three. What Sheldon is less known for is his development, in The Varieties of Human Temperament (1942), of constitutional psychology and of his finding correlations of eighty percent between the strengths of each component of the physical

constitution and a corresponding component of personality. The fat man
tends to love food, comfort, and company, the strong man physical
activity, and the thin man solitude and contemplation. All three are
needed, these talkers, doers, and thinkers.

Sheldon does not claim that a person's body type determines every
aspect of his behavior and gives cases of individuals with the same body
type but with quite different personalities. Still, the very broad
similarities observed among those of similar body types are striking. We
need not ask acceptance of Sheldon's results here--the older idea of
Montesquieu that climate determines the form of government will do--but
since Cattell upholds the importance of group genetic differences, this is
an illustration that may point up Cattell's biases. So when he decries
"women with extensive fore and aft projections" (351) and "the
overbreasted female of American Playboy pin-ups," (397) one suspects he is
simply stating his personal preference for ectomorphs, which is of course
his privilege.

Cattell, then, fails to carry the implications of bio-cultural
differences that he makes in the abstract over into the particular. For
long stretches, it seems as though Cattell thinks he already has the
answers, that his own particular bio-social type is the best one, and that
experimentation is quite pointless. It may well turn out that Prometheans
(Sheldon's 2 3 5 temperament, on his 1 to 7 scale for each of the three
dimensions) are the most progressive, but it could also turn out that a
society of Cattells would produce so many with Messiah complexes that
constant feuding would be the norm. I am referring here to Sheldon's
finding that 65 percent of paintings of Jesus depicted him as a 2 3 5 or
a 2 3 6. Judging from Cattell's photograph, his own type is close to a
2 3 5. (So, incidentally, is the present author.) Other societies of
different body types (somatotypes) will produce different excesses, but
within each society some sort of optimal diversity about a desired mean
might potentially be agreed upon.

These criticisms of Cattell, and pointing up of his biases, are not
crucially important to the present discussion. What counts, in the
metaphysics of liberty, is Cattell's idea of federalism, of different
peoples having different social contracts. Values are partly objective,
as in Cattell's maintenance values which all societies share, and partly
subjective, as in Cattell's experimental values which can be partly shaped
by group genetic differences. What we have is a kind of pluralism that
could be dubbed moral federalism.

A further criticism of Cattell is that, like nearly everyone else, he has produced a <u>one-planet book.</u> While he <u>is</u> a far more thoroughgoing advocate of diversity than almost anyone else, his fears of an irremediable breakdown are similar to Buchanan's fears of the erosion of public capital. [49] But it would take only one or a few space colonies pursuing Beyondism for it to take hold, while all the rest could sink into hedonistic stagnation or retrogression. [50] More difficult still for any social theory in general and for multi-generational contractarian theory in particular, is that while the future can be taken into account, one basically relies upon current knowledge. If the future is progressive, future generations will know far more than we do and tear up any contract we sign, or philosophy we espouse, as being hopelessly outdated. While we might try, with Nietzsche, to build the house for the superman--or fabricate him out of silicon--we are stuck with only a very poor conception of what the superman would be.

6.5 The Ontology of Federalism

What exactly is a federated political order in Mario Bunge's terms? Recall that the composition of a system, social or otherwise, is the list of the system's parts. Now in Bunge's Chinese-box ontology, the parts exist on several layers. A social system may be conceptually decomposed to people, at the living layer, to all the molecules of all the people at the chemical level, and so forth. (FW 29-30) In a federated social system, there is also a country layer, into which the federation of countries is decomposed before decomposing to individuals.

Speaking of countries as units courts metaphysical confusion, the dangers of which are explored by Viktor Vanberg, "Organizational Goals and Organizations as Constitutional Systems" (1983). Vanberg argues that the notion of the goal of an organization is held to be both indispensable and problematic in that it suggests that an organization and its goals exist in a reified ontological realm apart from the individuals in the organization and the separate goals which each of them hold. Vanberg would rather conceive of an organization as being a constituted set of rules that regulate the actions and goal-seeking of the members, who need not have any goals in common.

Vanberg's formulation seems to get around the metaphysical problems. Nevertheless, few are going to adopt his circumlocutions when statements like "All institutions outlive their usefulness" are much more compact and

economical to use and furthermore get the message across. [51] But what
does this statement mean? Recall that the structure of a social system is
limited by natural laws, including the laws of social systems. Even
without government, there are customs, regularities, and predictable
behavior that Buchanan calls "ordered anarchy." Much of this order has
roots going back beyond mammalia. In formal organizations, ordered
anarchy is supplemented by man-made rules. The workings of the
organization, constrained by the laws of reality, can go contrary to the
hopes and expectations of individuals. The time may come when the
organization is counter-productive to all concerned but where there is no
easy way out. This situation is called a dead end or a cul-de-sac by most
and the "transitional gains trap" by Gordon Tullock (1975). There may be
a way out, but only through wholesale reform. The "law" that all
institutions outlive their usefulness is a claim that such is always bound
to happen. The law is probably just a very strong tendency, [52] but
institutions can outlive their usefulness because of the difference
between scientific laws and man-made rules. The connection between the
two is tenuous, and we apprehend these connections oftentimes at best
dimly. Omniscient beings would never fall into a cul-de-sac.

Nevertheless, countries are organized systems and it is worth
asking whether it is metaphysically sinful to attribute goals, actions,
interests, etc., to them rather than just restricting such terms to
individuals. Any answer will be arbitrary, for reality is constantly
changing and the things in it shifting, to a certain degree, from one
ontological category to another. Gordon Tullock argues, in
Coordination without Command: The Organization of Insect Societies
(unpublished MS, c. 1960), that for at least some purposes an ant hill can
be regarded as a single organism and the individual ants as cells. When
it comes to corals, distinguishing individuals within a coral becomes very
problematic. By the same token and again for some purposes, individual
humans can be thought of as cells of an organism called a country.

When metaphor stretches into reification is not always clear.
Is a country somehow a "natural" unit? Recall Bunge's definition of a
natural kind from Chapter 3, "Thing," of his furniture book: A natural
kind is a set of things that obeys a scientific law or several such laws
conjointly. A law, in turn, describes the possible states or changes of
states of certain things. Bunge advances this definition of natural kind
to distinguish purely arbitrary sets of things from sets that fall under

various laws of science. Electrons clearly constitute a natural kind, but our knowledge of social laws is so poor that it is hard to say whether countries are.

Fortunately, there is another way to look at whether countries are natural kinds. This is to take a leaf from biological taxonomy. Given a taxonomy of species, one could expect a natural grouping to conform to certain statistical patterns (such as the size distribution of species in a genus) that are the results of orderly probability processes of evolution (such as the birth and death of species, the Founding Paper whereof being Yule 1924). If, for example, all genera under consideration consisted of exactly three species, the hand of the taxonomist would be evident in producing such a "rational" pattern.

An easy test for countries has to do with a stochastic process similar to Yule's and is given as the so-called rank-size rule, whereby the rank times the population is a constant. China times its population = India times twice its population = the Soviet Union times thrice its population, and so on. This rule works rather well, taking one country with another. China has about twenty times as many people as No. 20 (Egypt), and about forty times as many as No. 40 (Kenya). Actually, India is too big and the Soviet Union too small, [53] but the United States is quite close. A better fit can be had if an exponent to size other than one is used. Invoking more complicated rules can improve the fit even better. In any case, there is evidence of some sort that countries are as natural as biological species.

6.6 Problems for Contractarianism in the Composition of Countries

Countries may be natural, but the placement of boundaries has been a source of extreme friction down through the ages. Men are not necessarily the most quarrelsome animals, but only they can form social contracts, much as other animals act as if they did. [54] Judging from the amount of bloodshed, the composition of a social system is a much more contentious issue than a constitution of man-made rules designed to affect the structure of the system. Bloodshed is arguably a poor basis for judging approximation to unanimity, however, and coercion inside a system may simply be cheaper, as seems to be the case with animal societies generally. Nevertheless, the composition of countries will be less tractable than internal laws, if conceptual agreement is harder to achieve in the former case. This is almost certainly the case, since every border

change is bound to make someone worse off, with practically no exceptions.
Revisionist historians maintain that the plebiscite in Austria following
the Anschluss of 1938 was only a little less popular than the vote of
approval showed, but it is hard to come up with another instance of a
quasi-unanimous border change. In any event, third nations by no means
approved, let alone all the people in all the third nations.

A unanimous federal order requires many simultaneous unanimities on
the part of each person regarding: (1) his own country's constitution for
internal affairs, (2) the country to which he belongs, (3) the country to
which each other person belongs, (4) every other country's constitution,
and (5) every country's constitutional machinery for making international
law, including the provisions for border changes. It would help if each
person delegated to his government the power to form an international
constitution, which could (among other things) change his citizenship.
In such a case, nations could act as units with respect to other nations.

Buchanan swept the difficulties away in a paragraph quoted above
(from LL 103) by assuming freedom of migration. In reality such multiple
unanimities forthcoming are wildly improbable. Even if countries
miraculously went against the record of all history and allowed free
migration, they would no longer have contiguous borders. Pushed to the
limit, individuals could secede from all states, with anarchy resulting.

In "Public Finance and Academic Freedom" (1979a) and elsewhere
Buchanan called himself a pessimist, but he is a great optimist when it
comes to the possibility of agreeing on reforms. He is not so great an
optimist that he drops "quasi" from "quasi-unanimity," and he realizes
that reforms will have to be thoroughgoing indeed to make everyone better
off. Still, the last chapter of The Limits of Liberty, "Beyond
Pragmatism: Prospects for Constitutional Revolution," is not a litany
of despair. Buchanan's optimism leads him to think that, while perfect
unanimity may not be achievable, only a small dent in the ideal will have
to be made in order to get on with the serious business of making
improvements. He would be far less sanguine were he to concentrate on the
composition of countries as opposed to their man-made rules for altering
their structures. Buchanan may well have to depart far from unanimity to
get an international federated order and may even adopt a simple majority
rule. Simple majorities, after all, have the pleasing property that some
decision will be reached and the logjam broken. Buchanan, despite what
Warren Samuels and Leland Yeager say (as was discussed in Chapter 1), does
not want to freeze the universe to the status quo.

Majority rule is not sacrosanct and by no means the best possible rule from anyone's standpoint, as Buchanan and Tullock so well argued in The Calculus of Consent. It is an ethical assumption, and if majority rule can be entertained as a method for deciding on the composition of countries, so can many others. One such rule is to group people by some sort of criterion of naturalness. Possible criteria are language, religion, race, and political homogeneity. African dictators rarely want to cede territory but they frequently want to extend their rule over the remainder of the tribes they govern. Hitler's major foreign policy aim was to put all German speakers in Europe into one country, with the curious exceptions of Switzerland and the Tyrol region of Italy. Religion is a major factor in India, Pakistan, and Bangladesh. The South tried to secede from the Union over political differences. On the other hand, over time, a territory, once seized, can become integrated into the whole, as Scotland perhaps has with England. There are Scots separatists today, but they are in a minority.

A multi-national country is one made up of several natural groupings called nations. The Union of Soviet Socialist Republics is one such, the United States of America another. The United Kingdom perhaps no longer is, while China has been a One for millennia. Ayn Rand, in "Global Balkanization" (1977), has argued that free societies best contain multi-national frictions, but other factors include the degree of centralization. Other hypotheses can be put forth, and a unanimitarian's objective would be to put knowledge on the matter to good use when designing a constitutional world government.

Some problems of the composition of countries are just plain intractable and the unanimitarian is bound to be sorely disappointed despite his best efforts to come up with a solution everyone could agree upon. In this case, a unanimitarian qua unanimitarian has to remain silent about one far-from-unanimous proposal versus another. But there is a dubious way out, frequently seized upon. Under a not very thick veil of ignorance, I would surely prefer a social contract that empowered the government to retrieve stolen property. The veil need be only so thick that I would not know in advance that I was to be one of the relatively few criminals who would oppose the restoration of stolen property. As with individuals, so with nations. Hitler, on this reading, was not wrong to try to restore Germany's boundaries to the status quo ante of 1914. (Such a reenlarged Germany was considered a threat to peace by many, but that is another issue.) The rectitude of taking back Alsace-Lorraine is

ambiguous, but that region has been war booty ever since the death of
Charlemagne's grandson, Lothair. (Maybe by this time there exists a
conceptual contract between France and Germany that to the victor belongs
this particular spoil!) This way out is dubious, however, since any
expansionist power can trump up an excuse of collective security to
justify its territorial grabs.

Other times, no one is in the right. Take the case of Northern
Ireland: The Southern Irish hold that Northern Ireland would belong to
them had England not taken over their island in violation of unanimity (to
put it mildly), while the Scots Irish who have lived there for hundreds of
years point out that their ancestors were forced to go there by the
English. When it comes to trying to restore what would have been had a
(conceptual) social contract continued (or even existed in the first
place), the possibilities for hypocrisy, self-delusion, and just plain
lying are stupendous. The unanimity ideal, like any other, can be
stretched beyond the breaking point.

6.7 Evolutionary Morality

Biological evolution is very definitely a testable theory, one
moreover that has passed the test. In a classic 1924 paper, G. Udny Yule
considered the size distribution of species in a genus and conceived the
first birth and death probability process, now known by his name, to
generate this skewed size distribution. Yule hypothesized that species
split in two at one random rate and become extinct at another. He
compared the theory against reality--made a postdiction--and got a good
fit. As far as I know, Yule's paper has never been cited by evolutionists
in their debate with Creationists, who construe an ambiguous passage in
Genesis, "And God said, Let the earth bring forth the living creature
after his kind, cattle, and creeping thing, and beast of the earth after
his kind: and it was so" (1:24), to deny both the initial evolution of
these beasts and any subsequent speciation after the Sixth Day.

Darwin himself noted the increasing complexity of life forms in the
fossil record as time marched on. Today, we would add increasing order,
organization, and information (negentropy). Peacocke 1984 describes and
discusses these different directions, each of which comes somewhat at the
expense of the other three. He also discusses problems of quantification
and adds that there may be other dimensions. Hence, evolutionary advance
is not uniform. Hence, it is open-ended. And hence, while evolution

might be directed, it cannot be perfectly planned and predicted. Evolutionary theory is very much a framework in which the facts of biology are to be placed and fossils to be interpreted rather than a science so rigidly mechanistic that man could have been predicted upon the appearance of the first hesitant mammal. Evolutionary theory could indeed be called metaphysical, but in the good sense of being very general science like Bunge's ontology. Happily, the theory makes enough contacts with quite hard facts (such are fossils!), as Yule's paper showed, that the framework is a science rather than a set of assumptions so broad as to be untestable (metaphysical in the bad sense).

So what is Cattell up to when he calls for an evolutionary ethics? Is he just jumping on a bandwagon, hooking a prestige word onto his personal preferences? Is he calling for an incorporation of what is known about human nature as a product of evolution into ethical deliberations, as seems to be absent from several of this book's authors? Is he urging us to get realistic and stop planning utopias that go against real constraints of biology? Could he be telling economists that their ever-ready notions of constraints, like production frontiers, are far too abstract? After all, Veblen's classic 1919 paper, "Why Economics Is Not an Evolutionary Science," is still very much worth reading.

An evolutionary morality can mean just about anything. Marx, for example, had very definite ideas on how societies evolve. I shall propose a definition, but first a passage from Lon Fuller, The Morality of Law (1964:9,10,27,28):

As we consider the whole range of moral issues, we may conveniently imagine a kind of scale or yardstick which begins at the bottom with the most obvious demands of social living and extends upward to the highest reaches of human aspiration. Somewhere along this scale there is an invisible pointer that marks the dividing line where the pressure of duty leaves off and the challenge of excellence begins. The whole field of moral argument is dominated by a great undeclared war over the location of this pointer. There are those who struggle to push it upward; others work to pull it down. Those whom we regard as being unpleasantly--or at least, inconveniently--moralistic are forever trying to inch the pointer upward so as to expand the area of duty. Instead of inviting us to join them in realizing a pattern of life

they consider worthy of human nature, they try to bludgeon us into
a belief we are duty bound to embrace this pattern. All of us have
probably been subjected to some variation of this technique at one
time or another. Too long an exposure to it may leave in the victim
a lifelong distaste for the whole notion of moral duty.

If the morality of duty reaches upward beyond its proper
sphere the iron hand of imposed obligation may stifle experiment,
inspiration, and spontaneity. If the morality of aspiration invades
the province of duty, men may begin to weigh and qualify their
obligations by standards of their own and we may end with the poet
tossing his wife into the river in the belief--perhaps quite
justified--that he will be able to write better poetry in her
absence.

Fuller's morality of duty, at the minimum of "the most obvious
demands of social living," corresponds with what Ayn Rand (1961) calls the
(mere) "survival of man" and which I shall call the morality of survival.
Fuller's morality of aspiration corresponds with Ayn Rand's "survival of
man qua man." This I shall call a morality of evolution, the reason being
that, like evolution, the paths to excellence are open-ended and extend
along multiple dimensions, not unlike those of biological evolution, of
increased complexity, order, organization, and information. Again, there
are trade offs: Excellence does not consist entirely in piling up
information; to be excellent, information needs to be organized. One
could make similar analogies and play with them indefinitely and indeed
generate a great deal of debate. What counts is that the pursuit of
excellence is just as uncertain as that of biological advance and can only
partly be directed.

Fuller has apparently mixed up levels of systems, for he speaks of
duty in relation to "the demands of social living," while he refers to
individuals when speaking of aspirations. Let us fill in the other
combinations and speak, in my terminology, of moralities of survival both
for the individual (system of cells) and for the social system, as well as
of moralities of evolution for both. So an individual can just barely
keep going or reach out for excellence in one of many ways, and so also a
society can just barely survive in all due obscurity, by adhering only to
Cattell's maintenance values, or it can reach out for excellence, by
adopting a successful set of experimental values.

The problem with the last lies in avoiding holistic talk, and this is

done by insisting that a society's experimental values redound to the
benefit of its members. Now what benefit consists of is problematic.
Economists, when speaking of benefits, usually have in mind revealed
preferences and the construction of a utility function out of such
preferences when constraints are varied. This is of course all static
and, while useful for some purposes, it is easily subject to misuse and a
far cry from Buchanan's 1978 statement, "Man wants freedom to become the
man he wants to become." It is the job of an evolutionary ethic
(Cattell's, but also Fuller's morality of aspiration and Ayn Rand's
virtues of rationality, productivity, and pride) to say something about
what sort of man he _ought_ to try to become. But if we emphasize the _he_ in
Buchanan's statement, it is the job of an evolutionary ethical theorist to
persuade the individual of the merits of his particular version of such an
ethic.

I could solve this problem merely by choosing the evolutionary ethic
I like best and insist that New Contractarian Man holds it or that people
behind the veil of ignorance would choose it. Making any such
presumptions is decidedly premature, but it is not necessarily forever
preposterous. Here's why: Social psychology is an immature discipline;
in fact, a living person, Raymond Cattell, is one of its pioneers. As
social psychology approaches being a science, its conclusions will become
increasingly accepted (but remember that individual differences will
remain). Even then, though, we are a long way from a _political_ contract.
This contract is not about what the good life is, nor even about how
people ought to interact with one another. Rather, it is about empowering
a government under a constitution, and in its two aspects, the protective
and productive states. Recall Buchanan's statement that men live together
to pursue their _invididual_ objectives, not to strive toward "some
transcendental common bliss." (LL 1) If it were not for the facts that,
in living _together_, individuals and individual objectives change and also
that individuals strive to change themselves into (at least somewhat)
different individuals, designing the constitution would be comparatively
straightforward and we would remain in a world not too much more
complicated than that of The Calculus of Consent. Chaining Leviathan
would remain a problem, as would be designing legislative rules to protect
new kinds of property and to specify the duration of patents and
copyrights. But in a world where there is such a thing as _social_
psychology, a feedback from what Bunge calls the social structure to the
individual, matters become more subtle. The structure can do more than

help or hinder people in achieving their separate objectives. It can goad
them into becoming better persons, or it can bring out the worst and
foster degeneracy.

Now some people are so far sunk in degeneracy that their every act
reveals a preference to become more degenerate. These are not the men
Buchanan probably had in mind when he was speaking of the freedom to
become the men they want to become. Nor did Frank Knight (1935) when he
spoke of men wanting better wants, nor myself when speaking of New
Contractarian Man. Can their consent honestly be excluded from the
unanimity criterion for a social contract? One excuse for doing so is to
suppose that men sunk this far are in fact sunk so farther also that they
are incapable of forming an opinion about the social contract: they do not
and can not consent, but neither can they object. In particular, they
will not object to a social structure that does not actively aid and abet
further degeneration, whether of themselves or others. But here's the
rub: the drug addicts among the degenerate will very likely object
strenuously to laws controlling drugs, even if everyone else prefers such
maternalism to protect them from degeneracy. A libertarian compromise
would allow each person to go to Hell in his own way, which will please
the addicts, but also to go to Heaven in his own way.

However this problem might be handled or ignored, an individual
adopting a personal evolutionary ethic will persist at or desist from
certain actions, but this does not mean he advocates forcefully
prescribing or proscribing them for others. Indeed, one of the features
of an evolutionary ethic is precisely the open-ended character of
evolutionary advance: Advances might be characterized along the axes of
complexity, order, organization, and information, but they cannot be
reduced to a single scale. Nor can anyone know for sure beforehand
whether his plan of action will result in advance. That only the
individual in question can acquire certain kinds of information to guide
him in intelligent planning, information that might better lead to advance
and which is not available to others, in particular to central planners,
is not only a principle tirelessly advocated by Hayek, but also a feature
of all animals with plastic neuronal systems, i.e., animals capable of
learning. (Recall the section, "Bunge on Mind," in Chapter 3.)

An evolutionary ethic at the social system level is one that
facilitates and promotes the realization of the diverse evolutionary
ethics of individuals. This goes beyond Buchanan's 1975 formulation in
Limits, that all that counts is what the contractors unanimously agree

upon, and goes in the direction of his 1978 statement, "Man wants freedom to become the man he wants to become." Recall however that Buchanan explicitly stated that a social contract is the "first leap out of the anarchist jungle," not the best leap, even from an internal point of view. His 1975 and 1978 positions can be reconciled by claiming that the agreements men in fact will reach will provide for the freedom men need to change themselves. I am sure Buchanan is aware of the existence of some men who are apparently hopelessly degenerate and want only to degenerate still further. I am only a little less sure that, excepting certain kinds of genetic, congenital, or infant mishaps, he has significant hopes that a good many, if not most, of these men could have been rescued from a life of degeneration and would have come to be grateful for it. His previously mentioned pessimism, I think I can say, is not over the hopelessness of the human condition as it applies to individual men nearly so much as over the prospects of a critical mass of men coming together to stage a constitutional revolution. As I said earlier, reforms have a habit of getting bogged down and few will volunteer their own turf first.

Although Buchanan has never himself put his 1975 and 1978 positions together, neither has he retracted the first sentence of Limits, "Those who seek specific descriptions of the 'good society' will not find them here." But can his use of "quasi-unanimity" and "conceptual contract" become a loophole into which an evolutionary ethic at the social system level can be wedged? Yes, of course, if the number of the incurably degenerate is minute and if it is the case that most men want in fact to become better men, in the sense of holding or wanting to hold an individual evolutionary ethic, even if not self-described as such. Buchanan says men want freedom, but to what extent they also want their government to restrict them for their own good (better: betterment) depends on the chainability of Leviathan. And this depends on their knowledge of the lessons of history, some of which may be codified and systematized by the very public choice theory Buchanan has pioneered. Buchanan may not be ready to give his own vision of the good society, but he and his colleagues do have something to say about the feasible society. And so does social psychology as it comes out of its infancy (ceases to be infantile, a charge Cattell is willing to heap on economics, on page 331 of his book, but apparently not on his own field?).

But remember we are after "good government," not the "good society," and that we are thinking about a political contract, rather than a social contract in the wider sense. After all, the power of government to bring

about chosen end states is limited enough as it is, controlling even so apparently simple a thing as the money supply (no matter how measured or mismeasured) being a notorious example. (But ponder Vining 1984.) Hayek, for one, is convinced the government should not even try here, at least given governments as they exist today, and should get out of the money business altogether. That governments can actively nudge people towards virtue, or into adopting personal evolutionary ethics, seems very much less feasible than their keeping the money supply on target, but I must add that governments are quite successful in promoting attitudes favoring their expansion and in fostering a rent-seeking mentality.

So like Buchanan, I am no great optimist when it comes to government actively promoting virtue. The immediate reason is the problem of chaining the state; at present we just try to close up potential loopholes leading to Leviathan. [55] But perhaps the better reason is that we simply know very little about what it takes for government to actively promote virtue, even if we had nailed down anything like an adequate conception of it in the first place. My own analogy with biological advance along the lines of complexity, order, organization, and information is just a suggestion about how virtue might be given some metaphysical content beyond the quest to fulfill what Unger calls arbitrary desires.

Now the general thrust of economic theory is that a regime of property rights will indeed reduce potential conflicts among men, in that having these rights in place is more to the long-run interests of each man than violations may benefit him in the short run. Ayn Rand (1961:31) states that these long-run interests are not to be equated with whims, but it is not clear that Unger equates what he calls arbitrary desires with whims either. Rather, he may be taken as saying that the long-run desires men have are not to be grounded in any essential human nature, that one man's life goals are random with respect to anyone else's. They are, to the extent mandated by biochemical individuality, the diversity of individual histories, and the open-ended texture of human choice (i.e., heredity, environment, and free will). It is the job of evolutionary biologists, neuropsychologists, and social scientists to characterize these variations and also to nail down what men have in common.

Philosophers can try to clarify the issues, but scientists are the ones to answer them. [56] At present, it is safe to say that neither economics nor social psychology is enough of a science to advance much of a prescription for a positive role of government, beyond the protective

state, in the encouragement of evolutionary advance of individuals. That this situation might change cannot be ruled out on metaphysical grounds, but social contractors must act in the present and it is very difficult to conceive of even New Contractarian Men coming anywhere near unanimous agreement at the present time. This should be obvious in view of the current, irreconcilable strife over the public schools.

Cattell's Beyondism, however, is not a blueprint for the good society. He does go beyond the opening sentence of Limits in stating his opinions based upon his study of social psychology (which is certainly not appreciably less "infantile" than Cattell thinks economics is), but he could have been just as reticent as Buchanan. In fact, by sheer sentence count he spends very much less time on specifics than in beating a drum for federalism. One could, if one wished, view Cattell's specifics as tentative illustrations that the findings of his own social science need not be wholly useless.

Beyondism is mostly a (meta-) blueprint for a society of societies in a cooperatively competitive federal order. I spoke earlier of several levels of consent required for such an order. Given the strife among men that goes well back before recorded history, even a token approximation to unanimity seems outstandingly unlikely. But does not a good deal of this strife stem from bad metaphysics, from the supposition that one's own way of life is, in every one of its details, some sort of higher Truth, a Truth moreover of such pressing importance that one's group must not just be patient in hopes that the rest of the world will come to see its obvious merits, but rather must start waging war? Let me impose one final requirement upon New Contractarian Man: He need not be a good metaphysician, but he must not be an intolerant one.

6.8 Conclusion

So what have we learned? Possibly only that six very diverse authors (born in six different countries) can be brought together, as Buchanan would say, conceptually, or as Bunge said (WS 158), "It is possible to synthesize a variety of philosophical isms, provided the result is a coherent conceptual system rather than an eclectic bag." From Bunge (born in Argentina) we learned that the world comes in layers, with the higher layers rooted in the lower ones but emergent relative to them. In particular, values are tied to individuals and not transcendent over them in some holistic reification called society. From Buchanan (United

States), that the test of good government is the (ideally) unanimous consent of the governed and not whether that government pursues objectives exterior to individuals and their values. From Unger (Brazil), the paradoxes associated with abstracting the individual out of the social system of which he is a part. From Hayek (Austria), a sense of limits on the humanly calculable and hence an overriding need for abstract rules. From Ayn Rand (Russia), a reestablishment of the pre-modern sense of the end nature of man as a rational being, leading to a harmony of men's interests in a social order that protects rights. And from Cattell (England), an empirical approach to human nature and the spirit of evolutionary experimentation in a world federalist order.

Along the way, I have criticized my various authors. Buchanan's constitutional contractarianism suffers from the fact that strict individualism must be tempered by placing restrictions on the social contractors, lest the social contract fall apart. Unger suffers from pushing out the paradoxes of modern individualism so far that the ordinary business of life could not possibly go on. Hayek suffers from so sweeping an insistence on abstract rules that no room is left for a role for fairness as a public good. Ayn Rand, like Unger and Hayek, suffers from an excess of deduction, in her case, too much on man the rational being and too little on man the rational animal, a product of biological evolution. By contrast, I made no real criticisms of Bunge. I do have several--the chief one is that the world is not quite so neatly ordered in layers as he (in what he cheerfully admits is just the beginning of scientific metaphysics) seems to imagine--but they are not germane to the discussion here. Nor were the criticisms of Cattell I did make germane to his overall conception of federalism and an evolutionary ethics.

My achievement, if such it be, has been to exploit Bunge to extend Buchanan's contractarianism in the direction of a meta-contract, if you will, for evolutionary federalism. There are many holes in my arguments, the attempted plugging of which would take at least another book and which, for now, I have swept under the rug. But two are glaring: One is the fact that the social contract is a historical fiction, to which I can only plead again that this fiction not be stretched immoderately, to presume a degree of consent far removed from actuality. Contractarian theory can be used by us to justify to ourselves our enforcing the law against recalcitrants. But it should not be overused. The second hole is that nothing is said about comparing governments to which consent is not close to being unanimous. The hope is that such a situation will not arise

or, if it does, its subjects amicably regroup into two or more countries where unanimous consent is much more closely approximated.

Towards this hope, I have invented New Contractarian Man, a fiction also, but one I hope will not forever be too farfetched. Tolerance of other groups of social contractors was the final virtue I placed on New Contractarian Man. This seems wildly unrealistic in today's world, but I lay this partly at the foot of a bad metaphysics that encourages a wholly premature presumption that one's own way of life is universally valid. Evolutionary federalism blocks this: Evolutionary, in that any such presumption of finality is premature; federalism, in that no solution is universal. Evolutionary federalism is universalist in that all New Contractarian Men are to agree to the metaphysical tolerance to make it go, but it is a universalist philosophy of particularism.

ENDNOTES

CHAPTER 1: JAMES McGILL BUCHANAN AND INDIVIDUALISM (Pages 1-30)

1. (p.4) Buchanan is not concerned with the issue of social welfare function, or how to rank all possible rules and/or outcomes. Indeed, he has criticized the whole concept many times, at least as far back as 1954. There has been considerable refinement of the notion of a social welfare function, some of which have been described as individualistic. The rule of unanimity (the Pareto principle in its strongest form) that Buchanan uses in Limits is decidedly individualistic. It would be interesting to argue about which of the two-to-the-continuum many social welfare functions are to be called individualistic (or for that matter whether there is only a finite number of them, given the mere ten billion or so neurons in the human brain). For present purposes, however, Buchanan is interested only in the one social contract that emerges.

2. (p.12) It might be objected, at this point, that a good many dictators have been widely and wildly popular. Mayor Daley was a man who got things done, and even if he stretched the law, it can be argued, he enjoyed nearly unanimous support. Then why did he have to resort to such high-handed methods, including getting the dead to rise from their graves to attest to his high qualifications, to get reelected? The arguments go back and forth. Whatever the case with Richard Daley, it would seem that the losers under dictatorships are a whole lot worse off than losers under a majoritarian democracy.

3. (p. 15) The quotation is rarely given accurately. The Oxford Dictionary of Quotations, 2nd ed. (London: Oxford University Press, 1955), p. 167:26, quotes John Philpot Curran (1750-1817) as saying in a speech on the right of election of Lord Mayor of Dublin on July 10, 1790: "The condition upon which God hath given liberty to man is eternal vigilance; which condition if he break, servitude is at once the consequence of his crime, and the punishment of his guilt."

4. (p. 24) A modification is necessary here. Many laws, most especially in the fine details, are rather arbitrary but nevertheless necessary to coordinate expectations. The classic example is that of requiring driving on the left side of the road, which is arbitrary; what is necessary is

that everyone drive on the same side, whether left or right. Other arbitrary laws will appear biased or unfair and efforts to correct the alleged unfairnesses will be mounted. In some cases, the laws will be flouted and not enforced. What is not generally realized is that, in an economy where prices are free to change, biases will be corrected for, albeit not completely.

CHAPTER 2: ROBERTO MANGABIERA UNGER AND COLLECTIVISM (Pages 31-53)

5. (p. 31) Unger calls the post-medieval world view "liberalism," which he conceives broadly to encompass both the exponents of natural rights and of twentieth century liberal interventionism. I shall refer to both views as "individualism" instead in order to provide continuity with the last chapter.

6. (p. 36) Lewis Carroll, Through the Looking Glass and What Alice Found There, ch. 6, "Humpty Dumpty," with Illustrations by John Tenniel (London: Macmillan, 1872) in The Philosopher's Alice, with an Introduction and Notes by Peter Heath (New York: St. Martin's Press, 1974). Heath gives an extended note here, which begins: "This famous passage has immortalized Humpty Dumpty among philosophers of language as the leading exponent of what might be called 'subjective nominalism,' a theory in which two familiar views about language are somewhat extravagantly amalgamated" (p. 192). See also The Annotated Alice, with an Introduction and Notes by Martin Gardner (New York: Clarkson N. Potter, 1960). Both books contain the texts of the two Alice books and the Tenniel illustrations.

7. (p. 37) This is not completely true. One of the first half-dozen paradoxes of set theory was Bertrand Russell's set of all sets that do not belong to themselves as members. Thus, the set of all numbers, itself not a number, belongs to the Russell set, while the set of all concepts, itself a concept, does not. The paradox is that the Russell set itself belongs to the Russell set if and only if it does not. The standard way out of this dilemma, called "the limitation of size doctrine," is to disallow the aggregation of so many things into a set in the first place, that is, to decree that the Russell set is not a set at all, in other words to decree that our main intuitions about the formation of aggregates of sets is wrong. One other possible way out of this paradox, which to my knowledge has never been tried, is to modify an axiom of set theory that

seems entirely obvious, namely the Axiom of Extensionality, which states that two sets are equal if and only if they have the same members. This axiom states, essentially, that all sets are well-defined. But Russell's set is far from well-defined and in fact keeps on growing. (But, then, neither is economics well-defined. As remarked above, the field has lost a great deal of its moral content while seizing territory from political science and sociobiology.)

8. (p. 37) The Founding Papers of pragmatism are Charles Sanders Peirce, "The Fixation of Belief," Popular Science Monthly 12 (1877): 1-15, "How to Make Our Ideas Clear," ibid. 12 (1878): 286-302, and "What Pragmatism Is," The Monist 15 (1905): 161-81. The papers have been reprinted many times, e.g., H.S. Thayer, ed., Pragmatism: The Classic Writings, with an Introduction and Commentary by the editor, prepared under the editorial supervision of Robert Paul Wolff (New York: New American Library, Mentor Books, 1970).

9. (p. 38) See The New Encyclopaedia Britannica in 30 Volumes, 15 ed. (Chicago: Encyclopaedia Britannica, Inc., 1974), Micropaedia 5:891-92, s.v., "Milky Way," and Macropaedia 7:833-49, s.v., "Galaxy, The."

10. (p. 43) Note this well: The envious are predisposed to hold that the rich got that way by crooked means. In a free society, this accusation is not very easy to get away with. In a mixed economy, it is true that many of the wealthy are recipients of political pull. This, however, should not be overstressed, since under competitive rent-seeking the successful have to invest, at the margin, just as much effort to obtain their successes as in an unregulated economy. Resentment of the successful individual is called for only when new rents are obtained. That the rules of the game may need drastic modification is no excuse for envy.

11. (p. 49) There seems to be no positive content to assigning praise or blame to the random processes of recombination of genetic material employed in bisexual reproduction--only certain higher animals are praiseworthy or blameworthy--but there is a certain case for saying unanimity might be achievable on some limited minimum income plan as a public goods (why public?) insurance measure, coupled with means test and possible (temporary) sterilization.

12. (p. 50) I have quoted page one often enough!

CHAPTER 3: MARIO AUGUSTO BUNGE AND SCIENTIFIC METAPHYSICS (Pages 55-81)

13. (p. 64) David B. Tanner has spoken to me of his experiments in physics at the University of Florida. They consist in measuring physical properties of small molecules. With enough data collected, chemists can try to make guesses and extrapolations to predict physical properties of other chemical compounds. Tanner tells me that we are now able to project the remarkably high freezing point of water within a factor of two, based upon data such as he has been collecting and upon quantum mechanical considerations. As more data become available, physicists may be able to make a partial (epistemological) reduction of chemistry to the physics of quantum mechanics. A full epistemological reduction, however, is at best something for the remote future.

14. (p. 68) $3 = \{\emptyset, \{\emptyset\}, \{\emptyset, \{\emptyset\}\}\}$.

15. (p. 72) The Oxford Dictionary of Quotations, 2nd ed. (Oxford: Oxford University Press, 1955), s.v., Mrs. Edmund Craster, page 166:23.

16. (p. 75) Pages 191, 194, 209, 221, and 242, respectively. I retain his punctuation.

17. (p. 76) Defining a legal system consistent with Bunge's notion of the structure of a social system is not as automatic as it might first seem, because man-made laws differ from natural laws, especially since man-made laws can be broken. Recall that the structure of a system is the set of relations among the system's parts (and between the parts of the system and the parts of the environment). The relations, known and unknown, specify what is possible in two senses: they limit both the possible states of the system and possible changes of states. So once a specific state is in being, only certain trajectories to certain other states are possible. Making a choice (in fact, just letting things happen) forecloses certain possibilities and allows others that would notehave been possible under other choices. Thus, when a legislature exercises its choice and passes a minimum wage law, individuals have changed expectations about what would happen to them should they hire a man below the minimum wage. They may still do so--natural laws, including those

about social systems, do not forbid it--but they run the risk of being
punished. Some will break the law, or so economic theory predicts, as it
also predicts more unemployment. But laws of social systems, as Karen
Vaughn pointed out (personal communication), are not as absolute as laws
of physical and chemical systems, since men have free will (which, it will
be recalled, is a feature of Bunge's metaphysics). The expected effects
of minimum wage laws are consequently only highly probable.

This is only a sketch of how the notion of man-made laws might be
incorporated into Bunge's structure of a social system, and much further
work needs to be done, in particular with regards to the notions of power
and sovereignty in legal philosophy. My own suspicion is that there will
be in practice no absolute center of power that is not subject to check by
other power blocs, despite what the paper documents say. (Just how pieces
of paper affect behavior is another topic about which a metaphysician
ought to have something to say.) These problems in legal philosophy
become especially acute when considering federalism, as we shall do in
Chapter 6. Frenkel 1986 gives three conceptions of sovereignty in a
federation: that the central government is sovereign, that central and
state governments are sovereign in their respective spheres (but he notes
that the two spheres are always complexly interlinked), and that the
constitution that arches over both is the soveriegn. He notes (page 75),
"It is obvious that an author's preferences for one or the other doctrine
often run parallel to his more or less centralizing bias." See also
Ostrom 1971.

I cheerfully admit my own bias is strongly decentralist, and the type
of world federalism Raymond Cattell espouses that will be described in
Chapter 6 would grant only very limited powers to the central authority.
However, I want to avoid converting my biases into metaphysical
conclusions by semantic trickery. I cannot yield to this tempation,
though, until I discover or someday work up a description of sovereignty
compatible with Bunge's conception of the structure of a social system.

CHAPTER 4: FRIEDRICH AUGUST VON HAYEK AND THE MIRAGE OF SOCIAL JUSTICE
            (Pages 83-99)

18. (p. 86) I have been searching for a possible test for the existence
of God, gods, or just some being or organizing entity beyond this planet
ever since I rejected Christianity on grounds of lack of evidence at age
14. The whole notion of god is at least confused, if not downright

contradictory (George Smith 1974), and the burden of proof <u>and</u> concept
clarification clearly rests upon those who make extraordinary claims.
Nevertheless, to conceive of such a test is important for one's
self-assurance that one's own atheism is not purely dogmatic. Hume's
famous argument that human error, self-deception, and fraud can never be
decisively eliminated before accepting miracles as miraculous is, of
course, well made but still not absolutely decisive.

Here is a possible case for theism I have invented: There are gaps
in the fossil record, especially from genera on up, that are far from
being explained by current evolutionary theory. Michael Denton (1985)
argues that each of the genera (e.g., those comprising dogs and cats and
cows) are sui generis Platonic types, in that while each genus of mammal
comprises species close to each other, the genera are all equidistant (on
a variety of measures) from each other. So also with orders among
birds and reptiles. Higher up, mammals, birds, and reptiles, as
groups, are again roughly equidistant from each other. This clustering is
hierarchical in form and goes all the way up the chain of life. (Indeed,
Linnaeus was a Creationist.) Saltationist theories can account for some
of the gaps in the fossil record, but (according to Denton) so far
saltationist theory is largely ad hoc regards mechanisms and, in my view,
solves the problem of life's hierarchy only by relocating the mystery to
the apparent hierarchical clustering of ecological niches.

Even assuming Denton's highly controversial book has merits—I am
invoking it for its metaphysical import—such clustering now more and more
appears to be a pervasive feature of the universe, not only in life forms
but also in the grand structure of the universe of stars, galaxies, galaxy
clusters, superclusters, and possibly up further. (Cities, highway
networks, and languages are among many other phenomena that are also
heirarchically clustered.) The great Benoit Mandelbrot has described
random fractal processes that lead to hierarchical clustering in
"Subordination; Spatial Levy Dusts; Ordered Galaxies," Chapter 32 of his
The Fractal Geometry of Nature (1983). Mandelbrot's concerns are more
mathematical than empirical scientific, and the investigation of
empirical stochastic generators of hierarchies has barely begun. Once
this science of fractal processes has advanced considerably, it may be
argued that some clustering can be plausibly accounted for by processes
running on their own, while others (life, perhaps) need something else,
perhaps some thing or force that could be described as teleological, a
concept itself that needs much further exactification. There would then

be the possibility of deism. Needless to say, this is far removed from establishing the truths of Christianity or any other historic religion, especially as regards their moral aspects.

Mandelbrot's work may come to have large implications for the most basic science. (Recall that Bunge only briefly touched upon scientific laws operating at all levels of his ontology and mentioned the principle of least effort. Adding such laws will move ontology from the rather abstract science he presented in Furniture to a still general but less abstract description of this reality.) In particular, a modified version of Platonic essentialism, that of evolving hierarchies of types, may come to be recognized as a pervasive feature of reality on all levels. This is quite compatible with epistemological essentialism, as in Rand (1966-67) and Bunge's "working definitions" (1967a).

19. (p. 86) Indeed many conservative writers cynically urge that citizens accept the supernatural so as to reduce their excessive quarrelsomeness. As far as I know, no one has ever adopted a supernatural metaphysic on this ground, and it is a puzzle why such cynical arguments continue to be repeatedly advanced. The answer may be desperation or an inability to develop a secular ethic that will steer the middle ground "Between Anarchy and Leviathan," the subtitle of The Limits of Liberty.

20. (p. 87) It is a delicate question whether irrational individuals can be said to have consented to a social contract, or whether their consent is required. This is part of a more general problem of how to deal with the inhuman, non-human, sub-human, and yet-to-be human (infants?). There are two extremes: the authorities classing everyone who disagrees with their rule as insane or sub-human, or giving full recognition (under strict unanimity, the veto power) to those with the craziest beliefs.

What about Christianity? The religion is openly irrational, contradictory, even anti-rational. It is an elementary (meta-)theorem in logic that once a system contains a contradiction, every sentence (and its contrary) can be proven. Fortunately, the human brain is not a perfect logical machine and is spared the instantaneous global cancer resulting from a contradiction. Nevertheless, those who openly maintain contradictions (whether from a belief in Scripture or otherwise) and do not seek to resolve them are unpredictable. It is a difficult question what minimal requirements of rationality should be made for one to qualify for membership in the polity, and I have no answer.

From the Good Book itself:

Irrational: "He that believeth on him is not condemned: but he that believeth not is condemned already, because he hath not believed in the name of [whatever that means] the only begotten Son of God" (John 3:18, i.e., belief, not the evidence, is the requirement for salvation).

Contradictory: "One of themselves, even a prophet of their own, said, The Cretians are alway liars, evil beasts, slow bellies. This witness is true...." (Titus 1:12–13, i.e., if Cretans always lie, then the Cretan's saying so cannot be true. But Paul says the witness is true. This is the famous paradox of Epimenides.)

Anti-rational: "Verily I say unto you, Whosoever shall not receive the kingdom of God as a little child, he shall not enter therein" (Mark 10:15, i.e., credulity is the highest virtue).

21. (p. 87) I might add that creatures with bigger brains or who had a better science of calculating remote effects could form a larger social justice social contract group. I suspect that the computational tasks would grow at least exponentially with the size of the group but that the ability to develop a science of remote effects would also grow very rapidly as a function of average brain size. So I have no formula for the maximum size of a case-by-case social justice social contract group as a function of brain size. Needless to say, there is really no exact dividing line cutting off populations over a certain size from having a tolerably near-unanimous social contract.

22. (p. 88) What about a society where there are sharp differences of opinion on how the world works? A social contract will be far more achievable if people differ only in their subjective trade-offs (including their risk aversion to Leviathan) than if they also disagree anent matters of fact. Such factual disagreement can be mundane, regarding, say, the consequences of doubling the life of patents, or even the effect of inherited wealth upon concentration of wealth and economic mobility in future generations and the reasons for the perpetuation of poverty in families. It can be over a fundamental conception of the way the economy operates, e.g., Friedman's sovereign consumer vs. Galbraith's manipulated one (see Breit 1984). It can enshrine free will or embrace various kinds of determinism, which Bunge (1959) correctly calls fatalism, all mutually antagonistic. Or it can combine all approaches and assess their relative

and changing strengths.

But a deeper cleavage is ontological. Those who see man as serving God's glory or some transcending social justice are going to have the severest difficulty agreeing with those who root values in individuals.

23. (p. 89) On the other hand, there can be a feeling that the market fails to pay secretaries and janitors, say, enough. If these are purely arbitrary feelings, they are unlikely to be persuasive. What needs to be done is to give reasons that pinpoint the failure. One possible reason is an externality argument, but this can be handled by Buchanan's productive state that subsidizes the production of public goods. Another is that some sort of "prejudice" is at work, in which case there are unexploited opportunities for unprejudiced entrepreneurs. But entrepreneurship is not a free good, whence the issue becomes one of why correcting the alleged prejudice in question is especially urgent. The opportunity cost is failing to correct any number of other alleged prejudices, many of which will not be immediately visible. We must beware of fashions (and the potential for rent-seeking) here.

In many cases, the initial sense of injustice may be tempered by a greater understanding of how markets work, especially how they tend to erode certain kinds of prejudice, and eventually give way to a willingness to abide by abstract rules and not pay the price of continuous interference with market results. Passions may also cool as general outrage about prejudice gives way to a search for the factors responsible for the apparent underpayment of secretaries and janitors. Thus one may come to hold that employers are not engaging in discrimination--that is, the market itself is working--but rather the educational system is at fault. The great Frank Knight repeatedly asked whether the market was being criticized for doing what it was supposed to do or for failing to do what it was supposed to do.

24. (p. 90) There are other possibilities, and rational bargaining theory is a complicated and strife-ridden field. I reproduce in an appendix my Public Choice review of David Gauthier's Morals by Agreement (1986). I cannot make use of his reasoning in the text, because I find his assumptions considerably more heroic than those I have made about New Contractarian Man. But his book will be of enough interest to the present readers, since it too deals with The Limits of Liberty, to merit the appended review.

25. (p. 90) The way regressivity is usually defined. Or they could institute a flat "one man, one tax" rule. I have argued that "true" justice must recognize the innate worth of all human lives and that protection of life is therefore of equal value to all humans, whence justice demands they all pay the same tax. Exaggerating perhaps only slightly Gordon Tullock's Economics of Income Redistribution (1983) and claiming that five percent of government spending constitutes vertical redistribution, fifteen percent traditional public goods, and eighty percent horizontal redistribution to pressure groups, eliminating the eighty percent would result in a head tax of $1200 per year, per man, woman, and child. No one has accepted my conception of true justice, but no one has gone beyond argumentum ad disgustum either. Neither has anyone argued that reducing taxes to a $1200 flat tax would not boost economic growth enormously.

26. (p. 91) According to the great Nietzsche, the philosopher's world is not peopled with wives either:

> Thus the philosopher abhors marriage, together with that which might persuade to it--marriage being a hinderance and calamity on his path to the optimum. What great philosopher hitherto has been married? Heraclitus, Plato, Descartes, Spinoza, Leibnitz, Kant, Schopenhauer--they were not; more, one cannot even imagine them married. A married philosopher belongs in comedy, that is my proposition--and as for that exception, Socrates--the malicious Socrates, it would seem, married ironically, just to demonstrate this proposition. (On the Genealogy of Morals, Third Essay, Section 7, Walter Kaufmann translation)

27. (p. 92) Alas, these ignoramuses know all about rates of return on all kinds of investments, from here to eternity!

28. (p. 97) Has anyone investigated the consequences of (say) Knut Wicksell's five-sixths majority rule with freedom of contract for representation? I know of no case where there is this freedom, but I don't think restrictions have been examined from a public choice perspective as collectively helping along certain ends. Under freedom of contract, a politician could organize the teachers' lobby across states and specialize in just that one issue. He could roll logs with the lawyers' politician, and all could bargain with those that specialized in geographic blocks. I

predict the upshot would be a vast increase in the number of politicians and an underrepresentation of geographical interests. Article I, Section 2 of our Constitution limits the number of Representatives to one for every thirty thousand citizens. This could allow for about eight thousand Representatives, and it is an interesting question why this number is currently only 435. Certainly, one would not expect the House to want to expand its membership and so dilute each incumbent's power, but neither has the House chosen to let the number shrink through retirements and deaths. Perhaps the reason is just the persistence of a hitherto unexamined tradition, and I hope I haven't let loose a suggestion that could have quite harmful consequences.

29. (p. 98) The notion of cycling elites goes back to Pareto. What is remarkable is the speed-up of cycling. The third cycling (fourth, if we include the American Revolution itself) is now underway in American history. By contrast Quigley (1961) reports two for all of Western civilization (from feudalism degenerated into chivalry to trade capitalism and from trade capitalism degenerated into mercantilism to industrial capitalism) but never a cycling for any other civilization, just degeneration, often culminating in outside conquest.

CHAPTER 5: AYN RAND AND NATURAL RIGHTS (Pages 101-112)

30. (p. 103) This means that men deliberate as well as choose. Julian Jaynes, in The Origin of Consciousness in the Breakdown of the Bicameral Mind (1976), makes a highly controversial argument that deliberation (i.e., consciousness) was unknown before the Dorian invasions of Greece. If Jaynes is right and if deliberation rather than merely choosing is to be the criterion for rationality, then natural rights came into existence only during historical times. As rationality came in by evolutionary degrees, one might also argue that rights came in by degrees. I am not necessarily endorsing Jaynes here, merely pointing out the metaphysical implications of a theory that could be true regards the origin and existence of rights.

In this context it is worth noting that Ayn Rand (1973b) once said, "I am not a student of the theory of evolution and, therefore, I am neither its supporter nor its opponent." Nathaniel Branden (1982) noted her refusal to endorse biological evolution during all the years of their friendship but did not speculate upon the reason why. I think her refusal

stemmed from her excessively deductivist approach, which resulted in her
regarding man, not as a product of evolution, but as something
holistically different in kind from other animals. Bunge's ontology might
have saved the day by regarding deliberative behavior as an emergent
property, but this could have resulted in Ayn Rand's adopting the thesis
here, that societies are emergent relative to individuals.

31. (p. 101) Robert Nozick (1974:25) recognizes a similar problem, when
he considers that some are going to benefit more from having their rights
protected than others and that therefore any scheme for the protection of
rights will be redistributive. This line of reasoning has much less
force, however, when it is realized that there is a large random component
to having one's rights violated and that protection can be regarded as a
form of insurance. Regards perfection, Harry Binswanger (1981) argues
that perfection is a normative and hence contextual concept and not a
metaphysical and Platonic one: "In its rational meaning, the concept of
perfection denotes not the unimprovable but the best possible in a given
context," whence a billiard ball can be perfectly spherical to the naked
eye but not under a microscope. Binswanger's major point is that moral
perfection, in a human context, is "The Possible Dream," title of his
article.

32. (p. 107) Similarly, Noam Chomsky created quite a stir in linguistics
when he argued that the human brain is such that all languages will
display similar features in their grammars. The reason for the
controversy is that "liberal" environmentalists make, in Unger's
terminology, a radical separation of heredity and environment, so that the
products of culture can be completely arbitrary. Twenty years later, what
the Germans called the Zeitgeist, what Alfred North Whitehead called the
climate of opinion, and what Thomas Kuhn belatedly called a paradigm has
changed and environmentalism is now regarded as merely an extreme case.
The search is on to find and assess the nature and range of language
universals.

33. (p. 107) The Founding Papers of pragmatism are Charles Sanders
Peirce, "The Fixation of Belief" (1877), "How to Make Our Ideas Clear"
(1878), and "What Pragmatism Is" (1905). These papers have been reprinted
many times, e.g., Thayer 1970.
      For the notion of a working definition and its relationship to

essences, I have used Bunge's two-volume 1967 study, Scientific Research.
Ten years later, in his furniture book (p. 96), he propounded the
ontological thesis that "all properties are essential--which is to say
lawful." The problem is that we can know only some of the properties "out
there" (as Buchanan would have it) that something has, while the idea of a
working definition ties in with whatever theories we have at hand and is
hence more relevant to epistemology. It is not infrequent that a man
forgets what he said earlier and better. Ayn Rand takes a view remarkably
similar to the earlier Bunge in her Introduction to Objectivist
Epistemology (1966-67).

34. (p. 108) Ayn Rand (1966-67:69) states that "the essence of a concept
is that fundamental characteristic(s) of its units on which the greatest
number of other characteristics depend, and which distinguishes these
units from all other existents within the field of man's knowledge." The
difficulty is the "s" in parentheses: when does one stop adding
characteristics to the essence? The answer is not obvious, nor is the
formation of units in her sentence. I should note that when she speaks of
man as essentially rational (p. 58) the term "does not mean 'acting
invariably in accordance with reason'; it means 'possessing the faculty of
reason.'" However, the capacity to reason comes in degrees, and some
certifiable members of homo sapiens almost entirely lack that capacity.
It remains difficult to derive absolute rights from a highly variable
capacity.

35. (p. 111) Ayn Rand never explains why thinking in man must be
voluntary. An evolutionary explanation is in order and one is advanced by
V.C. Wynne-Edwards 1963: "Compliance with the social code can be made
obligatory and automatic, and it probably is so in almost all animals that
possess social homeostatic systems at all. In at least some of the
mammals, on the contrary, the individual has been released from this rigid
compulsion, probably because a certain amount of intelligent individual
enterprise has proved advantageous to the group." Such an explanation
invokes group selection and is bound to be controversial. An alternative
explanation might be that a) thinking requires work (uses up costly brain
chemicals) and b) free-will feedback circuitry allows the animal (or maybe
just certain humans) to choose both whether to think and what to think
about. Far less brain hardware, in other words, may be required by taking
the free will route. Now if Jaynes is right, we may just have been lucky

to have a capacity for free will already in place, though it may not have
been activated until the Dorian invasions. This is, I hasten to add, all
speculation: I include it for its evolutionary and metaphysical
implications.

> CHAPTER 6:   RAYMOND BERNARD CATTELL AND EVOLUTIONARY FEDERALISM
> (Pages 113-141)

36. (p. 120) See George W. Barlow and James Silverberg, eds.,
Sociobiology: Beyond Nature-Nurture? (1980). My reading of this book
supports Gordon Tullock's general observation (personal communication)
that the debate is over which very narrow conditions, if any, make group
selection possible.

37. (p. 120) Genuine cooperative altruistic behavior becomes possible
where there is reduced "genetic competition among the cooperators," in the
words of Donald T. Campbell (1975). Group selection, not of people but of
their moralities, is espoused by Hayek in his epilogue, "The Three Sources
of Human Values," in Law, Legislation and Liberty, vol. 3: The Political
Order of a Free People (1979).

38. (p. 121) Page 322. Unfortunately, this is holistic language, but
Cattell speaks more the language of Bunge and of emergent systemic
properties when he states, "Individual and group are links in an endless
causally interacting chain, each indispensable to the other." (166)

39. (p. 121) Cattell is far more prepared to admit the role of biological
factors in human history than is currently fashionable, but for him race
means primarily the new races that will be formed under Beyondism. He
decries both present-day racists as being presumptuous regarding
superiority and inferiority and "ignoracists" who deny the importance of
racial factors altogether.

40. (p. 121) Cattell recognizes the problems large groups have in
ensuring compliance that Buchanan discusses in Limits and at length in
"Ethical Rules, Expected Values, and Large Numbers" (1965).

41. (p. 121) Compare Buchanan: "Each man counts for one, and that is
that." (LL 2)

42. (p. 122) Page 244. He claims puberty is fifteen years too early, given today's educational requirements. (371)

43. (p. 122) Page 244. Aggressiveness, which correlates with cultural creativity, is hardly the same thing as pugnacity, as he explains on p. 190.

44. (p. 122) Page 193. On p. 258, he claims that "duties are the truly important aspect of rights," but he sometimes seems to equate altruism with self-restraint (e.g., on p. 250).

45. (p. 122) Page 394. In economics, he regards the consumption side—what money is spent on—as just as important as the production side. (192)

46. (p. 122) Page 453. "The greatest danger to [a Beyondist] future lies in man hedonistically betraying himself."

47. (p. 123) More troublesome still, his idea that the communications media should act "responsibly," and be subject to control if need be (441), would be vetoed, I daresay, by an easy majority of the present readers.

48. (p. 124) But why hasn't the promised sequel to his book appeared? The present writer feels that his continued psychological work which appeared instead is a comparative waste of time. At a more personal level, Cattell is quite fond of poetry and quotes it often. The present writer thinks it too is a waste of time, while Beethoven's chamber music is not only one of life's greatest joys but a spur to continue forging ahead.

49. (p. 127) The seventh chapter of Limits is entitled "Law as Public Capital."

50. (p. 127) Cattell fears that the reason why we have not found any intelligent life in the universe is that every society lapsed into hedonism and not a single one adopted Beyondism.

51. (p. 128) Metaphysically much more confusing is the German political geographer Freidrich Ratzel's notion of a state's needing a raison d'être

around a particular, distinctive "idea." See Richard Hartshorne, "The
Functional Approach in Political Geography," presidential address before
the Association of Political Geographers at its Forty-Sixth Annual Meeting
in Worcester, Mass., April 7, 1950, reprinted in Martin Ira Glassner and
Harm J. de Blij, Systematic Political Geography, 3rd ed. (New York: John
Wiley & Sons, 1980), pp. 128-152, esp. pp. 139-142.

52. (p. 128) But is this claim about the state's need for a raison d'etre
a law? Consider Hartshorne, op. cit., p. 139: "Unless Austria-Hungary,
[Hugo] Hassinger wrote after the First World War, had been able to
discover and establish a raison d'être, a justification for existence,
even without the calamity of the war, it could not long have continued to
exist." Vanberg would have difficulties with this statement, indeed, but
it does make some sort of sense. It is a job of philosophers to drag as
much sense out of statements as possible, which does not seem to be very
far in the case of, say, "Ex-sistent Dasein is the letting-be of what-is"
(Martin Heidegger, quoted by Mario Bunge, Scientific Research, 2 vol.
(Berlin: Springer- Verlag, 1967a), 1:118).

53. (p. 129) This is not to predict that the Soviets are going to go
grab a piece of India. They may, but for a much better reason than the
aesthetic aim of having the world conform to the rank-size rule, namely
food. Nels Winkless III and Iben Browning, Climate and the Affairs of Men
(New York: Harper Magazine Press, 1975), argue that the world gets colder
every eight hundred years and corresponding invasions have taken place, at
least as far back as history records. The wars of the twentieth century,
the authors claim, are right on schedule, with worse cold, and worse wars,
to come.

54. (p. 129) We let pass the issue of "conceptual" contracts in other
species, as well as symbiotic arrangements between species, being mindful
that such a study could be extremely fruitful in generating ideas. See,
for example, Robert Ardrey, The Social Contract: A Personal Inquiry into
the Evolutionary Source of Order and Disorder (Patterson, N.J.: Atheneum,
1970; New York: Dell, 1974).

55. (p. 138) Among Objectivists a glaring loophole has appeared, one that
I had not expected quite so soon after the death of Ayn Rand in 1982.

Binswanger 1987 states that American businessmen advocating protectionist
legislation "want to hobble the foreign runners in the race, to hobble
them either by force (tariffs) or fraud (conning Americans into believing
that buying foreign products damages our economy)." Objectivists
certainly want to punish fraud, but if this urging Americans to buy
American products is to be classified as fraud, what is to prevent
cracking down on those who peddle philosophies conflicting with
Objectivism as frauds? Libel laws, which Objectivists also support, raise
another issue: Given that a business's reputation is a form of property,
won't its own misrepresentations be punished adequately in the market?

56. (p. 138) Recall Bunge (FW 153): "We shall not list the kinds of
constituents of the world but shall leave that task to the special
sciences. For no sooner does the metaphysician pronounce the world to be
'made of' such and such kinds, than the scientist discovers that some of
the alleged species are empty or that others are missing from the
metaphysician's list."

APPENDIX 1

EGALITARIANISM AS A MORALITY RACKET

Why does public education persist, despite all the preaching of
free-market economists, with their mighty arsenal of moral and economic
arguments both, and despite the common experience of all mankind that
governments do things incompetently? Public choice theory has a
marvelously simple answer: politics is at bottom an economic game and it
just so happens that the coalition, the pressure group favoring the public
education Establishment is far more organized than students and taxpayers.
Just how it came about that the education Establishment overcame its
internal free-rider problem is not a question for pure public choice
theory as such, but it manifestly did happen.

Hartmut Kliemt, a philosopher at the University of Mainz, has thrown
a monkey wrench into this sort of simple explanation. He has come along
with no less than the first major new concept in public choice theory
since rent-seeking, namely what he calls the "veil of insignificance," a
term inspired by John Rawls's "veil of ignorance." Taking the fact that
one's vote has a negligible chance of overturning an election, Kliemt
argues that it is practically costless to vote for what one thinks is
right rather than what is actually in one's self-interest.

So if people do have moral scruples, and it is manifest that they do,
the challenge now confronting public choice theory is to explain why they
ever, or at least more than rarely, vote in their self-interest, as they
also manifestly do. The world is a messy place, with both scruples and
self-interest running at a steady clip, and no doubt this upsets public
choice theorists who would rather not have the random noise of morals
cluttering up an ideal world of Perfect Public Choice, any more than
antitrust lawyers like the messy world of real competition as opposed to
the ideal world of Perfect Competition. (I am going to propose a new
definition of competition in a paper, "Beyond Mechanism and Spiritualism,"
on Tuesday.) We need, in short, what our distinguished former President,
Bob Tollison, has called "an economic theory of words," or in other words
an explanation of how morals and ideologies operate.

To get at this problem we need to get a handle on human nature and
morals. Men, far beyond the animals, are good at forming concepts.
Ideally, the concepts should be checked to see whether they make useful
working definitions for scientific theories and the same theories checked

against the facts. Doing all this checking takes hard work and determined
persistence. The scientific mind-set is a wonderful but fragile flower
which came into being in the European Middle Ages and is still being
refined.

Making concepts is a necessary activity and some of us pile them up
merrily without pausing to check them. We have moved from the elementary
observation that <u>some</u> events have causes to reifying a god that is the
cause of everything and from the observation that some things are
beneficial to some people to reifying an Absolute Good. Economists
generally avoid these reifications; instead they can often fail to
acknowledge the reality of something by engaging in reductionism, or what
Mario Bunge calls ontological bulldozing. Thus a society is nothing but a
heap of people and there is no such thing as social justice. The better
description is that a society is a <u>system</u> of interacting people, but one
searches in vain for methodological individualists to say this. As far as
social justice goes, it often sounds like a mysterious reification of
something never very clear, but sense can be made of how <u>individuals</u> react
to <u>collective</u> measures of the performance of an economic system, examples
being the economic growth rate and the concentration of income. If Hayek
himself has not ridiculed such examples, his followers have.

But concept-making, as I have said, takes hard work. Most of us
most of the time just borrow the concepts others have worked out. Such
conformity is, for obvious cost-benefit reasons, almost totally
inevitable, and praise be to those hardy souls that press on on their own.
It is moral concepts that are at issue here, in regard to Hartmut Kliemt's
veil of insignificance. The public choice question is <u>who</u> controls the
ideas on what is right that lead voters to vote against their self-
interest?

The first place to look is the rent-seekers themselves.

Physicians obviously stand to gain from gettin people to believe that
there is an objective, minimum standard of medical care, not a spurious
reification which just so happens to maximize the income of the existing
pressure group of doctors. Actually, the medical Establishment has gone
even further and has persuaded millions of people to believe that no one
should ever want less than The Best, in capital letters, in medical
treatment. Every economist knows that The Best could not be purchased by
the entire GNP and that there are infinitely fine trade-offs between

quality and price.

Yet the medical racket persists. What is astonishing is that the
veil of insignificance reinforces self-interest. While we might and do
find a senior citizen voting for a politician advocating cuts in Social
Security, a voter taken in by the medical Establishment is not only
convinced he wants only The Best but thinks regulation is the way to
get it.

This is vastly more true of education. Most people are horrified at
the prospect of privatizing education. They genuinely believe that hordes
of people would never learn to read or write, and never mind that the
public schools graduate hordes of functional illiterates right now and
largely kill off any remaining desire to learn, which really takes some
doing, given our innate need and even compulsion to learn. Social chaos
would result, so most people have been led to think, and so they continue
to vote for public education out of their own perceived interests. They
would like reforms, to be sure, but not privatization. The exceptions are
scarce.

On top of this is moral intimidation. People are led to believe that
public education, for all its faults, is morally right on the grounds that
the poor deserve public support. This is where egalitarianism comes in,
and egalitarianism is the chief morality racket today. It is exploited to
the hilt by the education Establishment. Now an awfully good case can be
made that the poor would get better educated if the government would get
out of the road, but so greatly are people intimidated that they fear that
even one poor person would not get an education. Again, never mind that
millions of the poor are ill-served by the public schools right now.

How can this morality racket work? It works by metaphysical and
epistemological terror. Equality is left very ill-defined. Douglas Rae
and his colleagues in their 1981 book Equalities have distinguished 720
species of equality. Which of these equalities is the right one? How
much levelling is desirable? Gordon Tullock, as most of you I am sure
know, has been pestering liberals for years to get them to specify just
what concentration of income they think best, with nary a specific answer.

What it has come down to is that the voters, under the veil of
insignificance, have no clear idea of which or how much equality is
morally right and find it very difficult to oppose any growth in
egalitarian programs, especially in education. It takes hard thinking, in
the face of all the propaganda, to come up with the right kind and amount
of equality independently, and one risks the scorn of liberals, who always

want more of it. The education Establishment benefits hugely from this
confusion and the fear spread thereby of never doing enough. What is
more, they have, as no other group has, the terrible, terrible, and
dangerous power over the upbringing of youth.

One final remark, to tie things together. At the beginning, I
mentioned the internal free-rider problem. Again, morality is the key.
Morality allows people inside the rent-seeking group to swallow their own
propaganda, to believe they are truly working for the public good. E.O.
Wilson has pointed out that all social vertebrates are hypocrites. This
means both that social vertebrates have consciences and that these
consciences can be subverted. I wish to add that this subversion is
rarely total, even if it comes close for doctors and educators. Bob
Tollison has wondered whether the little education that squeaks out of
public schools (his example was actually defense) is just an incidental
by-product of rent-seeking. He is turning the whole idea of public goods
upside down. I see his point, a frightening point, and my explanation is
that hypocrisy is not total, that some conscience is left unsubverted, and
hence we don't fully live in the world of Perfect Public Choice. Coming
at it from a different way, perhaps Public Choice Man would be a perfect
cynic. In this case, what might happen is that rent-seekers get duped by
their own propaganda, whereupon public goods manage to get out.

This, then, is Bob Tollison's economic theory of words. Men need to
conceptualize things, in particular in regards to morals. But thinking is
hard work, and most of us most of the time just accept what we learn and
accept even oversimplified ideologies like extremely vague egalitarianism.
Under the veil of insignificance we often vote with our conscience, which
we did not wholly develop ourselves. Others have an interest, a public
choice or economic interest if you will, in directing this development of
conscience for their own private interests. And it is the public
education Establishment that has, far more than any other group, the power
to do so.

Address read at an invited session, "Economics of Education," at the
annual convention of the Southern Economic Association on November 23,
1986, in New Orleans.

APPENDIX 2

Review (from <u>Public Choice</u> 56 (1):84–88 (January 1988)) of Robert H.
Frank, <u>Choosing the Right Pond: Human Behavior and the Quest for Status</u>.
New York: Oxford University Press, 1985, 306 pp., $22.95.

What people say they want, think they want, really want, and ought
to want, what they try to get and what they really get, are six different
things. Sorting them out is the main job, maybe the only job, of social
science. Economics mostly studies the connections between the last two:
what they try to get (the choices people make) and what they really get.
Economics actually only studies a subset of the last two, that which is
produced and exchanged in markets, and public choice theory extends this
study to non-markets. The first four, the wants and their formation, are
left to the other social sciences, especially psychology and sociology.

Economists usually take wants as "given." In practice, this means
that the strength of a person's wants is straightaway for absolute
amounts of various goods, whether these goods are to be consumed right
away or to be used to produce other goods, such as ingredients used in a
recipe. People are implicitly held to be autonomous; the utility of my
consumption of a good depends only on the absolute quantity and not at
all upon the quantity of my consumption relative to that of others. We
all know, of course, that this is plainly not so, but for the most part
economists rarely study the matter of relative consumption.

Along comes a book to incorporate relative consumption into economic
theory, Robert Frank's <u>Choosing the Right Pond</u>. The book discusses the
omnipresent quest for status in human affairs, how people sort themselves
out into separate, local hierarchies, how this implies that wages are far
more compressed than marginal productivity alone would prescribe, and
most importantly for public choice theorists, how there come to be the
manifold collective restrictions on unlimited status-seeking that we
observe. The reasons usually offered for these restrictions, what people
<u>say</u> they want, are not what they <u>really</u> want. It is Frank's hope that if
people understood what restrictions they <u>really</u> wanted, namely to put
brakes upon status seeking, they would go about it better.

<u>Choosing the Right Pond</u> is successful in showing that in the
dividing up of an industry into firms, the market place does help people
get what they <u>really</u> want. We all know that microeconomic theory often
does just this. We all know that theory teaches (preaches?) that firms

really want to maximize profits and that the way to do it is to set prices at marginal cost. What we further know is that firms rarely actually know their own marginal costs but that even so, economic forces will make price equal to them. Never mind myriad objections of and qualifications to this theory; the theory is nevertheless helpful, even if not the entire truth.

Choosing stays within the neoclassical orthodoxy but extends its logic of utility functions to incorporate the human desire for status. The extension is done in a wholly orthodox way. To accomplish the job, Frank supposes not just that people value status but also that they are somewhat myopic about it. People are rarely concerned with where they stand relative to all inhabitants of the Earth (and why don't people rest content with having big brains and opposable thumbs, placing all of us very near the top of the animal kingdom?). Rather, they compare themselves with their neighbors, residential neighbors partly, but also with coworkers.

Given that people vary in their demand for status, Frank's main conclusion follows that the structure of firms in an industry will respond to this variation in demand. The argument is straightforward: a first person who cares greatly about relative status will work for less in a firm where his income is relatively higher in that firm. Contrariwise, a second person who cares little about status will accept a relatively low position in a firm that pays him more.

Firms will specialize in attracting workers of different levels of productivity. Persons with a given level of productivity and a great concern for status will go to work for firms with lower productivity, achieve a relatively high status there, but be paid less than their marginal product. Conversely, those with a low concern for status will go to work for firms with high productivity, achieve a relatively low status, and be paid more than their marginal product. The upshot is that within each firm there will be a tendency (sometimes strong) to offer compressed wage schedules that do not fully reflect internal differences in productivity. "Firms may be thought of as posting menus (their wage schedules) of wage-status combinations they have to offer" (p. 55).

In addition to theoretical considerations, Frank investigates actual cases and finds, for example, that car dealers in upstate New York reward a salesman who generates an extra dollar in gross commissions only 24 cents more in wages. On the other hand, in real estate firms, whose salesmen are not so visible to each other, the figure is 50 to 70 cents.

Frank gives a host of other examples, from university professors getting
research monies to the singularly compressed salaries of top federal
government executives.

Frank next argues that, while individuals are myopic, in that they
compare relative status more with their co-workers than with everyone
generally, they are not so myopic that relative status outside the
workplace is wholly unimportant. We might see, for example, a
segregation of shopping centers into those selling low- and those selling
high-priced goods. A person with a given level of income would patronize
one or the other shopping center depending on the strength of his desire
to be seen as a conspicuous consumer. In other cases, however, market
segregation and ensuing compressions will be impractical, due to
transactions costs or economies of scale. This sets the stage for
collective action for direct redistribution to achieve what the market
cannot. (Frank's arguments here are somewhat difficult to follow, as he
overlays them with different ones on high transactions costs of mutual
agreements to put brakes on status-seeking. See below.) But emulation
can be a powerful motive to work harder, so a balance must be struck. On
the other hand, as Frank notes, every society seeks to informally
suppress envy (which used to be regarded as the deadliest of the seven
deadly sins) through socialization of its members, whence I add that
government action may not be needed on a major scale.

Frank says, "I did not intend to claim that the income distribution
we currently have in the United States is just" (p. 127). It is a large
step between what we ought to want (justice) and what we get. Indeed,
there is a large gap between what we try to get, as embodied in our
Constitution (which is far from the ideal of unanimity of James M.
Buchanan's The Limits of Liberty), and what we have got, which is a
government whose main function today (as the public choice literature
often argues) is to redistribute wealth and income among organized
pressure groups. Besides, no two persons agree on what our Constitution
aims for.

Along with all this, Frank argues from sociobiological and
neurological considerations that the drive for status is innate but, also
and importantly, that it can be counterproductive or at best futile, at
least in modern society. Resources are invested in climbing up the totem
pole. They are countered by expenditures of others to do just the same,
with the result that relative positions are left largely unchanged. In
many cases, from the arms race between nations to conspicuous consumption

and the chasing after college degrees within a nation, an agreement might be
negotiated to limit status-seeking. Here, Frank's contention is that we
really want to limit this seeking and that many of the laws we get reflect
this.

Much of the book is given over to discussing legislation that has
the effect of limiting status-seeking, a good example being occupational
safety laws. The argument is that workers really want safe workplaces
but that the scramble to provide a better start in life for their
children would lead them to accept less safe, higher paying jobs than
would be the case if they could somehow collectively agree upon limiting
the status questing so that relative positioning would stay the same.
Now after Robert Frank came along to point this out, it all sounds
plausible. But: how do people get from what they really want but don't
know they want to the laws that implement what they really want?

The public choice student asks, what sort of constitutional rules
might they set up? How might, not just some level of safety measures be
adopted, but an optimal (in some sense) level be put into being? What
will keep OSHA bureaucrats at bay? And given powers under a constitution
to limit status-seeking generally--and our government has undertaken these
powers even if the Constitution of 1789 did not exactly provide for
them--how will laws in specific cases overshoot or undershoot the mark?
The invisible political hand must work miraculously indeed if an inchoate
desire (inchoate until Frank's ideas filter down) works out to something
even occasionally approaching an optimum. Frank's answer is that, given
conscious recognition of the desirability of putting brakes on
status-seeking, we would do far better to tax conspicuous consumption
goods directly and avoid round-about measures such as OSHA. So, ideally,
there will be no OSHA bureaucrats to keep at bay.

It would be silly to berate the author for not having provided a
complete theory to explain every piece of legislation, some of whose side
effects limit status-seeking. Public choice theory is, after all, a
perspective. It gives partial explanations of some things, not total
explanations of everything. The reader may feel that Frank can get
carried away, rather too often seeing an unconscious intent to limit
status-seeking as being the major operative force behind a piece of
legislation whose secondary effects of limiting status-seeking are rather
minor. Nevertheless, the author argues well that much status-seeking is
zero sum in nature and that collective limits on it can often be
desirable, though he realizes that the quest for status up to a certain

point furnishes a powerful drive for economic progress.

Frank expounds various other theses in later chapters. In Chapter 8, he argues that, inasmuch as incomes are bunched closer together at the lower end of the spectrum, apparent status increases by way of conspicious consumption are greater, dollar for dollar at the lower end, which is why we observe relatively more spending and less saving at the lower end. He also argues that trade unions can and do internalize the negative externalities of treadmill conspicious consumption by collective bargaining arrangements that channel cash incomes into such things as health care and retirement plans. In Chapter 9, he argues that the left's critique of capitalism is simply contrary to all evidence when claiming the economy is not competitive but that there is an imbalance of power held by corporations. By organizing, workers really only harm themselves, as far as cash wages go. However, they can use this organizing to collectively limit status seeking and the "alienation" that results. The benefits here could outweigh the lower money wages, but this will be more likely if the workers conciously realized that this is what they really want to do rather than to combat a spurious imbalance of corporate power.

Chapter 10 surveys various ethical restrictions limiting the use of money which have the effect of reducing status seeking, which again is what people really want. In particular, Frank observes that public financing of education (whether governments should operate schools is an entirely different matter) reduces the positioning advantages parents can obtain for their children by paying for private education. In this regard I note that, as government aid to students has increased, so have the relative costs of private versus public colleges. Far greater than the effect of reducing positioning expenditures, I suspect, is simply the effect of getting more students listening to professors. Indeed, colleges, and especially college administrators, complain far more loudly about proposals to reduce student aid than do the students themselves or their parents.

The last two chapters give a general overview of the limits of government maternalism and the tendency for government to grow out of bounds and calls for a tax, not on all income, but on the consumption of positional goods. Frank would have a political constitution that would "mimic as closely as possible the decisions that citizens would reach themselves if they could negotiate costlessly with one another in a hypothetical restricted environment" (p. 242). The current welfare state

does some of these things poorly, but what he calls a "libertarian
welfare state" would do them ideally. He calls such a state
"libertarian" to emphasize that it is only giving people what they
really want.

Frank will get many protests from libertarians here (isn't the word
far too stretched as it is?), but he is arguing for an ideal, one of
political freedom under an ideally unanimously agreed-upon constitution,
as well as for the traditional individual freedoms. Skeptics, including
perhaps the bulk of public choice scholars, will doubt whether any
constitution that provides a government so powerful as to be able to
restrict status seeking will be able to keep Leviathan at bay.
Choosing the Right Pond, beyond extending neoclassical economics to
explain how the market oftentimes takes status into account, is thus
provocative in seeking to justify certain aspects of government action as
doing the same. Frank offers for now only a vague evolutionism to
explain what are now side consequences, and he never says just how far
such restrictions should go before they turn off a major force for
economic progress. These are topics for a second book.

APPENDIX 3

Review (from <u>Public Choice</u> 56(1):88-96 (January 1988)) of David Gauthier,
<u>Morals by Agreement</u>. Oxford: Clarendon Press, 1986, 367 pp., $39.95.

    <u>Morals by Agreement</u> is the mirror image of <u>Thecalculusofconsent</u>.
That book looked at what happens after the social contract is signed, at
the kinds of laws that will be passed by rational persons acting under a
constitution. <u>Morals</u> goes up to the social contract and asks what kind
of agreement might be reached by rational people in the first place. The
books intersect at the word consent and go in opposite directions.

    Public choice theory has moved so far from its roots in consent that
Buchanan and Tullock's book has indeed become a single word. It is an
image and conjures up not consent so much as a founding study of how
pressure groups exploit the coercive power of the state for special
privileges. Buchanan almost alone, most notably in <u>The Limits of Liberty</u>
(1975), has stuck with the idea of unanimous agreement, but even in that
book he is largely concerned with what happens once an agreement is made.
For him, just about any agreement will do, and a chief concern is in
keeping the agreement, preventing the subversion of a constitutional
order by a creeping Leviathan.

    David Gauthier, a philosopher at the University of Pittsburgh, now
joins Buchanan in his concern with the concept of consent and thus goes
back to the roots of public choice theory, but from a mirror image
perspective. Buchanan takes the social contractors to be rational, but
only in a loose and perhaps nearly tautological way, since his general
concern is with what flows from the agreement, not what leads up to it.
Such vagueness in the concept of rationality will not suffice for
Gauthier's purposes. Since every concept gets fuzzy as approached
closely enough, and since concepts are refined only until marginal costs
start exceeding marginal benefits, Gauthier spends far more time than
Buchanan on what rationality is.

    <u>Morals</u> and <u>Limits</u> thus complement each other. (It is also true that
<u>Morals</u> compliments <u>Limits</u> by devoting an important section to it, of
which more anon.) The complementation is, however, far from complete.
Economists will find that Gauthier's conception of rationality seems
hyper-rational, that Gauthier's people suffer from few of the
information, decision, and bargaining costs economists deal with so

regularly. On the other hand, philosophers want to specify in some detail just what sort of social contract rational men will agree upon and not rest content with just about any old agreement that happens along, as Buchanan would seem to. Morals by Agreement, which term no doubt will come to loom as large in the philosophical landscape as John Rawls' "veil of ignorance," is a first attempt by a philosopher to bridge the gap between economics and ethics. It will not be the last.

Gauthier defends a subjectivist view of value, preference, and expected utility under risk and uncertainty with which economists will be largely familiar and have few quarrels. He states the usual properties of completeness, transitivity, and so forth, with the only problematic assumption being that rational choices must be considered ones, thus allowing for irrationality in choice based upon incorrect beliefs. Gauthier then introduces some examples from game theory, especially regards mixed strategies that rely upon selecting among pure strategies in fixed proportions by using a randomizing device.

In using game theory, Gauthier makes assumptions economists would regard as heroic. Not only are the exact conditions of the game known to all parties in perfect detail, but also all players know each others' payoff schedules. It can often happen, as in the Prisoners' Dilemma, that the joint strategy the players settle into in equilibrium, while optimal, is not utility maximizing, in the sense that all might have done better by their own lights (or at least no one would have come out worse) if only they could have coordinated their strategies. The rules of the game would have to be modified, of course, but men make up new rules as well as carry out actions under old rules.

The crucial idea in Morals is that morality consists precisely and entirely of adopting new rules, generally in the form of placing constraints upon allowable strategies, so as to make the optimal joint strategies utility maximizing (Pareto optimal). Now many philosophers, but not enough economists, are going to protest that morality consists of exhortations to excellence that go beyond confining behavior, but still it is true that constraints are a very large part of morality. Gauthier's argument is that it is possible to justify these constraints, not by any appeal to God or natural law, or to any feelings of benevolence, but purely by a joint recognition by rational men that these constraints can further their interests. This may seem wholly obvious, at least for idealized Game Theoretic Man (but is it true for actual man?). What Gauthier does is flesh out this picture by giving details

about these agreements.

Gauthier holds that, given the so-called "perfectly" competitive market, the rationalities of individual optimization and utility maximization coincide, whence there is no need for moral constraints. Here Gauthier shamefully and shamelessly invokes the neoclassical orthodoxy, and for this reason his treatment is weak. While it can be rigorously proven that the coincidence Gauthier speaks of does hold under conditions of "perfect" competition, these conditions rarely hold in the market. Game Theoretic Man may be thoroughly informed and rational but may still affect prices by his actions. What is needed is a sense of when the two rationalities coincide, in cases where competition is cut-throat but not "perfect." The neo-Austrians proclaim but have not established that laissez-faire without antitrust legislation invariably generates the coincidence. The mathematics would have to be multi- if not infinitely dimensional, since under dynamic competition the products change, and the neo-Austrians disdain mathematics anyhow, which is too bad. We badly need a notion of Pareto optimality under conditions of dynamic competition that will go far beyond Alice-in-Wonderland "perfect" competition, but will stop short, perhaps far short, of saying that Pareto optimality always holds no matter what, even under competitive rent-seeking for regulation.

Gauthier himself is not to be blamed for the shortcomings of economic theory, even if he might have noted them. But a much deeper issue is that a free market is not a free good. It is not "given." If the rules of a free market are not enforced, then it may often be rational for men to disregard them, whence the market will not be a morally neutral zone after all. Besides, there are many free markets. Exact definitions of property rights will have to be debated and chosen among. Economists will surely want to add their thoughts here, but as we shall see Gauthier will argue that rational men will spontaneously obey the rules of the market, thus obviating any need for enforcement.

Gauthier then proceeds to discuss situations where (moral) constraints, in addition to those of a "given" market, can improve outcomes. Players will bargain over which constraints to cooperatively adopt. To study this a theory of rational bargaining is needed to derive mutually rational constraints. Unfortunately, "the general theory of rational bargaining is underdeveloped territory" (p. 129), and so Gauthier will by no means be able to propound a complete and comprehensive theory. He discusses a hypothetical example of players

having knowledge of the situation, including the initial bargaining
position, the set of possible outcomes, and the players' utility
schedules. Given that the aim is to choose a point on the Pareto
frontier, which one will be chosen? The answer depends critically on a
principle of Frederik Zeuthen from 1930, which states that the ratios
between the difference of the best point on the Pareto frontier from his
perspective to the bargained point, on the one hand, and the difference
between the best point and the starting point, on the other, must be
equal in the utility dimensions for all players. This is called "minimax
relative concession," but unfortunately Gauthier does not argue for the
merits of Zeuthen's Principle beyond noting that minimax relative
concession is independent of the choice of utility scales and does not
invoke interpersonal comparisons of utility.

What is going to generate far more controversy than invoking
Zeuthen's Principle is Gauthier's argument that rational men will comply
with their agreements. His argument boils down to the assertion that
people can force themselves to abide by their agreements over the long
haul, which is quite a statement about human psychology indeed.
Moreover, they can detect the sincerity of others to do likewise. These
seem to be new assumptions about human rationality, psychology, and
capacity, on top of full knowledge of the game and of others' utilities.
Gauthier's justification of all this by way of group selection of
societal indoctrination is by means of essentially sociobiological
arguments but is not terribly robust. While small departures from
absolute rationality weaken conclusions in, say, economic theory only
modestly, here it would seem that it would take only a very small
departure from Gauthier's new assertions about human nature and capacities
for detecting cheating to bring about a collapse of the game into
instability. He says, "our ideal would be a society in which the
coercive enforcement of such decisions would be unnecessary" (p. 164),
but the bald fact is that every society has such enforcement mechanisms,
often of a draconian sort. Gauthier is more right than perhaps he
realizes when he says that the Hobbist "sovereign makes morality,
understood as a constraint on each person's endeavor to maximize his own
utility, as unnecessary as does the market" (p. 164).

One could also ask whether there is any real agreement at all, in
the sense of a meeting of the minds. Given all of Gauthier's
assumptions, the outcome is already predetermined, and so there need not
be even any communication let alone any agreement. The same can be said

for Rawls' social contract. Again, an economist, dealing regularly with
agreement and negotiation costs, is more likely to ask whether Gauthier's
agreements are realistic.

So far, Gauthier has dealt with what he calls the internal
rationality of cooperation, which has to do with the formation of and
adherence to agreements made from a given starting point. His next task
is to examine the starting point itself and consider when it is rational
to begin the bargaining in the first place. He strives to set up
criteria here for the external rationality of cooperation, to say when
the starting point is just in a rational sense, as he conceives of
rationality. He develops a modified version of John Locke's famous
proviso, that there "be enough, and as good left for others," to serve as
an external constraint upon the initial endowments one may bring to the
bargaining table.

As mentioned earlier, Gauthier has an extended discussion of James
M. Buchanan's The Limits of Liberty, which regards any so-called justice
of the initial starting point in a state of nature, out of which a social
contract might emerge, as irrelevant. For Gauthier, this is decidedly
not so. In many cases, he claims, it would not be rational for parties
in an unfair position initially to adhere to the agreement, what is
unfair being decided by the proviso. I find Gauthier's criticisms of
Limits to be not entirely convincing, for reasons an economist would spot
more readily than a philosopher. Gauthier, as I argued earlier, went
beyond even Game Theoretic Man in order to conclude that men will
rationally adhere to their agreements. He goes further yet in his
development of the logic of external rationality.

After an introductory chapter, The Limits of Liberty considers two
persons in a state of nature and one good, which falls from Heaven,
perhaps unequally, upon the two. The two persons may attempt to seize
each other's holdings and exert efforts to prevent same. Buchanan
supposes that some "anarchist equilibrium" among predation, protection
(negative production), consumption, and (presumably) leisure will emerge.
Buchanan envisions that the two anarchists, reflecting upon their
situation, may come to negotiate a peace pact, "the first leap out of the
anarchist jungle," to better their mutual lots. The requirement for any
agreement, Buchanan argues, is that what is better is to be viewed
from the anarchist equilibrium.

This is precisely what Gauthier disputes. He maintains that the
initial point for bargaining should be the shares of goods from Heaven

and that it would not be rational for anyone to expect to hold onto the
fruits of predation. Now, Buchanan says that the party that did come out
better because of his superior talents at predation can always threaten
to plunge the society back into the Hobbist jungle, to which Gauthier
states flatly, "the threat is unreal" (p. 196). Being unreal, therefore,
no such agreement from the anarchist equilibrium will be signed by
rational actors.

This is the crux of the matter, but is it true? In the paragraph
before he stated "the threat is unreal," Gauthier jumped ahead three
chapters in Limits to Buchanan's discussion of the prospect for the
social contract being renegotiated if the underlying anarchist
equilibrium had changed in the meantime. Ideally, perhaps, men should
live up to their agreements, but if some think they might do better by
plunging society back into anarchy and emerging with a new (and for them
a better) social contract, why, they might just do so. What Gauthier is
apparently assuming is that, once an agreement to stop predation is
reached, those who got the better end of the stick by virtue of their
predatory abilities will throw these abilities irrevocably away. Now,
there may very well be some partial truth in this assertion. After all,
we were speaking of an anarchist equilibrium, and an economist, but not
necessarily a philosopher, will note that there are ongoing maintenance
costs of keeping up one's capital of predatory capacity. Bows and maybe
even arrows deteriorate, as do archery skills. Indeed, a main (if not
the main) objective in reaching an agreement is to eliminate these
ongoing expenditures.

But a certain amount of human and non-human capital for predation
will remain. Gauthier might have a way out of this, however, which
follows from his picking up a remark in Limits that side payments might
be necessary to get the social contract off the ground. This way out may
be to use said side payments to destroy predation capital or at least to
somehow equalize advantages so that the new anarchist equilibrium will be
the hypothetical equilibrium in a state of magical enforcement of no
coercion at no cost by the Lord. It is by no means necessarily the case
that those on the short end of the stick have enough to trade to bring
this equalizing about nor that rational individuals will consent to the
brain damage that would equalize predatory capital, especially as damaged
brains would be less productive all around. It is one thing to idealize
men as rational, having full knowledge of the situation and each other's
utilities, and able to detect one another's sincerity to abide by

agreements. But it is entirely something else to suppose that predatory
capital in the state of nature is structured in a quite specific way,
seemingly ad hoc just to derive a desired conclusion.

Unfortunately, I am unable to say how serious a defect the implicit
assumptions about predatory capital will be to Gauthier's argument in
practice. Given that moving from the state of nature to civil society is
beneficial to everyone, it may be possible (at least in some (rare?)
cases) to treat differences in predatory capital as part of the manna
falling from Heaven, and take rights to the converted plus original manna
as the state-of-nature starting point. If so, we might continue to
follow Gauthier, who proceeds to clarify what the proviso that defines
this starting point is. Gauthier modifies Locke's proviso "so that it
prohibits worsening the situation of another person, except to avoid
worsening one's own through interaction with that person" (p. 205). This
would require compensation for negative externalities, but would allow
appropriation from the commons provided that others will be made better
off through market exchanges with the new owner. This specification of
Locke's proviso, which I am simplifying but I hope not oversimplifying, is
necessary lest Locke be read strictly to mean that appropriation is rarely
ever justifiable.

Gauthier then attempts to justify adherence to the proviso (before
the bargaining over morals begins) as rational, still however not by
dealing with predatory capital. He wraps up this discussion with yet
another expansion of the concept of rationality, this time having to do
with the instrumental ability to get what one wants. He makes the
astonishing claim that "we suppose that the unequal rationality brought
about by technological differences between societies is accidental" (p.
231), and concludes that "morals arise in and from rational agreement of
equals" (p. 232, my emphasis). At bottom, I cannot but conclude that
Gauthier's justification of the proviso rests upon a kind of highly
falsifiable egalitarianism.

It may however simply be that some sort of egalitarianism is needed
to derive any morality that pretends to be universal. Otherwise, there
could be situations that Gauthier mentions briefly where it would be
entirely rational for one group to systematically exploit another.
Granted, but what if such exploitation is rational? (It has occurred
often enough.) Gauthier is unclear here. Instead, he argues that his
scheme of universalist rationality (a person "chooses the proviso as
constraining interactions among all mankind" (p. 261, my emphasis))

comports with a modification of Rawls' "reflective equilibrium," which
Gauthier dubs "the Archimedian point." But for all his criticisms of
Rawls' egalitarianism, I am not at all sure how much Gauthier's
egalitarianism would differ.

In practice, also, Gauthier may be assuming less subjectivism than
his theory calls for. In many places throughout his book, an economist
aware of the limits of his discipline (alas, not very many economists!)
may think Gauthier overly restricts values to the market. This is
especially apparent in Chapter 9, where Gauthier defends the seizure of
land from the American Indians by Europeans. To justify this seizure,
Gauthier claims that the land under capitalist cultivation made the
Indians better off, as required by his proviso. To do this, Gauthier
overrates increased longevity and underrates Indian lifestyles: "These
old ways were effectively doomed by the arrival of the Europeans....The
effect of European incursion was to turn cultural practices that had been
necessary into a form of play" (p. 296). By not recognizing the utility
value of play, as an economist would (or should), Gauthier is here
abandoning subjectivism for intrinsicism.

In several ways, then, Gauthier is out-economizing (out-econom*ism*-
izing) economists. He assumes no lack of information about the structure
of the game; he assumes people can read one another's utility functions;
he assumes one can tell whether another will hold to his bargains; and he
assumes that communitarian values and lifestyles are unimportant. For an
excellent critique of the premises of modern individualism, see Roberto
Mangabeira Unger, Knowledge and Politics.

On the other hand, Gauthier has not gone completely over to
decreeing that ethics is "a kind of glorified economics," as Frank Knight
had put it in The Ethics of Competition. He is aware that values are not
formed in a social vacuum, that "men want to have better wants" (Knight
again), and that "man wants freedom to become the man he wants to become"
(Buchanan, in "Natural and Artifactual Man"). Be that as it may,
Morals by Agreement is certainly a stimulating book. It is densely
written and demands attentive reading, yet it rarely drags, a
considerable achievement for a work of philosophy. At last a philosopher
has troubled himself to contemplate economics and connect it to ethics.
(Most philosophy of economics has to do with how far economics is a
science. The trick is to avoid rigid isms without embracing an
eclecticism so broad as to constitute anarchy.) My essential reaction is
that the first contribution by a philosopher toward linking ethics and

economics (<u>Limits</u> being the first such contribution by an economist) is
still the first contribution, and that it ought to stimulate more
contributions. The next step, I think, is to relax, not the unreal
assumption that men are rational, so much as the other assumptions of
Game Theoretic Man, especially the ones about his fantastic knowledge of
other people.

We need, in short, an ethic for <u>homo ignoramus</u>. Or rather, many
ethics. Philosophers are entirely too prone to searching for one big
system for all mankind, and so are economists and public choice
theorists. Very little time is spent examining America's great
contribution to politics, federalism. I daresay even Game Theoretic Men
would have their quarrels and might well split up into cooperativly
competing countries. As we go on moving into the era of cyborgs, genetic
engineering, and space travel, searching for universalist answers looks
more than a bit odd.

CONTRACTING FOR NATURAL RIGHTS
(reprinted from Vera Lex 8 (1988))

"With the clash of authority came the end of authority." Thus wrote
H.L. Mencken in 1908 in the first biography of Nietzsche in English, and
quite possibly still the best. He was speaking of Nietzsche's early
rejection of religion on the grounds that there could not be more than
one absolute Truth, but the statement may apply to natural rights
doctrines as well. There are just too many philosophers laying down
diverse pronouncements, each of them final, about which of the various
natural rights are the true ones. Might it not be better for the people
themselves to make up their own minds about which rights, whether they
call them natural or not, to protect? After all and unless we believe
society is some god or some transcendental object and rights only a
manifestation of its glory, then rights ought to benefit people. And who
is in a better position to know which rights are beneficial than the
people themselves?

Thus, the justification of the idea of a social contract is that the
people have decided upon it. Yet "authorities" known as philosophers
take over the interpretation of this idea and tell the people what they
have agreed to. Thomas Hobbes, for example, tells them that they are so
frightfully warlike that the only right they have kept is to remove a
sovereign who fails to keep the peace. John Locke, who holds a less
fearsome view of human nature, lets them keep a good deal more. John
Rawls, as East Coast liberals read him, says the people have agreed to
East Coast liberalism, though my own reading of A Theory of Justice makes
me think he moved in a libertarian direction during the twenty years he
spent writing it. (I got this impression by reading it cover to cover in
a week, or about 1/1040 the time he spent writing it.)

This all would seem to mean the end of authority, too, in that even
the Mayflower Compact could no doubt be regarded as coerced, surely so
far as the children on board were concerned, to say nothing of those yet
unborn. But we can move away from authority in the direction of realism,
and such is the perspective an economist can give, a perspective which I
shall herein explore under the name of economic contractarianism. My
basis here is James M. Buchanan's magnum opus, The Limits of Liberty
(1975). He sees the social contract as economists see contracts: as

agreement, exchange, bargain, compromise. Before the agreement, there is
what he dubs an "anarchist equilibrium" of production, predation, and
protection. Anarchists in a state of nature might negotiate a peace pact
to reduce predation and protection, so as to better concentrate on
production. Such a pact is not likely to be self-enforcing, and so they
will empower a government to enforce the pact. Just what pact will come
about, that is, what rights will be protected, is up to the anarchists.
No pact, and the state of nature persists.

In the strict historical sense, we are still in a state of nature,
because there are always enough people around (it only takes one) who are
simply disagreeable, thus blocking any agreement. But we can assess how
closely any situation approximates unanimity. Compromises can be made,
and we don't have to wait for everyone to agree with every jot and tittle
that John Rawls, or John Locke, or Thomas Hobbes wrote. Maybe even this
distinguished trio could come to some sort of agreement, if only to stop
fighting one day a week and hold a pow-wow on the ideal social contract.
Buchanan very definitely recognizes that a social contract need not at all
be the best one possible.

Buchanan has also distinguished the protective from the productive
state, in which a government goes beyond protecting rights to engage in
producing public goods. The people don't decide for all time what goods
the government will provide and how they will be paid for. This is
asking too much. Rather they set up a constitution that grants limited
authority to pass legislation under a set of rules. Thus the
contractarian productive state solves the problem of providing such
public goods as national defense and sanitation, before which
libertarians must usually modify their position. It is true that not
everyone will approve every publicly financed scheme, but they could
agree to a set of legislative rules that will benefit everyone over the
long haul. Some public goods may be judged as "necessary," but most will
not, and the quantities of all will be decided on the basis of individual
values and trade-offs. Natural rights theories do not offer much of a
method or solution here.

On the other hand, natural rights theories can have their uses when
it comes to setting up the rules for the protective state. Authorities
continue to clash, but the basic idea behind natural rights theories,
that the broad features of human nature determine natural rights, is
certainly worthy of attention. The important point is that the social
contractors see that they merely need to get out of the state of anarchy

and do not have to resolve the clash of authorities perfectly and for all
time. They may agree that reason is man's tool for survival and that
this implies the protection of life, liberty, property, and the pursuit
of happiness. They need not agree upon the existence of "positive
welfare rights" (e.g., a guaranteed minimum income paid for by taxes) to
tax monies nor on redistributive schemes for "social justice."
Philosophers certainly have not established even negative rights (e.g.,
property rights) absolutely--in other words, they continue to clash--and
a great deal of philosophy is given over to replacing big holes in their
arguments with little holes. In all strict logic, a hole is a hole, but
the contractors will not wait around in a state of anarchy until the
authorities stop clashing: At some point they will decide that some
alleged rights have been established plausibly enough and set up a
protective state. As it happens, the case for negative rights has been
far better made than that for positive rights and redistribution. It
would seem that the unanimity ideal--that an agreement be a genuine
meeting of the minds--is an excuse for the minimal libertarian state.
Two replies: First, advocates of positive rights had better get busy and
cook up far more persuasive arguments than they have to date, and second,
the productive state goes beyond libertarian minimalism anyhow.

     The economist's contractarian approach has a further advantage over
a natural rights approach, in that it pays attention to institutional
design. While natural rights authorities clash over whether, say,
intellectual property (patents, copyrights, trademarks, and trade
secrets) is a genuine natural right, social contractors can simply(!)
weigh costs and benefits of establishing rights in intellectual property.
Moreover, they can empower a legislature to set the duration of patents,
something that natural rights theories are utterly incapable of doing.
Social contractors can also set up machinery to make trade-offs between
the costly accumulation of evidence in criminal cases and the probability
of wrongful conviction. Economists habitually, even compulsively, reckon
with trade-offs, a perspective generally absent among philosophers.

     The social contractors, as I have said, are something approximating
real people, who may disagree with one another, but hopefully not so much
that there is no prospect of moving out of the state of nature. They are
also real in that they will act on inconclusive arguments and information
and not delay moving out of the state of nature indefinitely. They can
agree upon the machinery of both the protective and the productive state.
Can they also agree upon schemes to establish social justice and

redistribution? In one sense, of course they can: they can agree upon
whatever they wish. But are they likely to? To answer this, we have to
make some assumptions about the contractors. Let us assume, rather
heroically, that the contractors are all good economists and have studied
the applications of economics to political markets, called Public Choice
theory. They have enough appreciation of how a constitution may be
expected to work out that their signing of the contract will be informed.
They will also be sure to build in constitutional safeguards to ward off
the ever-present threat of Leviathan. They are also metaphysical
individualists, in that they do not grant the existence of a
transcendental entity called society, which has values of its own apart
from those of the individuals that compose it. Moreover, they have
absorbed the lessons of Friedrich Hayek's The Mirage of Social Justice
(1976) and realize that remote consequences of human action so far dwarf
immediate ones that it is futile to try to calculate the corrections
necessary to bring rewards in line with gut feelings about desert on a
case-by-case basis. They will cheerfully pay the price of living in a
society controlled by abstract rules and suppress their desire to take
away even the high incomes of rock "musicians."

In short, these contractors are economists who have absorbed not
only the logic of the market but also the creative aspects of capitalism
emphasized by Ludwig von Mises, Friedrich Hayek, and others of the
so-called Austrian School of economics. Natural rights theories are
often greatly informed by economics, so the two approaches overlap quite
considerably on what human nature consists of. Nevertheless, there is
some room for social justice or redistribution, though not of the sort to
attempt to rectify each and every discrepancy between reward and desert.
Social justice can become an issue, not because the original social
contract is unfair--after all, everyone benefits from moving out of the
state of nature and the workings of competition will erode initial
privileges over time anyhow--but because new members are added
involuntarily to the society by birth. (I hold that voluntary
immigration is up to the contractors.) Inheritance laws that forbid the
alienation of property and are designed to perpetuate family wealth, such
as primogeniture laws or even provisions like the entail that allow such
perpetuation, can be viewed as unfair to involuntary entrants. And it
may be felt that rich parents provide their children with an unfairly
large head start in life, by way both of gifts of capital and the
provision of education and otherwise superior upbringing.

However and as it happens in the United States, movements to
confiscate inheritance have never been very robust and have been
restricted to moderately graduated inheritance and gift taxes and public
financing of education. (Hayek himself approves of the latter,
surprisingly for a man supposed to be a libertarian. Whether the
government should operate schools, as opposed to financing vouchers, is
another issue.) Evidently, Americans hold that the incentive to pass
wealth on to one's offspring is a powerful factor in its creation and
choose to balance this against any unfairness, with the result being only
moderately graduated inheritance and gift taxes.

I will not try to argue that the observed inheritance taxes and
public support for education can be justified on the basis of an historic
social contract, far from it; but the important points from a
contractarian perspective are that it is up to the people to decide how
to treat new entrants and it is up to them to decide what the trade-offs
are to be between pursuing their own conception of social justice and
their many other objectives. Social justice is neither something
existing outside of individual values, nor is it to be pursued at the
expense of everything else. The pursuit of any goal without limit will
doom liberty.

A few other points: (1) The other kind of justice, impartial
administration of laws, is a noble ideal, but the very existence of public
goods, prisoners' dilemmas, and externalities, as well as the sheer
finitude of the human brain, render perfect neutrality unworkable.
Besides, the social contract is supposed to change things. (2) In a
market economy, alleged biases in the law, e.g., rental contracts
favoring landlords over tenants, will very often get corrected by market
mechanisms, e.g., by rents going down. (3) Legislators and bureaucrats
can try to help the poor, but the voters can and do respond by electing
politicians to change marginal tax rates. In other words, in well-oiled
political markets, voters get the amount of redistribution they
themselves want. (4) Arguments that, say, school teachers are unjustly
underpaid are usually just so many arbitrary assertions or else involve
externalities and public goods, which is a matter for the productive
state to handle, not so much a matter of social justice. (5) While the
protective and productive states, under a well-designed constitution, are
positive-sum games, they quickly become negative when social justice
becomes thought of as an unlimited, transcendental objective. Since
people never do agree on the transcendental, the free society degenerates

into what Ayn Rand called "the aristocracy of pull."

In sum, the economist-contractarian perspective is not dissimilar from natural rights approaches, but the former has several advantages: (1) It lets the people act while authorities clash, adopting whatever sorts of natural rights arguments they see fit as a basis for their social contract. (2) It can take public goods into account. (3) It can deal with specific questions of institutional design in deciding which rights to protect and how much. The right to privacy, for example, comes into being when people conceptualize it (a process still going on) and seriously want it. (4) It allows for trade-offs. (5) It can advance a limited conception of social justice to take care of babies. (6) It makes a point of recognizing that people differ and need to bargain as opposed to finding some external truth. (7) It is constantly on the lookout for Leviathan. But above all, economic contractarianism is pluralistic: Different peoples will care differently about different rights and can arrange themselves accordingly. It rests upon the greatest tribute to the genius of our Founding Fathers, namely federalism. It assumes and makes room for a tolerance that, unhappily, most authorities cannot abide. No mean advantage, this, to allow for experiment and improvement.

BIBLIOGRAPHY

Key to the Four Most-Cited Books

FW   The Furniture of the World (1977) by Mario Bunge
KP   Knowledge and Politics (1975) by Roberto Mangabeira Unger
LL   The Limits of Liberty (1975) by James M. Buchanan
WS   A World of Systems (1979) by Mario Bunge

Works cited, followed by cross-references or page references to the text

Ardrey, Robert 1970. The Social Contract: A Personal Inquiry into the
    Evolutionary Source of Order and Disorder. Patterson, NJ: Atheneum;
    mass paperback, New York: Dell, 1974. 158
Arnold, Magda B. 1960. Emotion and Personality, 2 vol. New York:
    Columbia University Press. 105
Barlow, George W., and Silverberg, James, eds. 1980. Sociobiology: Beyond
    Nature/Nurture? Boulder: Westview Press. 156
Bellah, Robert N.; Madsen, Richard; Sullivan, William M.; Swidler, Ann;
    and Tipton, Steven M. 1985. Habits of the Heart: Individualism and
    Commitment in American Life. Berkeley: University of California
    Press. 113
Bible 1611. King James Version. xi 132 149 150 and disguised passim
Binswanger, Harry 1981. "The Possible Dream." The Objectivist Forum 2:
    February and April. 154
_____ 1987. "'Buy American' is Un-American." The Objectivist Forum 8:
    April. 159
Branden, Nathaniel 1982. "The Benefits and Hazards of the Philosophy of
    Ayn Rand." Lecture Tape. Los Angeles: The Biocentric Institute. 153
Breit, William 1984. "Galbraith and Friedman: Two Versions of Economic
    Reality." Journal of Post Keynesian Economics 3: 18–29. 150
Brennan, H. Geoffrey, and Buchanan, James M. 1982. "Is Public Choice
    Immoral?" Paper presented at the Public Choice Society Meetings in
    San Antonio, in March. 47
Brown, Lawrence R. 1963. The Might of the West. New York: Ivan Obolensky;
    reprinted, Washington: Joseph J. Binns, 1979. 47
Buchanan, James M. 1965. "Ethical Rules, Expected Values, and Large
    Numbers." Ethics 76: 1–13; reprinted in 1977, pp. 151–68. 156
_____ 1966. "Economics and Its Scientific Neighbors." In Krupp 1966,
    pp. 166–83; reprinted in 1979b, pp. 115–42. 57
_____ 1968. "An Economist's Approach to 'Scientific Politics.'" In
    Parsons 1968, pp. 77–88; reprinted in Buchanan 1979b, pp. 143–59. 1
_____ 1969a. Cost and Choice: An Inquiry into Economic Theory.
    Chicago: Markham Publishing Co.; paperback, Chicago: The University
    of Chicago Press, Midway Reprints, 1978. 91 113
_____ 1969b. "Is Economics the Science of Choice?" In Streissler
    1969; reprinted in Buchanan 1979b, pp. 39–63, and again in Buchanan
    1987, pp. 35–50. 57
_____ 1975. The Limits of Liberty: Between Anarchy and Leviathan.
    Chicago: University of Chicago Press; paperback as A Phoenix Book,
    1978. 1–30 (=Chapter 1) 31 33 36 42–44 49–52 57 86 91 97–99 110–111
    125 130 135–37 139 143 149 151 156–57 167 171 175 176 179 181
_____ 1977. Freedom in Constitutional Contract: Perspectives of a
    Political Economist. College Station: Texas A&M University Press.
    Buchanan 1965

Buchanan 1978. "Natural and Artifactual Man." Lecture presented at the
    Liberty Fund Series Conference in Blacksburg, VA, in July; printed in
    1979b, pp. 93–112. 105 119 135–37 178 All references are to the
    sentence, "Man wants freedom to become the man he wants to become."
_____ 1979a. "Public Finance and Academic Freedom." In 1979b, pp.
    252–70. 130
_____ 1979b. What Should Economists Do? With a Preface by H. Geoffrey
    Brennan and Robert D. Tollison. Indianapolis: Liberty Press.
    Buchanan 1968, 1969b, 1978, and 1979a
_____ 1984. "Victorian Norms, Keynesianism, and the Fiscal Whirlwind."
    Typescript. 91
_____ 1985. "Public Debt and Capital Formation." In Lee 1985.
    Reprinted in Buchanan 1986a, pp. 195–209. 91
_____ 1986a. Liberty, Market, and State: Political Economy in the
    1980s. New York: New York University Press. Buchanan 1985
_____ 1986b. "Better than Plowing." Banca Nazionale del Lavoro
    Quarterly Review 159: 359–75. 20
_____ 1987. Economics: Between Predictive Science and Moral
    Philosophy. Compiled and Prefaced by Robert D. Tollison and Viktor
    J. Vanberg. College Station: Texas A&M Press. Buchanan 1969b
Buchanan, James M. and Faith, Roger L. 1980. "Subjective Elements in
    Rawlsian Contractual Agreement in Distributional Rules." Economic
    Inquiry 18: 23–38. 92
Buchanan, James M., and Samuels, Warren J. 1980. "On Some Fundamental
    Issues in Political Economy: An Exchange of Correspondence." In
    Samuels 1980, pp. 517–40. 21
Buchanan, James M.; Tollison, Robert D.; and Tullock, Gordon, eds. 1980.
    Toward a Theory of the Rent-Seeking Society. College Station: Texas
    A&M University Press. Tullock 1975
Buchanan, James M., and Tullock, Gordon 1962. The Calculus of Consent:
    Logical Foundations of Constitutional Democracy. Ann Arbor:
    University of Michigan Press; Ann Arbor Paperback, 1965. 1–3 8 11 13
    47 90 131 135 171
Bunge, Mario 1974–??. Treatise on Basic Philosophy. Dordrecht, Holland:
    D. Reidel. 55–81 (=Chapter 2)
                          Volumes 1 and 2
                          (Semantics I and II)
            Sense and Reference (1974, 180 pp.)
            Interpretation and Truth (1974, 210 pp.)
                          Volumes 3 and 4
                          (Ontology I and II)
            The Furniture of the World (1977, 352 pp.) 37 55–62 73 78 95 102
                                                       127–28 159
            A World of Systems (1979, 314 pp.)   62–80 103 105 119 139
                          Volumes 5, 6, and 7
            (Epistemology and Methodology I, II, and III)
            Exploring the World (1983, 404 pp.)
            Understanding the World (1983, 296 pp.)
            Philosophy of Science and Technology (1985, 263 + 341 pp.)
                  Part 1: Formal and Physical Sciences
                  Part 2: Life Science, Social Science and Technology
                          Volume 8
                          (Ethics)
            The Good and the Right (too long forthcoming!)

_____ 1959. Causality: The Place of the Causal Principle in Modern
    Science. Cambridge: Harvard University Press; paperback as Causality
    and Modern Science, New York: Dover, 3rd rev. ed., 1979. 150

Bunge 1967a. Scientific Research, 2 vol. Berlin: Springer-Verlag.
      113 149 155 158
_____ 1967b. Foundations of Physics. New York: Springer-Verlag. 60
_____ 1980. The Mind-Body Problem: A Psycho-Biological Approach.
      Elmsford, N.Y.: Pergamon Press. 66
_____ 1981. Scientific Materialism. Dordrecht: D.Reidel. 68
Campbell, Donald T. 1975. "On the Conflicts between Biological and Social
      Evolution and between Psychology and Moral Tradition." Presidential
      Address before the American Psychological Association at its meeting
      in Chicago in August; printed in American Psychologist 30: 1103–26;
      reprinted in Zygon 11: 167–208 (1976), along with discussions by
      others, other than those in subsequent issues of American
      Psychologist. 156
Carroll, Lewis 1872. Through the Looking Glass and What Alice Found
      There. With Illustrations by John Tenniel. London: Macmillan. See
      also The Philosopher's Alice, with an Introduction and Notes by Peter
      Heath (New York: St. Martin's Press, 1974), and The Annotated Alice,
      with an Introduction and Notes by Martin Gardner (New York: Clarkson
      N. Potter, 1960). Both books contain the texts of the two Alice
      books and the Tenniel illustrations. 36–37 144
Cattell, Raymond B. 1972. A New Morality from Science: Beyondism.
      Elmsford, N.Y.: Pergamon Press. 119–27 (in chapter 6) 156–57
Coon, Carleton S. 1962. The Origin of Races. New York: Alfred A. Knopf.
      74
Coulson, N.J., "Islamic Law." In Derrett 1968. 33
Cuddihy, John Murray 1974. The Ordeal of Civility: Freud, Marx,
      Levi-Strauss, and the Jewish Struggle with Modernity. New York:
      Basic Books; paperback, New York: Dell, 1976. 40
Darwin, Charles 1859. On the Origin of Species by Means of Natural
      Selection, or the Preservation of Favoured Races in the Struggle
      for Life. London: John Murray. 117
DeNicola, Daniel R. 1976. "Genetics, Justice, and Respect for Human
      Life." Zygon 11: 115–37. 92
Denton, Michael 1985. Evolution: A Theory in Crisis. Bethesda: Adler &
      Adler. 148
Derrett, J. Duncan M. 1968. An Introduction to Legal Systems. New York:
      Friedrich A. Praeger. Coulson 1968
Dimond, Stuart J. 1979 "Symmetry and Asymmetry in the Vertebrate Brain."
      In Oakley and Plotkin 1979. 38–39
Downs, Anthony 1957. An Economic Theory of Democracy. New York: Harper
      and Row; paperback, 1965. 1
Dumézil, Georges 1959. Gods of the Ancient Northmen. Edited and
      translated from the 1959 French original by Einar Haugen, with an
      Introduction by C. Scott Littleton and Udo Strutynski. Los Angeles:
      University of California Press, 1973. 40
Encyclopaedia Britannica in 30 Volumes, The New, 15th ed. Chicago:
      Encyclopaedia Britannica, Inc., 1974: Micropaedia 5:891–92, s.v.,
      "Milky Way," and Macropaedia 7:833–849, s.v., "Galaxy, The." 145
Fletcher, Joseph 1974. The Ethics of Genetic Control: Ending
      Reproductive Roulette. With a Foreword by Joshua Lederberg. New
      York: Anchor Books (paperback). 92
Frank, Robert H. 1985. Choosing the Right Pond: Human Behavior and the
      Quest for Status. New York: Oxford University Press. 165–70 (App. 2)
Frenkel, Max 1986. Federal Theory. Canberra: Center for Research on
      Federal Financial Relations, The Australian National University. 147
Fuller, Lon L. 1964. The Morality of Law. New Haven: Yale University
      Press. Paged according to the 2nd and paperback edition, 1969.
      133–34

Gardner, Martin 1960. The Annotated Alice. Contains the text of both
    Lewis Carroll Alice books, with an Introduction and Notes by Gardner,
    and the Tenniel illustrations. New York: Clarkson N. Potter. 144
Gauthier, David 1986. Morals by Agreement. New York: Oxford University
    Press. 151, 171-79 (App. 3)
Glassner, Martin Ira, and de Blij, Harm J. 1980. Systematic Political
    Geography, 3rd ed. New York: John Wiley & Sons. 158. Hartshorne 1950
Hartshorne, Richard 1950. "The Functional Approach in Political
    Geography." Presidential Address before the Association of Political
    Geographers at its Forty-Sixth Annual Meeting in Worcester, MA, on
    April 7. Reprinted in Glassner and de Blij 1980. 158
Hayek, Friedrich A. 1944. The Road to Serfdom. Chicago: University of
    Chicago Press; paperback as A Phoenix Book, by 1963. 106
_____ 1976. Law, Legislation and Liberty, vol. 2: The Mirage of
    Social Justice. Chicago: University of Chicago Press; paperback as A
    Phoenix Book, 1978. 83-91 184
_____ 1979. Law, Legislation and Liberty, vol. 3: The Political Order
    of a Free People. Chicago: University of Chicago Press, paperback as
    A Phoenix Book, 1981. 156
Heath, Peter 1974. The Philosopher's Alice. Contains the text of both
    Lewis Carroll Alice books, with an Introduction and Notes by Heath,
    and the Tenniel illustrations. New York: St. Martin's Press. 144
Hobbes, Thomas 1651. Leviathan, or The Matter, Forme, and Power of a
    Commonwealth, Ecclesiasticall and Civil. London: Andrew Crooke.
    11 36 40 87
Hume, David 1739. A Treatise of Human Nature, Being an Attempt to
    Introduce the Experimental Methods of Reasoning into Moral Subjects.
    London at the White-Hart, near Mercer's-Chapelin, Cheapside: John
    Noon. 40
Ijiri, Yuji, and Simon, Herbert A. 1977 Skew Distributions and the Sizes
    of Business Firms. Amsterdam: North-Holland Publishing Co. Simon
    1967
Jaynes, Julian 1976. The Origin of Consciousness in the Breakdown of the
    Bicameral Mind. Boston: Houghton Mifflin. 39 153
Kliemt, Hartmut 1986. "The Veil of Insignificance." European Journal of
    Political Economy 2/3:333-44. 97 161-64 (App. 1)
Knight, Frank Hyneman 1935. The Ethics of Competition and Other Essays.
    New York: Harper & Brothers. 136 178
Kohn, Alfie 1986. No Contest: The Case against Competition. Boston:
    Houghton Mifflin. 113
Kripke, Saul 1971. "Identity and Necessity." In Munitz 1971, pp. 135-64.
    67
Krupp, Sherman Roy, ed. 1966. The Structure of Economic Science: Essays
    on Methodology. Engelwood Cliffs: Prentice Hall. Buchanan 1966
Lee, Dwight R., ed. 1985. The Political Economy of Capital Formation:
    Direct and Indirect Effects of Taxation. San Francisco: Pacific
    Institute. Buchanan 1985
_____ 1987. "Getting More from Less, with a Notable Exception."
    Third Annual Lecture in the Virginia Political Economy Lectures,
    George Mason Univeristy, March 19. Printed as a pamphlet, Fairfax:
    Center for Study of Public Choice, George Mason Univeristy. 114
Littleton, C. Scott 1973. The New Comparative Mythology: An
    Anthropological Assessment of the Theories of Georges Dumézil. Los
    Angeles: University of California Press, revised and paperback ed.
    40
Lumsden, Charles J., and Wilson, Edward O. 1981. Genes, Mind, and
    Culture: The Coevolutionary Process. Cambridge: Harvard University
    Press. 107

MacIntyre, Alasdair 1981. After Virtue: A Study in Moral Theory. Notre
    Dame: University of Notre Dame Press. 113
Mandelbrot, Benoit 1982. The Fractal Geometry of Nature. New York: W.H.
    Freeman; second printing with an Added Appendix, 1983. 148
Mencken, H.L. 1908. The Philosophy of Friedrich Nietzsche. Boston: John
    W. Luce & Co. 109 181
_____ 1927. "On Metaphysicians." In Prejudices: Sixth Series. New
    York: Alfred A. Knopf, pp. 79-85. 1
_____ 1928. Notes on Democracy. New York: Alfred A. Knopf. 2 17
Mises, Ludwig von 1949. Human Action: A Treatise on Economics. New
    Haven: Yale University Press. 105
Munitz, Milton K., ed. 1971. Identity and Individuation. New York: New
    York University Press. Kripke 1971
Nietzsche, Friedrich 1877. On the Genealogy of Morals. In Basic Writings
    of Nietzsche, translated from the German and edited with Commentaries
    by Walter Kaufmann (New York: Modern Library, 1968). 152
Nisbet, Robert A. 1953. The Quest for Community. Oxford: Oxford
    University Press. 117
Nozick, Robert 1974. Anarchy, State, and Utopia. New York: Basic Books.
    Issued simultaneously in its Harper Torchbooks paperback series.
    95 113 154
Oakley, David A. 1979. "Cerebral Cortex and Adaptive Behaviour." In
    Oakley and Plotkin 1979, pp. 154-88. 74
Oakley, David A., and Plotkin, H.C. 1979. Brain, Behaviour and Evolution.
    London: Methuen & Co. Dimond 1979, Oakley 1979, and Yeo 1979
Ortner, Donald J., ed. How Humans Adapt: A Biocultural Odyssey.
    Washington: Smithsonian Institution Press. 92
Ostrom, Vincent 1971. The Political Theory of a Compound Republic:
    A Reconstruction of the Logical Foundations of American Democracy as
    Presented in The Federalist. Blacksburg: Center for Study of Public
    Choice, Virginia Polytechnic Institute and State University. 147
Oxford Dictionary of Quotations, The 1955. London: Oxford University
    Press, 2nd ed. 143 146
Pagels, Elaine 1979. The Gnostic Gospels. New York: Random House;
    paperback as a Vintage Book, 1981. 39
Parsons, M., ed. 1968. Perspectives in the Study of Politics. Chicago:
    Rand-McNally. Buchanan 1968
Peacocke, Arthur 1984. "Thermodynamics and Life." Zygon 19: 395-432.
    132
Peirce, Charles S. 1877. "The Fixation of Belief." Popular Science
    Monthly 12: 1-15. 145 154
_____ 1878. "How to Make Our Ideas Clear." Popular Science Monthly
    12: 286-302. 145 154
_____ 1905. "What Pragmatism Is." The Monist 15: 161-181. These
    three papers have been reprinted many times, e.g., Thayer 1970.
    145 154
Popper, Karl R., and Eccles, John C. 1977. The Self and Its Brain.
    Berlin: Springer-Verlag; paperback, London: Routledge and Kegan Paul,
    1983. 67
Quigley, Carroll 1961. The Evolution of Civilizations: An Introduction to
    Historical Analysis. New York: Macmillan; paperback, Indianapolis:
    Liberty Press, 1979. 153
Rae, Douglas W.; Yates, Douglas T., Jr.; Hochschild, Jennifer L.; Monroe,
    Joseph; and Fessler, Carol 1981. Equalities. Cambridge: Harvard
    University Press. 163
Rand, Ayn 1961. "The Objectivist Ethics." Paper delivered at a University
    of Wisconsin Symposium on "Ethics in Our Time" in Madison, on
    February 9, 1961. Printed in 1964c, pp. 13-34. 103 114 134 138

Rand 1962. "The 'Conflicts' of Men's Interersts." The Objectivist
    Newsletter 1: August. Reprinted in 1964c, pp. 50-56. 104
_____ 1963. "The Nature of Government." The Objectivist Newsletter
    2: December. Reprinted in 1974c, pp. 107-115. 114
_____ 1964a. "Government Financing in a Free Society." The
    Objectivist Newsletter 3: February. Reprinted in 1964c, pp. 116-20.
    114
_____ 1964b. "Patents and Copyrights." The Objectivist Newsletter 3:
    May. 108
_____ 1964c. The Virtue of Selfishness: A New Concept of Egoism.
    With Additional Articles by Nathaniel Branden. New York: New
    American Library, Signet Books (paperback). References in the text
    to articles reprinted in this book use its pagination. 105. Rand
    1961, 1962, 1963, and 1964a
_____ 1966-67. Introduction to Objectivist Epistemology. The
    Objectivist 1: July-December and 2: January-February; mass paperback,
    with an Additional Article by Leonard Peikoff, New York: New American
    Library, Signet Books, 1979. 149 155
_____ 1971. "The Age of Envy." The Objectivist 9: July and August;
    reprinted in 1975, pp. 152-86, but not in the first (1971)
    editon. 17
_____ 1973a. "An Untitled Letter." The Ayn Rand Letter 2: January 29,
    February 12, and February 26; reprinted in 1982, pp. 102-19. 93
_____ 1973b. "The Missing Link." The Ayn Rand Letter 2: May 7 and May
    21; reprinted in 1982, pp. 35-45. 153
_____ 1975. The New Left: The Anti-Industrial Revolution. 2nd revised
    ed., New York: New American Library, Signet Books (mass paperbeck),
    1975. Rand 1971
_____ 1977. "Global Balkanization." Lecture delivered at the Ford
    Hall Forum, Boston, April 10; printed as a pamphlet, Palo Alto, CA:
    Palo Alto Book Service, 1977. 131
_____ 1982. Philosophy: Who Needs It. With an Introduction by Leonard
    Peikoff. New York: Bobbs-Merrill; mass paperback, New York: New
    American Library: Signet, 1984. Rand 1973a and 1973b
Rawls, John 1971. A Theory of Justice. Cambridge: Harvard University
    Press. 19 93 109 181
Rothbard, Murray N. 1962. Man, Economy, and State: A Treatise on
    Economic Principles, 2 vol. New York: Van Nostrand. 105 108
Samuels, Warren J., ed. 1980. The Methodology of Economic Thought. New
    Brunswick, N.J.: Transaction Books. Buchanan and Samuels 1980
Schoeck, Helmut 1966. Envy: A Theory of Social Behaviour, trans. from the
    German Der Neid (1966) by Michael Glenny and Betty Ross. New York:
    Harcourt, Brace and World, 1970. 20
Schumpeter, Joseph A. 1942. Capitalism, Socialism and Democracy. New
    York: Harper & Brothers; paperback of 3rd ed. (1950), New York:
    Harper & Row: Harper Torchbooks, 1962. 2
Schwartz, Peter 1986. Libertarianism, the Perversion of Liberty. New
    York: The Intellectual Activist. 109
Sheldon, William H. 1942. The Varieties of Temperament: A Psychology of
    Constitutional Differences. With the Collaboration of S.S. Stevens.
    New York: Harper & Brothers. 125-26
Shub, David 1950. Lenin: A Biography, abridged by Donald Porter Geddes.
    New York: New American Library, Mentor Books (paperback). 11
Simis, Konstantin M. 1982. U.S.S.R.: The Corrupt Society: The Secret
    World of Soviet Capitalism. Translated from the Russian by Jacqueline
    Edwards and Mitchell Schneider. New York: Simon and Schuster. 110
Simon, Herbert A. 1967. "A Model of Business Firm Growth." Econometrica
    35: 348-55; reprinted in Ijiri and Simon 1977, pp. 171-81. 7

Smith, Adam 1776. An Inquiry into the Nature and Causes of the Wealth of
    Nations. 2 vols. London, in the Strand: W. Strahan and T. Cadell.
    52
Smith, George H. 1974. Atheism: The Case against God. New York: Nash
    Publishing Co.; paperback reprint, Buffalo: Prometheus Books, 1979.
    148
Streissler, Erich, ed. 1969. Roads to Freedom: Essays in Honor of F.A.
    Hayek. London: Routledge & Kegan Paul. Buchanan 1969b
Thayer, H.S., ed. 1970. Pragmatism: The Classic Writings. With an
    Introduction and Commentary by the editor, prepared under the
    editorial supervision of Robert Paul Wolff. New York: New American
    Library, Mentor Books (paperback). 145 154. Peirce 1877, 1878, and
    1905
Tullock, Gordon c. 1960. Coordination without Command: The Organization
    of Insect Societies. Typescript. 128
_____ 1975. "The Transitional Gains Trap." The Bell Journal of
    Economics 6: 671-78; reprinted in Buchanan, Tollison, and Tullock
    1980, pp. 211-21. 128
_____ 1983. Economics of Income Redistribution. Boston:
    Kluwer-Nijhof. 52 85 88 94 152
Unger, Roberto Mangabeira 1975. Knowledge and Politics. New York: Free
    Press. 30, 31-52 (=Chapter 2) 59 91 104 113 178
_____ 1984. Passions: An Essay on Personality. New York: Free Press.
    117
Vanberg, Viktor 1983. "Organizational Goals and Organizations as
    Constitutional Systems." Paper read and discussed at a seminar of
    the Center for Study of Public Choice, George Mason University, on
    December 7. The paper was adopted from the author's
    "Organisationzeile und individuelle Interessen," Soziale Welt 34
    (1983): 171-87. 127 158
Vaughn, Karen I. 1983. "Can There Be a Constitutional Political
    Economy?" Typescript, dated November 9. Fairfax: George Mason
    University. 13-15
Veblen, Thorstein 1919. "Why Economics is Not an Evolutionary Science."
    Reprinted in The Portable Veblen, edited and with an Introduction by
    Max Lerner (New York: Viking Press, 1948). 133
Vining, Rutledge 1984. On Appraising the Performance of an Economic
    System: What an Economic System Is, and the Norms Implied in
    Observers' Adverse Reactions to the Outcome of its Working.
    Cambridge: Cambridge University Press. 138 My first academic article
    is a review of this book in Public Choice 47(3) (1985):533-34
Weber, Max 1918. "Politics as a Vocation." Speech at Munich University.
    In From Max Weber: Essays in Sociology, translated, edited, and with
    an Introduction by H.H. Gerth and C. Wright Mills (New York: Oxford
    Univeristy Press, 1946), pp. 77-128. 2
Whitaker, Robert W. 1976. A Plague on Both Your Houses. Washington: R.B.
    Luce. 98
Winkless, Nels, III, and Browning, Iben 1975. Climate and the Affairs of
    Men. New York: Harper Magazine Press. 158
Wynne-Edwards, V.C. 1963. "Intergroup Selection in the Evolution of
    Social Systems." Nature 200: 623-26. 155
Yeager, Leland B. 1983. "Contract and Truth Judgment in Policy
    Espousal." Typescript, dated June 3. The author discussed his paper
    at a seminar of the Center for Study of Market Processes, George
    Mason University, in October. 25-28
Yeo, Christopher H. 1979. "The Anatomy of Vertebrate Nervous Systems: An
    Evolutionary and Developmental Perspective." In Oakley and Plotkin,
    1979, pp. 28-51. 117

Yule, G. Udny 1924. "A Mathematical Theory of Evolution, Based upon the
    Conclusions of Dr. J.C. Willis, F.R.S." Philosophical Transactions
    of the Royal Society, London, ser. B. 213: 21-87. 129 132-33

ABOUT THE AUTHOR

Frank Forman was born in Kansas City, Mo., on October 28, 1944, and
moved with his family to Colorado Springs when he was 10. His forebears
were Protestant, mostly British, and came to the New World in the
seventeenth and eighteenth centuries. His great-great-grandparents were
Kansas pioneers.

He majored in mathematics as an undergraduate at the University of
Virginia and received a B.A. in 1966. Continuing at U.Va., he turned to
economics, became a Ph.D. candidate, and earned an M.A. degree in 1968.
His doctoral candidacy was transferred to George Mason University in 1983,
where he began his dissertation anew under Professor James M. Buchanan,
one of whose students he had been at U.Va. He received his degree, the
third Ph.D. in George Mason's history, in 1985. This book is an expansion
of his dissertation.

From 1969 to 1984, he worked as a research economist at the Civil
Aeronautics Board, where he was in favor of airline deregulation before
the word was coined. In 1985, having helped work himself out of a job, he
found another one at the U.S. Department of Education. The views
expressed in this book are not necessarily those of the Department or the
U.S. Government.

He gave an invited address on his dissertation at the 54th annual
conference of the Southern Economic Association on November 15, 1984, in
Atlanta. He has since given five more addresses at academic conventions
and has had published four book reviews in Public Choice and one article
in Vera Lex. The appendicies to this book are drawn from these sources.

His hobbies are jogging, mathematical logic, and collecting early
recordings of classical instrumental music. He is a member of the
Association for Recorded Sound Collections, the H.L. Mencken Society, the
American Running and Fitness Association (charter member), and the Public
Choice Society.

He married Sarah Stirling Banks on February 2, 1968, and they have
two children, Alice Gillette, born on January 8, 1976, and Adelaide
Willoughby, born on March 24, 1978. They live in Bethesda, Maryland.

NAME INDEX

Alice 36-37 144 173
*Ardrey, Robert 1908-80 158
 Aristotle of Stagirus aka The
  Philosopher 384-322 B.C. 106 114
  118
*Arnold, Magda Blondiau Barta 1903-
  105

*Barlow, George Webber 1926- 156
 Beethoven, Ludwig van 1770-1827
  57 157
*Bellah, Robert Neely 1927-
  113 115
 Berzelius, Jöns Jakob 1779-1848
  64
*Binswanger, Harry 154 159
 Blumenthal, Nathaniel 1930- under
  his pen name * Nathaniel Branden
*Branden, Nathaniel [pen name of
  Nathaniel Blumenthal] 1930- 153
  and under * Rand 1964c 105
*Breit, William 1933- 150
*Brennan, H. Geoffrey 1944- 47 and
  under * Buchanan 1979b 47
*Brown, Lawrence R. c. 1904-86 47
 Browning, Iben 1918- under
  * Winkless and Browning 1975 158
*Buchanan, James McGill, Jr. 1919-
  ix 1-30 (=Chapter 1) 33 34 36
  41-45 47 49-52 55 57 73 81 86
  90-93 97-98 101 104-105 108
  110-11 113-14 119 121-25 127-28
  130-31 135-40 143 153 155-56
  160-61 167 171-72 175-76 178-79
  181-82 and also under * Brennan
  and Buchanan 1982
*Bunge, Mario Augusto 1919- vii-ix
  xi 1 28 31 37-38 53 55-81
  (=Chapter 2) 83 86 90 93 95 102
  103 105 109 113 115 119 123-24
  127-28 133 135-36 139-40 150
  155-56 158-59 162
 Burke, Edmund 1729-97 117

*Campbell, Donald Thomas 1916- 156
 Canute the Great of Denmark and
  England ?-1035 53
*Carroll, Lewis [pen name of
  Charles Lutwidge Dodgson] 1832-98
  36-37 144
*Cattell, Raymond Bernard 1905- ix
  18 45 52-53 103 112 119-27 (in
  Chapter 6) 133-35 137 139-40
  156-57

 Charlemagne of the Holy Roman
  Empire aka Big Chuck 742-814 132
 Chomsky, Avram Noam 1928- 154
*Coon, Carleton Stevens, Sr.
  1904-81 74
 Copernicus, Nicolaus 1473-1543 vii
*Coulson, Noel James 1928-86 33
 Craster, Mrs. Edmund ?-1874 72
*Cuddihy, John Murray 1922- 40
 Curran, John Philpot 1750-1817 143

 Daley, Richard Joseph 1902-1976
  143
*Darwin, Charles Robert 1809-82
  117 132
 de Blij, Harm Jan 1935- under
  * Glassner and de Blij 1980 158
 deity 60
 demiurge 36 39
*DeNicola, Daniel R. 92
*Denton, Michael J. 148
*Derrett, John Duncan Martin 1922-
  under * Coulson 1968 33
 Descartes, Rene 1596-1650 152
 deus 4
*Dimond, Stuart J. 1938- 38-39
 Dodgson, Charles Lutwidge 1832-98
  under his pen name * Lewis
  Carroll 36-37 144
 Donne, John 1572-1631 113
*Downs, Anthony J. 1930- 1
*Dumézil, Georges Edmond Raoul
  1898-1986 40

 Eccles, John Carew 1903- and *
  under Popper and Eccles 1977 67
 Edwards, Jacqueline under
  * Simis 1982 110
 Elster, Jon 1940- 116 118
 Epimenides fl. 6th cent. B.C. 150

 Faith, Roger L. 1945- under
  * Buchanan and Faith 1980 92
 Fessler, Carol under * Rae 1981
  163
 First Cause vii
*Fletcher, Joseph Francis, III
  1905- 92
 Forman, Frank Shane, III, 1944-
  102 126
 Founding Fathers 15 19 186
*Frank, Robert H. 1945- 165-70
  (App. 2)

* means referenced in the bibliography under that name.

GLOSSARY

Pareto optimality

Vilfredo Pareto (1848-1923) was generally unwilling to compare the happiness of one man with another or to say that one man's benefit could outweigh another's loss, no matter how great the benefit to the one or how small the loss to the other. He was not such a misanthrope, however, to refrain from concluding that a change that led to at least one man's being better off but to no one's being made worse off was an unambiguous improvement. Such a change has become known as a Pareto improvement. When it finally comes that no further Pareto improvements are possible (that is, when any further change must lead to at least one man's being made worse off) the whole situation is called "Pareto optimal" (sometimes "Pareto efficient") and is said to be on the "Pareto frontier." It may often be the case that compensation can be paid by the bettered parties to those made worse off by the proposed change so that in the end the change becomes a genuine Pareto improvement. Some economists have denied the need to actually carry out the compensation and have been roundly and tirelessly criticized by Buchanan for it.

Rent-seeking

Rent, or rather differential rent, is a technical economic concept that means, not payment to a landlord, but the difference between the actual payment made for use of a resource and what would be paid in the resource's second highest use. Thus, my landlord's differential rent is my rent check minus what he could get by using the property as, say, a parking lot. Such a rent might come about by the special action of a zoning board. Differential rents may also come about because of a person's unique talents or a natural monopoly. The term rent-seeking is generally limited, however, to seeking after transfers, restrictions on competition, or other special dispensations from government. As such, it is almost always used pejoratively.

SUBJECT INDEX

Notices: 1. The subjects include -isms, -ists, and near synonyms.
        2. Chapters and subchapters are given in parentheses.

MAN AS A PART OF NATURE SUBINDEX

DIVINE SUBINDEX

And look under "religion" in the subject index for many more references.

THEORY AND DECISION LIBRARY

SERIES A: PHILOSOPHY AND METHODOLOGY OF THE SOCIAL
SCIENCES

Already published:

Conscience: An Interdisciplinary View
Edited by Gerhard Zecha and Paul Weingartner
ISBN 90–277–2452–0

Cognitive Strategies in Stochastic Thinking
by Roland W. Scholz
ISBN 90–277–2454–7

Comparing Voting Systems
by Hannu Nurmi
ISBN 90–277–2600–0

Evolutionary Theory in Social Science
Edited by Michael Schmid and Franz M. Wuketits
ISBN 90–277–2612–4